Federalism and the Role of the State

Edited by Herman Bakvis and William M. Chandler

What differences does federalism make? Is federalism useful and workable? What can we learn from the varying forms it takes in different countries? The rise of the positive state – affecting both economic life and social welfare – has proceeded apace and substantially affected the practice of federalism in a number of states. This volume brings together a number of comparative studies designed to explore conflict patterns, institutional arrangements, and policy-making within Canada and other federal states, including the United States, Australia, and West Germany.

This collection focuses on the many and varied problems associated with the massive increase in the scale of government. Federal states face more complex processes of adaptation than non-federal systems: the division of authority among multiple levels of government established along territorial/regional lines has vastly complicated the rise of the activist, interventionist state. The growth of governments at all levels has expanded the scale and scope of public control and increased the complexity of political and bureaucratic processes. It has brought interdependence and entanglement among different levels and has rendered inadequate such traditional analytical tools as water-tight compartments and degree of centralization/decentralization.

This volume compares stresses and strains – and fruitful adaptations – in several traditional federal systems, considers federalization in Belgium and regionalization in France, and looks at possible alternatives to federalism such as corporatism and consociationalism. It thereby presents several perspectives whereby the reader can judge the relevance and workability of federalism, in Canada and elsewhere, and the likelihood of its survival and adaptation in the years to come.

Federalism and the Role of the State

EDITED BY
HERMAN BAKVIS
AND WILLIAM M. CHANDLER

UNIVERSITY OF TORONTO PRESS

Toronto Buffalo London

© University of Toronto Press 1987
Toronto Buffalo London
Printed in Canada

ISBN 0-8020-2599-4 (cloth)
ISBN 0-8020-6621-6 (paper)

Printed on acid-free paper

Canadian Cataloguing in Publication Data

Main entry under title:
Federalism and the role of the state
Includes index.
ISBN 0-8020-2599-4 (bound). – ISBN 0-8020-6621-6 (pbk.)

1. Federal government. 2. Federal government –
Canada. I. Bakvis, Herman, 1948–   .
II. Chandler, William M., 1940–   .

JC355.F42 1987   321.02   C87-093565-8

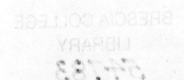

Contents

Preface / vii

1 Federalism and Comparative Analysis / 3
HERMAN BAKVIS AND WILLIAM M. CHANDLER

PART I
THEMES IN MODERN FEDERALISM

2 Federal Societies, Institutions, and Politics / 15
ROGER GIBBINS

3 Legitimacy, Democracy, and Federalism / 32
THOMAS O. HUEGLIN

PART II
INSTITUTIONS AND CONSTITUTIONAL PROCESS

4 Federalization and Federalism: Belgium and Canada / 57
MAUREEN COVELL

5 Second Chambers / 82
CAMPBELL SHARMAN

6 Bicameralism: Canadian Senate Reform in Comparative Perspective / 101
AREND LIJPHART

7 Judicial Review and Modern Federalism:
Canada and the United States / 113
JENNIFER SMITH

8 Regionalization and Decentralization / 127
ARTHUR BENZ

PART III
POLICY AND POLITICS IN FEDERAL SYSTEMS

9 Federalism and Political Parties / 149
WILLIAM M. CHANDLER

10 Federalism and Interest Group Organization / 171
WILLIAM D. COLEMAN

11 Federalism and Agricultural Policy / 188
GRACE SKOGSTAD

12 Federalism and the Canadian Economic Union / 216
MICHAEL J. TREBILCOCK

13 The Workability of Executive Federalism in Canada / 236
J. STEFAN DUPRÉ

14 Managing Intergovernmental Relations / 259
JOHN WARHURST

PART IV
CONCLUSIONS: THE FUTURE OF FEDERALISM?

15 Alternative Models of Governance: Federalism, Consociationalism, and
Corporatism / 279
HERMAN BAKVIS

16 The Future of Federalism / 306
HERMAN BAKVIS AND WILLIAM M. CHANDLER

Note on Contributors / 319

Preface

The essays commissioned for this volume are concerned with the significance of federalism for the workings of the modern state. Canadians will recognize the issues associated with this theme as perennial objects of political debate. However, the approach adopted throughout the book differs from our usual expectations about discussions of this quintessentially Canadian subject. Virtually all the contributors to this volume are comparativists by training and inclination. This is reflected in the comparative tone found in almost every chapter. Each focuses on some dilemma or question recurrent in modern federalism, which the author treats, explicitly or implicitly, within a comparative framework. This is not mere happenstance but rather the product of a belief, shared by editors and contributors alike, that one of the best ways to understand political phenomena within one's own country or culture is by reference to similar or contrasting experiences elsewhere.

The variety of relevant topics and the range of possible comparisons are enormous and have by no means been exhausted within this set of essays. We trust, however, that what follows will at a minimum demonstrate the value of various comparative approaches for generating fresh insights and new perspectives to old questions while simultaneously prompting new questions and debates for future research.

In our effort to unite these comparative essays within a single cover, we are deeply indebted to a number of people. First and foremost we thank our contributors. They were patient in the face of delays but expeditious in meeting deadlines and in making adjustments to fit the needs of the volume as a whole. Above all, it was their readiness to employ their expertise, based on a wide variety of federal experiences, to craft new perspectives on their respective topics that made the volume possible.

For his expert advice in steering the volume through the many phases of editorial revision, we are particularly grateful to Virgil Duff of the University of Toronto Press. All portions of the book benefited considerably from the valuable suggestions for change made by anonymous readers for the Press and the Social Science Federation of Canada. The judicious copy-editing of John Parry, also for the Press, proved extremely helpful in the final stages. Beyond their own essays, William Coleman and Grace Skogstad generously provided valuable comments on the chapters written by the editors. Marsha Chandler and Julia Eastman, by providing advice and encouragement from start to finish, convinced us of the worth of the project. Finally, we gratefully acknowledge the assistance of the Social Science Federation of Canada in granting financial support through funds provided by the Social Sciences and Humanities Research Council of Canada.

FEDERALISM AND THE ROLE OF THE STATE

1 / Federalism and Comparative Analysis

HERMAN BAKVIS

WILLIAM M. CHANDLER

Social change always creates challenges to established traditions. The post-industrial era has brought with it new values and demands that not only have enhanced the role of the modern state but also have raised doubts about the viability of institutions devised in an era of limited government. Nevertheless, federalism as a form of governance has successfully adapted itself to these challenges. Any comparative survey of federal régimes will confirm that they are alive and surprisingly healthy. Also, it appears that the rise of the positive state has helped to preserve and promote the federal form of government.

The reasons for this are many and varied,[1] but certainly one key element is to be found in the growth of activities undertaken by the modern state. This has fostered both large and unmanageable bureaucracies, regardless of régime type, and, in federal systems, an increase in the complexity of intergovernmental relations. This trend has, at the same time, facilitated separation and differentiation in the bases of political and bureaucratic power. Moreover, in federal systems these power bases have become increasingly lodged in the constituent units rather than the central government. Thus while organizational complexity and the multiplicity of power relationships are common to both federal and unitary systems, it is primarily in federal systems that there is greater opportunity for, and likelihood of, the devolution of power to lower and more manageable levels.

This proposition does not presume that all modern governments should become more federal in form or that federalism is in some sense preferable. Its stress is simply on the view that federalism should not be regarded as a remnant from the past or as an obsolescent form of governance in danger of being eroded by the forces of capitalism, as Harold Laski and others believed a half-century ago.[2] As chapter 2 in this volume, by Roger Gibbins, points out, pre-existing federal arrangements have proved remarkably adaptable to the changing requirements of modern industrial societies.

What continues to distinguish federal from so-called unitary states is the degree to which conflicts and relationships are formalized and shaped through constitutional-legal means. As Ivo Duchacek notes, in federal systems territorial conflict patterns tend to have a more public character and are widely seen as politically legitimate, and in many instances federal institutions provide incentives for structuring group/class conflicts along territorial lines.[3] Further, within most federal arrangements it is usually difficult for one level of government to exercise direct hierarchical control over another in order to resolve minor, let alone major differences. While this allows the separate levels of government flexibility in responding to the needs and demands of multiple constituencies, it also poses problems for the co-ordination of policies that cut across two or more jurisdictional areas. Thus, while in both federal and non-federal systems the critical issues are often related to the marshalling and co-ordination of resources and the setting of common goals, in the federal state hierarchical control mechanisms tend to be relatively weak. Indeed, goals themselves may vary between federal and non-federal systems.

In short, as political observers we have little difficulty in acknowledging what J. Stefan Dupré in this volume (chapter 13) has identified as the issues of the 'workability of federalism.' This may be seen as a subset of the general dilemma of governance in advanced industrial societies. We must also admit, given the increasing complexity of the modern state, that our understanding of these issues within the context of federal arrangements remains both rudimentary and unsatisfactory.

Nearly two decades ago William Riker and Vincent Ostrom debated the questions does federalism exist and does it matter?[4] Today, on the basis of additional research and in light of the apparent health of federal democracies, we can be reasonably assured that federalism will continue to exist and that it will continue to matter. However, we are now faced with a newer and probably more difficult research problem, for it is no longer simply a matter of whether federalism makes a difference but rather how and how well it works. As well, discussion of these issues has been rendered more complicated by changing perceptions of the links between federal states and federal societies. As sensitivity has developed to the questions of how and in what ways federalism matters, and to the manner in which federalism sustains itself, the traditional assumption of a close link between federal societies and federal states has been gradually losing its significance. Clearly, in some cases regional cleavages have weakened or disappeared over time, but federal institutions have remained in place.

In other cases, like Canada, regional and linguistic forces have continued to exert a centrifugal effect in reinforcing regionalist politics. But even here, the state is commonly understood to play an autonomous role in shaping the processes and the effects of federalism. By and large the Livingston view,[5] in which the process and policy of federal régimes are held to be products of territorially identified social forces, has been displaced by the so-called state-centred model, which holds that federalism is largely the result not of societies but of constitutions and the policy-making élites working within them.[6] Thus in the disciplines of political science, public administration, and economics, increasing attention has been focused on the political and administrative structures of the state and the manner in which autonomous state actions shape the social and economic environment.

Research agendas rarely stand still, however. Recent writings, including a number of the chapters in this volume, suggest not only that there are distinct limits to the autonomy of the state but that these limits are often due to state actions themselves, which, by creating new interdependencies between the federal state and society, serve to constrain the freedom of decision-makers. In addition, as will become evident in the chapters that follow, efforts to redesign the federal state often have unanticipated consequences. More generally, these new interdependencies, in combination with the kinds of policy issues that confront the modern federal state, raise new questions about the workability of present-day federal institutions.

Comparative Strategies

In this volume our essential task is to cast the themes of governability and workability within the context of federal arrangements. Regardless of how one chooses to formulate these themes, they are at base comparative questions requiring comparative responses. Our concern for fostering comparison in the study of federalism is also propelled by recognition of the relative lack of convincing comparative analysis in much of the traditional literature on federalism.

There are at least two reasons why we should be dissatisfied with traditional analyses. First, although the concept of federalism is inherently comparative, by far the largest part of in-depth research on federalism has been carried on within national boundaries with a view to dealing with a problem or a set of problems peculiar to each system. While one can note a valuable comparative emphasis in the early works of Friedrich, Corry, and Wheare and more recently those of Livingston, Riker, and Watts, with a few notable exceptions this tradition appears to have faded.[7] Today we most often find federalism treated as a dimension of domestic politics and within-system analysis. Thus the Canadian literature on federalism is of considerable interest in Canada but is generally neglected elsewhere. The same is broadly true for works on West German, American, and Australian federalism.

Second, there is a common preoccupation with definitional issues and with matching cases to some test of the ideal federal order. This has generated a tradition of asking whether A is more federal than B, or whether C, D, and E are really federal systems at all. While of some pedagogical value, this emphasis can divert attention away from those issues having substantial consequences for the workings of federal arrangements.

In short, questions and propositions concerning the actual operation of federations have significance extending well beyond the bounds of any single system. Further, although the problems and issues of a given federation may take on forms unique to that system, they nevertheless frequently relate to some basic strains or dimensions common to several systems. More often than not, an understanding of these common properties can place seemingly unique and discrete phenomena in a different light. All but one of the chapters in this volume rely explicitly on a comparative framework to elucidate aspects of federalism that would otherwise go unnoticed. 'Comparative framework,' however, implies no single approach but rather a variety of different research strategies. The remainder of this chapter is consecrated, therefore, to a brief review of what these approaches entail.

Strategies of analysis used by the contributors range from those that compare unitary and federal systems to those that develop side-by-side comparisons of two or more federal régimes and finally to those that are essentially one-system studies but with distinct comparative reference points. The study of West Germany and France by Arthur Benz (Chapter 8) constitutes an excellent example of the first type of comparison. Attempts to implement a degree of decentralization are examined in a federal and a unitary system respectively in order to estimate the extent to which pre-existing state structures can affect the substantive outcomes of initiatives for institutional change. The study by Maureen Covell (chapter 4) involves a direct comparison between Canada and Belgium. The latter, formally a unitary system, is in the process of acquiring federal institutions and practices, largely in response to pressures from the two main regionally based linguistic groupings. Although the two countries differ in obvious ways, specific dilemmas are often remarkably similar – for example, the difficulties of dealing with linguistic minorities (the Flemish in Brussels, the anglophones in Montreal) and the entrepreneurial role of politicians and the constraints they face in dealing with their own colleagues as well as with their counterparts in the other linguistic communities.

Within the second approach is Lijphart's study of bicameralism (chapter

6) in which the nature of the comparison allows for a wide range of variation among variables that are readily quantifiable, in this instance the extent of regional overrepresentation. Also in this category is Coleman's inquiry (chapter 10) into the link between federalism and interest-group organization. His analysis is structured on a four-way comparison involving a functional federal régime, the Federal Republic of Germany, two jurisdictional federations, Switzerland and Canada, and a 'union state,' the United Kingdom.[8] The study by Bakvis (chapter 15) on two alternative modes of governance, corporatism and consociationalism, employs a similar approach.

For many comparativists, the preferred approach involves the so-called most-similar systems design, where the main features of the countries in question are close to identical, save the independent and dependent variables under investigation.[9] In this volume chapter 5, by Campbell Sharman, on the reform of second chambers comes closest to this ideal strategy. Unfortunately, this state of affairs obtains but rarely. Most political scientists are willing to settle for what Anthony Birch has called 'the existence of somewhat similar arrangements,' where one takes account of the differences that could affect the outcome in question, in addition to the primary ones relating to federal structure.[10] Several chapters, such as those on government-society relations, political parties, and the management of intergovernmental relations, exemplify this strategy. The common element in these analyses is the use of two or three federal systems that share either institutional, cultural, or socio-economic characteristics. The alternative approach, the most-different-systems design,[11] involves the strategy of testing whether the same pattern holds in widely different circumstances. Lijphart's chapter (6), as well as Coleman's (10) on pressure groups, draws in part on this technique. So too does Thomas Hueglin (chapter 3) in his discussion of the increasingly evident contradictions within federal democracies associated with the rise of the post-industrial state. Those chapters that depend on a somewhat-similar-systems design attempt to identify the essential differences *among* systems, that is, those particular features that may account for differences in institutional processes or policy outcomes. Those chapters adopting the alternative approach have as their aim the identification of *common* patterns that exist despite dissimilarities in political traditions, institutions, policy processes, and social structure.

One further approach, though not used explicitly here, is entitled deviant-case analysis. Here an unusual or extreme case is examined in order to discern or observe patterns that might be latent or partially hidden in other systems.[12] Some of the authors do examine federal systems where specific institutions or practices currently exist, the object being to note how similar practices or institutions might operate in Canada. This is essentially the question asked by Jennifer Smith concerning the jurisdictional consequences of a more activist Canadian supreme court (chapter 7).

Answers provided through comparative analysis, while rarely definitive, are nonetheless valuable either because they indicate that certain practices or outcomes constitute universal patterns or because they reflect conditions within one system that are in fact unique. For example, Canada is one of the few federations lacking a strong second chamber for the representation of regional interests. Those who see federalism primarily in terms of power-sharing would argue that second chambers may serve to foster decision-making by consensus rather than by majority rule. As well, insight into the costs and benefits of a popularly elected second chamber can be gained through a comparison with Australia, a federation based on the Westminster model within which an American-style senate has been implanted. Sharman's discussion (chapter 5) of the constitutional dilemmas in Australia, the incentives that are provided to political parties for pursuing certain strategies, and the changes that can occur in the representation of state-government interests, as opposed to party interests, is highly suggestive and will help inform Canadian debate about the prospects and possible outcomes of having an elected Senate.

John Warhurst's analysis (chapter 14) of intergovernmental relations in Australia and Canada shows how in the former country intergovernmental affairs agencies or bureaus may reduce conflict between the state and Commonwealth governments, while in the latter they often appear to exacerbate conflict. He argues further that the positive role of these agencies in Australia can be attributed in part to their early development during an era of co-operative federalism. It appears that the circumstances under which important institutions come of age have a distinct bearing on the role they subsequently play in the management of intergovernmental conflicts. The Australian experience suggests how a heritage of institutionalized co-operative relations may persist despite intensification of conflict at some later stage. By contrast, in Canada these institutional mechanisms were created largely as instruments to defend and pursue provincial and federal interests at a time when there were major disagreements between governments, with the result that these mechanisms do not carry within them a tradition of co-operative behaviour.

Lessons may also flow in the other direction. Maureen Covell (chapter 4) notes how Belgium could benefit from Canadian experience in designing appropriate institutions and fiscal arrangements. Findings elsewhere, while less clear in their implications, may also be instructive. Grace Skogstad (chapter 11) notes that in spite of quite different systems of representation and approaches to agricultural policy in the United States and Canada, involving the so-called intra- versus inter-state distinction (whereby local/ regional interests are seen as being represented much more directly in central institutions in the United States), the ultimate consequence for both farmers and consumers in the two countries are roughly similar, suggesting inherent limitations in the effects of institutional and policy design.

The various contributions that follow, although varied in their policy and institutional foci, may usefully be grouped in four main parts. The first deals with two of the broadest core themes in federal analysis: the continuing viability of federal arrangements in the face of changes in social structure and the question of the quality of democratic life in the post-industrial era of executive federalism. The second part is focused on institutions and processes, encompassing such topics as the roles of second chambers and judicial review in federations, the institutional mechanisms involved in the conduct of intergovernmental relations, and the manner in which either centralization or decentralization might be best achieved in light of extensive interdependencies between central and constituent units. In the third part most of the chapters share a common concern with the question of whether federalism makes a difference. They do so with respect to specific policy areas ranging from economic union to agricultural policy, and to questions of political representation through political parties and pressure groups. Two of the chapters are concerned with the actual conduct and management of intergovernmental relations and include discussions of health care policy and fiscal relations.

The concluding part weighs alternative forms of governance and assesses the prospects of the federal form, both in broad outline and in regard to specific designs and consequences. We note further how differences between countries in the way citizens conceive of and interact with the state, and in the extent to which they are willing to accord legitimacy to the various institutions and branches of the state, affect the roles we expect the federal state to perform in Canada and elsewhere. Although some may believe that at present the Canadian federation is experiencing a crisis of 'workability' and that interdependencies within and outside the federal state prevent policy-makers at both levels of government from taking effective action, one of the lessons illustrated by the comparative analyses found in this volume is that this conundrum neither is nor need become a consequence of the federal arrangement alone.

NOTES

1 Daniel J. Elazar 'Constitutionalism, Federalism, and the Post-Industrial Ameri-

can Polity' in S.M. Lipset (ed) *The Third Century: America as a Post-Industrial Society* (Stanford: Hoover Institution Press 1979) 79–107; Sydney Tarrow 'Introduction' in Tarrow et al (eds) *Territorial Politics in Industrial Nations* (New York: Praeger 1978) 1–27; S. Rokkan and D. Urwin 'Introduction: Centres and Peripheries in Western Europe' in S. Rokkan and D. Urwin (eds) *The Politics of Territorial Identity: Studies in European Regionalism* (London: Sage 1982) 1–18; L.J. Sharpe (ed) *Decentralist Trends in Western Democracies* (London: Sage 1979); Henry Teune 'Decentralization and Economic Growth' *The Annals of the American Academy of Political and Social Science* 459 (January 1982) 93–102

2 Harold J. Laski 'The Obsolescence of Federalism' *New Republic* 3 May 1939, 367–9

3 Ivo D. Duchacek *Comparative Federalism: The Territorial Dimension of Politics* (New York: Holt, Rinehart and Winston 1970)

4 William H. Riker 'Six Books in Search of a Subject or Does Federalism Exist and Does It Matter?' *Comparative Politics* 1 (1969) 135–45; Vincent Ostrom 'Can Federalism Make a Difference?' *Publius* 3 (1973) 197–232

5 William S. Livingston *Federalism and Constitutional Change* (Oxford: Clarendon 1956)

6 Alan C. Cairns 'The Governments and Societies of Canadian Federalism' *Canadian Journal of Political Science* 10 (1977) 695–726; Donald V. Smiley 'Federal States and Federal Societies, with Special Reference to Canada' *International Political Science Review* 5 (1984) 443–54

7 K.C. Wheare *Federal Government* (Oxford: Clarendon 1946); C.J. Friedrich *Constitutional Government and Democracy: Theory and Practice in Europe and America* rev ed (Boston: Ginn 1950); J.A. Corry and J.E. Hodgetts *Democratic Governments and Politics* (Toronto: University of Toronto Press 1946); Livingston *Federalism and Constitutional Change*; William H. Riker *Federalism: Origin, Operation, Significance* (Boston: Little and Brown 1964); R.L. Watts *New Federations: Experiments in the Commonwealth* (Oxford: Clarendon 1966). Exceptions include Roger Gibbins *Regionalism: Territorial Politics in Canada and the United States* (Toronto: Butterworths 1982); D.V. Smiley and R.L. Watts *Intrastate Federalism in Canada*, vol. 39 of the research studies prepared for the Royal Commission on the Economic Union and Development Prospects for Canada (Toronto: University of Toronto Press, 1985).

8 By 'union state' is meant one that is not fully unitary, that is, where integration, both formally and informally, is less than perfect but that at the same time does not qualify as a federal arrangement. See S. Rokkan and D. Urwin 'Introduction: Centres and Peripheries in Western Europe' 11

9 A. Przeworski and H. Teune *The Logic of Comparative Social Inquiry* (New York: Wiley 1970) chap 1

10 A.H. Birch 'Approaches to the Study of Federalism' in Wildavsky (ed) *American Federalism in Perspective* (Boston: Little, Brown 1967) 77
11 A. Przeworski and H. Teune *The Logic of Comparative Social Inquiry* chap 2
12 Arend Lijphart 'The Comparable Cases Strategy in Comparative Research' *Comparative Political Studies* 8 (1975) 160–1. See also G. Molnar 'Deviant Case Analysis in Social Science' *Politics* 2 (1967) 1–11.

Part One

THEMES IN
MODERN FEDERALISM

2 / Federal Societies, Institutions, and Politics

ROGER GIBBINS

One of the most difficult problems for students of federalism arises from the vast scope of the subject matter. In the Canadian case, for example, the study of federalism leaves few aspects of political life untouched. Depending upon one's specific orientation, the study of federalism could encompass national parliamentary institutions, the formal constitutional structures of the Canadian federal state, the relationship between the franco-phone and anglophone communities, territorial conflict in both the western and Atlantic peripheries, intergovernmental relations, judicial decision-making, and party politics, including both national organizations and the complex relations between national and provincial parties sharing a common party label. Indeed, given a bit of imagination there are few aspects of Canadian political life that could not be brought under the umbrella of federalism.

Thus if we are to come to grips with such an all-encompassing term as *federalism*, we must begin by breaking it into smaller, more easily digested chunks. To use a simple analogy, we might think of a federal system as a large and complex jigsaw puzzle. While we ultimately want to put the puzzle together, to get some sense of the federal whole, we must begin with smaller, albeit central pieces and determine how these are related one to another. In this chapter, three pieces of the federal jigsaw puzzle are identified and their interrelationships explored. More specifically, the chapter will examine federal societies, institutions, and politics.

A federal society is one in which there are significant territorial cleavages that may or may not be reinforced by linguistic, religious, or ethnic divisions. The term *federal institutions* will be used to embrace both institutional and constitutional elements. The former encompass institutional mechanisms designed to give expression to cleavages within a federal society; these would include, for example, territorial representation in second chambers such as the US Senate. The latter encompass the formal constitutional society of the federal state, with particular reference to the division of powers between the national and sub-national governments. The term *federal politics*, which may appear very global, refers in this particular discussion to the political parties and private groups that energize the more formal institutional structures of federal states.

Admittedly, these are rather large pieces that could readily be dismembered into smaller components. By breaking the federal jigsaw puzzle into large sections rather than into a multitude of smaller pieces, we have simplified a complex political world. If, however, we concentrate on these larger sections and on the interplay among the three, the broad outlines of contemporary federal states can be brought into focus. Indeed, one might argue that the essence of federalism is to be found in the interplay among these three factors, in their complex and reciprocal interaction. Of particular importance is the changing nature of this interaction over time as federal societies are transformed by social change and as federal institutions both shape and adjust to social change.

As we will see, the relation between federal societies and federal institutions changes dramatically as federal systems move through time. The commonsensical assumption that federal institutions reflect federal societies offers little insight into the contemporary character of federal states.

The Origin of Federal States

When federal states come into existence it seems reasonable to assume that they do so because of a pre-existing federal society, that federal institutions are adopted in order to reflect the federal nature of the underlying society. In the Canadian case, for example, the historical record leaves little doubt that federalism was adopted because of the need to accommodate the divergent interests of the francophone-Catholic and anglophone-Protestant communities, although the size of the new country, the rudimentary state of transportation and communication facilities, the American model to the south, pre-existing territorial governments in Nova Scotia and New Brunswick, and the underdeveloped state of municipal institutions in Lower Canada and the Maritimes[1] all played contributing roles.

Sir John A. Macdonald, the chief architect of Confederation, stated: 'I have always contended that if we could agree to have one government and one parliament, legislating for the whole of these peoples, it would be the best, the cheapest, the most vigorous, and the strongest system of government we could adopt.'[2] A unitary state was not to be, however, for it could not accommodate the two religious-linguistic communities. Its inability to do so had been forcefully demonstrated by the failure of the Act of Union of 1841. The act had brought Lower Canada (now Quebec) and Upper Canada (now Ontario) together within the confines of a unitary, albeit still colonial state. This unitary state not only failed to correspond with the federal society of the times but had been explicitly designed as a counter-weight to that society, as a political instrument to facilitate the assimilation of French Canadians into the English-Canadian community. In practice, however, political institutions were soon modified to incorporate an informal administrative division of powers. Macdonald, for example, served as the attorney general for Canada West (formerly Upper Canada) rather than for the province of Canada as a whole, even though the constitutional structure of the colony was in no sense federal. This informal federalism helped lay the foundation for the formal federal state that was put into place by the Constitution Act (formerly the British North America Act) of 1867.

One might assume from this the necessity of fitting political institutions to the underlying social order. We must be cautious, however, in generalizing too broadly from the Canadian experience. Indeed, while the federal nature of Canadian society was of pressing interest to politicians from the province of Canada, it was much less so to Maritime politicians, who were more concerned that pre-existing governments be incorporated within the constitutional framework of Confederation. Federalism, in other words, was desired not because it would reflect distinctive colonial societies in Nova Scotia and New Brunswick but rather because it would reflect and preserve pre-existing political institutions. A federal constitution was the cart to an institutional, not a social horse.

In the case of the United States, federalism emerged primarily because the eastern seaboard had been carved up into discrete colonial entities. Having declared their independence from Great Britain, the thirteen colonies were reluctant to surrender that independence to a new national government, even an American one.[3] Thus the 1781 Articles of Confederation created an extremely weak national government in which the unicameral Continental Congress was controlled and virtually immobilized by the states; each state had one vote, and each had the right to veto any tax proposed by Congress. Except under narrowly defined conditions, Congress could not directly govern the citizens of any state; national legislation could be brought to bear on individual Americans only through the willing co-operation of the states. As article 11 declared, each state retained 'its sovereignty, freedom, and independence.' When the Articles eventually failed and a new federal constitution was put in place in 1789, the state governments were retained intact while a new national government was created and superimposed. The point to be stressed is that the American federal system did not arise because of a territorially segmented society, such as that in the province of Canada. Rather, it came about because American territory had already been divided politically. Federalism was designed to protect pre-existing political divisions rather than to reflect a federal society.

This general line of argument takes on additional force when Australia is examined. Here again, federalism did not arise because the citizens of Queensland formed a society clearly distinct from that formed by the citizens of New South Wales or Western Australia. Federalism emerged because Australia had previously been partitioned into distinct colonial segments that then sought to protect their political integrity within the context of a new and broader Australian state. Federal institutions did not emerge in order to reflect and protect a federal society. In Australia, as in the United States, federalism had political rather than social roots.

Whatever the sources of federalism, it may still seem reasonable to assume that some rough initial symmetry will exist between the nature of the underlying society and that of the new federal institutions. To a degree, federal institutions will 'reflect' the nature of the society, although some cases may mirror colonial divisions rather than sociological forms of segmentation. Federal institutions, however, do more than reflect; they also reinforce those cleavages that gave impetus to federalism in the first place. Social groups, such as francophones within Quebec, may use new sub-national governments to protect and promote their own interests and distinctive identity. Where social segmentation is of little initial consequence, federalism may create the governmental foundations upon which distinctive social systems can be constructed. Federalism therefore not only reinforces pre-existing social divisions but also fosters new lines of social cleavage paralleling the institutional divisions of the federal state.

The capacity of political institutions to shape their social environment has been captured by Alan Cairns's notion of 'governmental societies.'[4] As Cairns points out, governments are not passive reflectors of their society; they reach out and shape that society and its economic foundations in numerous ways: 'It is no longer meaningful or appropriate to think of ... economies and societies at the provincial and national levels as logically prior to governments. To an indeterminant, but undoubtedly significant extent they are the consequences of past government activity, and will increasingly be so in the future.'[5] Sub-national loyalties are created and nurtured by sub-national governments; provincial or state flags, symbols, slogans, and seals are created, idiosyncratic social services are provided, and both licence plates and drivers' licences are used to confirm sub-national territorial identifications. Thus we have a reciprocal and reinforcing relation; federal cleavages within the society foster a federal system of government, which in turn reinforces the initial cleavages and, in many cases, creates new cleavages or at the very least sub-national identifications where none existed before.

This last point is illustrated by the imposition of state and provincial boundaries across the central plains of North America. If we look, for example, at the boundaries separating South Dakota, Nebraska, Iowa, Kansas, Missouri, and Oklahoma, they are little more than surveyor lines imposed upon the expanse of the plains, lines that do not reflect any preexisting geographical boundaries, much less social segmentation. Nonetheless, these states today possess distinctive histories, political personalities, and symbols, coupled with a sense of loyalty to and identification with the states shared by their inhabitants. North of the 49th parallel, which in itself was initially a political barrier rather than a reflection of social segmentation, the boundary separating Alberta and Saskatchewan was determined by little more than the fear of Canada's prime minister at the time, Wilfrid Laurier, that the transformation of the Northwest Territories into a single prairie province would create too powerful a political rival for Ontario and Quebec. Yet from the time of their creation in 1905, Alberta and Saskatchewan have followed quite different and even divergent political paths, and provincial identities within the two have become firmly entrenched. Today the provincial border between the two seems as natural and as immutable as that between Ontario and Quebec in 1867.

Once federal systems of government have been put in place, they structure not only the society but also politics along federal lines. Political parties, at least for the most part, develop the capacity to compete in both national and subnational elections.[6] Interest groups structure their organizations so that they can lobby effectively at both the national and subnational levels. Interest groups may also uphold and sustain the federal division of powers, using it as a shield to ward off the regulatory ambitions of the national government. As Truman has argued in the American context, 'the separate existence of the states . . . provides effective access to the whole governmental structure for interest groups whose tactics may be local or sectional but whose scope is national. Sectionalism . . . has frequently been a refuge for interests bent on defensive or evasive action, and the "states' rights" argument has often had about it an air more of expediency than of principle.'[7]

Political conflicts are moulded by the specific nature of federal institutions and the federal division of powers. To take but one recent example, energy politics in the United States has not had the same intergovernmental dimension that it has had in Canada because mineral rights in the United

States are largely held by those private individuals who own the surface land, rather than by provincial governments, as is the case in Canada. Thus energy-related wealth can be captured by Washington, should it wish to do so, through the conventional tools of corporate and personal income tax and without any federal raid on state revenues. In Canada, a large proportion of such wealth can be captured only from provincial governments rather than from individuals and corporations, a process that engendered the intense intergovernmental and regional conflict between the governments of Canada and Alberta during the 1970s and early 1980s. While wealthy individuals and large corporations are far from defenceless within the political arena, their power pales beside that of sub-national governments exercising constitutionally entrenched powers.

To this point, we have assumed that a rough initial symmetry exists within federal states, that federal institutions are created to reflect pre-existing social segmentation and/or to respect pre-existing political lines of demarcation such as might result from colonial experience. As Cairns has suggested, however, once federal systems are in place both national and sub-national governments will not only reflect but will also begin to shape their social and economic environments. The relation between federal societies and federal institutions thus becomes more interactive. The concept of governmental societies captures one side of that interaction – the impact of political institutions on social and economic change. It is now appropriate to examine the other side – the impact of social and economic change on the character of federal institutions.

Federal Systems and Social Change

Canada, Australia, and the United States are all relatively old federal states that have experienced a great deal of social and economic change. Indeed, to say that the United States of the 1980s bears little resemblance to the United States of the 1790s may seem a statement of the obvious. Nonetheless, it is important to reflect on the magnitude and scope of social change that federal systems have experienced over their lifetime; both have been immense. The direction of that change, moreover, has generally been such as to break down the distinctive character of sub-national societies and to create a more homogeneous national community.[8]

No country better exemplifies the nationalizing character of social change than does the United States. Note, for example, a 1906 address by US Secretary of State Elihu Root:

Our whole life has swung away from the old state centers and is crystallizing about national centers ... The people move in great throngs to and fro from state to state and across the states; the important news of each community is read at every breakfast table throughout the country; the interchange of thought and sentiment is universal; in the wide range of daily life and activity and interest the old lines between the states and the old barriers which kept the states as separate communities are completely lost from sight. The growth of national habits in the daily life of a homogeneous people keeps pace with the growth of a national sentiment.[9]

The pattern of change described by Root accelerated as the twentieth century unfolded, with the advent of radio, television, and a national entertainment industry. Geographical mobility, McWilliams notes, 'has weakened the attachments of Americans to home and place; for increasing numbers ... a state or city is only a location where one happens to live at the moment.'[10] As William Riker, one of America's foremost federal scholars, has observed, 'Our system for the exchange of ideas (television, radio, movies, magazines, newspapers, associations, etc.) is based on our national life and customs, not on provincial ones.'[11]

While one might argue that the extent and pace of nationalization have been somewhat less in Canada or somewhat greater in Australia, there is little question that the direction of social change has been the same. The question of interest here is how federal systems of government have adapted to rapid social change.

It should be stressed at the outset that the direction of political change has not been uniform across federal states. In the United States and Australia, the direction of change has been in line with the political modernization hypothesis advanced by Lipset and Rokkan. Urbanization and industrialization have led to the transfer of political loyalties from local communities to the national community. The powers of the central government have been progressively augmented, and territorially based political cleavages have been submerged beneath those relating to class and ideology.[12] In Canada, in contrast, similar patterns of social change have been accompanied by growth in the power and stature of provincial governments, by enhanced regional conflict, and, in some respects, by decentralization of the Canadian federal system.[13] Nonetheless, while the direction of adjustment in federal institutions may differ, similar mechanisms of adjustment have been employed. Of these, three warrant examination here; formal constitutional change, informal constitutional change, and changes in the nature of federal politics.

Formal Constitutional Change

The formal or written constitutions of federal states are not easily changed.

Amending formulas are by design cumbersome and difficult to mobilize. In the United States, for example, an amendment to the constitution requires the support of two-thirds of the members of both the Senate and the House of Representatives, plus ratification by three-quarters of the states. The prolonged and ultimately unsuccessful attempt to secure passage of the Equal Rights Amendment demonstrates how difficult the process can be.

This is not to suggest that formal constitutional change never occurs. The American constitution, for example, has been amended twenty-five times since 1789. The first twelve amendments, however, were adopted within a 'fine-tuning' period spread over the first fifteen years. In more recent times, amendments have been rare and, in most cases, have not affected the federal aspects of the constitution. In the wake of John F. Kennedy's assassination, the twenty-fifth amendment (1967) formalized the pattern of presidential succession beyond the vice-presidency. In the wake of the Civil Rights movement, the twenty-fourth amendment (1964) prohibited the use of poll taxes in federal elections. The twenty-third (1961) extended suffrage in presidential elections to the District of Columbia. The twenty-second (1951) limited the presidential term of office. The twenty-first (1933) repealed national prohibition. The twentieth (1933) addressed the presidential and congressional terms of office. The nineteenth (1920) granted women's suffrage. And the eighteenth (1919) imposed national prohibition. None of these amendments substantially altered the balance of powers and responsibilities between the state and national governments.

Prior to 1982, the written part of the Canadian constitution had been modified at the margins. In 1940, for example, an addition to the division of powers outlined in section 91 of the Constitution Act lodged responsibility for unemployment insurance with the federal government. On the whole, however, formal constitutional amendments are a rare phenomenon within federal states. While Canada's Constitution Act of 1982 may appear to be a major exception, the discussion below will suggest that it supports more than it contradicts this conclusion.

Informal Constitutional Change

In their practical operation, federal systems may depart quite dramatically from what their written constitutions would predict. Perhaps the greatest departures are to be found in the fiscal relations between national and subnational governments. As a general rule, national governments have turned out to have fiscal resources in excess of their legislative responsibilities as outlined in the federal division of powers. For their part, sub-national governments have tended to require fiscal transfers from the national government in order to meet their legislative responsibilities. (For example, fiscal transfers were built into the 1867 Constitution Act in the Canadian case.) As a direct consequence of this imbalance, national governments have been able to use their fiscal resources to intrude into the legislative domain of sub-national governments.

In 1902 Alfred Deakin, later prime minister of Australia, graphically captured the fear of fiscal intrusion: 'The rights of self-government of the States have been fondly supposed to be safe-guarded in the constitution. It has left them legally free, but financially bound to the chariot wheels of the Commonwealth. Their need will be its opportunity.'[14] Deakin's comment was prophetic, for by the 1970s the Commonwealth government was collecting five out of every six Australian tax dollars, and Commonwealth grants from Canberra to the states accounted for 60 per cent of state expenditures.

In the United States, the Great Depression of the 1930s prompted a massive increase in federal 'grants-in-aid' to both state and local governments. Washington's spending increased from 34 per cent of all government spending in 1932 to 55 per cent in 1936 and 83 per cent by the end of the Second World War.[15] Grant-in-aid programs entailed the payment of federal funds to state or local governments for a specified purpose, usually on the condition that the recipient meet minimum national standards and supply matching funds. Grant-in-aid programs thus enabled the federal government to legislate indirectly in state and local arenas through the specification of conditions for federal grants. Federal aid through grant-in-aid programs now constitutes more than one-third of the total revenue of state governments in the United States, as well as providing an important source of funds for municipal and county governments.[16]

In this way grant-in-aid programs and the accompanying growth in federal expenditures have reshaped the American federal system without any formal change to the constitutional structure of the American federal state. They have 'transformed intergovernmental relations, making state and local governments into client groups of federal programs and their chief executives into federal lobbyists.'[17] State and local governments have become increasingly tied to federal regulations, standards, and priorities as their own spending is tailored to attract matching funds from close to one thousand federal grant-in-aid programs that permeate virtually all state and local activities.[18]

The Canadian equivalent of Commonwealth grants and American grants-in-aid is the conditional grant, which came into full flower in the 1960s. Conditional grants entailed federal expenditures in provincial fields of jurisdiction, usually in health and welfare, along with the imposition of national standards and the need for matching provincial expenditures. However, there was a general retreat from conditional grants in the 1970s. Fiscal transfers from Ottawa to the provincial grant-in-aids (but not to local governments, as in the United States) remain, but they have increasingly assumed the form of unconditional grants for which national standards are not enforced[19] and matching provincial expenditures are not required.

This is the place not to assess whether conditional grants, grants-in-aid, and Commonwealth grants are good, bad, or indifferent for federal states, but rather to point out that they provide a great deal of informal constitutional flexibility. Where the constitutional division of powers may prohibit legislative activity by the national government, such grants provide a fiscal back door through which national governments can enter. Where sub-national governments are burdened with legislative responsibilities that outstrip their fiscal resources, such grants provide essential relief. Fiscally, then, federal systems have proved very adaptive to changing social conditions and changing public expectations. Fiscal flexibility has in turn reduced the need for more formal constitutional amendment, although the imbalance between the fiscal resources and the legislative responsibilities of sub-national governments has been an ongoing source of constitutional tension within at least the Canadian federal state.

Changes in the Nature of Federal Politics

Federal constitutions are brought to life by a variety of political actors within the federal state, among which political parties are of the greatest importance. Note, for example, Riker's argument that political parties play a critical role in the extent to which federal systems are centralized or decentralized: 'The federal relationship is centralized according to the degree to which the parties organized to operate the central government control the parties organized to operate the constituent governments. This amounts to the assertion that the proximate cause of variations in the degree of centralization (or peripheralization) in the constitutional structure of a federalism is the variation in degree of party centralization.'[20] Riker goes on to argue that whatever the social conditions sustaining the federal bargain, it is the structure of the party system 'which may be regarded as the main variable intervening between the background social conditions and the specific nature of the federal bargain.'[21]

Thus party systems have the potential to corrode or reinforce the federal division of powers. In the United States, for example, the electoral dominance of the Democratic and Republican parties in both state and national politics has blurred the federal division of powers. With the same parties competing in both state and national elections, and with the two campaigns frequently being waged at the same time and conducted through a common ballot, state and national party organizations tend to flow into one another despite the federal division of powers. This integrated party system facilitates the movement of political élites from state to national office, a tendency that is also encouraged by state-imposed constraints on the re-election of governors in some states and by an elected Senate which offers national offices of sufficient power and prestige to attract governors.

In Canada, conversely, the party system is structured so as to reinforce the constitutional division of powers. Provincial and national elections are conducted at different times through independent ballots. The party system lacks the symmetry of the American arrangement. Provincial parties with no federal counterparts or at least very weak federal counterparts are common – the Parti québécois, the Union nationale, British Columbia's Social Credit party – and national parties often lack viable provincial affiliates in parts of the country. Here, for example, we might note the absence of a Quebec Progressive Conservative party and the comatose state of the provincial Conservative and Liberal parties in British Columbia. Except for electoral defeat, Canadian premiers face no restrictions on their tenure of office and thus may enjoy an extended political career without any need to seek national office. More important, Canada has no elected office at the federal level comparable in power and prestige to that of a US Senator that might lure premiers from the substantial rewards, prestige, and electoral security of provincial politics. Thus one might argue that the Canadian party system promotes both a relatively decentralized federal system and the vigilant defence of the federal division of powers by provincial political élites.

Political parties can also be linked to the operation of federal states by the modernization thesis of Lipset and Rokkan, who argue that 'whatever the structure of the polity, parties have served as essential agents of mobilization and as such have helped to integrate local communities into the nation or broader federation.'[22] Lipset and Rokkan dealt primarily with the decline of territorial conflict in Western industrialized states, which corresponded with the emergence of national parties attempting to mobilize electoral support across the body politic. It is a thesis, however, that applies with particular force to federal states where territorial conflict plays a central role in shaping constitutional evolution. Here one can argue that national parties in federal states will chafe against the federal divisions of powers, although in the Canadian case provincial parties have found a vigorous defence of the federal division of powers to be an essential electoral tool. As Duchacek explains, 'a classic political party negates the federal idea of power dispersion, because political parties are deemed to aim primarily at aggregating and welding different elements of territorial and functional interests and powers into one phalanx, committed to a common goal and action under one leadership.'[23]

In summary, not only do constitutions shape the nature of party systems in federal states, party systems also shape the nature of the federal experience. Different party systems can accentuate centralizing aspects of some federal constitutions while all but negating the centralizing features of others. Party systems thus provide an important means of adaptation as federal systems confront rapidly changing social conditions. They have the capacity to adjust constitutional parameters to changing social conditions without the necessity of formal constitutional change.

Major Constitutional Change

The federal systems discussed in this chapter have been characterized by a high degree of constitutional stability. Their federal constitutions, once put into place, have proved very resistant to change. Even civil war in the United States did not fundamentally change the constitutional character of American federalism but rather served to confirm the constitutional principles put into place in 1789. The thirteenth amendment (1865) abolished slavery, while the fourteenth (1868) shifted the focus of citizenship from the states to the national community. 'All persons born or naturalized in the United States, and subject to the jurisdiction thereof, are citizens of the United States *and of the State wherein they reside*' (emphasis added). The third amendment emerging from the Civil War, and the fifteenth overall, declared in 1870 that 'the right of citizens of the United States to vote shall not be denied or abridged by the United States or any State on account of race, color, or previous condition of servitude.'

Typically federal systems have adjusted to social change through what have been termed *informal* constitutional changes, such as those entailed in conditional grants, Commonwealth grants, and grants-in-aid and through even more informal modifications in the structure and operation of parties and other political actors. Where these have proved sufficient to meet the challenge of changing social conditions, the constitutional parameters of the federal state have not come under attack and have not had to undergo fundamental change.

Over the last twenty-five years in Canada, however, the constitutional parameters of the federal state *have* come under persistent and vigorous attack. Indeed, by the early 1980s Canadians approached a national consensus that the federal system put into place in 1867 was no longer capable of handling political conflict between French and English, between the governments of Canada and of the provinces, and between the regional interests of the western and Atlantic peripheries and those of the central Canadian provinces. Within Quebec there was a growing nationalist movement which, in 1976, led to the election of a Parti québécois government committed to the withdrawal of Quebec from Confederation. In the west, alienation was pervasive and intense and, for the first time, was finding expression through small but vocal separatist organizations. On the east coast, conflict between Newfoundland and the federal government over the ownership of offshore resources was coming to a boil. More generally, expanding intergovernmental conflict led to an extensive re-examination of the federal division of powers and of existing mechanisms for regional representation within parliamentary institutions.

Recognition of the need for change led to a flood of reform proposals but not to any positive consensus on the direction of change. In Quebec, the Parti québécois proposed a form of sovereignty-association for Quebec, while more extreme nationalists called for complete independence and the government of Canada called for renewed federalism. The Task Force on National Unity called for a substantially decentralized federal system coupled with the reform of parliamentary institutions. In the west, reform proposals called for increased provincial control over natural resources and enhanced regional representation in the national government. Virtually every provincial government had reform proposals on the table, as did a plethora of private interests, including such groups as the Ontario Bar Association and the Canada West Foundation. There was, then, a broad-gauge and at times intensive search for constitutional reform.

It is useful here to stop and consider the assumptions that lay behind the Canadian constitutional debate. It was assumed, first of all, that the federal constitution no longer fitted the social and political realities of Canada. Indeed, the constitution itself was seen as one of the sources of strain, although by no means the only one, on national unity. It was also assumed that constitutional change could be used to overcome political problems, that the conflict between Quebec and the broader Canadian community could be addressed through modification in the division of powers, or that the regional conflict between the west and the broader national community could be addressed through improved channels of regional representation within national parliamentary institutions. Thus the federal constitution was not only a source of strain but also a solution. Through creative constitutional engineering, the national unity problems stemming from social and economic change could be contained and moderated. It was assumed, then, that constitutional change would have a direct impact on the nature of the society, that a new and different constitution could provide the national glue that had been found to be sorely lacking.[24]

It is thus of interest to examine the constitutional change that finally emerged from a protracted and often acrimonious constitutional process stretching from the late 1960s to the Constitutional Accord in November 1981 and the proclamation of the Constitution Act on 17 April 1982.[25] While this is not the place for a detailed examination of the Constitution Act,[26] a number of general conclusions can be drawn concerning constitutional change to Canadian federalism.

First and foremost, the act did *not* address the major strains in the federal system that had initially launched the search for a new constitution. The act did not modify the federal division of powers, apart from a relatively limited expansion in provincial control over non-renewable natural resources.[27] It did not redefine, and indeed did not even address, the position of Quebec within the Canadian federal state. Thus the major impetus behind constitutional change was not reflected in the new constitution, although one might argue that the act's silence on Quebec can be taken as endorsation for the vision of French Canada pursued by Pierre Trudeau. (This vision was centred on individual language rights common to both linguistic communities, rights that had been expressed through the 1969 Official Languages Act and that now find expression in sections 16 through 22 of the Charter of Rights and Freedoms.) There were no changes to parliamentary institutions that would enhance regional representation, no changes to the Senate, the electoral system, or the method of appointment to the Supreme Court and federal regulatory agencies. There was no change to the intergovernmental structure of the Canadian federal state, although there was agreement on an amending formula for the constitution.

All this is not to disparage the Constitution Act or to belittle the changes that did occur. There is little question, for instance, that the Charter of Rights and Freedoms has the potential to have a profound impact on Canadian political life. Nonetheless, the federal system per se emerged relatively unscathed and unaltered. This demonstrates how resistant federal systems are to formal constitutional amendment. Despite general consensus and abundant evidence that Canada's federal system was flawed, despite a raft of detailed and creative proposals for constitutional change, and despite serious political challenges to national unity arising in both Quebec and the west, the federal system was not restructured.

This suggests in turn that federal constitutions have a life of their own, that they have a resilience that makes them very resistant to social change. Because of this resilience, and because of the vast amount of social change that federal states such as Canada, Australia, and the United States have experienced since their creation, we should no longer expect any close fit between federal constitutions and societies. Federal constitutions have great staying power, but not because they accurately reflect social and economic realities. Rather, that staying power comes from the governments put into place by the initial federal constitution. Those governments have been able to survive substantial social change and indeed, as Cairns has suggested in the notion of governmental societies, have been able to shape that change to serve their own interests. Thus today the link between federal societies and federal constitutions has become not only reciprocal but tenuous. Federal systems persist because they exist, not because they necessarily reflect the society about them.

Here I would like to close by noting a comment by Alan Cairns on the Canadian experience leading up to the Constitution Act of 1982, and on the act itself:

What was in happier days described as the 'living Canadian constitution' still lives, modified in some ways, but still essentially much as before. Its survival is due at least as much to the difficulties of change and the profound disagreement about the desirable direction of change as to any massive support by elites or masses for the particulars of the existing constitutional system ... It survives because in competition with its rivals it alone possesses the supreme advantage of existence, and its continuation does not spell chaos for the private and public interests whose affairs it regulates and channels.[28]

To generalize further, we might conclude that federal systems, once put into place, are able to ensure their own survival. Thus the fact that the underlying federal society might be profoundly transformed is largely irrelevant to their continuation. Federalism persists in the United States and Australia not because of the federal nature of the underlying societies, but because the constitutional status quo is resistant to change. Federalism persists in Canada not because the particulars of the federal system square with the federal aspects of the society, but because the governments of the Canadian federal state are able to defend their constitutional position. In effect, then, the link between federal constitutions and federal societies becomes increasingly tenuous as time goes on.

NOTES

1 Bora Laskin *Canadian Constitutional Law* 2nd ed (Toronto: Carswell 1960) 3

2 P.B. Waite ed *The Confederation Debates in the Province of Canada, 1865* (Toronto: McClelland & Stewart 1963) 40
3 William Anderson *The Nation and the States, Rivals or Partners?* (Minneapolis: University of Minnesota Press 1955) 56
4 Alan C. Cairns 'The Governments and Societies of Canadian Federalism' *Canadian Journal of Political Science* 10 (1977) 695–726
5 Ibid 723
6 Here the American and Australian experiences have been more consistent than the Canadian case, where parties such as the Union nationale and the Parti québécois have enjoyed substantial provincial success while not entering the national electoral arena.
7 David B. Truman 'Federalism and the Party System' in Aaron Wildavsky ed *American Federalism in Perspective* (Boston: Little, Brown 1967) 92–3
8 This argument is pursued at greater length in Gibbins *Regionalism: Territorial Politics in Canada and the United States* (Toronto: Butterworths 1982).
9 Elihu Root *Addresses on Government and Citizenship* Robert Bacon and James Brown Scott (Cambridge: Harvard University Press 1916) 366–7
10 Wilson C. McWilliams 'The American Constitution' in Gerald M. Pomper et al *The Performance of American Government* (New York: The Free Press 1972) 32
11 William H. Riker *Democracy in the United States* 2nd ed (New York: Macmillan 1965) 287
12 See Stein Rokkan 'Electoral Mobilization, Party Competition, and National Integration' in Joseph LaPalombara and Myron Weiner eds *Political Parties and Political Development* (Princeton: Princeton University Press 1966) 241–66; and Seymour Martin Lipset and Stein Rokkan 'Cleavage Structures, Party Systems and Voter Alignments: An Introduction' in Lipset and Rokkan eds *Party Systems and Voter Alignments: Cross-National Perspectives* (New York: The Free Press 1967) 1–64
13 For an extended discussion of the Canadian and American contrast, see Gibbins *Regionalism*.
14 Cited in W.J. Bryt and Frank Crean *Government and Politics in Australia* (Sydney: McGraw-Hill 1972)
15 Gibbins *Regionalism* 15
16 Ira Sharkansky *The Maligned States: Policy Accomplishments, Problems, and Opportunities* 2nd ed (New York: McGraw-Hill 1978) 99
17 Donald H. Haider *When Governments Come to Washington: Governors, Mayors, and Intergovernmental Lobbying* (New York: The Free Press 1974) 93
18 William Simpson *Vision and Reality: The Evolution of American Government* (London: John Murray 1978) 178
19 The Canada Health Act, 1984, which imposed financial penalties on provincial

governments straying from the federal policy on extra billing, is an exception
here.

20 William H. Riker *Federalism: Origin, Operation, Significance* (Boston: Little,
Brown 1964) 129

21 Ibid 136

22 Lipset and Rokkan 'Cleavage Structures' 4

23 Ivo D. Duchacek *Comparative Federalism: The Territorial Dimension of Politics* (New York: Holt, Rinehart and Winston 1970) 331–2

24 The perspective of Quebec nationalists, of course, was quite different, as new
constitutional arrangements were seen as a solvent for the existing Canadian
federal state rather than as a strengthened bond.

25 With respect to the constitutional position of Canada's aboriginal peoples, the
process was not brought to a close by the Constitution Act but rather was
extended through section 35, which called for further constitutional negotiations
between aboriginal organizations and the governments of Canada.

26 For such an examination, see Keith Banting and Richard Simeon eds *And No
One Cheered: Federalism, Democracy and the Constitution Act* (Toronto:
Methuen 1983).

27 These changes are to be found in section 92A of the Constitution Act, 1982.

28 Alan Cairns 'The Politics of Constitutional Conservatism' in Banting and
Simeon eds *And No One Cheered* 53

3 / Legitimacy, Democracy, and Federalism

THOMAS O. HUEGLIN

The twentieth century will open the age of federalism, or else humanity will undergo another purgatory of a thousand years.

Pierre-Joseph Proudhon, 1863

I infer in a word that the epoch of federalism is over.

Harold Laski, 1939

Proudhon envisaged a world of socio-economic federalism set against the perils of class conflict in the nascent world of modern industrial capitalism.[1] Laski's cynical prediction was that political federalism would become helpless against the concentrated socio-economic power of giant capitalism.[2] Four decades after the great purgatory of the Second World War political federalism governs over approximately half of the world's territory and 40 per cent of its population.[3] Moreover, there are signs of de facto federalization in a growing number of non-federal states such as Spain, Belgium, and even France.

At the same time, some of the older and traditional federations seem to show signs of fatigue. In West Germany, for example, usually regarded as one of the most successful federations of the post–Second World War period, increasing criticism is voiced against the peculiar modes of political accommodation on which the success of federal stability has been based. These modes of centralized federal-state co-operation, known as inter-locking federalism, have turned out to be costly, inefficient, and prone to result in political immobilism. It was the goal of the constitutional reform of 1969 to raise the federal system's overall capacity to 'steer' the national economy by the introduction of 'joint tasks' and other means of formalized federal-state co-operation such as councils for financial planning and macroeconomic steering. This goal was not reached, and 'over-interlocking' is generally seen today as a serious systemic deficiency of West German federalism.[4]

By contrast, in the United States, still the acknowledged homeland and model of modern federalism, the death of 'old-style federalism' has been proclaimed. The states' share of power has been eroded by their dependence on the ever-growing grant-in-aid system. As a result, the national government possesses whatever degree of 'legal authority' it wishes to impose on states and localities, and the states' share of power rests upon the 'permission and permissiveness' of the national government.[5]

Finally, there is Canada, often neglected in comparative political inquiry, but recently receiving some attention because of the centrifugal dynamic in its federal system. Canadian students of federalism see their system as one of 'compounded crisis.'[6] The diagnosis includes a general decline of nationhood incurred by linguistic conflict, centre-periphery disparity, and the problems arising from economic dependence on the American neighbour. Of particular concern are the delegitimizing effects of executive federal-provincial diplomacy on the Canadian political community.[7] While inter-governmental co-ordination has become an increasing necessity, the result has often been 'federal-provincial paralysis' rather than successful collaboration.[8]

The problems of executive delegitimization and bureaucratic growth, of uneven economic development and regional discontent, and of newly asserted sub-national sociocultural identities are by no means confined to the federal world of institutionalized fragmentation. They are problems and conflicts endemic to advanced industrial societies. In the European context they have been identified as the systemic nexus of territory, economy, and identity.[9] And even in the United States regional discontent and 'state egotism' have been pointed out as a new threat to the national agenda of policy formation and economic recovery.[10] The heart of the matter is as old as the history of civilization. It is the dialectical tension between authority and liberty, efficient government organization and societal diversity, between the 'Mace and the maze.'[11] If the territorial dimension of politics thus reasserts itself in federal as well as in unitary political systems, the inevitable question is once again:

Does Federalism Matter?

No other country has had a longer political tradition of political accommodation between the Mace and the maze, between empire and regional particularism, than Germany. The three empires of Charlemagne, Bismarck, and Hitler are usually studied with awe as Teutonic manifestations of state power and bureaucratic order. Much less known and studied, though, is the fact that between the years 800 and 1945 Germany was governed in a centralized and unitary fashion only for the twelve years of Nazi totalitarianism. Consequently the rebirth of a democratically re-educated West Germany after the Second World War was accompanied with much hope in the federal traditions of the past. As Franz Jerusalem wrote in 1949, the natural form of political life, which had been destroyed by the modern centralized state, must be re-established: 'One glance at the basic forms of social life shows that all social life is federal by nature.'[12]

According to this view, federalism is in the first instance an organizational response to the pluralist nature and group structure of society,[13] a balance between individual and group liberties, established by agreement among compound majorities.[14] As a safeguard of society's structural maze against the power of the Mace, federalism consciously repudiates the idea of empire. As Donald V. Smiley pointed out: 'The justifications of federalism over a unitary system are political and the values furthered by federalism have nothing to do with rationalism in public policy. First, federalism is one of several possible devices for constraining political power, particularly executive power. Second, to the extent that within a nation attitudes and interests are not uniformly distributed on a territorial basis, federalism contributes to the responsiveness of government to the popular will.'[15] According to this argument, federalism may be costly and inefficient, but because it promotes freedom, these costs are acceptable. The partisans of the Mace have never accepted this view. William Riker, for example, sees federalism at best as a confusion of contradictory policies, and at worst as a tyranny by minority and 'impediment to the freedom of all.' The assertion that federalism promotes freedom is nothing but a 'hypocritical falsehood.'[16] Clearly placing individual liberty over group liberty, he sees majoritarian national government as invariably more efficient and democratic than a maze of local governments. The costs of federalism are not worth accepting – at least not in principle.

In practice federalism is not a free choice, but a function of the political power of territorial minorities, at least when war and other means of open coercion are excluded as possible options. Even Riker admits that while federalism is 'specious and unreasonable' in the United States and West Germany, it serves some purpose given the degree of societal fragmentation in Canada.[17] Canadians themselves are not always so sure about this. In a most influential refutation of Livingston's famous definition of federalism as a function of societies, Alan Cairns raises serious doubts as to whether Canadian federalism serves the interests of its societal fragments. The sociological perspective of federalism, he contends, pays inadequate attention to the political self-interests of powerful governments at both ends of the federal structure and to the 'capacity of government to make society responsive to its demands.'[18] From a class-analysis perspective the idea that federalism promotes freedom has been viewed even more sceptically. Canadian federalism in this view reflects the unequal power relations of a regionally fragmented class structure. Far from granting all regions an equal share, federalism rather increases inequality and dependence, because, in its essence, 'regionalism is an exploitative relationship.'[19]

At this point an important distinction must be made between federalism as ideology and federation as institution.[20] As ideology, federalism assumes that the retention of some degree of group liberty is a democratic requisite in territorially fragmented societies and that compound polities are better safeguards against the abuse of political power in general. Federation as institution commonly consists of two or three levels of government with overlapping jurisdictions. Neither level has the power entirely to dominate the other. National decision-making is therefore based on compound majoritarianism and usually dependent on political bargaining and compromise.

Federal legitimacy depends primarily on whether the premises of federalism as ideology are fulfilled, i.e. whether federations do indeed serve a societal desire for the retention of group liberty and identity and whether this retention does indeed contribute to the promotion of freedom by making governments more responsive to the popular will. The question of federal legitimacy, then, is one of congruence between form and content in federally organized polities. It is the contention of this essay, however, that federalism matters not only when it responds adequately to societal demands for group liberty but also when it satisfies the material needs of societies and individuals efficiently.

In post-war West Germany the 'equity of living conditions' has been a top priority of political federalism. An almost unitary degree of homogeneity has been reached because of the prosperous phase of national economic rebuilding. Political and social conflicts for the most part cut across region and are articulated through the channels of a strongly centralized and competitive party system, on the one hand, and through corporatist modes of interest intermediation among the dominant groups of society, on the other hand. The Bundesrat, West Germany's second parliamentary chamber, rarely has promoted regional interests and rather serves as an additional site of national policy formation. In times of divergent party majorities at both levels of government, this kind of 'intrastate federalism' has sometimes been used as an instrument by the opposition to obstruct federal policy-making.[21] Form and content of West German federal politics are therefore characterized by a high degree of non-congruence. It has even been suggested that the ultimate goal of federal politics in West Germany is to bypass and render superfluous the institutional forms of federalism.[22] If so, West German federalism may have become obsolescent as a safeguard of democratic legitimacy.

At first glance, similar patterns might be discerned in the case of the United States. Certainly the historic evolution of federal-state relations has enhanced the pre-eminence of the central government. Ironically, the heterogeneity and lack of self-co-ordination among the American states may have been the main reason for the creeping centralization and nationalization of American politics. Roger Gibbins attributes this nationalization to the effects of political and socioeconomic modernization, which gradually diminish the influx of territorial politics as a primordial source of conflict.[23] As recent western European experience shows, however, regionalism, while not primordial,[24] is far from dead. In the context of territory, economy, and identity, regionalism is a function of those centre-periphery relations newly created by modern industrial capitalism and its tendencies of sectoral and spatial concentration. The effective expansion of a capitalist economy and the creation of regional dependence simply are two sides of the same coin.

American federalism therefore needs re-examination. On the one hand, the recent rounds of proclaiming a new and even 'new-new' federalism must be taken with caution. Are the 'decongestion, devolution, decrementalism and deregulation' of intergovernmental relations[25] a real alternative to the long-term centralizing trend of American federalism, or are they just a tactical variegation within the framework of an unscathed federal prerogative using its spending power selectively by granting and withdrawing funds according to the interests of the national economy?[26] On the other hand, the noted increase of regional divisiveness over the asymmetry of growing fiscal burdens, demographic shifts from frostbelts to sunbelts, and the negative effects of the world economic crisis on the traditional centres of industrial production[27] has already had some impact on federal policy formation – as in the recent free trade discussion with Canada.

Concerns over the fate of the northwestern US lumber industry, for example, are no primordial outcry of narrow-minded senators resistant to modernization.[28] They reveal a deepening legitimation conflict between national and regional interests. A 'new-new' federalism committed only to the yardsticks of national industrial reconstruction and international economic competitiveness would doubtlessly increase that conflict.

In West Germany it is the centripetal party system that principally undermines the federal form of government. At the same time the policy immobilism of 'interlocking federalism' – which is a result of this incongruence of form and content – frustrates the expectations of the policymakers and the general public alike. In the United States, in contrast, the incongruence lies between increasing regional policy demands and the federal zero-sum game of macroeconomic selectivity. In both cases, the delegitimizing effects of federalism stem from the deficiencies of centripetal politics, and frustrated expectations are typically met with a populist rhetoric of bland generalizations.

The case of Canadian federalism is of an altogether different nature. The federal government in Canada does not have such unrestricted legal authority over provincial affairs as in the case of 'permissive federalism' in the United States, and it cannot rely on centralized national party machinery, as its West German counterpart can. The problem of Canadian federalism is its constitutionally entrenched centrifugalism. Because the provinces possess extensive jurisdiction over Canada's crucial natural resources, and because the French factor in Quebec serves as a permanent reminder of sociocultural diversity and economic disparity, unilateral federal efforts of macroeconomic planning and regulation are met by provincial resistance and occasionally even retaliation.[29] The issue of federal legitimacy emerges as one of 'regionalism versus rationalism.'[30] According to this view there is an unresolved conflict built into Canadian federalism between the economic rationalism of maximized nation-wide resource mobilization for the benefit of all Canadians (individual liberty) and the (irrational?) quest for provincialist self-determination (group liberty). The legitimacy of Canadian federalism is based on the perpetual compromise between the national claim of unity and the provincial claims of diversity. Delegitimization occurs when either order of government tries to impose its will unilaterally.

The discourse becomes even more complicated when we consider what and whom these manifestations of governmental power may represent. In a highly fragmented society like Canada, regional interests roughly correspond to manufacturing in central Canada and resource-based industries in the peripheries. Of course, some manufacturing sectors may decline while others grow; and the same is true in the resource-based industries because of the fluctuations and turbulences of world markets. Finally, manufacturing interests are closely tied to the availability of cheap resources, and the resource industries seek stability through industrial diversification.

As a result, regions – centres and peripheries – not only in Canada but in all advanced industrial societies are becoming simultaneously more autonomous and more interdependent. The centralized nation-state may lose its capacity 'to act as the arena for expressing and integrating regional views, or for defining a national interest that transcends region.' National policy formation degenerates into a kind of multiregional patchwork. It is therefore not surprising that, when 'listening to all the grievances, one sometimes gets the impression that all regions are "losers" in the Confederation balance sheet.'[31] This is the irrationality of the rational in highly complex socioeconomic systems.

What the advocates of national economic centripetalism have overlooked, then, is the apparent survival of another rationalism, based on the nexus of territory, economy, and identity. While there is certainly no 'small-is-beautiful' rationalism available that could relegitimize post-industrial societies in a world of ubiquitous interdependence, it must also be noted that centripetal economic determinism becomes obsolescent and irrational when 'peripheral predicaments and politicization emerge out of the incongruity between cultural, economic and political roles, an incongruity that has existed ... as long as there have been states.'[32] The legitimation crisis of federal systems does not stem from the fact that fragmented interest-group politics 'necessarily produce fragmented, particularistic programs'[33] but from the irrational 'smartness' of that kind of economic rationalism that seeks to graft the logic of nation-wide market mobilization onto a highly fragmented societal system.[34]

If political regionalism is a legitimate manifestation of the triadic nexus of territorial, economic, and identity interests in fragmented societies, where do the political will and legitimacy of the centre come from? According to federalism as ideology, its sources are the demands of individual liberty which cannot be satisfied by a confederal structure of group liberties. Indeed, the existence of 'multiple loyalties' is a major empirical given in fragmented societies such as Canada. While Canadians appear to be 'highly sensitized to regional differences,' these differences by no means eliminate other conflicts that cut across regions and are not perceived as conflicts of territorial group liberty.[35] This does not necessarily mean, of course, that such conflicts could not be regionally based and accommodated. Do a political will and interest exist that call for the nation-wide accommodation of such conflicts?

It was Immanuel Wallerstein's seminal contention that the economic interests of capitalism 'operate within an arena larger than that which any political entity can totally control' and that this 'gives capitalists a freedom of manoeuver that is structurally based.'[36] Economic interests initially aim at exploiting the domestic/regional market. But the consequent accumulation of surpluses soon allows them to exceed these markets and to widen the circle of influence and domination beyond the regional scope that politically sanctioned their success in the first place.[37] Within global competition and interdependence the nation-state is the political basis for the formation and expansion of economic interest. The regional circle of the triadic territory-economy-identity nexus is broken by a 'new trinity' of capital, state bureaucracy, and scientistic technocracy in the name of modernization. Modernization in this context means 'the attempt to rationalize an entire society, make it conform to a model designed to impose the most efficient use of available means for the achievement of particular ends, such as reindustrialization, military security, education for international competition, etc.'[38] Obviously there are winners and losers in such a rationalization scheme, and this is the source of social conflicts that can be both reinforcing and cross-cutting for territorial politics.

Of course, there is no guarantee that a highly decentralized form of regionalism should not result in an anachronistic fallback to an almost feudal degree of unrestrained provincialism. Province-building in Canada has been extensively criticized as such a fallback,[39] and Riker's criticism of state minority tyranny aims in the same direction. However, efficient modernization ultimately allows for the existence of only one rationale, and its main imperative is the 'curse of bigness':[40] the creation of one technocratic structure 'whose task is to rationalize the conditions that will preserve order, promote conditions favourable to capitalist enterprise, and strengthen ... power.'[41] As long as regions, provinces, and states remain dependent on central handouts according to a legally unrestricted allocative rationalism, we 'might go so far as to say that there can be no favourable conditions for autonomous economic development.'[42]

It is one of the crucial assumptions of federalism as ideology that the existence of a strong central government is the necessary safeguard of individual liberty against the excessive use of group liberties. But who holds in check the excesses of the centralized forces of modernization? Federal ideology refers to the notion of a social compact or covenant that stipulates that federal power has to be based on the consent of the constituent members. However, it is one of the most striking characteristics of the new trinity of capital, state, and technocracy that each of its elements depends 'only minimally, if at all, on the consent of the members of society.'[43] Thus it is a characteristic feature of capitalism that it transcends the political entities in which it operates and that it affects most; likewise, the federal executive bureaucracy typically avoids getting caught in the pitfalls of jurisdictional or parliamentary control; finally, science as the sacrosanct originator of techno-systemic requirements 'became the perfect incarnation of a conception of power that was to be generated independently of any social contract or democratic agreement.'[44]

The delegitimizing effects of such consent minimization affect all advanced capitalist systems. Can federalism make a difference, or has Laski's prophecy of the obsolescence of federalism reached its ultimate conclusion? At the crossroads of economic and legitimation crisis, the question of whether the old triad of territory, economy, and identity will become revitalized, or whether the new trinity of economic rationalism will prevail, is very much dependent on the structural contradictions and challenges in capitalist systems under conditions of socioeconomic contraction and sociopolitical fragmentation.

Industrial Democracy in Crisis

The economic rationalism of advanced industrial societies rests on one fundamental condition: the parallel growth of mass production and mass consumption.[45] Consequently, the regulatory task of the capitalist state must focus on the two functions of economic accumulation (supply side) and political legitimation (demand side). Under the impact of economic crisis and fiscal constraint, however, this double task of the interventionist welfare state becomes unmanageable. A general crisis of 'governability' is the inevitable result. It is usually explained as a crisis of overloaded governments that are no longer capable of satisfying the rising expectations of competing interest groups and parties.

Whether or not these rising expectations are in reality a 'misnomer for increased insecurity and structurally induced need,' the result is significant reduction of the system's conflict-resolving capacity. On the one hand, the state is under pressure from powerful economic interest groups to restore business confidence and the investment climate (accumulation function). On the other hand, the 'support systems of the welfare state' cannot simply be 'switched off' (legitimation function).[46] As a consequence, the capitalist state has to take refuge in two compromising and discriminating strategies: a greater degree of welfare spending selectivity according to the conflict-generating potential of the addressees, and a selective winner/loser scheme with regard to economic restructuring and industrial modernization. The latter has been described and propagated as the formation of a 'recessionary cartel'[47] in the case of the ailing North American economies, and it has been practised under the name of (selective) corporatist intermediation in the case of West Germany.[48]

The dilemma and contradiction of advanced industrial democracies then lie in the fact that both economic and political strategies increase rather than diminish the conflict potential. Available cures appear worse than the disease. The reason once again is the separation of form and content in complex industrial systems. Supply side economics, for example, is not based on any institutional guarantee that tax incentives are actually being used for consumption- and employment-intensive investment.[49] Neo-corporatist or recessionary cartel strategies are bound to be inefficient for the same reason. There is no institutional guarantee or control that the obstruction potential that brings the major participants to the negotiating table in the first place will be used in a way generally beneficial to societal, industrial, and market reconstruction. Narrowing 'the scope of political conflict admitted to democratic politics' by 'informal, highly inaccessible negotiations among poorly legitimated representatives of functional groups'[50] is likely to lead to a deepening of the crisis, as the power mechanism contracts 'so that an even smaller part of the entire social structure is directly determined by it.' A plausible result is the 'emergence of a bifurcated society organized around a shrinking capitalist core and an expanding periphery of non-market institutional arrangements and conditions of life.'[51]

If it is the 'trick of the state' to co-opt the shrinking capitalist core into a system of restricted political accommodation, then it is 'society's ruse' to autonomize the periphery which is no longer determined by it.[52] This is why the structural contradiction of advanced industrial democracies can be identified as a separation of form and content, between the political system, on the one hand, and the real world of social existence on the other. Here is where both liberal and Marxist analyses miss the point. The system of capitalist accumulation and reproduction is still based on the accommodation of class conflict, as in the case of corporatist interest intermediation. At the same time, however, the real world of social existence is increasingly determined by 'disparate as well as peripheral group conflicts' that are no longer primarily class-based. A new conflict line arises between the centres of capitalist accumulation and a growing periphery of unspecific and multiple interests. Given the asymmetry of this conflict one can no longer speak of a system of market competition. A new level of complexity leads to the formation of new 'personal and collective identities.'[53]

Such identities focus on new issues and living conditions that are not taken care of by the central system, such as environmental issues, peace, and the social consequences of marginalization. At the same time these collective identities are fostered by the retention of those collective memories that the systemic success of the modern nation-state tries to suppress but has not yet eradicated altogether: culture and region. These values become especially mobilized when uneven economic development is perceived as discriminatory. In other words, a revitalized triad of territory, economy, and identity may revolt against the new trinity of technocratic state capitalism.

The territorial dimension of fragmentation in highly complex societies leads back to the question of whether federation as an institutionalized form of political fragmentation can accommodate the conflicts and interests of fragmented societies. A reconciliation of form and content would require that either the form of government adapt to the fragmentizing societal dynamic (centrifugal federalism) or that this dynamic be tamed and brought into harmony with the systemic requirements of the contracting economic system (centripetal federalism). If societal fragmentation is persistent, however, and deepened by the constraints of the politics of scarcity, the latter strategy seems to be a doubtful path toward relegitimation of federalism.

Repercussions on Federal Legitimacy

The legitimacy of territorially fragmented democracies rests on two conditions: the political system must be perceived as sufficiently responsive to the demands and expectations of all regional groups, and the economic system must be sufficiently successful to compensate for structural disparities and inequalities. As Rokkan and Urwin show in the case of the territorial politics of western Europe, both conditions have been fulfilled only poorly throughout the phase of modern nation-state formation.

Economically, the benefits of industrial modernization spread unevenly. Regional policy was based on the false assumption that 'regional inequalities were not a direct and inevitable consequence of the economic system, that they would ultimately be eradicated by an improvement in the overall national economy.' Even when more deliberate efforts were made to overcome regional disparity by the creation of peripheral 'growth-poles,' the logic of regional policy remained unchanged: the cure for the regional disease had to come from the centre. While the economic welfare of peripheries was clearly improved by regional aid programs, regional policy more clearly failed 'in terms of enabling more of the indigenous peripheral population to live, work and enjoy within the periphery a standard of living comparable to that of more central regions.' In their analysis, Rokkan and Urwin come to the conclusion that regional politics can regain legitimacy only when the peripheries 'obtain the ability to control the appropriate means and instruments' allowing for autonomous economic development. Most important, they should 'receive the financial autonomy that centres have consistently refused to grant.'[54]

The discriminating effects of the politics of territory in modern industrial societies are more difficult to identify. Complex industrial societies are normally characterized by a polycentric economic structure based on the spatial distribution of resource-based (primary), industrial (secondary), and service/administrative (tertiary) activities. It is important to note that 'secondary sector activities can be spatially separated from centres of tertiary activity.' Likewise, resource bases and centres of industrial production can be separated. What this means is that the development of regional production centres (primary or secondary) is not necessarily a sufficient condition of political legitimacy. The overall system can still be perceived as insufficiently responsive to the demands and expectations of regional economic centres if the tertiary activities of the national economy, especially finance, trade, and transportation, are disproportionally concentrated elsewhere. Rokkan and Urwin conclude that it is a new 'quaternary sector, covering all the agencies responsible for the registration, handling and diffusion of decisions, orders, instructions and information across a wide territory' that is 'a more cogent indicator of centrality.'[55]

Federation as an auxiliary form of political accommodation in territorially fragmented societies can respond to the challenges of uneven economic development and political alienation by means of two institutional alternatives. It can incorporate the peripheries into central decision-making ('intrastate federalism'), or it can co-ordinate decision-making among relatively autonomous levels of government ('interstate federalism').[56] While intrastate federalism is a more or less clear case of centripetal federalism and decision-making, the dynamic of interstate federalism can be centripetal (aiming at harmonization and standardization) or centrifugal (aiming at diversification). The traditional logic of federal systems is to contain societal centrifugalism by varying degrees of political and economic centripetalism. Form and content of federal politics are in harmony when the balance between centrifugalism and centripetalism is congruent with the overlapping sets of differentiated expectations and multiple loyalties of the polity's federal segments.

As long as all expectations can be more or less satisfied and everybody can take home at least some sort of prize, as during the post-war decades of economic growth and prosperity, inevitable imbalances can be accommodated relatively easily. Under the condition of economic scarcity and fiscal constraint, however, the contradictions of capitalism in advanced industrial democracies spill over into the political fabric of federalism and federation. The logic of capitalist market systems has been impaired by two structural contradictions. On the one hand, the economic exchange relations between capital and labour, and those between producers and consumers, always had to be stabilized by non-market institutional arrangements. On the other hand, the political system always had to rely on power structures outside the institutional models provided by the architects of liberal democratic (party) competition. Under the recent conditions of persistent structural economic and fiscal crisis, a new dynamic seems to be set in motion by which the effort at system stabilization tends to increase rather than decrease the stability of those parts of the political and economic system that are no longer determined by the market exchange relationship and no longer controlled by its liberal democratic institutions. This is what Offe aptly calls the 'structural contradictions of late capitalism.'[57]

When federal efforts at containing the centrifugal effects of uneven economic development and regional disparity actually increase centre-periphery conflict, it is appropriate to speak of the contradictions and legitimation crisis of 'late federalism.'[58] Such a development was most obvious in Canada during the Trudeau era.

According to Pierre Trudeau's vision of federalism, a clear priority must be given to individual liberty over group liberty. Consequently it was the main reformist thrust of the Trudeau era that the centrifugal pressures created by powerful provincial governments must be 'contained, deflected, undermined, and attacked.'[59] Having entered the political stage with the conviction that Canadian federalism was bound to fail if strong centripetal 'counterweights' did not keep in check – and ultimately prevail over – the forces of provincialism,[60] Trudeau left the political stage sixteen years later reiterating the message for his successor even more bluntly: for a nationally justified purpose and benefit, the federal government should reach out, over the heads of multinational corporations and provincial premiers alike, and directly address the concerns of the Canadian people.[61]

As the Rokkan-Urwin analysis of territoriality in advanced industrial states has shown, the centripetal reaching out to the concerns of the people in the peripheries not only too often 'failed to live up to expectations and the claims made for them' but also 'brought into the open the more fundamental issue of how space is to be managed.'[62] Trudeau's centripetal reformism triggered the further intensification of federal-provincial conflict. Because regional policy formation remained based on centralist premises, the conditions for the further rise of provincialist aspirations became even more salient. Although the recent patriation of the Canadian constitution must be seen at least in part as a result of Trudeau's unilateral strategies,[63] it was nevertheless based on a compromise that essentially did not overcome the systemic contradictions and challenges of Canadian federalism.[64]

Provincialism and regionalism are not likely to disappear in the years to come, and 'Canadian history is littered with the broken dreams of centralizers.'[65] After its 1984 electoral victory, the new Conservative government set out to ease federal-provincial conflict by 'bringing the provinces back in.' As the free trade issue shows, this is easier said than done. In the volatile world of advanced international capitalism, national economic strategies will always produce a fragmenting effect by creating winners and losers. It seems that in a strongly regionalized federal economy such as Canada's, grand designs of national economic restructuring inevitably tend to arouse the resistance of at least some regions and provinces.

If the recent legitimation crisis of Canadian federalism mainly stems from centre-periphery polarization and the failure of federal institutions 'to represent and provide a forum for accommodation among competing regional interests,'[66] the delegitimizing effects of American centripetal federalism are much harder to detect. Mobilization of national consent is easier for the US presidential system of government than for the Canadian type of Westminster parliamentarianism with its lack of adequate intrastate representation. At the same time competitive and market-oriented US mass culture can accept more easily the existence of regional disparities. Moreover, patterns of centre-periphery disparity are more difficult to detect in a country of fifty states than in one of ten provinces with one of them, Ontario, in a clearly dominating position. This is why Riker found the maintenance of federalism justified in the case of Canada but 'specious and unreasonable' with regard to the United States.[67] He did so, however, in the mid-1960s, when faith in the economics and politics of scale was at its peak. Twenty years later, Etzioni argued that the American polity was threatened by a serious 'retreat from nation,' a decreasing willingness to attend 'shared concerns,' and a spectacular rise of 'regional and state egotism.'[68] Of the reasons given – decline of faith in national leadership, decline in unifying Cold War tensions, and economic crisis – only the last still seems valid under President Reagan's back-to-the-fifties approach to politics. The economic record, however, is mixed at best: a significant economic recovery on the one hand, achieved mainly through unprecedented military-cum-deficit spending,[69] and the continuing decline of social as well as regional segments of American society on the other.[70]

If these trends persist, they will even be reinforced by a 'new-new' federalism that tries to stimulate a regionally discriminating industrial restructuring program while at the same time cutting the transfers on which states and localities have come to depend. What the Reaganite version of federalism looks like is the abandoning of peripheral fiscal obligations in the name of greater state autonomy and for the sake of greater central budgetary flexibility: 'austerity equals decentralization.'[71] The United States may soon find itself in a legitimation crisis resulting from growing and deepening social polarization. Due to the contracting dynamic of modern capitalism, this polarization may well lead to the contradictory situation of regional dissent and an ever-increasing degree of federal centripetalization at the same time.

Among Western industrial nations, West Germany is perhaps the country with the lowest level of open regionalism. Its post-war reconstruction as an almost 'unitary federal state,'[72] and the phenomenal success of its 'economic miracle' during the phase of industrial rebuilding,[73] led to an almost unique degree of political homogenization. At the same time the traditional non-centralization and diversity of sociocultural life were maintained and preserved by the cultural autonomy of the Länder. A mutually reinforcing mobilization of economic and cultural grievances did not occur. Contrary to the United States and Canada, a centralized party system could reach out directly to the West German citizenry. Distributional conflicts remained regionally cross-cutting and class-based. They were muted by economic success and later, after the first serious recession in the mid-1960s, accommodated by corporatist intermediation (Concerted Action) between capital, labour, and the state. This accommodation was initially facilitated by a grand coalition government of conservatives and social democrats (1966–9), roughly resembling a similar compromise between business and labour interests.

At the same time a substantial constitutional reform took place that aimed at the further centripetalization of the West German federal system in the name of macroeconomic steering and Keynesian control of the national economy.[74] It included curtailment of the fiscal autonomy of the Länder and creation of 'joint tasks' in crucial policy areas such as regional development, infrastructure, and education.[75] The result was a new system of 'interlocking federalism' that essentially had to rely on collective bargaining between the federal and Land governments.

It was not until after the oil shock of 1973 that a more dramatic change began to take place. It can be characterized as a two-fold process of political polarization. Within the political institutions a growing degree of policy immobilism resulted from the fact that the conservative opposition had gained an obstructive majority in the Bundesrat that blocked or watered down the reformist political agenda of the social-liberal federal government. Outside the political institutions a rapidly increasing number of citizens' initiatives (Buergerinitiativen) was formed. These were single-issue movements for the promotion of environmentalist and other alternative political goals, and they were protest movements against the unison of West German party politics in a more general sense. As a result, the Green Party emerged as the collecting point of alternative interests and new collective identities.[76]

Until the mid-1970s, the main delegitimizing conflict lines of the West German political system can be seen correctly in the incongruence between the institutionalized federal structures and the centralized party system on the one hand,[77] and in the alienation between party politics and new social protest movements on the other.[78] The Green Party's spectacular success, especially in influencing and reshaping (informal) coalition structures and policy contents at the Land and local level of government, indicates, however, that a considerable revitalization of territorial politics may be imminent in West Germany as well. West German federalism has doubtlessly facilitated the political success of the Greens by allowing them to attack and compete with the established parties on a regional level. Once again the legitimation crisis of late federal systems appears as the contradictory consequence of centripetal systems stabilization. The centripetal concentration of a cartelized (party) élite on competitive (and immobilizing) federal policy formation according to the systemic requirements of the national economy has created an atmosphere of political disillusionment and prepared the grounds for regional protest politics.[79]

In comparative synopsis, then, the common denominator of the legitimation crisis in federal systems is the contradictory interdependence of centripetalism and centrifugalism. While common to all advanced industrial democracies, this conflict poses a particular challenge to federal systems, because only here can it find recourse to a structure of institutionalized fragmentation, and only here can it become mobilized further by the incongruence of federalism as ideology and federation as institution. Yet federalism and federation can be seen as particularly promising responses to the challenges of fragmentation. If an institutional formula can be found that responds adequately to the revitalized desire for group liberty, the reconciliation of form and content in the context of the territorial politics of fragmented societies seems possible.

Rebuilding the Federal Polity

Federalism as ideology holds that the retention of collective group liberties is a necessary constraint on centralized political power and contributes to the popular responsiveness of governments. For the sake of democracy, therefore, the economic and administrative rationalism of the Mace must be sacrificed. Critics of the federal maze, however, insist that a majoritarian national government is not only more rational and efficient but also, by enhancing individual liberty, more democratic. The question then is: does democracy matter? It has been the most fundamental and lasting fact of 2,000 years of Western civilization that always 'some are more equal than others.' One might say with some justification that the general degree of active citizens' participation in politics never again reached the level that it once had attained in classical Athens, at the very beginning of that civilization.

In the age of modern liberal mass democracy, governments increasingly rely on sources and channels of conflict regulation and policy formation other than the ritualized processes of democratic representation. In West Germany neocorporatist modes of interest intermediation have been criticized as a new form of functional representation and decision-making among a small number of participants seeking 'to keep their delicate exchange of proposals, information and threats as remote as possible from both the general public eye and from the segmental constituencies which participants represent.'[80] A similar case of such non-political decision-making can be made with regard to the American system of clientelism. It was Lowi's famous contention that American interest-group liberalism results in the 'atrophy of institutions of popular control' and the 'creation of new structures of privilege' and that this provides the system with 'stability by spreading a *sense* of representation at the expense of genuine flexibility, at the expense of democratic forms, and ultimately at the expense of legitimacy.'[81] Finally, federalism in Canada has been criticized in similar terms as bypassing the traditional forms of democratic legitimation and providing political coherence and unity through channels of executive bargaining that are 'two or three steps removed from any sort of popular control.'[82]

In other words, it appears to be very difficult to argue for or against federalism in terms of democratic legitimacy. Democracy as ideology is a poor yardstick to make a choice of preference between unitary or federal political institutions. The conflict between individual and group liberties transcends democratic values when it is governing élites and dominant classes who make the choice in any case. Likewise, however, the abstract criteria of functional efficiency and effectiveness are of little help in choosing between centripetalism and centrifugalism, because they 'always contain the implicit "for whom", "in whose eyes".'[83] What remains, then, is the question of whether and how the premises of federalism as ideology can be reconciled with the structural possibilities of federation as institution.

The essence of federalism as ideology is the belief in the existence of multiple loyalties and overlapping circles of social life. As a consequence, federalism is 'agnostic about community.'[84] Living together in a complex plurality of overlapping and interdependent communities does not allow for the simple majoritarianism of the centripetal and unitary nation-state. The political will of the widest circle of community instead arises from the compound majoritarianism and mutual bargaining among the members of this community. This belief in mutualism as a covenanted form of living together is, in fact, deeply rooted in the tradition of Western thought. It has been neglected by the economic rationalism of modern industrial societies because it is incompatible with the have-or-have-not ideology of capitalist zero-sum society.[85]

In federal systems political mutualism is frustrated mainly by the zero-sum competitiveness of different levels of government and by the centripetal imperative of maximized nation-wide resource mobilization, which creates a vicious circle of centre-periphery dependence and peripheral aggressiveness in return. In order to reconcile federal mutualism with federation as institution, this vicious circle must be broken. Dependence can be overcome only by a multilateral strategy of economic diversification and political autonomization. In other words, the 'new-new federalism' must have a real material and institutional basis approaching regional self-sufficiency. This would in particular include fiscal and administrative autonomy. Economically, local industries must be developed that can be based on local resources, tend to promote regional employment, and satisfy local needs.[86] Politically this means that a good deal of the quaternary sector's central powers have to be regionally redistributed in order to make the peripheries more independent from the interests of central élites and industries. The gain of political control over their own affairs could compensate the poorer regions for the continuation of some degree of transfer dependence. Moreover, the spirit of federal mutualism would probably be better served if fiscal equalization were organized by means of direct transfers from richer to poorer regions, states, or provinces, according to a periodically renegotiated formula. This type of 'brotherly' federalism is successfully practised in West Germany.[87] It contradicts the commonly held view that a central enforcer is inevitably needed to harmonize the economic and fiscal disparities of a federal system.

In terms of federation as institution the obvious consequence is a revival of confederal principles of political organization. This essentially includes the acceptance of an institutionalized system of 'concurrent majorities,' which means that decisions of the national majority can be vetoed by a (qualified) provincial or state majority and vice versa. Again the problem is how to harmonize the demands and expectations of the two majorities. In the case of Canada, it has been suggested to 'harness together at the national level both majorities' by creating an upper parliamentary chamber 'based on region or province rather than population,' in analogy to the American Senate and the (government-appointed) German Bundesrat.[88] As the unrestrained American centripetalism and the immobilism of the West German system of interlocking federalism show, however, such a reform toward more intrastate federalism does not replace the quintessential logic of confederal political practice: the necessity of political bargaining between territorial groups aiming at asymmetrical solutions policy by policy, issue by issue, and, in deeply fragmented federal systems, region by region, and province by province. If this is a 'messy' and 'untidy' solution from the perspective of centripetal systems rationalization, it may nevertheless turn out to be the only viable one. It may turn out even to be more efficient economically. Regional self-sufficiency is likely to reduce competitive conflict orientation among the members of the confederal federation, and the costs of co-ordinative bargaining may be lower than those of perpetual territorial conflict containment on behalf of an overburdened central government.

The argument for the retention of a federal political system is then ultimately not that it does or does not promote democratic freedom. The retention and maintenance of federal systems are based rather on the fact that territorial minorities have enough political power to resist the political will of a national majority. The question of federal legitimacy is therefore not whether federalism promotes freedom or not, but how democratic freedom can be improved within the parameters of existing federal systems. This question becomes all the more important when the politics of fragmentation in advanced industrial democracies implies the obsolescence of the traditional nation-state institutions, and federal solutions to the federal problems of fragmented societies may turn out to be not so much democratic solutions as politically viable ones. In the end federal solutions to federal problems may also be more efficient than the centripetal solutions of overburdened governments to the problems of fragmented societies. Admittedly this conclusion is rather speculative. But then this essay has been an exercise in federalism and democracy, and not in what mankind can realistically expect from its governments.

NOTES

1 Pierre-Joseph Proudhon *The Principle of Federation* ed and trans R. Vernon (Toronto: University of Toronto Press 1979) 70
2 Harold J. Laski 'The Obsolescence of Federalism' *The New Republic* 98 (3 May 1939) 367
3 Max Frenkel *Foederalismus und Bundesstaat* Band I *Foederalismus* (Bern: Lang 1984) 134–5
4 Fritz W. Scharpf et al *Politikverflechtung* (Kronberg: Scriptor 1976) 54–66
5 Michael D. Reagan and John G. Sanzone *The New Federalism* (New York: Oxford University Press 1981) 157–79
6 Donald V. Smiley *Canada in Question* (Toronto: McGraw-Hill/Ryerson 1980) 252–80

7 Richard Simeon *Federal-Provincial Diplomacy* (Toronto: University of Toronto Press 1973) 298–313
8 Alan C. Cairns 'The Other Crisis of Canadian Federalism' *Canadian Public Administration* (summer 1979) 177
9 Stein Rokkan and Derek W. Urwin *Economy Territory Identity* (London: Sage 1983)
10 See Amitai Etzioni *An Immodest Agenda* (New York: McGraw-Hill 1983) 163–82.
11 Richard Rose *The Territorial Dimension in Government* (Chatham: Chatham House 1982) 149–71
12 Franz W. Jerusalem *Die Staatsidee des Foederalismus* (Tuebingen: Mohr 1949) 6
13 See especially William S. Livingston 'A Note on the Nature of Federalism' in Aaron Wildavsky ed *American Federalism in Perspective* (Boston: Little, Brown 1967) 20–30.
14 See Daniel J. Elazar 'Confederation and Federal Liberty' *Publius* 12 no 4 (fall 1982) 4
15 Donald V. Smiley 'The Political Context of Resource Development in Canada' in Anthony Scott ed *Natural Resource Revenue: A Test of Federalism* (Vancouver: University of British Columbia Press 1976) 72
16 William H. Riker *Federalism* (Boston: Little, Brown 1964) 139–45
17 Ibid 151
18 Alan C. Cairns 'The Governments and Societies of Canadian Federalism' *Canadian Journal of Political Science* 10 no 4 (December 1977) 695–725
19 Wallace Clement 'Regionalism as Uneven Development: Class and Region in Canada' in *Perspectives on Regions and Regionalism in Canada* v (Ottawa: The Association for Canadian Studies 1983) 68–79
20 See Preston King *Federalism and Federation* (Baltimore: Johns Hopkins 1982).
21 See Gerhard Lehmbruch 'Party and Federation in Germany: A Developmental Dilemma' *Government and Opposition* 13 no 2 (spring 1978) 151–77.
22 See Wolfgang Zeh 'Entscheidungsmuster der Politikverflechtung und ihre verfassungsstrukturellen Zwaenge' in Fritz W. Scharpf et al *Politikverflechtung II* (Kronberg: Athenaeum 1977) 138.
23 Roger Gibbins *Regionalism* (Toronto: Butterworths 1982) 1–7
24 See Thomas O. Hueglin 'Regionalism in Western Europe: Conceptual Problems of a New Political Perspective' *Comparative Politics* 18 no 4 (July 1986) 439–58.
25 Deil S. Wright and Harvey L. White 'Federalism and Intergovernmental Relationships: Evolving Patterns and Changing Perspectives' in D.S. Wright and H.L. White eds *Federalism and Intergovernmental Relations* (Washington, DC: American Society for Public Administration 1984) 22
26 Cf Anthony Careless 'The Struggle for Jurisdiction: Regionalism versus

Rationalism' *Publius* 14 no 1 (winter 1984) 70.

27 Etzioni *An Immodest Agenda* 168–73

28 See 'The Threat to Free Trade' *Maclean's* 21 April 1986, 40–3

29 See John F. Conway *The West* (Toronto: Lorimer 1983) 208–17.

30 See Careless 'The Struggle for Jurisdiction' 61–77.

31 Richard Simeon *Intergovernmental Relations and the Challenges to Canadian Federalism* (Kingston: Institute of Intergovernmental Relations, Queen's University 1979) 6–7

32 Rokkan and Urwin *Economy Territory Identity* 192

33 Reagan and Sanzone *The New Federalism* 154

34 See Lester Thurow 'Industrial Policies: Smart Ones and Stupid Ones' *Whig Standard Magazine* 11 February 1984, 5–8

35 Richard Simeon and David J. Elkins 'Province, Nation, Country and Confederation' in D.J. Elkins and R. Simeon eds *Small Worlds* (Toronto: Methuen 1980) 285–309

36 Immanuel Wallerstein *The Modern World-System* (New York: Academic Press 1974) 348

37 Cf Eric Kierans *Globalism and the Nation-State* (Montreal: CBC Enterprises 1984) 83–4.

38 Sheldon S. Wolin 'From Progress to Modernization: The Conservative Turn' *Democracy* (fall 1983) 9–21

39 See Garth Stevenson *Unfulfilled Union* (Toronto: Gage 1982).

40 Cf Daniel J. Elazar 'Cursed by Bigness or toward a Post-Technocratic Federalism' *Publius* 3 no 2 (summer 1973) 239–98.

41 Wolin 'From Progress to Modernization' 17

42 Rokkan and Urwin *Economy Territory Identity* 177

43 Wolin 'From Progress to Modernization' 15

44 Ibid

45 Cf Alain Lipietz *The Globalisation of the General Crisis of Fordism* (Kingston: Programme of Studies in National and International Development, Department of Political Studies, Queen's University 1984) 164–70.

46 See Claus Offe *Contradictions of the Welfare State* (London: Hutchinson 1984) 164–70.

47 Thurow 'Industrial Policies' 6

48 See Josef Esser and Wolfgang Fach 'Korporatistische Krisenregulierung im "Modell Deutschland"' in Ulrich von Alemann ed *Neokorporatismus* (Frankfurt: Campus 1981) 158–77.

49 Fritz W. Scharpf 'Institutionelle Bedingungen der Arbeitsmarkt- und Beschaeftigungspolitik' *Aus Politik und Zeitgeschichte* 12 February 1983, 3–4

50 Offe *Contradictions* 165–8

51 Ibid 284–5

52 Cf Gerhard Willke *Entzauberung des Staates* (Koenigstein: Athenaeum 1983) 117–46
53 See Juergen Habermas *Theorie des kommunikativen Handelns* II (Frankfurt: Suhrkamp 1982) 489–593.
54 Rokkan and Urwin *Economy Territory Identity* 170–9
55 Ibid 6–14
56 See Roger Gibbins in this volume.
57 See Offe *Contradictions* 125–9.
58 See Wolfgang Zeh 'Spaetfoederalismus: Vereinigungs- oder Differenzierungs-foederalismus?' *Zeitschrift fuer Parlamentsfragen* 8 no 4 (December 1977) 475–90.
59 Alan Cairns 'Constitution-Making, Government Self-Interest, and the Problem of Legitimacy' in Allan Kornberg and Harold D. Clarke eds *Political Support in Canada: The Crisis Years* (Durham: Duke University Press 1983) 429
60 Pierre E. Trudeau *Federalism and the French Canadians* (Toronto: Macmillan, 1968) xxiii
61 Remarks by Prime Minister Pierre E. Trudeau, Liberal Party of Canada Leadership Convention, Ottawa, 14 June 1984
62 Rokkan and Urwin *Economy Territory Identity* 178–9
63 Cf Michael B. Stein 'Canadian Constitutional Reform, 1927–1982: A Comparative Case Analysis over Time' *Publius* 14 no 1 (winter 1984) 121–39.
64 See Keith Banting and Richard Simeon 'Federalism, Democracy and the Future' in K. Banting and R. Simeon eds *And No One Cheered* (Toronto: Methuen 1983) 348–59.
65 Ibid 353
66 Ibid 353–4
67 See above, note 17.
68 Etzioni *An Immodest Agenda* 163–5
69 See Gerd Junne 'Das amerikanische Ruestungsprogramm: Ein Substitut fuer Industriepolitik' *Leviathan* 85 no 1 (1985) 23–37.
70 See John L. Palmer and Isabel V. Sawhill eds *The Reagan Record* (Cambridge: Ballinger 1984)
71 Wright and White 'Federalism' 25
72 Konrad Hesse *Der unitarische Bundesstaat* (Karlsruhe: Mueller 1962)
73 See Joachim Hirsch 'Developments in the Political System of West Germany since 1945' in Richard Scase ed *The State in Western Europe* (London: Croom Helm 1980) 116–21.
74 Ibid 121–4
75 See Scharpf et al *Politikverflechtung* 71–235.
76 See Wolfgang Beywl 'Neue Selbstorganisationen' *Aus Politik und Zeitgeschichte* (17 March 1984) 15–29

54/Thomas O. Hueglin

77 See above, note 21.
78 Klaus von Beyme *Das politische System der Bundesrepublik Deutschland* (Muenchen: Piper 1979) 59–94
79 Cf William M. Chandler and Alan Siaroff 'Post-industrial Politics in Germany and the Origins of the Greens' *Comparative Politics* 18 no 3 (April 1986) 303–25.
80 Offe *Contradictions* 167
81 Theodore J. Lowi *The End of Liberalism* (New York: Norton 1979) 58–63
82 Leo Panitch 'The Role and Nature of the Canadian State' in L. Panitch ed *The Canadian State* (Toronto: University of Toronto Press 1977) 11
83 Richard Simeon 'Criteria for Choice in Federal Systems' *Queen's Law Journal* 8 no 1 (fall 1982) 149
84 Reginald Whitaker *Federalism and Democratic Theory* (Kingston: Institute of Intergovernmental Relations, Queen's University 1983) 45
85 See John Kincaid and Daniel J. Elazar eds *The Covenant Connection* (Carolina Academic Press, forthcoming).
86 Ralph Matthews *The Creation of Regional Dependency* (Toronto: University of Toronto Press 1983) 109–17
87 *Studies in Comparative Federalism: Australia, Canada, the United States and West Germany* (Washington, DC: Advisory Commission on Intergovernmental Relations 1981) 70
88 See Whitaker *Federalism* 41–2.

Part Two

INSTITUTIONS AND
CONSTITUTIONAL PROCESS

4 / Federalization and Federalism: Belgium and Canada

MAUREEN COVELL

In August 1980, the Belgian parliament passed a series of laws and constitutional amendments creating a new set of regional and cultural institutions and handing over to these institutions a portion of the powers of legislation and regulation held by the central government. With this move in the direction of federalization if not federalism, Belgium joined a European trend and became one of several formerly unitary countries to attempt to resolve problems created by regional/ethnic differences by giving increased autonomy to the groups based on these differences.[1] Will the creation of a new, sub-national level of government make it easier to resolve conflicts among a country's ethnic and/or regional groups? One possible strategy for attempting to answer this question is to examine the experience of countries like Canada that have adopted a federal structure as one device for the resolution of group conflict. However, there are several prior questions that must be answered before such a comparison is undertaken.

Are the transfers of power involved in these new regionalization plans real or simply mystifications designed to shift responsibility without sharing power? Do they represent an attempt to diminish the trouble-making potential of groups by co-opting their élites into newly created positions of privilege without power? If, as many writers on older federations argue, the maintenance of federal institutions depends as much on a balance between centrifugal and centripetal forces in political and social systems outside formal institutions, then the reality of the transfer of power may depend on pre- or post-federalization changes in these systems. What are the changes, and are they happening? Finally, is it useful to compare the history of older federations with the present and future of the newer federalizing systems? The literature on political change in advanced capitalist societies, particularly under current conditions of economic crisis, argues that these societies are undergoing a process of fragmentation. If so, federalization as the deintegration of formerly unitary states might represent a process quite unlike the federalization as integration that marks the origin of most of the older federations.[2] This chapter will examine the process of regionalization in Belgium in the light of these questions and explore the utility of comparisons with the Canadian experience of federalism for predicting the course and outcome of the process.

Belgium and Canada

To paraphrase an old saying, 'One person's ark is another's *Titanic*.' Certainly the institutional arrangements and political practices that Canada and Belgium have developed to deal with their common problem of ethnic fragmentation differ enough to suggest that a multitude of intervening variables must come between a societal 'problem' and an institutional 'solution.' On the surface, at least, the similarities between the two countries are striking. Each is divided into two major language groups possessing a territorial centre of gravity: Dutch-speaking and French-speaking in Belgium and anglophone and francophone in Canada. In each country the language groups are also perceived to have differing cultures, while differences in economic organization and degree of prosperity both reinforce the differences between the groups and create intra-group differences.[3] Both countries were born under circumstances in which exogenous factors such as great-power strategic interests were as important as nationalistic zeal. Neither country has an elaborate founding myth: 'national deal' rather than 'national dream' best describes the circumstances of the creation of each.[4] As in other divided countries, heroic moments of the past are perceived and reacted to differently by the constituent groups and often constitute a divisive rather than a unifying force. Finally, each country has developed a modern economy heavily dependent on external trade and investment. In spite of these similarities, each country developed different ways of dealing with the problems of governing a fragmented society. In the terms usually employed to discuss the organization of such countries Canada is a federation, by most measures one of the more decentralized of the world's federal polities. It is not, however, considered a consociational democracy – or, at best, only a partial or imperfect example of the species. Belgium, however, has been called 'not just a complete example of consociational democracy: it is the most perfect, most convincing, and most impressive example of a consociation.'[5] It is not, or at least was not until the 1980 revision of its constitution, a federal country.

Canada chose the federal option at the beginning of its life as an independent country after a short experiment (in Upper and Lower Canada) with a system of unitary government tempered with practices such as double majorities that later came to be considered 'consociational devices.' Although the separation of the united province of Canada into Ontario and Quebec has some elements of federalism as disintegration, in most respects the creation of the Dominion of Canada was a classic act of federation: the union of previously separate political entities, prompted by such considerations as economic development and defence. While the introduction of consociation-style devices has occasionally been proposed, often under the rubric of intrastate federalism, formal adoption of such devices has usually been rejected as inconsistent with the practices of parliamentary democracy.[6]

There is no record that federalism was even considered as an option at the 1831 convention that drew up the constitution for the new kingdom of the Belgians. This constitution established a unitary state whose centralization was diluted by considerable autonomy at the communal level.[7] Attempts to make this unitary state work in the face of Flemish-francophone differences led to introduction of such classic consociational devices as guaranteed language parity in the national cabinet. The federalist option was not seriously proposed until the 1930s and for years was rejected as unnecessary or even as a dangerous experiment precisely because of the depth of the division between the two groups.[8]

Why the Original Choices?

Studies of federalism as integration list several factors that might lead to the striking of a federal bargain among formerly separate units: a desire to create a larger economy, defence needs, and a desire to act with greater diplomatic weight in international arenas. These motives could, of course, lead also to creation of a unitary state, and there is less discussion in the literature of the reasons for choosing a federal form of government instead: size and diversity are the reasons usually given. Federalism is seen as a least common denominator, a recognition of the fact that the basis for a unitary system of government simply does not exist in a given society. On the score of size of territory, if not population, federalism is a more logical choice for Canada than for Belgium. On the score of diversity of population, federalism would appear to be a logical choice for both. There were other reasons behind the Belgian choice of a unitary state and the Canadian choice of the federal form.

There are two minor and one major reason for the choices made. The first minor reason is the international context. A small European nation, surrounded by unitary states, is likely to choose a similar form of organization. A large North American nation is more likely to be influenced by the United States, although in 1867 the American example was used to illustrate the dangers of too decentralized a federal organization as well as the fact that the federal form of organization did not necessarily prevent a state from achieving industrial and military prowess. (It is also true that Great Britain, while rejecting the federal form of organization for itself, was very fond of federalism in its colonies.)

Another reason lies in the very fact that the Canadian state as a whole was intended to be stronger than the Belgian state. In particular, areas of social control such as language use, education, and religion, which in Canada were given to the provinces, in Belgium were instead largely removed from the area of state regulation. The Belgian constitution does not separate church and state but requires the state to support any religious group with a certain minimum number of adherents. Education was largely church-run for most of the nineteenth century. The state network of schools was slow to develop, and even now a complex series of agreements prevents the government from giving its own network preferential treatment. Finally, the Belgian constitution made language use optional for both state and citizen. Thus, the major subjects on which centralized policy-making could be expected to create conflict were removed from the scope of this policy-making, even though they were not, as in Canada, given to another level of government.[9]

The major reason for the choices made by the two countries lay in the composition of their respective élites. The Canadian political élite of 1867 contained an important francophone element, and the anglophone section of the élite had separate geographical and economic bases which were often in competition with one another. The Belgian élite of 1830, however, was uniformly francophone and predominantly based in Brussels, although its wealth derived from 'the provinces': agricultural Flanders and industrializing Wallonia. Although the majority of the Belgian population was Dutch- (or Flemish-) speaking, French was the dominant language in the educational system and was the language of economic, social, and political power. As a result, only the élites from Flanders were normally bilingual; other élites spoke no Flemish or only enough to give orders to servants. The restricted suffrage of the period meant that the electorate, too, was predominantly francophone.[10] Thus linguistic and cultural diversity, though characteristic of the Belgian population as a whole, was not reflected in the composition of the Belgian political élite. Before federalism can be considered as a solution to the problems of governing a country characterized by ethnic and regional diversity, the problems themselves must both exist and be perceived as problems by political élites. This situation existed in Canada in 1867 but not in Belgium in 1832.

Belgium to 1980

Although the language-based divisions of the Belgian population were not an issue in 1832, they soon made an appearance in the political arena. As in Canada, the divisions became a permanent source of political conflict, sometimes quiescent but never eliminated. The emergence of the language issue as the major political conflict in Belgium in the 1960s did not represent the rebirth of a dead issue but rather the latest in a series of crises based on the language-region cleavage. These crises had each culminated in social changes and new legislation that contributed to the consolidation of the language communities and established their territorial basis.[11] Largely the result of pressure from the Flemish community, this legislation first introduced Dutch in official-language use in Flanders and then, in 1931–3, divided Belgium into two unilingual regions, Flanders and Wallonia, and one bilingual region, Brussels. The choice was the opposite of the one made at the national level in Canada and reflects the fact that in Belgium bilingualism worked to the disadvantage of the majority community. Unilingual regions are often cited as an example of 'segmental isolation,' a consociational device advocated as a way of dealing with this type of conflict. In Belgium, at least, the device is not the result of an inter-community compromise but represents a majoritarian move in the purest Westminster tradition. One effect of the laws was the tying of membership in a language community to residence in a given territory, a step that facilitated future development in a federalist direction. The consolidation of the Flemish community provoked a reactive Walloon prise de conscience and led to the first, Walloon proposals for a federal organization of the country. The language laws of 1961–3 furthered the process of identifying language groups with territory by permanently freezing the language frontier between the groups. Instead of being considered national property to be allocated to each group according to its proportion in the population, the territory of Flanders and Wallonia became inalienable.

The new institutions of 1980 have their roots in this process and in a prior constitutional revision of 1970. The 1970 revisions established Dutch and francophone cultural communities with some autonomy in such spheres as education and language use and gave the Dutch community some control over the propagation of the Dutch language in Brussels. In return, francophones obtained measures to protect themselves from the consequences of their position as a permanent minority. These included parity in the national cabinet and the creation of three economic regions, Flanders, Brussels, and Wallonia, with some control over economic affairs, which the Walloons in particular considered crucial to their survival. The 1970 constitutional revisions were part of a process of political separation of the two communities that was matched by differentiation elsewhere in society, particularly in the party system and the economy.

Previous solutions of conflicts based on religion and class had left Belgium with a system of strong, bureaucratized parties whose relationship with the population went far beyond that of merely getting out the vote: the famous 'pillars' of political sub-cultures of the Belgian political system. Because this relationship was only partially based on support of the ideological positions represented by the parties, the pillars were able to withstand post–Second World War secularizing forces. The arrival of the welfare state strengthened rather than weakened the parties because they were given the role of administering many of its policies, especially those that involved making payments to individuals and groups. If anything in the pre-1980 Belgian political scene resembled Canada's provinces, it was these parties, characterized by a long-time observer as 'vast clientelistic mini-welfare states.'[12] Traditionally the parties had differing strength in each region, but until the 1960s this was a factor for national unity. Each party had a 'little brother' in another region, and unity at the national level was seen as the best way of protecting the party's interest in the region where it was in a minority.

This situation changed in the 1960s, not because of changes in party standing but because differential economic development in Flanders and Wallonia meant that each wing of a given party came to represent different combinations of groups.[13] Economic differentiation of the regions also meant that similar groups, such as industrial workers, had different interests. A specifically political change also reduced centripetal forces in the system. The success of the Front démocratique des francophones (FDF) in Brussels reduced the capital's representation in the other parties. Politicians from Brussels, who had the greatest interest in the maintenance of a unitary state dominated by its capital, had often played the role of helpful fixer in intra-party language disputes. All these changes weakened the ability of the parties to maintain their unity in the face of the inter-community quarrels of the 1960s and 1970s. The first to split was the Catholic party (1968), the last the Socialist party (1978). The result was a regionalization of the party system that preceded the regionalization of the country. The political make-ups of the regions are now quite different, and parties' political fortunes vary according to region, although the regional versions of the

TABLE 1

Belgian political parties

Initials	Name (English translation)	% of vote in 1985 election	
		National	Regional*
Flanders			
CVP	Christelijke Volkspartij (Christian People's party)	21.3	34.6
SP	Socialistische Partij (Socialist party)	14.6	23.7
PVV	Partij voor Vrijheid en Vooruitgang (Party for Freedom and Progress)	10.7	17.3
VU	Volksunie (People's Union)	7.9	12.7
Wallonia			
PS	Parti socialiste (Socialist party)	13.8	39.4
PRL	Parti des réformes et de la liberté (Party for Reform and Liberty)	10.2	24.2
PSC	Parti social chrétien (Social Christian party)	8.0	22.6
ECOLO	Ecologistes	2.5	6.2
Brussels			
PRL			26.0
PS			14.8
FDF	Front démocratique des francophones (Francophone Democratic Front)		10.9
PSC			9.3
CVP			8.0

*SOURCE: Xavier Mabille and Evelyne Lentzen, 'Les élections du 13 octobre 1985' CRISP
Courrier Hebdomadaire 1095–6 (1985)

original parties still participate in governments together. See Table 1.

Another intersecting issue was the economic crisis of the 1970s and 1980s. Its impact differed in Flanders and Wallonia, as did its implications for the dominant parties of each region and the strategies they developed to deal with it. Wallonia, paying the price of its earlier industrialization, was massively hit. All Walloon parties were concerned with the problem, but the dominant Socialist party (PS) was faced with two problems: it was held responsible for the defence of working-class interests in the area, while the processes of deindustrialization left it with a shrinking and aging political base. The PS argued for job-maintaining infusions of money to the ailing industries. The crisis was less severe in Flanders: traditional industries such as textiles and coal were in trouble, but the industries created by post-war economic development were healthier. The dominant Catholic party was a cross-class alliance in which domestic capital was well represented. It opted for a policy of 'rationalization' which involved allowing dying industries to go bankrupt and giving aid only to 'healthy sectors' in supposed temporary difficulty.[14] These differences led to a dramatic change of the content of inter-community disputes. At the beginning of the 1960s, the dispute could be summarized by saying that the Flemish demands were cultural: conflicts of taste in the Simeon formula; Walloon demands were economic: conflicts of claim. By the time the new cultural and regional institutions began operation in 1981, both sides were preoccupied with economic questions.[15]

The New Institutions

The regional institutions set up by the special laws and constitutional revisions of 1980 have been well described by a Belgian observer: 'La complexité de nos institutions est à l'image du pays, et nul ne peut plus l'ignorer. Elle ne resulte pas d'une manque d'esprit de synthèse de la part de ses auteurs mais bien d'une absence de consensus sur certaines notions qui, de ce fait, pourront être interprétées differemment suivant les intérêts en cause.'[16] The complexities exist in several aspects of the new institutional framework. First, not only is the framework itself to be put in place according to a complicated schedule phased over several years; it still lacks some crucial components. Further, rather than set up a single sub-national level of government, the new laws divide the functions to be handled at this level into 'community' and 'regional' matters; divide the country into two communities, French and Dutch,[17] and three regions, Flanders, Brussels, and Wallonia; and establish separate institutions for each set of powers. Finally, the list of functions to be transferred is complicated and riddled with special cases and exceptions to such an extent that it seems to create interaction between national and sub-national levels as much as it lays the basis for separate action.

Because of failure to agree on the issues involved, the new institutional framework has two crucial gaps. First, as a result of Flemish-francophone quarrels over the future status of Brussels, the institutions for the Brussels economic region have not yet been established. Second, the community and regional executives were to be responsible to directly elected legislatures. The institutional space for these legislatures was to be created by abolishing the second house of the current national legislature, the Senate, and replacing it with a body concerned only with regional and community matters. The senators have resisted what they regard as demotion of their institution, and since, under the present constitution, the powers of Chamber and Senate are roughly equal, they have been able to block the proposed transformation.

The 1980 revisions provided for a three-phase transition period between the 1980 status quo and complete regionalization. The first phase was to last until the first general election after 1980, which took place in December 1981, the second for four years after the 1981 election. In the second phase, the regional and community councils are composed of members of the Chamber of Representatives and directly elected senators from the regions and communities. (The Belgian Senate is composed of three types of senator: those elected directly by the population, those elected by the provincial assemblies, and those co-opted by the members of the first two groups. The heir to the throne is also a senator.) Each directly elected senator and each representative is, therefore, a member of a community assembly and, except for those from Brussels, of a regional assembly, as well as of the national legislature. For the councils, phase II will last until reform of the Belgian Senate is completed. At this point members of the Chamber of Representatives will drop their regional responsibilities, and the Chamber will be the only legislative body at the national level.

In the first phase, the regional and community executives took the form of ministries of the national government. Phase II saw their separation from the national government, establishment of partial political responsibility to the regional and community assemblies, and creation of regional and community bureaucracies, formed by transferring civil servants from the national bureaucracy. During this period, the executives were composed on the basis of proportional representation of all parties in the assemblies. (For the composition of the executives in phase III see Table 2.)

Although the executives were supposedly politically responsible to the regional assemblies, the requirement of proportional representation of all parties effectively delayed the acquisition of one of the components of responsible government, the dependence of the executive on a political majority in the assembly for its survival. Although the assemblies could, techically, vote non-confidence either in the executive as a whole or in individual members of the executive, the fact that all major parties were represented on the executive made at least the first action improbable. The transition to the third phase occurred in 1986, after the October 1985 election. The composition of the new executives was negotiated as part of the overall government formation process and reproduces the Social Christian-Liberal coalition that exists at the national level.[18]

The transfer of civil servants was also supposed to occur in the second phase but has been subject to several political and practical difficulties. Often, of course, the practical difficulties have been exacerbated by political

TABLE 2

Regional and community executives

Party standing in council		Executive posts
Flemish council (185)		
CVP	74	CVP 6
SP	48	PVV 3
PVV	33	
VU	23	
Others	7	
French community council (133)		
PS	53	PRL 2
PRL	37	PSC 1
PSC	30	
Ecolo	7	
FDF	4	
Others (incl. VU)	2	
Walloon regional council (104)		
PS	47	PRL 3
PRL	26	PSC 3
PSC	26	
Ecolo	4	
VU	1	

NOTE: For acronyms see Table 1.

ones. First, the sub-national executives did not have the physical capacity to house their new bureaucracies, and, even now, most of their civil servants are still physically located in their national ministries of origin. This issue was complicated by political disputes over the location of the new regional and community capitals and by the reluctance of civil servants to accept the change in habits involved in relocation to another area of Brussels, to say nothing of exile to Ghent or Namur. Other practical difficulties involved disputes over facilities such as libraries and computer systems that were shared by several services. The transfer was not a priority for the new national government, and the office charged with negotiating and arranging it was grossly understaffed, while financial restrictions limited the ability of the sub-national governments to take independent action.[19]

Political problems also complicated the transfer. The national ministries were, naturally, reluctant to lose any posts; when the transfers became inevitable they tried to use them to get rid of as much deadwood as possible. The new regional ministries had, of course, directly conflicting goals. The new executives were also slow to set up the necessary organizational frameworks to receive their new personnel. Belgian civil servants, especially at the higher levels, have known party affiliations, and complex balancing of party strength in the bureaucracy is one national practice that has been directly reproduced at the lower levels. Inter-party disputes also complicated the actual transfers once they had been agreed on in principle. For example, the francophone national Ministry of Education, which had a Liberal minister after 1981, had to transfer functions and personnel to a French community dominated by Socialists. Since the Liberals and Socialists are rivals for control of the 'secular' branch of the Belgian education system, it is not surprising that the transition process moved slowly. Finally, philosophical disputes arose. Are juvenile offenders future criminals? If so, the personnel involved in administering programs dealing with them stay with the national Ministry of Justice. Are they, on the contrary, merely socially deprived? If so, the personnel should be transferred, along with other social welfare programs, to the community level. Not surprisingly, the minister of justice took the former philosophical position, the community executives the latter.

The institutional framework is complicated by the existence of two sets of sub-national institutions whose relationship is different in each community. The council of the Dutch community, which includes the Flemish of Brussels, and the Flemish regional council, which does not, have been merged and given a single executive. The members from Brussels can speak but not vote on questions falling under the jurisdiction of the regional council. However, in response to Walloon (and francophone Bruxellois) insistence, the council and executive of the Walloon region and the French community have been maintained as separate institutions, thereby preserving the institutional space for a separate Brussels regional council and executive. Disputes over the exact powers to be given to a future Brussels region and over the status to be accorded the Flemish minority in regional institutions have so far prevented establishment of the Brussels region. The 'Brussels Regional Executive' is still a ministry of the national government. These institutional complications mean that there are in practice three sub-national executives: a Flemish executive, a French community executive, and a Walloon regional executive.

Division of Powers

In any new case of federalization as deintegration, the division of powers between national and sub-national institutions is complicated by the difficulty of separating the functions of modern governments, which are interconnected in ways that are not always clearly understood either by observers or by participants, and which often take the form of overlapping programs whose

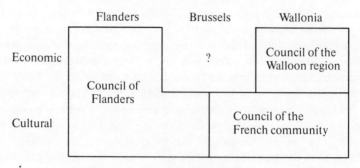

FIGURE 1
The new regional institutions

growth and even existence follow a political rather than a functional logic. In Belgium these complications have been multiplied by the decision to divide sub-national functions between community and regional institutions. The communities have been given not only cultural matters such as the regulation of language use but also what are called in Belgium 'personalizable matters': 'those matters which by their nature directly affect the individual in his community identity as determfined by language.'[20] Health care is one of the major personalizable matters. The regions are given economic functions. Naturally the two areas often overlap: employment policy is merely one of the more obvious cases. Often, to be effective, a single policy action requires community-region co-ordination. To give a minor example: the decision to put up a new stop sign is made by the communes, whose decisions are reviewed by the regions; the language of the sign is regulated by community laws.

These complications are exacerbated by the nature of the division of powers between national and sub-national institutions. Rather than handing whole areas of policy-making over to the sub-national institutions, the 1980 laws divide most policy areas between the two levels, leaving the national government the power to set standards and determine broad policy choices. For example, the revision gives the communities power over old age assistance but reserves to the national government the right to determine minimum payments, conditions for payment, and financing. The same situation applies in health care. Major areas of social assistance such as unemployment insurance remain at the national level. Similar provisions limit the ability of the regions to act alone in economic matters. The result of these partially given and partially withheld transfers is imbrication rather than separation between the two levels of government. Suspicion that this was the intent of the drafters is probably well founded.[21]

The system has a further set of institutions to manage this interdependence. At the level of the new institutions themselves there are commissions charged with promoting co-operation between communities, between regions, and between the Walloon region and the French community. (Co-operation between the Flemish region and community is an internal matter for the council of Flanders and the Flemish executive.) The constitution also requires a whole dictionary of different types of co-operation between national and regional levels. Co-ordination (concertation) is required on economic decisions that will affect other regions as well as on public borrowing. Association of the national government is required for international treaties undertaken by the regions or communities. The agreement (accord) of regional and national levels is required for changes in the list of national economic sectors. The state is to be informed by the regions about the management of communal organizations for the distribution of gas and electricity. Finally, the opinion (avis) of the region concerned must be followed in national decisions about the amalgamation of communes.

There are also specific institutions to handle conflicts between the sub-national level and the national level. A court of arbitration, composed of equal numbers of jurists and politicians, is to handle conflicts of competence between national and sub-national institutions and between community and regional institutions. 'Conflicts of interest' are handled by a co-ordination committee composed of the prime minister and three other members of the national government (linguistically balanced, of course) and the president and one other member of the executives of the French community and the Walloon region.

Transfer of Power?

To what degree has all this complicated legislation transferred significant powers to the sub-national level?[22] The political, social, and economic factors that might push the institutions' development in one direction or another will be dealt with in the next section: here we will concentrate on the texts. First, it could be argued that these texts give the regions and communities power only to alter policy at the margins, not to take independent action in any important area. The power to set the outlines of overall policy in most areas remains with the national level. For example, the current government has conducted a major revision of social policy, during which interest and party groups were much more extensively consulted than the communities. In the economic sphere, the national level controls not only monetary and fiscal policy but also five major industries (steel, textiles, shipbuilding, coal mining, and glass). These 'national sectors' are the traditional backbone of the Belgian economy; they are also all subject to such serious structural economic crises that their preservation will require sums beyond the powers of the regions to raise. Power of the purse without textual sanction has given the national government veto power over the economic reorganization plans required of communes in economic difficulty.

These restrictions on the financial powers of communities and regions constitute another argument that their real power is limited. Most of their income is derived from transfers of funds from the national government, whose total rises according to a formula based on the increase in the national budget.[23] The national government does not appear to have the power to hold back the grants, but delays in actual transfers of funds have already occurred for financial reasons, and it is not hard to imagine the same thing happening for political reasons. The communities and regions can also borrow money, subject to co-ordination with the national level, and impose taxes on activities in the areas under their control. However, they are specifically forbidden to move into tax fields already occupied by the national level, a significant limitation in any modern state. When the French community made a study of unoccupied fields of taxation, it found only one of any importance, the rental of video cassettes. (Their sale, of course, was already covered by the national-level value-added tax – VAT).[24]

However, it would be premature to argue that the transfer of functions is only a façade. Aside from the fact that the Canadian provinces evolved on the basis of a text that foresaw their future powers as of little more significance than those formally assigned to Belgium's regions and communities, there are several aspects of the 1980 laws that give the new level of government a power base with the potential for expansion. First, as argued earlier, political power in Belgium very largely rests on control of the distribution of money, in the form of social welfare benefits, subsidies to groups, and, in a period of economic crisis, rescue operations for enterprises.[25] The fact that the new laws hand over power to decide the actual allocation of money, if not to determine the policy behind the allocations, gives the regions and communities a base from which to form alliances to support the expansion of their power. In addition, the fact that the politicians at the head of the new institutions can articulate the interests of their groups, while those at the head of the national government must compromise, is also significant, particularly since real conflicts of interest among the regions exist and will probably continue.

Canadian Comparisons

While the years immediately following creation of new institutions set crucial precedents and patterns, this is also a period of considerable flux and uncertainty. Some studies of institutionalization suggest that it may take at least a generation for an 'institution' in the formal sense to become 'institutionalized' in any real sense; indeed, some suggest that it takes a generational change.[26] If this is true, it is obviously too early to say exactly what role the communities and regions will play in the Belgian political system. Although it is also too early to make a firm argument about how to compare them with older federations as integration, it is evident that several differences in circumstance separate the nineteenth-century experience of a country such as Canada from the contemporary experience of Belgium.[27]

First, the institutional landscape of modern capitalist societies is infinitely more crowded than that of their nineteenth-century predecessors. In the case of Canada, the federal framework preceded, and to a degree shaped, the development of most interest groups, to say nothing of the development of the national economy. Belgium's new institutions have not only to define their role vis-à-vis the national level but also to compete with other institutions for the allegiance of and control over their mass clientele. They have to persuade these institutions to alter long-standing habits of concentration on the national level of government. Second, while the older federations, like the newer ones, had to find a balance between centrifugal and centripetal forces, for most of the older federations the balance involved strengthening centripetal forces, at least in the earliest period. For the newer federations, it is the centrifugal forces that must be strengthened if the new institutions are to have any real effect on the operation of the political system.

Third and finally, modern political systems are subject to forces of fragmentation that challenge the problem-solving abilities of all levels of government. Transnational interdependence has moved many of the levers of economic and social control outside the nation-state altogether. Both national and sub-national levels in Belgium are restricted in several areas by the rules of the European Community. The modern crisis of confidence in the capacity of any institution to serve its clients hardly creates an auspicious environment for the launching of a new set of institutions. For these reasons, the early experience of countries such as Canada is only an imperfect guide to the future experience of the newer federations. However, the historical and contemporary experience of Canada and other federations can give us some general idea of the factors that will influence the development of the newer federations, even if we cannot say what precise form these factors will take in the future.

Disagreements about the nature of the federal experience in Canada have provided the bread and butter, to say nothing of the jam, of Canadian political scientists for the last several years. In spite of the apparent differences of opinion there is enough agreement to draw some generally accepted conclusions. Writers on Canadian federalism agree that the original federal bargain, and the divisions of functions and financial resources set out in the original text, are only a starting point. The text is merely part of a larger constitution that changes over time.[28] As one article on Canadian federalism points out: 'Only rarely has a Canadian government simultaneously possessed the constitutional jurisdiction, fiscal resources, and program design that matched its contemporary priorities for income distribution and social services. It is both the genius of Canadian federalism and the cause of much of its complexity that so many mechanisms have been developed to overcome these discontinuities.'[29] The Canadian experience suggests not only that the balance of power and function between national and subnational levels of government varies over time but also that this variation is not always unidirectional. Within an overall trend toward greater provincial power, alternating periods of domination of centrifugal and centripetal forces, of decentralization and centralization, can be discerned.

These movements of political power appear to depend on changes in several areas. The importance of societal factors is captured by the distinction between symmetrical and asymmetrical federations and societies. In a symmetrical federation the units resemble each other and, in miniature form, the nation. The dominance of centrifugal forces in Canadian federalism has been traced to the asymmetrical nature of its society. The provinces rest on different economies and have developed different political configurations that do not simply reproduce the national pattern.[30] While the degree to which the provinces have distinct political cultures has been disputed, certainly regional differences can be observed, and provinces are considered by their populations to be important objects of political attention and identification. If these differences are one of the main bases of decentralization in federations, then Belgium, too, is likely to move in this direction. The differences in economy and economic interest that exist among the Belgian regions are real and likely to increase. Although the existence of distinct political cultures has, as in Canada, been a matter of debate, at least the regions are perceived to have distinct identities, in itself an important point.[31] Pious Flanders, socialist Wallonia, cosmopolitan Brussels: each region has a fairly detailed image differentiating it from the others. What is lacking is a strong emphasis on regional over national identity and a belief that the region or community will be better able to solve pressing problems than the national government. The regional and community governments have all mounted campaigns to call attention to themselves, and a panel survey has found that identification with the sub-national level is increasing.[32]

Canadian experience further suggests that the mere existence of a sub-national level can provide the basis for further differentiation, provided the units have or can acquire the resources and scope of activity to attract able and ambitious politicians and bureaucrats to make their careers at this level.[33] The beginnings of institutional rivalry can be seen in Belgium, but the sub-national level is still perceived as subordinate, in career terms, to the national level. The first independent regional and community executives have had a rather mixed composition. Some of their members are simply pre-pensioners: people who needed only a few more years at ministerial rank to qualify for a minister's rather than an ordinary parliamentarian's pension and who either belonged to an opposition party or were felt to be already beyond the demands of ministerial office at the national level. In one case, a minister who was felt to have performed poorly at the national level was 'demoted' to a community executive. Other members of the executives have clear ambitions to move to the national level. These include young politicians for whom this is a first ministerial post and middle-level, mid-career politicians who see regional office as a base from which to mount a challenge for top-level national ministries, including the prime ministership. Finally, there are convinced regionalists and communitarians, often people of national stature, who have chosen to make their career at this level. These are still in the minority but are not always more extremely regionalist in their positions than those with national ambitions. Together the two groups constitute a core of people with at least a short-term interest in strengthening the sub-national level of the system.

Strengthening either level of a federal system appears also to depend on interaction among such factors as the important issues of the day, the nature and calculations of self-interest of organized groups, and the manoeuvring of those in charge of each level.[34] In Canada the regional basis for many interest groups, the fact that both economic and social issues divide the country into its regional or cultural components, and successful assertion of provincial control in many of these areas have constituted an important and mutually reinforcing combination of centrifugal forces.

In Belgium this combination has not yet come into existence. Regionalization was conceived in prosperity but born in poverty. The current recession has exacerbated regional differences, but the central government has used its control over financial resources to assert its primacy in shaping the response to the crisis. When disagreements over financing the deficits of industries in the national sectors led to demands that these sectors be regionalized, the government refused to do so and instead set up regional committees within the national government to handle these sections. The regional governments have played two major roles in the crisis. Their financial resources do allow them to make rescue attempts for some middle-sized and small enterprises, and their control over research and development and some aspects of investment incentives gives them a role in restructuring regional economies. As important, however, has been their role in putting pressure on the national government on behalf of regional industries and other interests.[35]

Belgian interest groups themselves reinforce the centripetal tendencies of the system. Although many interest groups exist only in a single region, and most of the national interest groups have been regionalized to some degree, they still interact mainly with the national level of government. They may cover their bets by making additional representations at the regional or community level, or turn to that level after being turned down at the national level, but there are not yet interest groups whose main focus of attention is at the sub-national level.

Another important determinant of the evolution of a federal state is the party system. Most studies of the Canadian federation agree that the fragmented nature of the Canadian party system has been one of the major contributors to the decentralization of the system as a whole. Not only are provinces often controlled by parties that do not exist at the national level, but within national parties the federal and provincial organizations lead almost totally separate existences. The party system therefore pays little role in tying the federation together.

In Belgium the party system is still a major centripetal force. Although there are no national parties that present candidates in all regions of the country, in another sense all parties, including the Belgian equivalents of the Parti québécois, are national.[36] All parties' main area of activity is still the national level, the same party executive names ministers to both national and sub-national levels, and there is no separate party organization with specifically sub-national functions. Although there are some signs of tensions between national and sub-national party leaders, the parties have so far been able to contain these tensions, and in a way that demonstrates the continuing dominance of national party interests. Flemish-francophone disputes remain a major threat to the cohesion of the current Social Christian–Liberal government, and Social Christian and Liberal members of regional executives who were threatening this cohesion (and the careers of the national level ministers) by strident articulations of regional interests have been called to heel by their parties. The centripetal functions of Belgian parties are likely to persist, and a shift in their role is likely to come only after a crucial institutional change: the introduction of direct elections to regional and community councils. Without separate sub-national elections, there is little incentive to develop a sub-national level of party organization, and no independent power base for party figures who want to make their career at this level.

Conflict Resolution

Can Belgians expect that federalization will make it easier to resolve conflicts between their language groups? Many writers on Canadian federalism argue that the existence of a provincial level of government has exacerbated the country's regional and language divisions by giving the groups involved an institutional power base and creating political élites with a vested interest in bad relations with the national government.[37] However, most people do not criticize trade unions for institutionalizing industrial conflict. To a certain degree, the answer to the question depends on whether regional and ethnic conflicts are perceived to be 'real' and not mystifications designed either to hide other conflicts or advance the careers of ambitious politicians. Like most political disputes, regional and ethnic conflicts probably contain elements of both reality and theatre. In Belgium the regions differ in economic terms, in language, and in historical and present relationship to the national state: it would be surprising if no conflicts resulted from these differences.

   If the conflicts are real, does institutionalizing them make them easier to handle or simply enshrine them 'so that our children will inherit them intact?'[38] On balance, it seems that federal institutions should ease the process of conflict resolution, at least of low- to medium-level conflicts. At the simplest level, federalism may lower the temperature of élite competition by multiplying the number of available political and bureaucratic posts. Federalization also multiplies the number of available arenas for negotiation. When lack of Liberal representation in the west lowered the capacity of national-level institutions for handling Canada's regional tensions, the possibility of federal-provincial negotiations provided a useful alternative. Federalism also reduces the number of topics on which it is necessary to arrive at interregional and inter-community agreement. One of the insights of consociational theory is its argument that attempting to reach agreement is itself a conflict-generating process. Finally, giving groups an institutional power base may make it easier for them to live together because each feels it can defend its interests when they are challenged. Certainly the Belgian political system has applied this principle in other areas. Institutionalized groups, strident articulation of conflict, and quiet accommodation have characterized Belgium's religious and class conflicts, and their extension to its regional conflicts is a new application but not a new mode of operation.

A more serious criticism of the impact of federalism is its effect on minority rights. Federalism is often advocated as a way of defending minority rights (assuming that some limits should be placed on majoritarianism), but Canadian experience suggests that at times it is an imperfect defence and that some of its operations threaten these rights. One way in which federalism allows minorities to defend their interests is by giving them smaller units in which they are majorities.[39] Since these units are rarely homogeneous, they will themselves contain minorities. The rights of linguistic minorities at the provincial level have been a perennial issue in Canadian politics, often spilling over and creating conflict at the national level. In Belgium the question of minority-language rights is less acute in Flanders and Wallonia but is at the root of the problem of Brussels.

If the divisions in a federal state also reflect cultural differences, questions of the treatment of political minorities are likely to arise. Most federations have mechanisms to allow the federal level to intervene to protect these minorities. In Canada the Supreme Court has been the major such mechanism, and the Charter of Rights may add to its ability to fulfil this role. In Belgium the main protection is likely to reside in the application of the Schools Pact and the Cultural Pact to the regional and community levels. These agreements are essentially non-aggression pacts signed by the country's major political parties, which are the institutional representatives of Belgium's cultural 'pillars.' The Schools Pact guarantees the separate existence of Catholic and state school systems, while the Cultural Pact enforces proportional representation of recognized groups in a whole series of activities. In addition, laws such as those controlling racial discrimination remain at the national level and are applicable in the regions.

Finally, federalism is not always a guarantee of protection for minorities at the national level. The existence of Quebec as a political unit has not allowed the Québécois to prevent the perpetuation of the British connection, participation in two world wars, and, most recently, the explicit denial of a Quebec veto over future constitutional revision. The existence of the prairie provinces as institutions did not protect farmers against the effects of eastern economic domination. It is too soon to say whether the existence of regions in Belgium will, for example, allow the Walloons to avert the economic collapse of their region. Federal institutions provide a tool for self-defence but no guarantee of success.

Conclusions

Whatever their other similarities and differences, the Canadian and Belgian experiences underline the necessity of analysing federalism as a complex and dynamic situation. Because they attempt to organize a whole polity, federal institutions even more than other types of institution are both dependent and independent variables. Their coverage means that they have to be analysed in their relationship with the whole system, but the act of analysis demands attention to more specific and limited questions like those addressed in this chapter. Since the questions are limited, the answers must be partial and conditional, a necessary but frustrating situation. A related paradox can be found in the comparative analysis of federal countries. Because federal institutions are part of a whole system that includes economic, social, and historical elements, their study compels close attention to the national context of their operation. The great variety of federal institutions and practices simply underlines the importance of national specificity. However, precisely because so many variables influence and are influenced by the existence of federalism, comparative analysis has a useful role to play in sorting out important from contingent variables, even though it involves stepping away from the specific toward more general concepts. The development of regionalization in formerly unitary countries like Belgium both adds to the variety of phenomena to be explained and increases the pool of cases available for comparison. It has been the purpose of this chapter to use the Canadian experience of federalism to illuminate the Belgian experience of federalization. However, it is one of the lessons of our own experience that a federal country is always 'federalizing.' Under these circumstances, an understanding of the Belgian experience adds useful light to our understanding of ourselves.

NOTES

1 For discussions of regionalization projects in Belgium and other countries see Keith G. Banting and Richard Simeon eds *The Politics of Constitutional Change in Industrial Nations: Redesigning the State* (London: Macmillan 1985).

2 This argument is made by Kenneth D. McRae 'Comment: Federation, Consociation, Corporatism – An Addendum to Arend Lijphart' *Canadian Journal of Political Science* 12 (1979) 517–22.

3 In both countries, economic and political divisions create 'regions' that do not correspond exactly to the divisions created by the language cleavage.

4 The term is that used by Michael Valpy and Robert Sheppard to describe the negotiations that led to the 1982 patriation of the Canadian constitution but could apply as well to the original Confederation bargain; Robert Sheppard and Michael Valpy *The National Deal: The Fight for a Canadian Constitution* (Toronto: Fleet Books 1982).

5 Arend Lijphart in Arend Lijphart ed *Conflict and Coexistence in Belgium: The Dynamics of a Culturally Divided Society* (Berkeley: University of California, Institute of International Studies 1981) 8. For further discussions of the relation between federalism and consociationalism, see Arend Lijphart 'Consociation and Federalism: Conceptual and Empirical Links' *Canadian Journal of Political Science* 12 (1979) 499–515 and McRae 'Comment' 517–22.

6 See Alan C. Cairns *From Intrastate to Interstate Federalism in Canada* (Kingston: Queen's University, Institute of Intergovernmental Relations, Discussion Paper No. 5, 1979).

7 See Aristide Zolberg 'Belgium' in Raymond Grew ed *Crises of Political Development in Europe and the United States* (Princeton: Princeton University Press 1978).

8 For a survey of early projects see 'Tableau synthétique des projets de fédéralisme de 1931 à nos jours' Centre de recherche et d'information socio-politique (CRISP) *Courrier Hebdomadaire* 129 (1961).

9 For a discussion of the Belgian constitution and its development, see Pierre Wigny *La troisième revision de la constitution belge* (Brussels: Emile Bruylant 1972).

10 For a discussion of the changing nature of the Belgian political élite, see Aristide Zolberg 'Les origines du clivage communautaire en Belgique. Esquisse d'une sociologie historique' *Recherches sociologiques* 7 (1976) 150–70.

11 For an overview, see Kenneth D. McRae *Conflict and Compromise in Multilingual Societies: Belgium* (Waterloo, Ont.: Wilfrid Laurier University Press 1986). The language conflict in Belgium has given rise to a large body of literature. See the bibliography in McRae, and the collections by Albert Verdoodt, *Bibliographie sur le problème linguistique belge* (Quebec: Centre international de recherche sur le bilinguisme 1973, 1983).

12 John Palmer 'On Leaving Brussels' *Brussels Bulletin* 26 April 1983. It was the general opinion of the 1970s that the pillars could be expected to dissolve under the pressure of post-industrial secularization. For a reconsideration of this point of view, see Luc Huyse 'Pillarization Reconsidered' *Acta Politica* 1983. The system is also described in Mark Elchardus 'Bureaukratisch patronage en etnolinguisme' *Res Publica* 20 (1978) 141–65.

13 For example, the Walloon Social Christians tend to recruit from a more conservative base than the Flemish Social Christians.

14 For a discussion of the different policies, see Michel Quévit 'Economic Competi-

tion, Regional Development and Power in Belgium' in Antoni Kuklinski ed *Polarized Development and Regional Policies* (New York: Mouton 1981) 357–77.

15 Jack Mintz and Richard Simeon *Conflict of Taste and Conflict of Claim in Federal Countries* (Kingston: Queen's University, Institute of Intergovernmental Relations, Discussion Paper No. 13, 1982). The authors argue that conflicts of claim are more difficult to resolve, and Belgian experience seems to bear this out.

16 Jacques Brassinne 'Les institutions de la Flandre, de la Communauté française, de la Région wallonne' (Brussels: CRISP, Dossier No. 14, 1981) 12. The information in this section is based in part on research undertaken in Brussels from March to July 1983 and supported by a Sabbatical Leave Fellowship and a Research Grant from the Social Sciences and Humanities Research Council of Canada.

17 There is also a German community (population: 60,000). Its institutions differ somewhat from those of the French and Dutch communities. See Jacques Brassinne and Yves Kreins 'La réforme de l'état et la communauté germanophone' CRISP *Courrier Hebdomadaire* Nos. 1028–9 (1984).

18 See Brassinne 'Les institutions.' Installing a Social Christian–Liberal executive in the Walloon region, in which the two parties did not really have a majority, involved the disqualification of a Volksunie (Flemish nationalist) representative elected in the region. The legality of this move was debatable, at least.

19 For an outline see 'Les ministères des communautés et des régions' (Brussels: Services of the Prime Minister 1982); J.L. De Brouwer 'La mise en place des administrations régionales et communautaires: quelques points de repères' (Brussels: CRISP *Courrier Hebdomadaire* No. 967, 1982). The executives have compensated by developing large ministerial cabinets. The size of the cabinets is difficult to estimate, but observers agree that they total almost as many members as the number of civil servants who will be transferred to the subnational bureaucracies.

20 See Jacques Brassinne 'Les matières "culturelles" + les matières "personnalisables": les matieres "communautaires"?' (Brussels: CRISP *Courrier Hebdomadaire* No. 889, 890–1, 1980). For further discussions of the division of powers, see Jean-Marie Van Bol 'Les matières communautaires et régionales' *Journal des tribunaux* 95 (1981) 633–42 and Hugo Van Hassel 'New Forms of Executive Regionalization in Belgium' mimeo (Leuven: Catholic University Public Management Training Centre 1982).

21 The original regionalization plans of 1978–9 did foresee the transfer of blocks of powers, and the change to interwoven powers was in part the result of urgings from ministers fearful of the centrifugal forces that might be set in operation by giving the regions and communities extensive powers of independent action.

22 If the intent of regionalization was to confuse the location of responsibility, it succeeded in the short run. In the period immediately following 1981, many groups routinely sent their dossiers to all three possible recipients.

23 Brassinne 'Les institutions' 24

24 The Walloon region has imposed a tax on water exports (which go mainly to Flanders) and off-track betting.

25 For a further description of the system, see M. Covell 'Ethnic Conflict, Representation, and the State in Belgium' in Paul Brass ed *Ethnic Conflict and the State* (London: Croom Helm 1985) 228–61.

26 Samuel P. Huntington *Political Order in Changing Societies* (New Haven: Yale University Press 1968) 13–14

27 For an earlier comparison see Ivo D. Duchacek *Comparative Federalism: The Territorial Dimension of Politics* (New York: Holt, Rinehart and Winston) 111–47.

28 Alan C. Cairns 'The Living Canadian Constitution' in J. Peter Meekison ed *Canadian Federalism: Myth or Reality* (Toronto: Methuen 1977) 86–99

29 D.M. Cameron and J.S. Dupré 'The Financial Framework of Income Distribution and Social Services,' quoted in Thomas O. Hueglin 'Trends of Federalist Accommodation in Canada and West Germany,' paper delivered at the Annual Meeting of the Canadian Political Science Association, 1984

30 C.C. Tarlton 'Symmetry and Asymmetry as Elements of Federalism' *Journal of Politics* 17 (1965) 861–74, quoted in Hueglin 'Trends of Federalist Accommodation.' For an analysis of the impact of economic differentiation on Canadian federalism, see Garth Stevenson *Unfulfilled Union: Canadian Federalism and National Unity* (Toronto: Gage 1982).

31 See Edwin R. Black *Divided Loyalties: Canadian Concepts of Confederation* (Montreal: McGill Queen's University Press 1975); David Elkins and Richard Simeon *Small Worlds: Parties and Provinces in Canadian Political Life* (Toronto: Methuen 1980).

32 See N. Delruelle-Vosswinkel and A.P. Frognier 'L'opinion publique et les problèmes communautaires' CRISP *Courrier Hebdomadaire* No. 880 (1980) and N. Delruelle-Vosswinkel et al 'L'opinion publique et les problèmes communautaires' CRISP *Courrier Hebdomadaire* No. 966 (1982). In the 1981 survey, 42 per cent of the Flemish interviewed, 25 per cent of the Brussels inhabitants, and 30 per cent of the Walloons gave their primary identification as members of a region or community. The proportion of respondents who identify first with the national level has not declined; rather, the regions and communities appear to have profited from a decline in identification with the local communes (*Courrier Hebdomadaire* No. 966, 11).

33 For an argument that these ambitions are the major reasons for centrifugal tendencies in Canada, see Albert Breton and Raymond Breton *Why Disunity? An*

Analysis of Linguistic and Regional Cleavages in Canada (Montreal: The Institute for Research on Public Policy 1980).

34 See Stevenson *Unfulfilled Union.*

35 J.M. Van Bol *Politique économique et pouvoir régional* (Louvain-la-Neuve: Ciaco 1982)

36 All of Belgium's 'federalist,' i.e. pro–regional autonomy parties, have participated in national governments, although with uniformly disastrous results for themselves.

37 See Stevenson *Unfulfilled Union.*

38 Solange Chaput-Rolland, cited in Roger Gibbins 'Constitutional Politics and the West' in Keith Banting and Richard Simeon eds *And No One Cheered: Federalism, Democracy and the Constitution Act* (Toronto: Methuen 1983) 119–32

39 A similar point is made in Stevenson *Unfulfilled Union* 17. It does seem a bit excessive to assume that the majorities will inevitably be oppressive: if this is indeed the case, movement to a unitary state is not likely to provide a solution.

5 / Second Chambers

CAMPBELL SHARMAN

In discussions of the formal characteristics of federal government it has often been noted that there is an association between federalism and bicameralism. Duchacek,[1] for example, made it a component of one of his ten yardsticks of federalism, and Wheare observed that, while there is no logical requirement for the national government of a federation to contain an upper house based on equal regional representation, 'it is often essential if federal government is to work well.'[2] Beyond these broad generalizations, however, the relationship between these two principles of organizing government appears confused and ambiguous. Both authors just mentioned qualify their comments on second chambers and federalism by noting that this characteristic may have more to do with the political conditions prevailing at the time of federal union or with ways in which regional components of the federation are represented in the national government than with any inherent connection between bicameralism and federalism. They also point out that, to the extent that second chambers are an avenue for regional representation in the national legislature, they may be less important than practices that require regional representation in the executive branch, especially in parliamentary régimes.[3]

Much of the difficulty in dealing with the topic can be traced to the fact that it involves four separate but closely related issues. The first is the nature of the political compromise that was necessary to secure a federal union in the first place. The second raises questions about the structure of federation, regional representation, and the meaning of a states' house in a national legislature. Third, there is the issue of the constitutional design of the national government. Since the notion of bicameralism brings with it a long tradition of upper houses as a component of limited government quite apart from the matter of federal representation, this issue encompasses the question of the extent to which bicameralism and federalism stem from similar philosophical assumptions about the nature of constitutionalism. Fourth and finally, whatever the intentions of the founders and the logic implicit in the design of a particular institution, there is the question of the evolution of upper houses as they respond to changing political and governmental contexts.

As much of what follows examines the interrelation of these issues, it may be helpful to look first at each in greater detail. The historical context of federal union is the most straightforward, since there is general agreement about the political constraints that may require the inclusion of an upper house. In Australia and the United States, an upper house embodying the principle of equal representation of the territorial units, notwithstanding disparities in their populations, was the price that the larger states had to pay for the participation of the smaller states in the federal union. In both countries the less populous regions feared that their interests would be swamped in a legislature composed of a popularly elected lower house alone, and the pressure of political expediency required a powerful second chamber based on equal state representation.[4] Similar forces were at work in the creation of the Swiss council of states in the constitution of 1848[5] and were an important component in the establishment of the West German Bundesrat in 1949.[6] In Canada, however, the terms of political debate at the time of Confederation were not ones that put provincial equality of representation in the national legislature as high on the agenda,[7] and the composition of the Canadian Senate, while based on regional representation, largely mirrored the dominance that the two largest provinces, Ontario and Quebec, had in the lower house by virtue of their population. In Australia, Switzerland, the United States, and, with some provisos, West Germany, the existence of powerful upper houses based on substantial equality of representation of the constituent states resulted from the ability of the smaller states to veto the creation of the federation, coupled with the fact that the politicians representing these states were prime actors in the negotiating process that established the federal union.

The second issue raises the question of the federal role of a second chamber in the national legislature. In those federations where equality of state representation was enshrined in the constitution there was clearly an intent that the upper house should be in some measure a microcosm of the federal union. But such a house of states is ambiguous both as to its governmental purpose and as to the nature of state representation. To take the first point, it is not clear whether the role of the upper house is to act as a potential check on the power of the national government as such, presumably in the interests of reserving to the states in general the fullest ambit of political influence, or whether the equal representation of the smaller states in the upper house is simply to ensure that whatever legislative action the national government takes, it needs the same consent of the residents of small states represented in the upper house as it does of the more populous states represented in the lower house. Is the upper house in a federation to be a states' house or just a small states' house? Any answer to this question is closely related to the second point.

When the constituent regional units are represented in the national legislature, what is it that is being represented? In the countries so far mentioned three answers are provided. The West German Bundesrat is composed of the delegates of the executives of the state governments who vote as a bloc on the instruction of each state cabinet.[8] In this case, the entities represented are the states themselves in the sense of the political and bureaucratic apparatus of the executive branch. The second answer is that originally provided in the United States and Switzerland, where representatives were chosen by state legislatures or by special procedures established by them. This form of indirect election gave state legislatures the ability to shape representation in the upper house, although, if state legislatures delegated their power to an increasingly broad franchise, this solution moved rapidly toward the third possibility.[9] This is the notion of states as aggregates of electors who vote directly to choose members of the second chamber. This system was the one adopted for the Australian Senate in 1901 and the US Senate after amendment to the constitution in 1913.

In the light of these observations it can be concluded that the federal role of a second chamber can range from being the forum for expressing the preferences of state governments or legislatures to being an institution directly reflecting a pattern of electoral preferences weighted in favour of the residents of the smaller units of the federation. All positions on this spectrum have in common the fact that they provide an opportunity for injecting the strongly felt preferences of particular regional aggregates into the national political process, although the nature, force, and political consequences of such preferences will vary markedly with the system of representation. It is for this reason that Canada stands out as being unusual, since, apart from the nominally regional composition of the Canadian Senate, the process of nomination by the national government precludes the Senate from being used as a federal institution in any of the senses used above.[10]

The third broad issue involves the constitutional design of the national government. Thus far, the focus of attention has been on upper houses as agencies of regional representation, however defined, in a federal union.

But bicameralism brings with it the theme of the separation of powers and limited government generally. This aspect of second chambers was mixed with the question of federalism in the debates over the US constitution, although the discussions on the theme of limited government were the more extensively and eloquently argued. In the *Federalist Papers*, for example, the Senate's function is seen as being that of a house of review coupled with its role as an element in the system of dividing power between the various branches of the national government.[11] The philosophical underpinnings of both federalism and bicameralism may be similar, particularly in the case of the United States, but the virtues of an upper house can be maintained quite independent of any commitment to federalism.

The constitutional role of upper houses can be seen as deriving from two distinct traditions. The first, already touched upon, is as a device to check the power of other elements in the governmental process to achieve a system of limited government. The second, much older tradition is that of a chamber to represent particular estates or community interests in a body with legislative functions. The British House of Lords is an example of such an institution that has persisted from medieval times, and the British notion of bicameralism exported to its colonies around the world has been based on this view. Colonial legislative councils in the nineteenth century were initially designed to give the colonial governor the benefit of the advice of powerful interests in the colony, not as a mechanism to achieve limited government.[12]

This is the tradition enshrined in the Canadian Senate[13] and goes much of the way to explain why elective bicameralism poses major structural problems for British-style parliamentary government. The idea of responsible parliamentary government, in which a monarchical form of executive is made responsive to the wishes of the majority in a popularly elected lower house, has the effect of fusing the executive and legislative branches of government. The rise of mass parties has ensured that British-style parliamentary systems have a strong tendency to become dominated by the executive branch, which can use the partisan majority on which it is based to inhibit or severely curtail any independent initiative taken by the legislature.[14]

In such a system, upper houses appear anomalous, since they are denied the legitimacy of popular representation reserved to the lower house and denied a legitimate base for effective opposition by the notion of parliamentary responsible government. Where powerful elected upper houses have been part of the constitutional structure of British-style parliamentary systems, as in Australia at both the national and state levels, there have been crises whenever a major conflict between the two houses has occurred.

An executive based on a partisan majority in the lower house has been faced with an upper house controlled by a hostile partisan majority. The problem has not simply been one of political disagreement between components of the legislature but has involved a clash between competing views of both constitutionalism and the legitimacy of executive dominance of the legislative process.[15] The executive has called on the right of popular support and the canons of responsible parliamentary government, while the upper house has claimed the right of legitimate opposition based on the full use of its constitutional powers.

The contest has been essentially about the scope of an executive based on a majority in the lower house to dominate the legislative process. While in the United States the dispersal of power inherent in the presidential system assumes that regular and continuing disagreements between the executive and the legislature are inevitable and even desirable, parliamentary systems have put a corresponding stress on the virtues of coherent government policy and the co-ordination of the legislative and executive branches. In such systems there is little room for the constitutional legitimacy of a powerful upper house with a mind of its own and a partisan backing at odds with the government of the day. The consequences of building a second chamber with such potential into a British-style system may be seen in the contentious role of the Australian Senate.

The Swiss and West German solutions to this structural problem should be noted. The Swiss in particular had no special commitment to bicameralism in the national government, but in view of the rival claims for representation in the proposed unicameral legislature between those who wanted representation purely on the basis of population and those who wanted equal representation for each canton, a compromise was struck which created the familiar pattern of a popular lower house coupled with a canton-based upper house. The problem of relations between the legislature and the executive appears to have been defused by the collegial nature of the executive, the existence of referendum procedures for the resolution of disputes, and the high value put on achieving a broad-based consensus that appears to characterize Swiss politics.[16]

The West German solution in 1949 was to couple a parliamentary system with an upper house, as noted above, representing the governments of the constituent states. This basis of representation in the Bundesrat makes it radically different from British-derived bicameralism, since the German model both presumes the possibility of conflict between a national executive based on a majority in the lower house and a differing state-based majority in the Bundesrat and implies that resolution of conflict will be by accommodation between the two levels of government within the national legislature. This requirement of consultation and accommodation is enhanced by the method of dividing government functions so that the states are disproportionately involved in the administration of all laws at whichever level they originate.[17] This means not that there is an absence of conflict but that such disputes as arise between the houses are seen as legitimate political differences and not as challenges to the underlying structure of government, even if the level of partisan disagreement is high. If constitutional disputes do occur over the scope of the power of the Bundesrat, this is simply one of a number of constitutional matters that can properly be resolved by the Constitutional Court.[18]

The position of the Bundesrat as a forum for the resolution of inter-governmental disputes in the West German federal system raises the general issue of the role of legislatures in intergovernmental relations in a federation. While the point is incidental to the main thrust of this essay, it has been observed by a number of authors that, while intergovernmental relations in the US system are characterized by a multiplicity of actors from both the legislative and executive branches,[19] such relations in federal systems with British-derived parliamentary governments and modern mass parties tend to be monopolized by the executive branch alone. This situation, which Smiley has aptly called 'executive federalism,'[20] is but another manifestation of the same logic that tends to deny legitimacy to autonomous initiatives by upper houses in such systems – partisan-based executive dominance of the legislature in the name of responsible government.[21]

Before leaving the question of constitutional design, brief reference should be made to bicameralism at the sub-national level in federations. The variation at this level is considerable, ranging from complete unicameralism in the Swiss cantons and the Canadian provinces, and the existence of a single bicameral state in West Germany (Bavaria), to bicameralism in Australia (except in Queensland) and the United States (except in Nebraska). While, as noted above, the experience of the United States is congruent with the rest of its constitutional tradition,[22] there is marked divergence between Australia and Canada, notwithstanding their similar colonial histories. Five of Canada's ten provinces had experience with upper houses, but these legislative councils were not composed of popularly elected members and were never more than minor appendages to the governmental process.[23] In Australia, however, all six states on achieving self-government were set up with powerful upper houses designed in large measure to be a conservative check on popularly elected lower houses. This produced considerable tension between the two chambers which periodically flared into major confron-tations between the government based in the lower house and an intransigent legislative council. These sporadic clashes have been a major characteristic of state government in Australia, a feature that has not diminished with the broadening of the franchise for upper houses.[24] Indeed, it might be argued that attempts to reform legislative councils by making them more representative and increasing their political weight may increase differences of opinion between the chambers rather than reduce them. This tendency may be exacerbated by the use of proportional representation, which may inject an element of diversity not found in the lower house.[25] Those legislative councils that were elected from the start of responsible government, albeit with the original franchise severely limited, have resisted abolition or the reduction of their powers much more successfully than the two legislative councils that began as appointed bodies (Queensland and New South Wales).[26] By the time Australia reached federation in 1901, most of its component states had had over forty years of experience of the difficulty of blending bicameralism with British-style parliamentary government.

The final issue involved in the examination of bicameralism concerns the evolution of upper houses and the question of the changes that have occurred in their role and functioning since their establishment. This is often framed as a contrast between the intentions of the founders and the actual experience of the chamber. In Australia, for example, many a first-year undergraduate student of political science has been told that the Australian Senate was intended as a states' house but has become a party house. Such sweeping comments, however, may distort both the historical events leading up to the foundation of the chamber and understanding of its subsequent operation. The design of political institutions is likely to be the result of compromise, and ambiguities in their structure may simply reflect a minimum acceptable agreement between competing points of view in the full appreciation that the legislature, once set up, will take on a life of its own. In a similar fashion, as mentioned above, such concepts as a states' house contain their own ambiguities, not all of which are inconsistent with the dominance of party.[27]

The general point is, nonetheless, important. When looking at an institution at any given time, there is a problem in distinguishing between those features that follow from the inherent logic of its structure and those that can be traced to the political context in which it operates. This is particularly so when the original design of the structure itself embodied conflicting principles. In the case of upper houses in federations, one of the more striking of such conflicts is the clash between the principle of regional representation and the creation of a national government. The US Senate, for example, owes its present importance and its character to its place as a major institution in the national government and as a forum for the resolution of national issues. While the state basis of its representation has clearly been a factor in shaping its character and the career patterns of its members, it is pre-eminently an institution with a national audience. No current commentator would regard it as a states' house in anything other than the basis of its electoral composition and, perhaps, in its patterns of partisanship.[28] It is certainly not a chamber that seeks to reduce the ambit of national government in the interests of preserving the widest possible scope for state governments. This is not to deny that it may be specially sensitive to the demands of those regional interests that are overrepresented in the Senate, but this is not peculiar to the Senate, nor are such interests treated differently from any other minority that may have a claim on the political vulnerability of senators.[29] The Senate is, in sum, a national institution first, and a federal one a very poor second. This has not simply been the result of changes in the nature of the political process in the United States but reflects the competing goals of national government and state autonomy that were present in the Senate's design, a competition in which the claims of national government have become dominant.

This nationalizing process inherent in the creation of national institutions can be seen at work in all federations. The Bundesrat is particularly interesting in this respect both because of the relative recency of its creation and because of its distinctive composition. Although the state governments have injected local concerns to some extent into national politics through state representation in the Bundesrat, this appears to have been more than offset by the introduction of national issues in state politics as a consequence of the partisan contest for control of the Bundesrat.[30]

The West German experience is also notable because it has brought the major area of growth in modern federations, that of executive intergovernmental relations, within the ambit of its national upper house to the extent that it represents the executive agencies of the regional governments. While the nationalizing process can be seen in operation, it is clearly moderated by the distinctive design of the Bundesrat and by the constitutional division of powers and functions.

The most striking constitutional ambiguity can, however, be found in the design of the Australian Senate. As touched on above, the creation of a popularly elected second chamber with almost the same powers as the lower house presumes a view of government that is compatible with the dispersal of power among a variety of agencies of government and accepts the possibility of partisan disagreements between the two parts of the legislature. Yet the British-style parliamentary government that was imported by implication into the newly created Commonwealth government of Australia assumed that an executive based on a majority in the lower house was to be the dominant force in the conduct of government. This potential for fundamental disagreement over the role of the Senate was canvassed at the time of the debates over federation, as was the likelihood of state loyalties being the major factor in determining majorities in the chamber. In the event, within a few years of federation, state particularisms had ceased to be the major divide in the Senate, but it took some seventy years for the more substantial ambiguity in the role of the Senate to produce a major confrontation between the rival philosophies of government, the American and the British, that had been discussed at its foundation.

The design of an upper house is only one of the components of its evolution, the other being its political environment. Second chambers in all the federations mentioned have been greatly influenced by the rise of the mass party as moderated by the federal structure of each system.[31] This has affected, in particular, the relationship between the chamber and the executive and the career patterns and aspirations of politicians and, above all, has determined whether the chamber has remained in the mainstream of political life. If, as with the Canadian Senate, partisan politics, as opposed to patronage, has largely passed the chamber by, it is doomed to play a minor role in the process of government, whatever its formal powers. But changes in political context do not have to be large to make an impact on an institution. The rise of new elements in the political process, or even small shifts in the conduct of politics, may make substantial alterations to the operation of a legislative body. The adoption of proportional representation in the Australian Senate, for example, when coupled with the subsequent emergence of minor parties, transformed the role of the chamber. In the continuing flow of politics, institutions are always making adjustments to new demands that are put upon them. Occasionally these adjustments trigger major changes in the institution that owe as much to the constitutional potential of the institution as they do to the particular political events that prompted the change.

For all these reasons, constitutional engineering is an imprecise science. Designing an institution is not only likely to be bedevilled by major differences over the goals and directions of change but is subject to all the uncertainty of trying to guess the political context, or range of contexts, in which the institution will operate. The debate over reform of the Canadian Senate is an excellent example of these difficulties. Some groups argue for the existence of a powerful upper house along the lines of the Australian or us Senate as a check on the dominance of the present parliamentary executive. Others want a chamber that will in some way represent the regional diversity of Canadian politics. This group is in turn divided between those who wish to see the regions represented in terms of the provincial governments along the lines of the Bundesrat and those who wish to see a new regionally

responsive Senate as a means of reducing the ability of provincial governments to claim to be the sole agents for the expression of regional diversity.
Yet others may wish to adopt some form of functional representation or
to make the Senate into a house of worthies.

Each of these views on the function of the Senate may have differing
prescriptions for the extent of legislative powers of the reconstituted chamber,
and its mode of election or nomination, and have in common only the
substantial inconsistency that exists between each proposal and any of the
others. And each must acknowledge that, unlike the original design of a
federal union when the principal body to be persuaded is a convention
of delegates, the redesigning of a part of the national government requires
the consent of both the unreformed chamber and the national government
of the day. As a final complication, changing one institution is likely to
cause reactions in other parts of the governmental process. The fact that
these adjustments may be delayed or subtle does not mean that they are
unimportant or can be ignored without risk. Thus, any substantial change
to the role of the Canadian Senate necessarily raises questions about the
modifications to the role of the House of Commons, the cabinet, and perhaps
even the governor-general, quite apart from the effects that a Senate with
strong regional representation might have on the party system and the federal
process generally.[32]

Thus far we have looked at one issue at a time in an attempt to analyse
the various perspectives from which the role of upper houses in federations
can be examined. It may be equally helpful to look at the experience of
a single system to illustrate the way in which these issues interact and to
give an idea of the complexity of the forces at work shaping any particular
institution.

The institution chosen for this purpose is the Australian Senate, since
it provides an example of the full range of themes discussed above and
has two further characteristics that make it useful as a case study. First,
it is the best illustration among the countries mentioned of inherent structural
ambiguity both toward regional representation in the national government
and, more acutely, between the British and US views of constitutionalism.
In contrast, the US Senate has a settled role: there is a basic compatibility
between the political assumptions underpinning both federalism and the
role of the Senate in the US political system. Not that evolution of the
role of the Senate is precluded, but it will take place within relatively narrow
parameters. Although much younger, the West German Bundesrat appears
to be in a similar position, that is, there is no internal contradiction within
its basic constitutional design likely to precipitate a rapid change in role.

This leads to the second reason for choosing the Australian Senate, since its inherent structural ambivalence, or rather the inconsistency between its structure and the constitutional framework to which it is intimately connected, has recently been demonstrated in a dramatic fashion. It has provided an example of rapid institutional evolution resulting from apparently minor changes to its political context over a period of fifteen years.

In the debates at the conventions that took place in Australia in the 1890s to discuss federal union, two groups of delegates were strongly committed to the existence of a powerful upper house. The first group consisted of those from the four smaller colonies who saw the absence of a Senate based on the principle of equal state representation as an invitation for the proposed federal union to be dominated by the two-thirds of the population who lived in the two largest colonies, New South Wales and Victoria. The second group comprised those who, mindful of the experience of colonial upper houses, favoured an upper house as a conservative device. Both groups had, however, to accommodate the widespread commitment among the delegates to the importance of direct popular participation in the choice of representatives to both houses of parliament. The constitution that came into force in 1901 reflected a compromise between these views.[33] The Senate was to have coequal power with the lower house, the House of Representatives, except for the initiation and amendment of money bills, and it was to be chosen on the basis of the same number of senators from each state, originally six, with half being elected every three years on the same franchise as the House of Representatives.

This arrangement, explicitly borrowed from the American system as was the general design of the federal division of powers, was coupled with British-style parliamentary government. It is clear from the debates at the Federal Conventions that it was generally assumed that, while formal executive power was placed by the constitution in the hands of the governor-general as the representative of the British Crown, this power was to be exercised on the advice of ministers chosen from that group that could maintain a majority in the House of Representatives. That is, it was taken for granted that the new Commonwealth government would operate on the same principles of responsible government that were well established at state level.

It is also clear that the potential for disagreement between these powerful chambers was well recognized. The delegates at the Federal Conventions were familiar with bicameral conflict in the colonies and built into the Commonwealth constitution procedures for the resolution of deadlocks between the houses. In case of persistent disagreement between the chambers over the passage of legislation, there was provision for a double dissolution at which all the members of both houses would stand for election. If the deadlock persisted, a joint sitting of both houses would be called, and the legislation would pass or fail on a division of the joint sitting. Other sections of the constitution make sense only on the presumption that the founders assumed continuing tension between the principle of parliamentary government based on popular majorities in the lower house and the competing principles of bicameralism and federal dispersion of power. The constitution provided for a nexus between the size of the Senate and the House of Representatives, requiring the latter to be as near as possible twice the size of the former, so that the Senate could not be swamped by the rapid growth of the House of Representatives alone but giving the House an edge in any deadlock between the houses that reached the stage of a joint sitting. In a similar fashion, the procedure for amending the constitution required the proposed amendment to be submitted to the voters at a referendum and to secure both an overall majority and majorities within a majority of states (that is, four of the six states).[34]

These provisions together with the general scheme of the Senate may be used as evidence for two rival propositions about the intentions of those who designed the constitution. The first proposition is that they indicate a willingness to accept that the new national government was going to be a hybrid, modified parliamentary system. The second is that these constitutional provisions were simply the result of piecemeal political compromise and reflect no more than an intention to leave the resolution of these contradictions to the future. Perhaps both these propositions are true; whatever the intention, the Senate was created in such a way as to permit subsequent evolution in widely divergent ways, depending on whether the federal, bicameral, or parliamentary themes became dominant.

In the early years after federation, the Senate struggled for a distinctive role, but after 1910 the emergence of a party system based on modern mass parties became the dominant factor shaping the activities of both houses of parliament.[35] In particular, loyalty to party meant that, with few exceptions, the potential for the Senate to act as a federal house reflecting coalitions between various state blocs of senators was not realized. The overrepresentation of the smaller states did, however, have a major effect on the composition of the parliamentary parties and, coupled with a party system firmly based at state level, has continued to make the Senate an avenue through which the national political process can be sensitized to state concerns.[36]

The potential for conflict between bicameralism and the notion of British-style responsible government was affected by the development of parties in a way that made the conflict more acute when differing partisan persuasions held majorities in the two chambers and substantially suppressed it when the same party had majorities in both houses. As a result, periods of quiescence were interspersed with short periods of strong partisan hostility, characterized by the opposition in the lower house attempting to use its partisan colleagues in the Senate to embarrass the government and prune its legislative program. While the Senate did develop a few mechanisms for the continuing review of executive actions, the major engine for independent action was partisan political advantage.

The effects of these periods of partisan hostility during the years up to 1949 were moderated by aspects of the electoral system by which the Senate was chosen. The system gave all a state's senate seats to the party that gained a majority of the votes in that state, with the consequence that not only was there likely to be a rough congruence between partisan support for the upper and lower houses but small shifts in the pattern of votes made dramatic changes to the partisan composition of the Senate.[37] If a party gained a majority of votes in all states at two elections in a row, there would be no opposition representation in the chamber at all. While this extreme case did indeed occur, the major result of these sudden changes in personnel and swings in partisan composition was a consequent reduction in the motivation for the partisan majority in the Senate at any time to set up the mechanisms to establish the Senate as an autonomous legislative body on a continuing basis. In the brief periods when the Senate had a hostile partisan majority, the major goal of the Senate was short-term political gain, and only once during the years up to 1949 was there a deadlock of sufficient duration and severity to precipitate double dissolution.

Although various proposals were made to alter the system of representation in the Senate, no action was taken until the expansion of parliament in 1949. The desire to increase the size of the House of Representatives and the consequent requirement to make a proportional increase in the size of the Senate led the government of the day to combine the increase in size with a system of proportional representation by single transferable vote (PR-STV) for the election of senators.[38] This measure had been advocated for many years as a way of reducing the violent swings in the partisan composition of the Senate, and its adoption for the 1949 election was marked by singularly little public debate over the likely consequences such a change might have on the role of the Senate.

Without wishing to become embroiled in the argument over the relationship between electoral systems and the party system, the adoption of PR-STV provided the context for a major alteration in the place of the Senate in the parliamentary process. For the first few years after 1949 the effect of PR-STV was much as had been expected; changes in the partisan composition of the Senate were very much reduced, with the two major party groupings having the closely balanced representation that matched their electoral support in the states. After 1960, however, a split in the Australian Labour party created a new party, the Democratic Labour party, which began to win seats in the Senate through the operation of PR-STV. By the late 1960s a combination of Democratic Labour senators and independents held the balance of power in the chamber. This led to a major growth in the activities and visibility of the Senate, so that by the early 1970s it had an established system of standing and special-purpose committees backed by the willingness of the chamber to modify or block any government legislation of which it did not approve.[39]

Matching this growth in influence was a change in the recruitment patterns for senators. Because of the way the ballot was arranged, the electoral system worked to create some safe seats for each of the major parties in each state delegation.[40] The result was to make a long-term career both possible and desirable for those who had the backing of the party machine in each state. As a seat in the Senate became a more prestigious acquisition, the calibre of senators increased, which had the incidental effect both of giving the Senate as a whole greater political weight and injecting people into it who had a strong link with the powerful state party machines.

A related effect of PR-STV was to reflect at the national level regional diversities in the states' party systems. Those minor-party and independent senators who have gained representation since the mid-1960s have all had strong regional variations in their bases of support, so that, at least in this sense, the Senate now mirrors a regional diversity not apparent in the House of Representatives.[41]

But it is the clash between bicameralism and executive dominance of the parliamentary process that led to the most dramatic developments. The constitutional crisis of 1975 sprang from many sources, but at base it was an extreme form of the contradiction between an independent legislative chamber and parliamentary government. The Senate, by refusing to pass a financial bill, contributed to the circumstances by which a government was forced to the polls at a time not of its choosing.[42] In the years that have passed since that event, the Senate has, in one sense, consolidated its independent position. Minor-party and independent senators have held the balance of power for much of the period, and mechanisms are now established for the executive to cope with an independent legislative body with a vigorous and autonomous committee system and to consult with the Senate over the shape of proposed government legislation. But the constitutional contradiction remains, and governments since 1975 have consistently backed measures that might work in the direction of lessening the political autonomy of the Senate and increasing the influence of the larger parties with a penchant for executive dominance.[43]

Returning to the broader theme raised at the beginning of this chapter, there remains the general question of the nature of the relationship between federalism and bicameralism. It is clear that there is no necessary relationship between the two, any more than any particular institutional arrangement can prescribe the precise form of the political processes that occur within it. This is especially true of attempts to design an upper house that will entrench a particular pattern of regional influence in the national government. While institutions may carry within them a structural logic that predisposes them to be sensitive to the demands of regions, this tendency may be more than countered by the influence of such nationalizing pressures as party and the very existence of a forum for nation-wide political debate.

Nevertheless, there is a connection between these two ways of organizing governmental structures. Federalism is not just a pattern of institutional arrangements or a mode of accommodating regional particularisms within one nation but should be seen as being based on a notion of constitutionalism that stresses the dispersal of power and the limitation of government.

Thus the existence of a powerful and autonomous upper house in a governmental system is an indication that the values implicit in federalism are pervasive in that system. The vigour and responsiveness of the American system is an example of this congruence, which, in a modified fashion, can be seen to apply in Switzerland and West Germany. The experience of Australia and Canada, however, shows that both federalism and bicameralism at the national level are inconsistent with several of the assumptions underpinning a British-derived system of parliamentary government and can coexist only with difficulty. A running compromise is necessary, centring on the place of the executive in the governmental system, and there is continuing pressure for the executive to distort the system by monopolizing both the process of federal interaction and the legislative process, thus stifling the governmental diversity on which bicameralism and federalism thrive. Bicameralism is the natural ally of federalism; both imply a preference for incremental rather than radical change, for negotiated rather than coerced solutions, and for responsiveness to a range of political preferences rather than the artificial simplicity of dichotomous choice.

NOTES

1 Ivo D. Duchacek *Comparative Federalism: The Territorial Dimension of Politics* (New York: Holt Rinehart & Winston 1970)

2 K.C. Wheare *Federal Government* 3rd ed (London: Oxford University Press 1953) 93

3 Duchacek *Comparative Federalism* 244–52

4 See, for example, L.F. Crisp *Australian National Government* 5th ed (Melbourne: Longman Cheshire 1983) chap 1, for the Australian Senate; and George H. Haynes *The Senate of the United States: Its History and Practice* (Boston: Houghton Mifflin 1983) chap 1, for the us Senate.

5 See George A. Codding *The Federal Government of Switzerland* (Boston: Houghton Mifflin 1961) 33.

6 Other factors were also at work, including a long tradition of regional representation in German national government: see Peter H. Merkl *The Origin of the West German Republic* (New York: Oxford University Press 1963). Note that state representation in the Bundesrat is not equal but weighted in favour of the small states. Article 51 of the Basic Law provides that no state has less than three votes in the Bundesrat; those with more than two million people have four votes, and those with more than six million have five.

7 See Roger Gibbins *Regionalism: Territorial Politics in Canada and the United States* (Toronto: Butterworths 1982).

8 See A.J. Burkett 'The West German Bundersrat' *The Parliamentarian* 56 (1978) 165–70, and note David P. Conradt *The German Polity* (New York: Longman 1978) 135–9.

9 Note Haynes *The Senate of the United States* chap 3 and Christopher Hughes *The Parliament of Switzerland* (London: Cassell 1962) 40–49.

10 'Thus while the Senate performs a number of useful legislative functions, effective territorial representation is not one'; Gibbins *Regionalism* 61.

11 See, for example, the argument of Madison in *The Federalist Papers* No 62.

12 That is, they had a significant executive role as well as a legislative one. This tradition can be found in the design of the us Senate, albeit in a much transformed manner: see Lindsay Rogers *The American Senate* (New York: Johnson Reprint 1968, originally published 1926) chap 3.

13 'The Senate of Canada was but the political heir of the nominated legislative councils of the various provinces under responsible government. Not one of these had been a co-equal partner with the elected assembly; not one had made or unmade Ministries; not one but was essentially a secondary legislative chamber'; Robert A. MacKay *The Unreformed Senate of Canada* rev ed (Toronto: McClelland & Stewart 1963) 51.

14 These developments have been lucidly traced by Samuel H. Beer *British Politics in the Collectivist Age* (New York: Vintage 1965).

15 See generally Arendt Lijphart *Democracies: Patterns of Majoritarian and Consensus Government in Twenty One Countries* (New Haven: Yale University Press 1984).

16 See Codding *The Federal Government of Switzerland* and Hughes *The Parliament of Switzerland*; and note Jean-Francois Aubert 'Switzerland' in David Butler and Austin Ranney eds *Referendums: A Comparative Study of Practice and Theory* (Washington, DC: American Enterprise Institute 1978) 39–66 and Harold E. Glass 'Ethnic Diversity, Elite Accommodation and Federalism in Switzerland' *Publius* 7 (1977) 31–48. For a note of caution, however, see Jürg Steiner and Robert H. Dorf 'Structure and Process in Consociationalism and Federalism' *Publius* 15 (1985) 49–56.

17 See Jörn Alwes 'Participation of the Laender in Decision-Making at the Federal Level with Special Reference to the Bundesrat' in R.L. Mathews ed *Federalism in Australia and the Federal Republic of Germany: A Comparative Study* (Canberra: Australian National University Press 1980) 31–43; Joan Rydon and H.A. Wolfsohn *Federalism in West Germany* Advisory Council for Inter-Government Relations Information Paper No 8 (Canberra: Australian Government Publishing Service 1980); and Gordon Smith *Democracy in Western Germany: Parties and Politics in the Federal Republic* (London: Heinemann 1979) 51–4.

18 On the recent history of such disagreements between the houses see Nevil Johnson *State and Government in the Federal Republic of Germany: The Executive at Work* 2nd ed (Oxford: Pergamon 1982) 125–32; see also Philip M. Blair *Federalism and Judicial Review in West Germany* (Oxford: Clarendon Press 1981).

19 Giving rise to Morton Grodzins's marble cake analogy: see generally Morton Grodzins *The American System: A New View of Government in the United States* ed Daniel J. Elazar (Chicago: Rand McNally 1966) and Deil S. Wright *Understanding Intergovernmental Relations* 2nd ed (Monterey, Calif.: Brooks-Cole 1982).

20 Donald V. Smiley *Canada in Question: Federalism in the Eighties* 3rd ed (Toronto: McGraw-Hill Ryerson 1980) chap 4. For two forcefully argued analyses of the undesirable consequences of this characteristic, note Jonathan Lemco and Peter Regenstreif 'The Fusion of Powers and the Crisis of Canadian Federalism' *Publius* 14 (1984) 109–20 and Mark Sproule-Jones 'The Enduring Colony? Political Institutions and Political Science in Canada' *Publius* 14 (1984) 93–108.

21 Note Campbell Sharman 'Parliaments and Commonwealth-State Relations' in J.R. Nethercote ed *Parliament and Bureaucracy* (Sydney: Hale & Iremonger 1982) 280–90.

22 On the variety within the US tradition, note the contributions to 'State Constitutional Design in Federal Systems,' a special issue of *Publius* 12 no 1 (winter 1982).

23 Note G.W. Kitchin 'The Abolition of Upper Chambers' in D.C. Rowat ed *Provincial Governments and Politics: Comparative Essays* 2nd ed (Ottawa: Department of Political Science, Carleton University 1973).

24 See S.R. Davis 'What Price Upper Houses in Australia?' and Joan Rydon

'Upper Houses – the Australian Experience,' both in G.S. Reid ed *The Role of Upper Houses Today: Proceedings of the Fourth Annual Workshop of the Australasian Study of Parliament Group* (Hobart: University of Tasmania 1983). Note also Western Australia, Royal Commission into Parliamentary Deadlocks *Report* (Perth: Western Australian Government Printer 1984–5).

25 See Campbell Sharman 'Diversity, Constitutionalism and Proportional Representation' in Michael James ed *The Constitutional Challenge: Essays on the Australian Constitution, Constitutionalism and Parliamentary Practice* (Sydney: Centre for Independent Studies 1983) 91–112.

26 Note C.N. Connolly 'The Origins of the Nominated Upper House in New South Wales' *Historical Studies* 20 (1982) 53–74.

27 See also Campbell Sharman 'The Australian Senate as a States House' *Politics* 12 no 2 (November 1977) 64–75, also published in Dean Jaensch ed *The Politics of 'New Federalism'* (Adelaide: Australian Political Studies Association 1977) 64–75. For the coexistence of partisan and regional loyalties note Hans-Peter Hertig 'Party Cohesion in the Swiss Parliament' *Legislative Studies Quarterly* 3 (1978) 63–81, particularly 69–71.

28 See, for example, Charles O. Jones *The United States Congress: People, Place and Policy* (Homewood, Ill.: Dorsey 1982). On the early modification of the Senate in this direction, note William H. Riker 'The Senate and American Federalism' *American Political Science Review* 49 (1955) 452–69. On the residual effects of small state overrepresentation note Robert A. Dahl *Democracy in the United States: Promise and Performance* 3rd ed (Chicago: Rand McNally 1976).

29 Note Gibbins *Regionalism*, particularly 46–58.

30 See Burkett 'The West German Bundesrat'; Rydon and Wolfsohn *Federalism in West Germany* 44–65; Smith *Democracy in Western Germany* 157–61; and generally Johnson *State and Government in the Federal Republic of Germany*.

31 See generally Chandler's article in this collection.

32 For a discussion of those issues see Donald Smiley *An Elected Senate for Canada? Clues from the Australian Experience* (Kingston, Ont.: Institute of Intergovernmental Relations, Queen's University, Discussion Paper No. 21, 1985) and Parliament of Canada, Special Joint Committee on Senate Reform *Report* (Ottawa: Queen's Printer 1984).

33 The process of compromise had been complex: see Peter Loveday 'The Federal Convention, An Analysis of the Voting' *Australian Journal of Politics and History* 18 (1972) 169–88; and, more generally, note J.A. La Nauze *The Making of the Australian Constitution* (Melbourne: Melbourne University Press 1972).

34 For full details of the structure and operation of the Senate see J.R. Odgers *Australian Senate Practice* 5th ed (Canberra: Australian Government Publishing Service 1976).

35 Note Dean Jaensch *The Australian Party System* (Sydney: George Allen & Unwin 1983) chap 2.
36 See Sharman 'The Australian Senate as a States House,' and note Jean Holmes and Campbell Sharman *The Australian Feder System* (Sydney: Allen & Unwin 1977) chap 4.
37 For details of the electoral system and patterns of partisan representation see Odgers *Australian Senate Practice*.
38 See ibid 94–101, and note H.R. Penniman ed *Australia at the Polls: The National Elections of 1980 and 1983* (Washington, DC: American Enterprise Institute 1983) Appendix B.
39 Note G.S. Reid 'The Trinitarian Struggle: Parliamentary-Executive Relationships' and David Solomon 'The Senate,' both in Henry Mayer and Helen Nelson eds *Australian Politics: A Third Reader* (Melbourne: Cheshire 1973); and Hugh V. Emy *The Politics of Australian Democracy: Fundamentals in Dispute* 2nd ed (Melbourne: Macmillan 1978) 200–7. On the committee system see John Uhr 'Parliament and Public Administration' in Nethercote ed *Parliament and Bureaucracy*.
40 See Campbell Sharman 'Diversity, Constitutionalism and Proportional Representation.'
41 This statement needs the qualification that the National Party, a rural-based party, is overrepresented in the House of Representatives as a consequence of its geographical concentration in electoral districts in some states.
42 This event has prompted a flood of publications. For brief background, note Leon D. Epstein 'The Australian Political System' in Penniman ed *Australia at the Polls* 37–47; and, on the role of the Senate, note Emy *The Politics of Australian Democracy* chap 5 and Geoffrey Sawer *Federation under Strain: Australia 1972–1975* (Melbourne: Melbourne University Press 1977), particularly chap 7.
43 Such moves have included attempts to change the terms of senators by constitutional amendment and aspects of recent legislation to amend the number of senators from each state and the mode of their election. On the constitutional issue see Campbell Sharman 'Referendum Puffery' *Australian Quarterly* 56 (1984) 20–9; and on the likely consequences of the electoral legislation, see Campbell Sharman 'The Senate Rise and Fall? Small Parties and the Balance of Power in the Senate' *Politics* 21 (November 1986) 20–31.

6 / Bicameralism: Canadian Senate Reform in Comparative Perspective

AREND LIJPHART

The purpose of this chapter[1] is to examine the organization of bicameral legislatures – the relative powers of the chambers and their respective composition – in comparative perspective, with special emphasis on the Canadian Senate and on the reforms proposed by the Special Joint Committee of the two Canadian legislative chambers in January 1984.[2] The significance of these proposals does not derive from the probability that they will be adopted in the near future. On the contrary, because this kind of reform – or any other plans for major changes in the Senate's powers or composition – can be adopted only by the onerous procedures of constitutional amendment, it is not very likely that a Senate reformed along the lines of the Special Joint Committee's suggestions will soon become a reality.[3] However, the debate on possible Senate reform is bound to continue, since the Senate as currently constituted is widely regarded as unsatisfactory. And the proposals by the Special Joint Committee are the most authoritative, elaborate, and detailed that have appeared so far.

The persistence of the debate on Senate reform is illustrated by the fact that the more recent report of the Royal Commission on the Economic Union and Development Prospects for Canada (Macdonald Commission), published in 1985, also includes a recommendation for fundamental reform of the Senate – quite similar, with one important exception to be discussed later, to the plan of the Special Joint Committee. The royal commission states emphatically that 'practically speaking, serious Senate reform is no longer a "non-starter".'[4]

The legislatures that will be included in this chapter's comparison are the bicameral parliaments of stable democracies, that is, all countries that have been democratic without interruption since approximately the end of the Second World War. This criterion yields a set of thirteen countries, most located in western Europe: the four large western European democracies (the United Kingdom, France, West Germany, and Italy), five smaller European countries (Ireland, the Netherlands, Belgium, Switzerland, and Austria), and four countries outside Europe (the United States, Japan, Australia, and, of course, Canada itself).

There are also eight countries, continually democratic since about 1945, that have unicameral parliaments. All five Nordic countries (Sweden, Norway, Denmark, Finland, and Iceland) belong to this group, as well as Israel, Luxembourg, and New Zealand. The legislatures of Norway and Iceland are sometimes erroneously regarded as bicameral. However, they are elected as one body, and only after their election do they divide themselves into two 'chambers': the Norwegian legislators choose one-fourth of their members to form a 'second chamber,' and their Icelandic counterparts separate out one-third of their members for the same purpose. The two Norwegian 'chambers' have joint legislative committees, and in both countries any disagreements are settled by a plenary meeting of all members of the legislature. Hence the second 'chamber' of these two legislatures is not a distinct chamber in its own right but merely a 'glorified committee' of a 'modified unicameral parliament.'[5]

This chapter will focus on bicameral legislatures, but bicameralism is not as common at the national level as is frequently assumed: eight out of twenty-one parliaments in the contemporary advanced industrialized democracies – almost two-fifths – are unicameral. The reason why this fact tends to be overlooked is that unicameral parliaments typically occur in the smaller countries. It should also be noted that there appears to be a trend toward unicameralism. Three countries have moved from bicameral to unicameral legislatures since the Second World War: New Zealand in 1950, Denmark in 1953, and Sweden in 1970.

Symmetrical v. Asymmetrical Bicameralism

In contrast with the homogeneous class of unicameral legislature, bicameral parliaments form a very heterogeneous group because their second chambers assume a great variety of forms and functions. The extent to which a second chamber plays a significant role in a country's political life depends largely on two factors: its powers relative to those of the first chamber, and its composition compared with that of the first chamber, that is, whether it is selected on the same or on a different basis. The first question will be discussed in this section, and the second in the next section.

The distribution of political power between the two chambers of a bicameral legislature depends on the formal powers bestowed upon them by the constitution and fundamental constitutional conventions and on the degree of democratic legitimacy of the second chamber. With regard to their formal powers, most second chambers are subordinate to first chambers. For instance, their negative votes on proposed legislation can often be overridden by the first chambers, and in parliamentary systems the cabinet is usually responsible primarily or exclusively to the first chamber. Only four of the thirteen bicameral parliaments have chambers with formally equal powers: the national legislatures of the United States, Italy, Belgium, and Switzerland.

The actual political significance of second chambers depends not only on their formal constitutional powers but also – and even more – on the degree of democratic legitimacy conferred by their method of selection. All first chambers are directly elected by the voters, but the members of several second chambers are elected indirectly (usually by legislatures at levels below that of the national government) or appointed (like the senators in Canada, some of the Irish senators, and life peers in the British House of Lords). Second chambers that are not directly elected lack the democratic legitimacy, and hence the real political influence, that popular election can confer. Conversely, the direct election of a second chamber may compensate to some extent for its limited formal power.

A three-fold classification of bicameral parliaments can be constructed on the basis of the above two considerations. The only fully symmetrical bicameral legislatures – those in which the two chambers are coequal in power – are the four, noted above, that have chambers with formally equal powers. The vast majority of the members of these four second chambers are also directly elected: the entire us Senate, virtually the entire Italian Senate and Swiss Council of States, and most Belgian senators.

The second category consists of four bicameral legislatures that are moderately asymmetrical: those of Australia, West Germany, Japan, and the Netherlands. The Australian and Japanese second chambers are elected directly. The Dutch parliament belongs to the category of moderate asymmetry in spite of the second chamber's indirect election by the provincial legislatures, because this chamber has an absolute veto power over all proposed legislation, including money bills, which cannot be overridden by the first chamber. The West German second chamber, the Bundesrat, does not owe its strength to either popular election or an absolute legislative veto but to the fact that it is a unique federal chamber, composed of representatives of the executives of the member states of the federation – usually ministers in the member state cabinets. Lewis J. Edinger exaggerates only slightly when he calls the Bundesrat 'one of the most powerful upper chambers in the world.'[6]

The third category of bicameral parliaments is characterized by extreme asymmetry between the first and second chambers. It includes the five national legislatures of Austria, Canada, France, Ireland, and the United Kingdom. In all five cases, the formal powers of the second chambers are inferior to those of the first chambers, and the methods by which they are selected – indirect election, appointment, or, in the case of the British House of Lords, appointment or heredity – further decrease their stature relative to the first chambers. The Canadian Senate provides a good example of the crucial importance of the method of selection: although it has considerable formal powers, equal to those of the House of Commons with the exception of money bills, the fact that senators are appointed deprives them of the democratic legitimacy to make use of these powers. Hence there can be no doubt that the Canadian case fits the category of extreme asymmetry.

How should the new Canadian Senate, as proposed by the Special Joint Committee on Senate Reform, be classified? Its formal powers will be drastically reduced. Only with regard to legislation of linguistic significance will its absolute veto be maintained (and on such matters an absolute veto will be added for the group of francophone senators). On all other non-financial bills it will merely have a suspensive veto of about seven to nine months. It will not be able to influence money bills or to threaten the life of a cabinet. This means that, with the exception of matters of linguistic importance, its formal powers will be even weaker than those of the British House of Lords, which can delay non-financial bills for a full year instead of seven to nine months and money bills for a month instead of not at all. The recommendation by the Macdonald Commission is almost identical to that of the Special Joint Committee in this respect, except that the former proposes an even shorter suspensive veto of only six months.

But these relatively weak formal powers are amply compensated by the shift from appointment to popular election – as envisaged by both the Special Joint Committee and the royal commission – which will give the Senate the democratic mandate that it now lacks. This change will move the Canadian parliament from the category of extremely asymmetrical bicameralism, in which none of the second chambers is directly elected, to the category of moderate asymmetry. Although the proposed reform clearly does not entail, and does not even approximate, symmetrical bicameralism, it clearly does signify, in the words of the Special Joint Committee, 'fundamental change' and 'vigorous action' as far as the relative powers of the two houses are concerned.[7] The next section will show that the committee's proposals for the composition of the new Senate are much less vigorous and adventurous.

Congruent v. Incongruent Bicameralism

Whether a second chamber is a meaningful political institution depends not only on its power but also on whether its composition is significantly different from that of the first chamber. For instance, Belgium and Italy have powerful second chambers, but they are elected in such a way that they tend to be carbon copies of the first chambers. This kind of bicameralism may be called congruent; it is only a small step from congruent bicameralism to unicameralism, and, apart from general limited-government considerations, it is hard to find good arguments for having a second chamber that is congruent with the first chamber. Strong bicameralism requires a second chamber that is as similar as possible to the first chamber as far as its powers are concerned but that is as dissimilar (incongruent) as possible in its composition.

The two main ways in which incongruence between first and second chambers may occur – or may be engineered – is that they may be elected by different electoral systems and that the second chambers may be designed in such a way as to overrepresent certain minorities; in particular, second chambers in federal systems tend to overrepresent the smaller component units of the federation. The thirteen democracies being compared in this chapter includ six federal and seven unitary systems. Five of the seven unitary systems – Belgium, Ireland, Italy, Japan, and the Netherlands – have bicameral parliaments that are congruent in both respects. With only slight variations, their two chambers are elected by proportional or semi-proportional methods in multi-member districts, which are generally favourable to the representation of minorities but do not provide overrepresentation of particular minority groups. Ireland's Senate appears to be an exception, since a large number of senators have to be elected from candidates nominated by vocational and cultural interest groups, but in the electoral college, composed of national and local legislators, party politics predominates. Hence, as the Irish political scientist Basil Chubb states, the Senate 'is composed largely of party politicians not very different from their colleagues' in the other chamber and, in many cases, 'with only tenuous connections with the interests they affect to represent.'[8]

The two exceptions – unitary systems with incongruent bicameralism – are Britain and France. The overrepresented minority in the British House of Lords is, of course, the nobility. The French Senate is elected by an electoral college in which the small communes, with less than one-third of the total population, have more than half the votes. On account of this rural overrepresentation, Maurice Duverger has called the Senate the 'Chamber of Agriculture.'[9]

Federal systems generally provide the more interesting examples of incongruence. Three of them – Australia, West Germany, and Switzerland – use proportional representation for the election of one chamber and majority methods for the other. In Australia, the first chamber is elected by the alternative vote, a majority system, and the federal chamber is elected by the single-transferable-vote form of proportional representation. In West Germany and Switzerland, the pattern is reversed: their first chambers are proportionally elected, and their federal chambers are chosen by majority methods – a two-ballot majority system in most of the Swiss cantons and indirect election by the governing majorities in the West German Länder. The United States uses the same electoral formula – plurality – for both the House of Representatives and the Senate, but there is a difference in district magnitude; representatives are elected in single-member districts, senators in two-member districts (states), although usually not at the same time. The Canadian case is irrelevant in this context, since its federal chamber is not elected at all, and Austria, with its two proportionally elected chambers, is the only clear exception among the six federations.

The new Canadian Senate, as proposed by the Special Joint Committee, would also be an exception: the committee proposes election in plurality single-member districts – exactly the same method as is used for the House of Commons. This recommendation is the least original and enterprising aspect of the committee's plans. Its arguments in favour of the single-member plurality method for the election of both houses, which it calls 'simple and satisfactory,'[10] partly reflect a conservative attitude but are also partly based on an erroneous appraisal of the political consequences of plurality and proportional representation.

First, the committee states that it is impressed by the argument that proportional representation for Senate elections 'would facilitate the emergence of purely regional parties.'[11] Proportional representation may indeed encourage minority parties, including those of regional minorities; plurality discourages minority parties except regional ones. For instance, in Britain, plurality hurts the dispersed Liberals but not the regionally concentrated Scottish Nationalists. And in Canada, too, regionally based third parties such as the Progressives in the 1920s and the Créditistes in the 1960s were helped considerably by the plurality system of elections.[12] Hence there is little difference between the two electoral systems as far as their effects on regional parties are concerned.

Second, the committee states that 'province-wide constituencies would not allow for regional representation within provinces; for example, almost all the senators elected from a province might come from the major urban areas, leaving rural areas unrepresented.' This is true only if the plurality method is applied in large province-wide districts; proportional representation in such large districts would facilitate the representation of rural minorities or any other kind of minority. The committee, of course, prefers plurality in much smaller, single-member districts and argues that one advantage of its preferred system is the following: 'The chances of linguistic and cultural minorities within each region electing one or more of their members would be greater if constituency boundaries were drawn so as to permit such representation.'[13] A more accurate way of expressing this 'advantage' is that, compared with proportional representation, the single-member district plurality system has the disadvantage of discouraging minority representation but that this disadvantage can be partly compensated by affirmative gerrymandering in favour of particular linguistic and cultural minorities.

Third and finally, compared with the plurality method, proportional representation gives political parties a much greater incentive to apply their energies even in areas where they are weak. The committee appears to recognize this fact but argues that 'if parties are incapable of electing members in a particular province, they should pull themselves together and change their attitudes. The electoral system should not be altered merely to compensate for the weaknesses and strategic errors of political parties.'[14] The more realistic view is that it would be a strategic mistake for a political party to use its necessarily limited resources in areas where its chances are minimal. The committee wants parties to be unselfish and to disregard such calculations of electoral advantage – a curious argument on the part of practical politicians!

It is in this respect that the royal commission's proposals are significantly different from – and much more innovative than – the Special Joint Committee's. The royal commission recommends the election of 138 of the senators by proportional representation in 23 six-member districts. The six senators from Yukon and the Northwest Territories would be elected in smaller districts (single-member or multi-member), depending on the division of the Northwest Territories.[15] Single-member districts necessarily entail plurality or majority methods, but the commission presumably intended any multi-member districts in the territories to apply proportional representation in the same way as the six-member districts in the provinces.

To what extent do the six federations apply the second dimension of incongruent bicameralism – the overrepresentation of the smaller component units of the federation in the second chamber? Equality of representation regardless of the component units' population constitutes the maximum extension of the principle of overrepresentation. Such parity is found in the second chambers of three federal systems: the United States and

Switzerland (two representatives per state or canton) and Australia (twelve representatives per state, recently increased from ten, but only two for each of the two territories). The German Bundesrat and the Canadian Senate are examples of federal chambers in which the component units are not equally represented but in which the smaller units are overrepresented and the larger ones underrepresented. Canada is not a perfect example, however, because the two largest provinces (Ontario and Quebec) are actually somewhat more favourably represented – that is, they have a larger Senate delegation relative to their populations – than the two provinces that are next in size (British Columbia and Alberta). Austria is the clear exception on this dimension of incongruence, too: its federal chamber has roughly proportional numbers of representatives from each of the Länder.

Table 1 presents the degree of overrepresentation of the most favourably represented units – generally the smaller ones – in a more precise way: in terms of the degree of inequality of representation caused by the preferential treatment of the small units. It shows the percentage of the membership of the federal chamber that represents the most favourably represented 5, 10, 25, and 50 per cent of the population. The following example illustrates how these percentages are calculated. Assume that the smallest and best represented state in a federation has 6 per cent of the total population and 10 out of 100 seats in the federal chamber, and that the second smallest and second best represented state has 8 per cent of the population and also 10 out of 100 federal chamber seats. Then the best represented 10 per cent of the total population are the 6 per cent in the smallest state plus half of the people in the second smallest state. Together these 10 per cent of the people have 15 per cent of the seats in the federal chamber. In the last column of Table 1, the Gini index of inequality is given for the different countries. This index is a summary measure of the degree of inequality which can range from zero when there is complete equality to a theoretical maximum approaching 1.00 when the most favourably represented state has all of the seats and the others get none.

Table 1 includes the relevant percentages and indices not only for the six federal chambers, based on the population figures and seat distributions in about 1980, but also for the new Canadian Senate proposed by the Special Joint Committee (designated in the table as Canada II) and for a hypothetical Canadian Senate with completely equal provincial representation (Canada III). The committee's recommendation is to give 12 senators to each of the seven middle-sized provinces, 24 to Ontario and Quebec, 6 to the smallest province of Prince Edward Island, and 4 and 2 to the Northwest Territories and Yukon respectively. The royal commission's proposal is based on virtually

TABLE 1

Inequality of representation in federal chambers, c. 1980

	Percentages of seats held by given percentages of the most favourably represented voters				Gini index of inequality
	5%	10%	25%	50%	
Canada III*	29.0	43.1	69.1	85.2	0.56
United States	28.2	39.5	60.6	82.9	0.50
Switzerland	26.7	38.9	60.4	81.1	0.48
Canada II†	21.8	34.0	56.5	74.2	0.39
Australia	21.3	30.4	55.3	75.7	0.39
West Germany‡	20.1	31.5	50.7	73.1	0.36
Canada I§	18.9	31.2	48.5	69.2	0.31
Austria	6.9	12.8	28.2	53.2	0.05

SOURCE: Adapted from Arend Lijphart *Democracies: Patterns of Majoritarian and Consensus Government in Twenty-One Countries* (New Haven: Yale University Press 1984) 174
*A hypothetical example of equal provincial representation in the Canadian Senate
§The Canadian Senate as currently constituted
†The new Canadian Senate as proposed by the Special Joint Committee
‡Excluding West Berlin

identical numbers. Such a distribution of seats would bring the Canadian Senate more in line with most of the other federal chambers. The table lists the federal chambers in decreasing order of inequality; the current Canadian Senate is almost at the bottom – only the Austrian second chamber, which is basically congruent with the first chamber, ranks lower – but the present Canadian Senate is much closer to the other federal chambers than to the Austrian one. The committee's proposal would move the Senate past the German Bundesrat to about the same level of inequality as the Australian Senate but still well below that of the US and Swiss federal chambers, with their completely equal state and cantonal representations.

The committee did consider the possibility of equal provincial representation in the new Canadian Senate but rejected it on the ground that 'the imbalance between the constituent units' is considerably more pronounced in Canada than in Australia, Switzerland, and the United States. As an example, the committee states that 'Canada's largest province, Ontario, has about 36 per cent of the country's population; in the United States, the largest state has only about 10 per cent.'[16] This example yields an exaggerated impression of the differences. A more appropriate comparison would be between the largest of Canada's ten provinces and the five largest of the fifty states in the US federal system: 36 per cent v. about 35 per cent. Nevertheless, it is true that equal provincial representation would give the

Canadian Senate an even higher level of inequality of representation than the US and Swiss federal chambers. The example in Table 1 – Canada III – is based on the assumption that each province would have ten senators and each territory two (as in the Australian Senate prior to its 1984 expansion). Canada III is at the top of the list, well ahead of the United States and Switzerland.

Conclusion

Measured on the several dimensions of symmetry and congruence, the Special Joint Committee's proposal entails a substantial – but not radical – upgrading of Canada's bicameralism. This conclusion is summarized in Table 2. The Canadian parliament would move from the incongruent and extremely asymmetrical category of bicameralism, also occupied by the legislatures of unitary Britain and France, to the incongruent and moderately asymmetrical category in the company of federal Australia and West Germany. This shift would bring Canada into greater conformity with most of the other federations, and Austria would be left even more clearly as a deviant case among the federal systems. The most daring and significant innovation is the introduction of the principle of direct election of the Senate, but at the same time the formal powers of the new Senate would be cut severely. On the two dimensions of incongruence, the degree of minority overrepresentation would be strengthened – here, too, to a level similar to that of the Australian and West German cases – but the single-member district plurality system proposed for the election of the Senate is essentially congruent with the electoral system for the House of Commons. It should be noted that the bicameralism proposed by the Macdonald Commission should be placed in the same general category of Table 2. However, the commission's advocacy of proportional representation entails a fully instead of partially incongruent Senate and hence a considerably stronger and more meaningful bicameralism.

The main reason for the Special Joint Committee's reluctance to propose more radical reforms appears to be its concern that a too strong Senate with potentially a different majority from that in the House of Commons could interfere with the orderly operation of parliamentary government: 'In a parliamentary system, a government cannot serve two masters, whose wills might on occasion be diametrically opposed.'[17] The Australian constitutional crisis of 1975, discussed by Campbell Sharman in his chapter in this book, shows that this fear is by no means imaginary.

Nevertheless, there is an even more fundamental reason for the committee's

TABLE 2

Types of bicameralism in thirteen contemporary democracies

	Symmetrical	Moderately asymmetrical	Extremely asymmetrical
Incongruent	*Switzerland* *United States*	*Australia* *Canada II*† *West Germany*	*Canada I** France *United Kingdom*
Congruent	Belgium Italy	Japan Netherlands	*Austria* Ireland

SOURCE: Adapted from Lijphart *Democracies* 99
NOTE: The federal systems are italicized.
*The Canadian Senate as currently constituted
†The new Canadian Senate as proposed by the Special Joint Committee

conservatism: the continuing strength of the majoritarian tradition in Canada. For instance, in the statement that 'a government cannot serve two masters,' the 'masters' are not the two legislative chambers but majorities in these chambers. The logical solution to the 'two masters' dilemma is to form a broad coalition so that the government has sufficient support in both houses; but this solution clashes with the majoritarian hostility to the notion of coalition government. A similar example is the committee's fear of 'the possibility, if not the probability, of our parliamentary institutions continually becoming deadlocked.'[18] But paralysis is not at all a necessary consequence of conflict between equally powerful institutions. The US federal government has operated for a long time under what William H. Riker calls a system of 'three legislative houses,'[19] – a separately elected president, Senate, and House of Representatives. The key to the success of this kind of symmetrical and incongruent tricameralism is not majority rule but the search for compromise and consensus. The committee's utter rejection of proportional representation also clearly emanates from the majoritarian impulse.

The Nobel Prize-winning economist Sir Arthur Lewis has compared the strong influence of the British majoritarian model in the former British dependencies to brainwashing, and he recommends that they undergo a cure of 'much un-brainwashing.'[20] In all fairness, however, it must be said that any bicameralism that is not completely asymmetrical or completely congruent entails a deviation from strict majority rule. By proposing a stronger bicameralism for Canada, the committee has shown itself to be at least somewhat 'liberated' from the majoritarian tradition.

NOTES

1 This chapter was written while I was a Guggenheim Fellow. I should like to express my gratitude to the Guggenheim Foundation for its generous support. Parts of the chapter are drawn from chapters 6 and 10 of my book *Democracies: Patterns of Majoritarian and Consensus Government in Twenty-One Countries* (New Haven: Yale University Press 1984).

2 Special Joint Committee on Senate Reform *Report of the Special Joint Committee of the Senate and of the House of Commons on Senate Reform* (Ottawa: Supply and Services 1984)

3 See D.V. Smiley and R.L. Watts *Intrastate Federalism in Canada*, vol. 39 in the Research Studies Commissioned by the Royal Commission on the Economic Union and Development Prospects for Canada (Toronto: University of Toronto Press 1985) 140–4.

4 Royal Commission on the Economic Union and Development Prospects for Canada *Report* (Ottawa: Supply and Services 1985) iii 87

5 Gordon Smith *Politics in Western Europe: A Comparative Analysis* 2nd ed (London: Heinemann 1976) 167; Arthur S. Banks and William Overstreet *Political Handbook of the World: 1980* (New York: McGraw-Hill 1980) 347

6 Lewis J. Edinger *Politics in Germany: Attitudes and Processes* (Boston: Little, Brown 1968) 202

7 Special Joint Committee *Report* 1

8 Basil Chubb *The Government and Politics of Ireland* (Stanford: Stanford University Press 1971) 205

9 Cited in John S. Ambler *The Government and Politics of France* (Boston: Houghton Mifflin 1971) 165

10 Special Joint Committee *Report* 25

11 Ibid 24

12 See Alan C. Cairns 'The Electoral System and the Party System in Canada, 1921–1965' *Canadian Journal of Political Science* 1 (March 1968) 55–80.

13 Special Joint Committee *Report* 25

14 Ibid 24–5

15 Royal Commission *Report* 89

16 Special Joint Committee *Report* 28

17 Ibid 29

18 Ibid 30

19 William H. Riker 'Electoral Systems and Constitutional Restraints' in Arend Lijphart and Bernard Grofman eds *Choosing an Electoral System: Issues and Alternatives* (New York: Praeger 1984) 109

20 W. Arthur Lewis *Politics in West Africa* (London: Allen and Unwin 1965) 55

7 / Judicial Review
and Modern Federalism:
Canada and
the United States

JENNIFER SMITH

The adoption of the Charter of Rights and Freedoms has focused more public attention on the judiciary than is usual in Canada. There is widespread recognition of the additional responsibility and power that the Charter places in the hands of the courts. Many Canadian expectations about an enhanced judicial presence are related to perceptions about the influence of the US Supreme Court in its handling of the Bill of Rights. This chapter, too, takes its bearings from the American experience but from a somewhat different vantage point. The Canadian Supreme Court may well attain something of the high profile of its American counterpart as it deals with Charter cases. My question concerns its role as 'umpire' of the federal system. Will jurisdictional cases continue to form a significant part of its constitutional work? More generally, does the advent of the Charter mean that jurisdictional questions will be overshadowed by rights questions?

American experience suggests that the jurisdictional issues peculiar to federal constitutions can run their course. Jurisdictional issues normally arise out of disputes about the powers these constitutions assign to different levels of government. The US Supreme Court continues to dispose of such cases, but their number and significance relative to those of disputes arising under the Bill of Rights have diminished considerably in the post–Second World War period, as a glance at the table of contents of any contemporary constitutional law text indicates. Are the factors that have contributed to this development also at work in Canada? In order to address this question it is useful to begin by comparing briefly both the governmental arrangements within which the Canadian and American appellate courts are located and the institutional features of each body. Is there anything about them that bears on the use of the judicial forum to settle conflicts of jurisdiction? Following this I look at the way in which the Canadian and American constitutions distribute legislative subject matters and their respective courts' interpretations of this. Does the Canadian case present more outstanding or unsettled jurisdictional questions? The Canadian Charter, the appearance of which marks an apparent shift toward the American constitutional model, is the subject of the third section of the article. Does it differ significantly in its essentials from the US Bill of Rights? Comparative analysis on these three points is hardly definitive. Yet as I hope to demonstrate, it does suggest that while jurisdictional conflicts and their resolution by the courts are likely to remain an important feature of Canadian constitutional affairs, Charter issues will easily rival them.

The Canadian and American Supreme Courts

From the point of view of governmental arrangements, Canada and the United States have always presented an interesting comparative study because they possess federal frameworks but different principles of government. American government is based on the doctrine of separate yet interlocking powers. The judiciary is possessed of constitutional standing equal to that of the other two branches of government, the executive and legislative branches. While the US Supreme Court is established by virtue of the constitution, its power of judicial review, that is, the power to review the constitutional validity of acts of Congress and the state legislatures, is not found there. The court itself, in a landmark decision written by Chief Justice John Marshall, successfully laid claim to precisely that power in the case of *Marbury* v. *Madison* (1803). Although he did not use the word 'umpire,' Marshall's concept of the court's role was rather like that of a referee or impartial third party judging the claims of the constitution, on the one side, and those of an impugned law, on the other.[1] The concept of the judiciary as referee or umpire prevails today, especially in the context of jurisdictional disputes between governments.

By way of contrast the Canadian judiciary operates within a parliamentary form of government that, in theory at least, is not hospitable to the concept of judicial review. The reason is the principle of parliamentary supremacy, which denies to courts the power to review and invalidate legislative enactments. The authority of the parliamentary model at the time of Confederation helps account for the fact that, despite the federal aspect of the new political arrangements, the constitution provided only that Parliament, at its own choosing, might establish a general court of appeal, and eight years passed before it did so in 1875. The question of judicial review was also complicated by the role of the Judicial Committee of the Privy Council, the final appellate court for the colonies of the British Empire.

Under Britain's Colonial Laws Validity Act, colonial statutes in conflict with imperial laws extending to the colony were invalid. The Judicial Committee customarily reviewed the validity of such statutes in appeals brought before it, and colonial courts came to exercise the same review power. Accordingly Barry Strayer has argued that the origins of judicial review in Canada are to be found in its colonial past, not the logic of federalism.[2] Paul Weiler attributes the relatively non-controversial character of the review function to the same legal tradition.[3] Certainly the new Supreme Court had no qualms about it. In *Valin* v. *Langlois* (1879), Chief Justice Ritchie emphasized the great responsibility shouldered by 'those called on ... to declare authoritatively the principles by which both federal and local legislation are governed.'[4] Of course the responsibility of the chief justice and his colleagues was lightened somewhat by the fact that their decisions, unlike those of their American counterparts, were open to appeal. The Supreme Court of Canada did not become the country's highest appellate court until 1949, when appeals to the Judicial Committee were abolished.

In addition to the fact that it is a creature of Parliament, the court has other features that are consistent with parliamentary form. One of these is the way in which its nine members are selected. They are appointed by the federal executive in a process that includes some informal consultation but is not open to public scrutiny. By contrast, the American process is open to public scrutiny. Appointments to the nine-member court belong to the president, subject to confirmation by the Senate. Presidents normally nominate individuals from their own party, or at least individuals whose viewpoints appear to coincide with their own. The Senate is interested as well in the political views of nominees, and the confirmation stage is an opportunity to ascertain them. Only occasionally has the Senate refused to confirm a president's nominee. Two of President Nixon's candidates, federal judges Clement F. Haynsworth and G. Harrold Carswell, were rejected, in part because of allegations of pro-segregation bias in some of their decisions. The Senate's participation offers the occasion for public scrutiny, and it also serves as an avenue for state influence, at least to the extent that senators feel compelled to take state interest into account. Again by contrast, the Canadian process clearly favours the federal government, a point that has provoked some disgruntlement, notably on the part of provincial governments. Constitutional scholars are not as troubled. Peter Russell finds 'no discernible constitutional orientation' among most appointees. Peter Hogg stresses the balance in orientation evident in the court's decisions over time.[5] Certainly the visible lack of balance in the mode of selection has not inhibited the court in playing an active role in policing jurisdictional boundaries.

Another feature linked to the parliamentary form of government that distinguishes the two courts is the reference mechanism. A reminder of earlier notions of the subordinate role of the Canadian Supreme Court, the mechanism obliges the court to advise the federal government on any question referred to it by order-in-council.[6] Understandably the provinces initially took a dim view of this, especially since the government could refer provincial as well as federal laws to the court for a ruling on their validity. In the event, Parliament's competence to include the reference device among the court's functions was tested before the Judicial Committee in *Attorney General for Ontario* v. *Attorney General for Canada* (1912). The intervening provinces argued that it was an executive function and therefore a violation of section 101 of the Constitution Act, 1867, which permits Parliament to establish tribunals possessed of judicial powers only. In his judgment for the committee, Earl Loreburn, LC, appeared to accept their view of the court's task in the reference case as merely advisory, hence non-judicial, but he did not consider this fatal to its judicial status. The committee itself, he pointed out, was bound by the same obligation to answer questions referred to it by the British government yet on that account was not considered any less a court.[7] Thus Parliament's competence to treat the court as an adviser in reference cases was affirmed. In this respect, of course, the Supreme Court of Canada differs from its American counterpart. In its decision in *Muskrat* v. *United States* (1911), the US Supreme Court rejected the attempt of Congress to require it to undertake a task that the court considered non-judicial on the ground that it did not involve an actual case or controversy.[8] It has preserved for itself a strictly judicial or adjudicatory power, refusing to aid Congress by determining questions of constitutional validity not arising out of concrete disputes.

Settled v. Unsettled Jurisdictional Questions

Some of the features noted here that distinguish the Canadian from the US Supreme Court suggest that the latter is the more suitably designed for the role of umpire of a federal system. Thus these features cannot account for the fact that its activity in this respect is less vital than it used to be and certainly less vital than that of the Canadian court now. Does the distribution of legislative powers as set out in each constitution offer an explanation? The short answer is no, unless of course the distribution is viewed in the light of judicial interpretation. The US constitution specifies the powers of Congress only. The residual or remaining powers belong to the states. As originally drafted, the constitution did not state this. It was spelled out in 1791 in the tenth amendment: 'The powers not delegated to the United States by the Constitution, nor prohibited by it to the States are reserved to the States respectively, or to the people.'

In the first decades of the republic, the court was busy exploring and defining the scope of Congress's legislative competence over and against that of the state legislatures. While the weight of its earlier rulings favoured Congress, there were periods, particularly toward the end of the nineteenth century and the early years of the twentieth century, when the states fared rather well. Thus the general trend toward centralization on which almost all observers agree masks an enormously complex history of judicial tacking on a variety of jurisdictional questions. It also overlooks a point of some significance for the Canadian case, namely, the development of settled doctrines. In the course of resolving federal-state disputes, the American court has developed broadly accepted lines of interpretation, many of which favour Congress. Constitutional law on the tenth amendment illustrates this.

The meaning of the tenth amendment immediately proved controversial. It does not appear to limit federal powers, since it expressly excepts powers delegated to the United States. Yet states' rights enthusiasts viewed it as a barrier to the use of federal powers authorized elsewhere. According to them such powers are limited by those reserved to the states in the tenth amendment, in which case there must be some prior notion of what is properly reserved. In *Hammer* v. *Dagenhart* (1918), the Supreme Court included the age at which children are permitted to work in factories and struck down a federal statute designed to discourage child labour by forbidding interstate transportation of goods produced by children below given ages. Speaking for the majority, Justice Day stated: 'In interpreting the Constitution it must never be forgotten that the nation is made up of states, to which are intrusted the powers of local government. And to them and to the people the powers not expressly delegated to the national government are reserved.'

In dissent, Justice Holmes expressed the view that local powers are limited by those assigned to Congress: 'I should have thought that the most conspicuous decisions of this court had made it clear that the power to regulate commerce and other constitutional powers could not be cut down or qualified by the fact that it might interfere with the carrying out of the domestic policy of any state.'[9] Holmes's view ultimately prevailed. *United States* v. *Darby Lumber Co.* (1941) concerned the federal Fair Labor Standards Act, 1938, which set minimum wages for a forty-hour work week and for overtime in some interstate businesses. The court upheld the act as a valid exercise of Congress's trade and commerce power and, more important, openly repudiated Justice Day's reasoning in *Hammer* v. *Dagen-*

hart, terming it a 'departure from the principles which have prevailed in the interpretation of the commerce clause both before and since the decision.' Justice Stone reiterated the principle that Holmes had set out: 'The power of Congress under the commerce clause is plenary to exclude any article from interstate commerce subject only to the specific prohibitions of the Constitution.' On the meaning of the tenth amendment, Stone commented that it merely expressed a 'truism that all is retained which has not been surrendered.'[10]

Another issue settled early on in favour of the national government concerned the relation between the powers assigned Congress in article 1, section 8, and the last clause of that section, which authorizes Congress 'to make all laws which shall be necessary and proper for carrying into execution the foregoing powers.' The Jeffersonians and the Federalists disputed the 'necessary and proper clause' almost immediately, the former giving it a limited construction, the latter taking a broader view. The issue was joined over Congress's authority to establish the Bank of the United States, which it exercised in 1816. In *McCulloch* v. *Maryland* (1819), Chief Justice Marshall upheld the act as a valid exercise of the power implied by Congress's specified financial powers, arguing that such powers require 'ample means for their execution.' On the meaning of the contentious clause, he rejected the Jeffersonian position: 'Let the end be legitimate, let it be within the scope of the constitution, and all means which are appropriate, which are plainly adapted to that end, which are not prohibited, but consistent with the letter and spirit of the constitution, are constitutional.'[11] For the most part this broad view has prevailed.

In the Canadian case less is settled, and not necessarily in Parliament's favour. Sections 91 and 92 of the Constitution Act, 1867, enumerate the subject matters belonging to Parliament and the provincial legislatures respectively. Section 91 lists a host of financial, commercial, and transportation matters, all pertaining to the national economy, as well as broad military and enforcement matters. It is prefaced by a well-known clause enabling Parliament to legislate for the 'Peace, Order, and good Government' of Canada in relation to all matters not assigned exclusively to the provinces. The shorter section 92, in contrast, enumerates items supposed at the time of Confederation to be of a local nature, for example, hospitals, municipal institutions, and local business. There are other signs of the central government's dominance, such as section 90, which confers on it the power to disallow provincial laws at any time within one year of their passage. However, the Judicial Committee was inclined to take a large view of section 92 matters. In a series of well-known cases in Canadian constitutional law it enhanced both the constitutional status and the legislative sphere of the provinces. So much is beyond doubt. It is harder to determine the committee's doctrinal legacy, in part because at different times it entertained conflicting interpretations of sections 91 and 92 without achieving a satisfactory resolution. The clearest example concerns the peace, order, and good government clause.

In one of its earliest cases, *Russell* v. *The Queen* (1882), the committee seemed disposed to treat the opening words of section 91 as a general grant of power, and the items enumerated thereafter as examples of that power. Subsequently it changed tack, and in a series of decisions culminating in 1896 in the *Local Prohibition* case it developed a 'three-compartment' doctrine, so-called because it separates the opening words from the rest of section 91 and, of course, section 92. In accordance with this doctrine, the committee subordinated the peace, order and good government clause to the enumerated matters in section 91, in effect transforming it into a residual power. Only matters of a general nature unspecified in sections 91 and 92 and not affecting section 92 could find a home in the general grant of power. Lord Watson explained the rationale behind this: 'If it were once conceded that the Parliament of Canada has authority to make laws applicable to the whole Dominion, in relation to matters which in each province are substantially of local or private interest, upon the assumption that these matters also concern the peace, order, and good government of the Dominion, there is hardly a subject enumerated in s. 92 upon which it might not legislate, to the exclusion of the provincial legislatures.'[12]

Eventually the committee resurrected peace, order, and good government as a resource power for Parliament during national emergencies. As it turned out, this was not the end of the matter. In the *Canada Temperance Federation* case, decided in 1946, the committee returned to the approach taken in the *Russell* case and argued that the subject matter of legislation, not the existence of an emergency, is the proper test of its validity. Speaking for the committee, Viscount Simon enunciated a national interest standard to describe legislation within Parliament's competence: 'If it is such that it goes beyond local or provincial concern or interests and must from its inherent nature be the concern of the Dominion as a whole ... then it will fall within the competence of the Dominion Parliament as a matter affecting the peace, order and good government of Canada, though it may in another aspect touch on matters specially reserved to the provincial legislatures.'[13]

When appeals to the Judicial Committee were abolished and the Supreme Court became Canada's final appellate court, it was in a position to settle the meaning of the peace, order, and good government clause. But it is not clear that it has. In the *Johannesson* case decided in 1952, *Munro*

v. *National Capital Commission* in 1966, and the *Offshore Minerals Reference* in 1967, the court used Simon's inherent national interest test to invoke the general clause as a ground of federal legislation.

But in 1976, in the *Anti-Inflation Reference*, the Supreme Court returned to the emergency doctrine, indeed, gave it new life. At issue was the federal Anti-Inflation Act, 1975, which provided for a temporary but comprehensive program of wage and price controls that applied not only to the federal public sector and those of the provinces choosing to opt into the scheme but also to designated areas of the private sector as well. Thus it affected a host of economic activities normally thought to come under provincial jurisdiction in relation to property and civil rights. It was open to the court to sustain the act as a valid exercise of Parliament's general power understood in terms of the national interest test. Instead it sustained the act as a valid exercise of the general power during emergencies – in this instance a peacetime emergency. The latter point is significant, since the Judicial Committee, taking a narrower view of what constitutes an emergency, had used the doctrine to uphold federal enactments only in times of war. Moreover, in the *Anti-Inflation* case it was the Supreme Court, not the federal government, that insisted on the existence of an emergency. The irony is that Justice Beetz, who gave the fullest account of the doctrine, dissented from the view of the majority that it was applicable in the circumstances.[14]

In his critique of the Supreme Court's record as umpire of the federal system, Paul Weiler states: 'The Court is holding legislation valid or invalid on the basis of standards which it is making up as it goes along.'[15] This interpretation indicates considerable unease with the quality of judge-made constitutional policy. According to Weiler, the determination of jurisdictional competence is a complex and demanding undertaking requiring that judges have access to a great variety of relevant materials and the expertise to assess them. In his view they cannot possibly meet these requirements. First, the adversary process of adjudication is designed to uncover the facts in a case, not to encourage wide-ranging discussion and deliberation preparatory to forming policy on broad economic or social questions. The process is too narrowly focused. Second, the judges, normally recruited from the legal profession, are unlikely to have the kind of background enabling them to think in public policy terms. Weiler's controversial conclusion is that Canadian federalism would do well without a judicial umpire at all. He is willing to rely on intergovernmental negotiations combined with compromise at the political level.[16]

For the purposes of my argument Weiler's conclusion is less important than the reasoning he uses to reach it. As indicated, he identifies two institutional factors that inhibit the court in its policy-making function.

Too often the result is a kind of *ad hocery*, a reliance on discrete legal rules and materials that prevents the development of broader legal principles that are relevant to changing economic and social conditions and that together clarify the underlying structure and purpose of various areas of the law. And it is these legal principles, as Weiler points out, that ought to form the 'touchstone by which judicial innovation is carried on, both in creating new rules and in altering or abolishing the old ones.'[17] Without them there is no touchstone, which reinforces my earlier point about the lack of settled doctrine.

The Supreme Court's failure to develop a theory on the division of powers and its relation to the peace, order, and good government clause certainly gives its constitutional decisions an edge. This is heightened by the highly competitive nature of federal-provincial relations. As noted earlier, the Judicial Committee tended to take a favourable view of provincial claims. In particular it made much of two provincial heads, namely, 92(13), 'Property and Civil Rights in the Province,' and 92(16) 'Generally all Matters of a merely local or private Nature in the Province.' The result during the committee's tenure was a much more balanced distribution of powers in constitutional law than the bare words of sections 91 and 92 appear to intend. According to both Peter Russell and Peter Hogg, the Supreme Court has maintained the balance, thereby sustaining the conditions of competitive federalism. In his recent review of the court's record, Russell cites many examples of this, among them the interesting trio of decisions on the high matter of constitutional amendment. In the 1980 *Senate Reference*, the court ruled that Parliament's amending power under the old section 91(1) of the British North America Act did not encompass substantive reform of the Senate. A year later, in the *Patriation Reference*, it reached the nice conclusion that while constitutional convention prescribed substantial provincial consent, there was nothing in law preventing the federal government from unilaterally pursuing constitutional changes affecting the provinces. The last decision in the set went against the one province, Quebec, that has not yet consented to the constitutional changes adopted in 1982 in the wake of the *Patriation Reference*. In *Re Objection to a Resolution to Amend the Constitution* (1982), the court rejected Quebec's contention that, in accordance with constitutional convention, it possessed a veto on constitutional change affecting it. 'Uncanny' is the word Russell uses to typify the balance reached in these and other decisions he canvasses.

Litigation is a more promising course of action for governments in a competitive federalism than in a federalism dominated by one level of government. Russell draws this conclusion, and for the obvious reason: 'Whatever side you are on in a constitutional dispute over the division of powers, the record of balance makes it reasonable to believe you might win.'[18] The success of jurisdictional arguments can only encourage lawyers to continue to resort to their use. I would add that the lack of settled doctrine reinforces the habit. Russell adds weight to this contention when he remarks: 'It is not easy to find evidence that the balance is the result of the conscious intentions of the justices.' Only very occasionally, he notes, have individual judges treated the importance of jurisdictional balance in Canadian federalism, or the legal principles of federalism, to use Weiler's terms.[19] Russell cites other factors to account for the court's active federal role, including the increasingly litigious nature of Canadian society, fuelled in part by the expansion of the legal profession, and, in cases like the *Patriation Reference*, the breakdown of political negotiations between governments.[20] It is possible that the very balance to which Russell draws attention works against negotiation.

Rights Cases v. Jurisdictional Cases

The decline of the US Supreme Court's role as umpire of the federal system as yet finds no parallel in Canada. Will the advent of the Charter change this? Are there already signs of change? Russell thinks not. Having demonstrated the extent to which the court has triumphed over those who thought they could see an end to its umpiring role, he concludes that this role will remain vital. I am inclined to agree, primarily because of the constitutional competitiveness of the two levels of government. They possess substantial spheres of jurisdiction in which they are accustomed to manoeuvre and therefore have a great deal at stake when these spheres are contested. Added to this is the bureaucratic dynamic Alan Cairns has described. Canada's governmental bureaucracies, he writes, represent a 'permanent, expansive aspect of government.'[21] They are inclined to defend their turf when challenged, and the likelihood of that is enhanced, not diminished, by the increasing interdependence of modern governments within a technological environment.

The communications field, not identified as a discrete subject matter at Confederation, is an example. It has all kinds of ramifications for areas as disparate as security and culture and is subject to continual technological advance. It has required the courts to assign responsibility for new activities among competing governments, as the Judicial Committee did in the *Radio* case in 1932, and has imparted some urgency to the driest of technical matters. As Russell points out, Quebec's attempt to control the licensing of cable television operators in the province, denied by the court in 1978 in the use of *Public Service Board* v. *Dionne*, was a matter of cultural policy.[22] Nevertheless, it is likely that jurisdictional cases will take a back seat to Charter cases in the immediate future. Indeed, it is already happening. There are a number of reasons for this, one of the most important being the attitude of the judges themselves.

One of the great differences between the US Bill of Rights and the Canadian Charter is timing. The charter has appeared at a time when legal scholars have long since exploded the notion that the practice of judicial review is a matter of discovering the objective or true meaning of the words of the law and applying them to the case. The reality of judicial interpretation, of the meaning judges choose to give these words, is inescapable when the choices they make and the reasoning they employ in arriving at them are often controversial. Thus it was clear to almost everyone that in adopting the Charter in 1982, Canadian governments were handing the courts, especially the Supreme Court, a powerful instrument to police legislative activity and through it the boundaries of public policy. It is particularly clear to the Supreme Court judges themselves, as the Charter decisions handed down thus far indicate.

Two features of these decisions immediately impress the reader. One is the determination and openness with which the judges are prepared to tackle the Charter. The other is their own sense of the enormity of judicial scope the Charter gives them. An example of the first is Chief Justice Dickson's opinion for the majority in *The Queen* v. *Big M. Drug Mart Ltd* (1985). At issue was the validity of the federal Lord's Day Act, a Sunday observance law, in light of section 2(a) of the Charter, which guarantees 'freedom of conscience and religion.' In a wide-ranging and compelling opinion, the chief justice includes a section on the concept of freedom of religion and the purpose of protecting it. Here he argues that to determine the meaning of a guaranteed right or freedom the courts must ascertain the purpose for which it is secured in the light of 'the character and the larger objects of the *Charter* itself,' the express words used to denote the concept, its historical usage, and, where applicable, its relation to other rights and freedoms enshrined in the document. It is a comprehensive mode of analysis aimed at a 'generous' as opposed to 'legalistic' interpretation of the Charter, and also an unencumbered one, as his pursuit of it in this particular case illustrates.[23]

Justice Lamer's opinion in *Reference Re British Columbia Motor Vehicle Act* (1985) conveys a very clear appreciation of the extent to which the Charter extends the scope of judicial review. The case involved section 7 of the Charter, which asserts a right to life, liberty, and security of the person and a right not to be deprived of these things 'except in accordance with the principles of fundamental justice.' Lamer's opening remarks are of interest here because he feels compelled to consider the 'very legitimacy of constitutional adjudication under the Charter.' He notes the view taken by some that unless the courts narrowly construe section 7, especially the phrase 'principles of fundamental justice,' in procedural as opposed to substantive terms, they will risk questioning the wisdom of public policy. They will form a kind of 'super-legislature,' a position to which their unrepresentative status in no way entitles them in a liberal democracy. In response, Lamer argues that the fact of the Charter's entrenchment has put paid to this debate: 'It ought not to be forgotten that the historic decision to entrench the Charter in our Constitution was taken not by the courts but by the elected representatives of the people of Canada. It was those representatives who extended the scope of constitutional adjudication and entrusted the courts with this new and onerous responsibility. Adjudication under the Charter must be approached free of any lingering doubts as to its legitimacy.'[24] On the question of procedure versus content, he points out that in jurisdicational questions, the courts have customarily measured the content of impugned laws against the strictures of the constitution, without judging the merits of those laws. And they will do the same thing in relation to questions arising under the Charter. What is new about the Charter is that it 'has sanctioned the process of constitutional adjudication and has extended its scope so as to encompass a broader range of values.'[25] Individual rights as well as jurisdictional boundaries are now the occasion of judicial review.

There are other reasons for thinking that Charter issues will pre-empt jurisdictional ones. One has to do with the broad nature of many of its clauses. For example, the provision on equality rights in section 15 surpasses the equal protection provision of the US Bill of Rights by providing for equality before and under the law and providing a list of grounds on which discrimination is prohibited. It also cites conditions under which 'affirmative action' programs that might appear to be discriminatory are permitted. The sweeping section 24(1) on enforcement has no American parallel. It permits courts of competent jurisdiction to enforce Charter rights through remedies they deem 'appropriate and just in the circumstances.' Presumably they can develop new remedies if they choose not to rely on traditional ones. These examples serve to indicate that much is new in the Charter, and not only from the standpoint of Canadian law. Indeed, as Ronald Cheffins and Patricia Johnson point out, so much is new that not even American decisions, such a seemingly obvious resource in the light of American experience with the Bill of Rights, can be a reliable guide.[26] Thus there is a great deal to test in the Charter and an understandable desire on the part of the legal profession to test it. This eagerness on the part of the profession, also noted by Cheffins and Johnson, is of course another reason to expect that the courts will be busy with the Charter.[27]

In conclusion, while I agree with Russell that the Canadian Supreme Court is unlikely to shed its ongoing and still vital role as umpire of the federal system, I also think that it is important to grasp the significance of the sense of excitement the Charter has engendered. One indicator of it would be a desire to develop a distinctly Canadian approach to the Charter, and there is some evidence of this in the opinion of Justice Lamer referred to earlier. To return for a moment to his discussion of the phrase 'principles of fundamental justice,' he questions the utility of debating whether it ought to be interpreted in substantive or strictly procedural terms. In part this is because the 'substantive/procedural dichotomy' is an American one, developed in American legal doctrine and debate and related to problems of judicial review of the American constitution. Lamer reminds us of differences between the two constitutions, including two 'internal checks and balances' in the Charter peculiar to it alone, namely, section 1, which subjects its guarantees to 'such reasonable limits prescribed by law as can be demonstrably justified in a free and democratic society,' and section 33, which permits the legislatures to override some of its guarantees under specified conditions. He then states: 'We would, in my view, do our own Constitution a disservice to simply allow the American debate to define the issue for us, all the while ignoring the truly fundamental structural differences between the two constitutions.'[28] To the extent that this view is shared by other members of the Court, it indicates that, in relation to the Charter, the court is not only undeterred by its 'new and onerous responsibility' but prepared to develop its own approach where necessary. Canadian lawyers are likely to give it many opportunities.

NOTES

1 P.A. Freund, A.E. Sutherland, M. DeWolfe Howe, E.J. Brown, eds *Constitutional Law: Cases and Other Problems* I (Boston: Little, Brown 1967) 10
2 B.L. Strayer *Judicial Review of Legislation in Canada* (Toronto: University of Toronto Press 1968) 15
3 Paul Weiler *In the Last Resort: A Critical Study of the Supreme Court of Canada* (Toronto: Carswell/Methuen 1974) 165
4 Strayer *Judicial Review* 20–1
5 'Is the Supreme Court of Canada Biased in Constitutional Cases?' *Canadian Bar Review* 57 (1979) 721
6 Jennifer Smith 'The Origins of Judicial Review in Canada' *Canadian Journal of*

Political Science 16 (March 1983) 125, 131–2
7 [1912] App. Cas. 585 (PC)
8 Strayer *Judicial Review* 93–4
9 Freund et al *Constitutional Law* 232, 233
10 Ibid 297, 296, 299
11 Ibid 138–9
12 *Attorney-General for Ontario* v. *Attorney-General for the Dominion* (1896) 1 Olmsted 356
13 *Attorney-General for Ontario* v. *Canada Temperence Federation* (1946) 3 Olmsted 437
14 *Reference Re Anti-Inflation Act* (1976) 2 SCR 373
15 Weiler *In the Last Resort* 173
16 Ibid 174 5
17 Ibid 52
18 'The Supreme Court and Federal-Provincial Relations: The Political Use of Legal Resources' *Canadian Public Policy* 11 no 2 (June 1985) 164
19 Ibid
20 Ibid 168
21 'The Governments and Societies of Canadian Federalism' *Canadian Journal of Political Science* 10 no 4 (December 1977) 704
22 'The Supreme Court and Federal-Provincial Relations' 164
23 58 NR 81 (SCC) at 112
24 *Reference Re Section 94(2) of the Motor Vehicle Act (British Columbia)* (1985) 63 NR 266 (SCC); 36 MVR 240 (SCC) at 250
25 36 MVR 240 (SCC) at 249
26 *The Revised Canadian Constitution* (Toronto: McGraw-Hill Ryerson 1986) 131, 139
27 Ibid 131–2
28 *Reference Re British Columbia Motor Vehicle Act* (1985) 36 MVR 240 (SCC) at 251

8 / Regionalization and Decentralization

ARTHUR BENZ

In many Western countries we currently find serious concern with decentralization and regionalization of political and administrative systems. Regionalization in Italy and Spain, the socialist project in France, constitutional change in Belgium,[1] the 'new federalism' proclaimed by President Reagan in the United States, and last but not least the policies of debureaucratization and deregulation in the Federal Republic of Germany indicate a general tendency toward decline of centralized, hierarchical structures.[2] Decentralization has become a 'theme in vogue' taken up by many political leaders. At the same time various socioeconomic developments (e.g. territorial differentiation of economic problems, changing values, regionalist and social movements) have led to demands for decentralization and regionalization and have helped to initiate reforms of the governmental system. In Canada, where the attrition of the power of the federal government has been a long-standing trend, these socioeconomic developments gave impetus to regionalism in the provinces.[3]

A profound analysis of these tendencies suggests that they result from various, highly complex processes. It is not only that different policies sail under the flag of decentralization and regionalization and affect the system in different ways, but also that the assessment of these processes is rendered even more difficult by the fact that various, partly contradictory forces often yield effects not intended by the original programs.

This chapter deals with the distinctive approaches, processes, effects and prospects of policies aimed at decentralization and regionalization. Particular emphasis will be placed on tracing the difficulties in implementing such policies. After specifying the intended goals of decentralization and regionalization programs, subsequent sections will focus on the analysis of processes of decentralization and regionalization in two different political systems.

By comparing decentralization policies in France and in West Germany, I will seek to demonstrate how the effects of decentralization and regionalization are dependent on structural dynamics, that is, the outcome of internal structural adaptations and external pressure for change. It is suggested that federal systems are more flexible than unitary systems and are better able to react to demands for decentralization by adapting their decision structures during processes of problem-solving. Reform of the power structures in unitary systems, however, is more difficult, with decentralization often leading to unexpected results. Further, in many cases the rhetoric of decentralization is only of symbolic relevance and may in fact disguise centralist trends.

Arguments for Regionalization and Decentralization

The growing demand for regionalization and decentralization in recent years can be interpreted as the political reaction to the nearly continuous process of centralization and bureaucratization that marks the formation and development of the welfare state. Disillusionment with the effects of central planning, the crises of the central-rule-approach in policy-making (problems of implementation), the intricacies of 'marble cake federalism,' and the likelihood of political stalemates as the result of increasing entanglement of different levels of government,[4] have all given rise to an extensive discussion about the necessity of and means for decentralizing the political system and the creation of regional forms of problem-solving.

The demands for regionalization and decentralization can be found in political programs of diverse ideological tendencies and are the object of inquiries across a variety of disciplines. The wide scope of discussion has, however, not always led to a greater conceptual clarity and has added to a shifting in levels of argument. With some simplification four major reasons for the decentralization and/or regionalization of the political and administrative system can be identified.

1 The economic theory of federalism refers to the greater capacity of regional and local levels of government to react to particular substantive differences in the preferences of citizens. In the face of the high costs of centralized policy-making, the main argument for regionalization is the productive competition between decentralized units with a greater capacity to consider interests and to achieve and process information.[5]

2 Closely linked to this are the arguments advanced by liberal politicians and experts, for whom decentralization means the strengthening of private autonomy and political self-government and the establishment of market-like processes in the political system. In this way, political decisions are

intended to be more democratic, processes more open to citizens, and civic freedom greater.

3 The rise of regionalist movements in many European countries and in Canada has focused renewed attention on regional variations in socio-economic, ethnic, and cultural characteristics. Pursuing the goal of cultural self-realization and identity, regionalist spokesmen call for regional autonomy and self-government. Particularly when such ideas are not advanced by genuinely disadvantaged regional minorities – as in West Germany – they are often connected with a conservative, parochial renaissance contrasting the security and transparency of small social contexts against the complexity and impenetrability of national and supranational interdependencies.

4 Finally, decentralization is conceived as a vital element of an 'alternative politics.' In contrast to the established dominance of centralized distributive politics, decentralization in this variant is geared to the genuine needs and wants of individuals. Thus, it is regarded as largely linked to responsiveness, 'grass roots,' and participatory democracy; it means social services and self-help in small social networks and constitutes an important element of a participatory, ecologically oriented policy approach.

In all these approaches, decentralization and regionalization are intended to endow the decentralized level of government (states, regions, local government) with greater autonomy. They require disentanglement of inter-governmental relations in the federal system. Beyond this, decentralization and regionalization could also be understood as expanded participation of regional and local governments in policy-making of the central government. Although the normative debate is focused on decentralization in the sense of transfer of functions and resources to autonomous units, in reality the second form of decentralization may even be more important for analysing the real changes that have taken place over time.

In order to assess whether the hopes pinned on decentralization and regionalization are justified we must leave the level of abstract and nor-matively oriented debate. Aside from the problem that it is almost im-possible to identify a necessary or optimal degree of centralization or decentralization that is generally applicable for all policy arenas, we should focus our attention on the barriers to successful regionalization and decentralization. Every governmental system – be it unitary or federal – is characterized by internal tensions between central, regional, and local units that are interested in maintenance of domain and power. Further, intergovernmental relations are influenced by external factors that limit the scope of structural reforms. Formulation and implementation of policies aimed at decentralization and regionalization therefore are in large part determined by structural dynamics of the intergovernmental system.

The Dynamics of the Intergovernmental System –
Elements of a Theoretical Approach

For analysing the structural dynamics of intergovernmental systems and
the processes of centralization and decentralization I refer to a 'dialectical'
model of organizations and interorganizational systems.[6] With some modifications, we can apply this theoretical approach to study the dynamic
processes of change in intergovernmental relations. In analytical terms I
suggest distinguishing three aspects of system structures.[7]

The political-economic basis of the organizational structure is the *power
and resource structure* formed by the distribution of legally defined authority,
financial resources, political support, information, etc, between different
levels of government.

The *interaction structure* comprises the individual attitudes, action strategies, interests, and goals of the actors in the system, which are to be co-
ordinated into collective actions. In the context of this chapter, we have
to analyse the interaction structure between federal/central government,
state/regional government, and local government.[8]

The principles of co-ordinating and regulating individual actions (e.g.
hierarchical or co-operative; authority or consensus; standardized or
problem-oriented) are the content of a cognitive-normative organizational
'superstructure,' comprising both the 'rules of the game'[9] and the 'institutionalized thought structure,'[10] which we can call the 'organizational
paradigm.'[11]

The organizational paradigm arises from social processes in the system
based on the existing power and resource structure. It has to accomplish
a dual function. On the one hand, it regulates the processes of interaction
and co-ordination of individual activities of the members of the organization,
i.e. the policies of different levels of government, thus influencing the
interaction structure. On the other hand, it legitimizes the existing power
and resource structure of the system.

Although the three analytical levels of the system structure normally tend
to achieve a state of equilibrium, they are not completely dependent on
each other but can to a certain degree vary autonomously. Thus, tensions
and contradictions are created in the system that can trigger structural
changes and constitute momenta of dynamic processes. 'An organization
as a part of the social world is always in a state of becoming; it is not
a fixed and determined entity.'[12] As social constructs they represent only
provisional institutionalizations requiring that structural tensions and contradictions latently recurring in the processes of problem-solving have to
be permanently dealt with. In many welfare states this phenomenon can

be observed, for example, when centralized planning approaches come into contradiction with specific local interests, thus creating problems of implementation and increasing demands for decentralization.

Ultimately, all structural variations are determined by the existing power and resource structure. This does not, however, imply a deterministic approach in a crudely Marxist way. The political and economic basis can be changed by two processes. If there is a change in the organizational paradigm – which itself arises out of processes of interaction – the existing mode of legitimizing the power and resource structure will lose its effect. The revival of regionalism, which challenges centralist trends, presents a good example of this process. In this case, structural change proceeds from an alteration in the cognitive and normative framework of co-operation. The power and resource structure is in the second place significantly affected by the processes of resource flows between the organization and its environment. The governmental system is dependent on resource acquisition from the economic system and needs political support from society. Hence, different units of the system are affected in different ways so that shifts in resource flows directly influence the power and resource structure of the political and administrative system.[13] This point needs to be stressed. Reforms aimed at decentralization will be rendered more difficult by economic tendencies that favour the central government and diminish the resource basis of regional and local governments.

Although ultimately dependent on the distribution of power and resources, the focal point of structural change is the organizational paradigm. Whether the changes are produced in processes of interaction (e.g. changed interests of actors, perception of insufficient output) or whether there are changes in the distribution of power and resources, the primary result is tensions in the system that are the momenta of the process of change. These changes remain latent as long as the rules, norms, and collective patterns of orientations, which form the organizational paradigm, are constant. It is quite possible that the impulse to change will not be effective. In this case, the structure of the system would be in a state of contradiction, with the organizational paradigm screening the real problems, antagonisms, or power relations. This means that decentralization and regionalization would serve only symbolic political purposes. If the tensions in the inter-organizational political and administrative system rise to a level at which they are evident to all actors and therefore cannot be concealed, they will generate a 'climate of reform'[14] which creates the conditions for a paradigmatic change. As a rule, a competing organizational paradigm will emerge, challenging the established normative order.

Alterations of the organizational paradigm will not necessarily be initiated by hierarchical decisions of an agency empowered to rearrange the organizational structures; they will result rather from a political struggle among the advocates of competing paradigmatic approaches. The formulation and implementation of reform conceptions should, therefore, be regarded as a political process in which the aspirations and interests of different levels of government are at stake as well as the maintenance or realization of power positions.

An alternative organizational paradigm challenging the established order, if it is to become effective, will have to define the changed functions, policy norms, and action orientations in a distinct and simple manner. Possible changes must be clearly marked, and their value and foreseeable benefits must be pitched at a very high level in order to justify the political cost of structural transformation. For this reason, alternative organizational paradigms tend to be formulated in an extreme fashion. The difference between the alternative and the established paradigm creates the 'energies of reform' necessary as impulses for change. Under specific conditions, these energies can lead to structural overreactions in processes of revolutionary changes. However, internal counterforces based on the existing power and resource structure usually operate toward weakening the reform impulses, particularly during the process of establishing the new organizational paradigm.

The institutionalization of a new organizational paradigm, that is, enforcing a new normative and cognitive framework, is a complex process. Indeed, paradigmatic change can release considerable energies for reform, but at the very outset of implementing reform the new organizational paradigm will be challenged. The clearer the formulation of the elements of the new organizational paradigm, the more distinct become the benefits and costs for the different units in the system during the process of institutionalization. The winners and losers can now be identified more clearly. In such a situation, there exists a contradiction between a fundamental consensus about the necessity and utility of structural changes expressed in the new organizational paradigm, on the one hand, and the individual cost-benefit calculations with respect to domain and power maintenance of the agencies affected by the reform, on the other. This explains the process of reaction and adaptation in the system by which the scope of the reform is challenged. The consequences are retardation in effecting the reforms; partial revocations of proposed reform projects; modification of intended reforms in the processes of bargaining; and inhibition of the implementation of structural transformations.

The processes of internal adaptation may continue even after the institutional rearrangement is implemented by the establishment of the organizational paradigm. The introduction of binding definitions of problems, patterns of interpretation, and action norms does not mean that the organizational paradigm regulates the interactions in the organization completely. It only defines a framework designed to channel the actions and attitudes of the members and units of the organization. But this framework will always be trespassed and challenged. Particularly if the energies of reform released by a paradigmatic change lead to structural overreaction, internal adaptation will generally follow – often with a time lag. These are processes in which the defeated reformers try to adapt their strategies and to undermine the new organizational rules to accord with their own interests.[15]

Thus, in the process of structural change, the power and resource structure has a dual effect. On the one hand, it may delay the institutional rearrangement and act upon it in such a way that only marginal deviations from the organizational status quo will follow. On the other hand, it may cause subsequent alteration of the original structural reforms by adapting the strategies of action or by mobilizing hitherto latent potentials of power and influence. Thus the dialectics of the structural dynamics predominantly result in a cyclical but not continuous process of change.

Every social organization can be considered as a dynamic system moved by tensions and contradictions. So, too, can unitary and federal systems. Hence, we can analyse the process of regionalization and decentralization in France and West Germany applying this theoretical framework.

Regionalization and Decentralization in Unitary and Federal States

As shown in the first section, there is a growing demand for decentralization and regionalization. This development must be interpreted against the backdrop of economic and socio-cultural characteristics that are common to most Western welfare states. Economic recession, technological change, environmental problems, changes in value patterns are – generally speaking – the predominant tendencies. These conditions challenge the viability of centralized policy-making structures and seem to call for decentralization of political and administrative structures. The reasons for this can be summarized as follows: overload of the central government entailing policy stalemates and insufficient implementation; necessity of a differentiated and problem-oriented public policy; possibilities of applying small, resource-saving technologies; and growing demands for direct citizen participation in the formulation of policies. To illustrate the structural reactions of different governmental systems, I refer to two cases: decentralization under the French Socialist government and decentralization and regionalization in West Germany.[16]

Decentralization and Regionalization in a Unitary System (France)

The French political system is considered to be highly centralized. Nevertheless, there are strong territorial units at the departmental level. The structure of the system is much more complicated than the notion of the unitary state might suggest.[17]

At the local level, there are approximately 36,000 communes governed by elected mayors and elected councils. Although the French constitution declares the communes autonomous institutions, they have always been highly dependent on central administrative agencies. Until 1982, the prefect of the department, a central government official, was entitled to exercise a far-reaching control (tutelle) over the acts and activities of the communes. Besides, the fiscal resources available to the communes were very limited; in most cases they had to apply for special grants from the central government.

The commune and the departments had a dual status. On the one hand, they were autonomous units with a certain degree of sovereignty – although in fact they were dependent upon central grants. On the other hand, they were territorial divisions of the French Republic and as such units of the national government. The mayor and the prefect were both representatives of the central government and heads of the local and departmental administration respectively. For the implementation of its policies at the level of the communes and departments, the central government had instituted the services extérieurs of the ministries.

The centralized structure of the French political and administrative system was based on a traditional ideology of equality, uniformity, and support for the nation-state. The 1964 and 1972 reforms that established regional units should not be regarded as breaches of this tradition. They were means of improving the functional capacities of the centre in alliance with new peripheral élites rather than devices for increasing the independence of the periphery.[18] To be sure, the communes and departments were not colonies of Paris. The prefects and the external services of the ministries were dependent upon the locally elected members of the departmental councils (conseil généraux), particularly the so-called notables.[19] The notables are persons who hold offices at both the decentralized (local and/or departmental) and the central level of the state. This accumulation of offices (cumul des mandats) allows the notables to operate at several levels, thus playing a decisive role in integrating political demands. They are seen as the focal points in a differentiated inter-organizational system in which decisions are made through bargaining and mutual adjustment.[20]

Critics of the French political and administrative system describe it as closed, highly selective, immobile, and conservative. At the same time, however, a British observer regards it as well adapted to the needs of a modern welfare state and able to accommodate to changing conditions.[21] With respect to policies aiming at decentralization, it is important to note that the actors of the system did not plead for reform. Above all, as Thoenig states, local leaders 'do not consider the present situation to be critical and in need of change. Indeed they tend to be conservative and are rather sceptical about major decentralization reforms. They do not wish any fundamental alteration of the decision-making system.'[22] Thus all actors participating in the process of intergovernmental policy-making have benefited from the status quo.

It might – in the context of this chapter – be very instructive to investigate the long-standing policy debate over decentralization and regionalization in the French system and the failure to achieve substantial change in the first twenty years of the Fifth Republic. Obviously, the élitist power structure was an effective barrier to decentralization, although an organizational paradigm of decentralization emerged from time to time. Above all, there was a discrepancy between the paradigmatic changes promoted by regionalist politicians and the technocratic approach of the reform projects of the central government.

When the Socialists came to power in 1981, they represented widespread concern for decentralization and regionalization. The 'Projet socialiste' of 1980 presented decentralization as the most urgent step in the process of reforming society and the decisive measure in breaking up the existing power structures. Decentralization should not only contribute to democracy, thus facilitating citizen participation, but also increase the effectiveness of government by reducing the load on the centre. Although the project of decentralization is also aimed at strengthening the influence of the socialist councillors at the local and departmental level – whose connections with the system of notables were comparatively weaker – and thus at stabilizing the power of the Socialist party, it nevertheless indicates a paradigmatic change by emphasizing pluralist ideas, by the commitment to autogestion (self-government) at the decentralized levels, and by rejecting centralist structure.

The decentralization of the French political and administrative system is intended to be a political decentralization. It aims at strengthening the political influence of the local councils and the conseils généraux of the departments, at enhancing the scope of self-government at the decentralized level, and at curtailing the power of the central bureaucracy. The first law passed in March 1982 after a stormy discussion between the Socialist government and the opposition-controlled Senate abolished the 'tutelle' and reduced the control over local authorities to a subsequent inspection of legal, technical, and financial aspects. Thus the autonomy of the communes has been considerably extended in formal terms. Decisive changes have taken place at the departmental level. The prefect, who became the Commissaire de la République, has ceased to be the executive of the departmental council and is now the representative of the central government in the department. The directly elected departmental councils have gained importance, being now endowed with their own competences. The power of the Commissaire de la République over the external services of the ministries has been strengthened, since he now is the administrative co-ordinator in the previously fragmented decentralized public bureaucracies. The regional units were turned into territorial governments (collectivités territoriales) with directly elected assemblies.

The first 'projet de loi' of the decentralization scheme provides a framework to be fleshed out by subequent laws. The most important is the law concerning the tasks and responsibilities of the 'collectivités territoriales' adopted in March 1983. It lays down the principle of separation of functions and stipulates that decentralization of functions is to be accompanied by transfer of appropriate financial resources. The new tasks of the communes concern above all urban and local planning, the right to issue planning permission, and the planning and implementation of local infrastructures; the departments became responsible for redistributive services, social benefits, allocation of housing subsidies, and reallocation of resources among rural communes; and the regions are to fulfil functions concerning economic planning, co-ordination of regional infrastructure, and professional training. All three levels now have the right to give subsidies to ailing industrial firms.

With respect to changes in the power and resource structure, the transfer of financial means from the central government to the decentralized levels is particularly important. Instead of the variety of specific grants there are now block grants for revenue (Dotation globale de fonctionnement since 1979) and capital (Dotation globale d'équipement) spending. The taxes for vehicles and driving licences are assigned to the departments and regions. The Socialist government intended to regulate, definitively the distribution of finances in a further law, but this objective was not met.

The decentralization of the French centralist state means the establishment of a new organizational paradigm, which is incompatible with the existing power and resource structure. Although the old system had also shown tendencies toward weakening hierarchical regulation and control (viz. the influence of the notables and the mayors of the big cities), the now-realized decentralization is aimed at changing the élitist structure of the French administration. Above all, the reform is intended to undermine the power of the notables. This point turned out to be the decisive problem of decentralization.

My theoretical approach presented earlier explains the processes of structural adaptation that have occurred during and after the implementation of decentralization. The Commissaire de la République, the former prefect, has found ways to regain power over the local and departmental administration. In co-operation with the still-influential notables, he seems to form the focus of the co-ordination of local policies. Further, the communes do not have the administrative capacities and finances necessary to cope with their new tasks. The deterioration of economic conditions and the decline in the financial resources of the central government made a further transfer of funds to the decentralized units impossible. The failure to separate clearly functional responsibilities between the levels of government and increasing entanglement of resources, resulting, for example, from the contracts between central and regional or departmental governments (contrats de plan), have made it possible for the central government to regain control over the decentralized authorities via processes of co-ordination and by financial incentives.

Since about 1983, enthusiasm for reform has waned. There has been growing concern for current economic and social problems and for crisis management. More and more, central authorities have been unwilling to pass on responsibilities and resources to lower levels. These developments have created difficulties in implementing decentralization and have increased opposition to reform. However, decentralization and regionalization have not been without success. They have changed the intergovernmental system to a considerable degree, although reform has not resulted in greater autonomy of the decentralized authorities, as was originally intended. It has led to more intensive intergovernmental co-operation and interdependences between central and local jurisdictions, which enable communes, departments, and regions to influence policy-making at the central level.

Decentralization and Regionalization in a Federal System (West Germany)

West Germany has a well-established tradition of local self-government and federalism. The federal structure of the state emerged from a situation of high territorial fragmentation at the beginning of the nineteenth century.

At that time, concurrently, the cities gained importance as centres of expanding industrialization. The establishment of municipal self-government in 1808 can be considered as an expansion of bourgeois emancipation from the authoritarian state dominated by the aristocracy.

The development of the social service state in the nineteenth century and, particularly, of the welfare state in the twentieth century led to growing interdependence of the functions of the central and the decentralized governments. To an increasing extent, the state and local administrations became integrated into the economic and social policies of the federal government. The functions exclusively exercised by the states were diminished more and more.

After the centralizing epoch of the National Socialist state, federal institutions and local self-government were restored in 1949. In legal terms, the federal government was confined to legislative functions, while the states (Länder) became responsible for most of the administrative functions and some special legislative functions. The municipalities were entitled to deal with all local affairs with their autonomy being limited only by law.

But this form of 'layer-cake federalism' with separation of functions soon began to dissolve, particularly, since the end of the 1960s, in times of economic recession, when central planning and regulation were adopted. The results of these developments were expansion of forms of intergovernmental policy-making between federal, state, and local governments; establishment of hierarchical planning systems, integrating central and decentralized policies (e.g. budget planning, planning of infrastructure, territorial planning); extension of revenue-sharing and grant systems; commitment of state and local governments to national economic goals; and latent centralization of functions, with simultaneous decentralization of policy implementation, to name but the most important structural characteristics of West German co-operative federalism.

These tendencies toward policy entanglement and centralization were criticized for reducing the capacity of the governmental system to solve problems and its ability to adapt to changed situations and for contributing to political stalemates. This assessment was put forward by case studies related to specific policy fields.[23] A dynamic perspective, however, reveals processes of structural changes in the federal system that can be interpreted as reactions of the system to changed problems and situations.

In West Germany the structural reaction to demands for decentralization can be characterized as symbolic decentralization and internal adaptation. In terms of the outlined theoretical approach, changes are restricted to the organizational paradigm and to the interaction structure, i.e. to changes in the strategies of both central and decentralized units without major shifts in the structure of power and resources. On the one hand, while policies aimed at decentralization and regionalization are pursued and carried out with considerable fanfare, the real effects of these policies are marginal. The lessening of state control over local governments has hardly any impact on policy-making in the municipalities; decentralization schemes in areas of joint decision-making between federal and state governments (for example, hospital planning, road construction) are blocked in political bargaining processes or have been implemented in a form that deviates only slightly from the status quo. On the other hand, the federal system does not remain in a stable state but is marked by informal structural changes that proceed in an unstructured and unanticipated fashion. This can be illustrated in the discussions of decentralization and regionalization in specific policy arenas.

In recent years, an organizational paradigm of decentralization has developed that competes with the established paradigm of centralization. It has been generated in extensive discussion in both social science and political and administrative practice and challenges the existing order of central regulation, bureaucratization, policy entanglement, deductive planning, and technocratic policy. There are calls for decentralized problem-solving in small territorial units; co-operative decision-making on the basis of consensus; problem orientation instead of standardization; inductive planning and decentralized horizontal co-ordination; participation of the people directly affected; and policy implementation on the basis of persuasion. The elements of this paradigm of decentralization constitute a far-reaching consensus. Decentralization and regionalization (as a special form of decentralization) are widely accepted norms for the fashioning of political, administrative, and social structures. Nevertheless, the effect on the federal structure of the state is ambivalent.

Obviously, a far-reaching restructuring of the federal system in West Germany is less probable. The reform era of the 1970s has been followed by a period of conservation and stabilization. Nevertheless, there are structural changes in several policy fields. Projects of decentralizing politics are discussed and partly implemented. The most revealing example is energy policy. With the assistance of the federal government, integrated energy plans are passed by regional and municipal governments. These plans have no legal basis; they constitute informal arrangements between public authorities and private companies but still may form an important element in a resource-saving and environment-protecting energy policy. Other forms of decentralization can be found in housing policy, economic policy, and territorial planning, to name but a few. With respect to housing policy and economic policy, centralized problem-solving strategies are still dominant. But the more the territorial incidence of national developments or policies varies at the regional or local level, the more decentralized policy-making is gaining in importance. To a growing extent, local and regional authorities pursue active housing and economic policies to solve special problems in their domain. Often analysed as deficient in implementation of central programs, these forms of decentralized policy-making can be viewed as politics from below aiming not only at filling the gaps in central policies but also at realizing local and regional interests more or less in confrontation with the central government.[24]

In the field of territorial planning, decentralization is both the result of politics from below and of overload from above, reflected in an inability of central authorities to resolve conflicts. On the one hand, the municipalities participate more actively in the planning process at the regional and state level and are very successful in turning the regions into arenas for aggregating and carrying out local interests. On the other hand, approaches of central planning have not proved to be very effective. Ambitious forms of integrative territorial planning have failed because of stalemates in the processes of decision-making; problem-solving has actually largely devolved upon the regional planning authorities.[25]

As to relations between the states and the federal government, decentralist tendencies also seem to predominate. The state governments emphasize their independence within the federal system and strive against expansion of intergovernmental relations. At the same time, both executives and parliaments of the states try to gain influence in co-operative federalism. The activities and initiatives of some chiefs of state government in policy domains formerly occupied by the federal government point to the fact that centralist tendencies in the West German federal system are replaced by decentralized trends. Up to now, however, only the responsibility for planning and financing hospitals has reverted to the states. Although founded on a new paradigm of decentralization, most of these tendencies toward decentralization and regionalization remain informal processes, which change only the mode of interaction. At the level of the power and resource structures, centralist forces have emerged since the end of the 1970s. Changes in the financial structure of the federal system were chargeable to the municipalities. Between 1981 and 1983 most states reduced their grants to local governments, while the specific grants for investments were subject to even larger cuts. The restrictive budgeting of the federal government led to considerable disadvantages for the municipalities, especially in the face of the increasing need for social service expenditures.

Does this mean that regionalization and decentralization can be interpreted as merely symbolic policies? Inspection of policies of debureaucratization and deregulation of the federal and state governments, which are proclaimed with considerable publicity but lack effectiveness, seems to suggest this contention. Government committees have been established to evaluate the need for and effectiveness of existing laws and decrees, but no structural changes of bureaucratic administration and only unimportant reductions of centralist regulation have followed as yet. The only result seems to be internal administrative rationalization. There are also indications that decentralization is primarily an attempt of the central government to discharge its unwanted responsibilities and to resolve the problems of financing at the expense of the decentralized units.

In spite of this, decentralization and regionalization are gaining in significance. While they may be viewed by the federal and state governments as strategies aimed at discharging responsibilities and, therefore, to a wide extent only of symbolic relevance, they may gradually evolve into structural changes. To the extent that decentralized units use their right to participate in central policy-making and implement central programs in a creative manner, they can contribute to the break-up of the established paradigm of centralization and regain lost problem-solving powers. Empirical studies of the dynamics of central-local relations[26] confirm the assumption that West Germany's federal system is being adapted to changed conditions in a pragmatic way and without major upheavals in the political and administrative structures.

This view is further supported by the fact that the West German government has not had to deal with regionalist movements. Likewise, the social movements that emerged in the 1970s are likely to be integrated into the political system. And so far the growing problems of economic, social, and environmental developments in the big cities have not yet led to disintegrative processes: they were dealt with in various forms of central-local co-operation, with the decentralized units often being in a position to exercise considerable influence.

Prospects of Decentralization and Regionalization

The comparison of regionalization and decentralization in two different political systems illustrates the logic of the processes of structural change in the political and administrative system. The two cases exhibit significant differences in coping with pressure for restructuring the system. In France we can observe an attempt to realize political decentralization, while in West Germany we see pragmatic adaptation of the federal structure, accompanied by a symbolic policy of debureaucratization and decentralization. My argument is that these differences can be explained by the differences in the system structures – unitary on the one hand and federal on the other hand.

A centralized system is characterized by a hierarchical, monistic power structure that can be legitimized only by an organizational paradigm of centralization. Although sociological interpretations of French politics have often concealed decentralizing elements, the system still can be viewed as a closed, highly selective, élitist structure resistant to change. The decentralization program pursued by the Socialist government was intended to break up these structures and to establish autonomous political units at the decentralized level. This can be done only by institutionalizing a new organizational paradigm of decentralization. The difficulties in accomplishing such a reform are largely due to the divergence between the existing power and resource structure and the new organizational paradigm, which requires considerable energies for reform. In this case, it is quite likely that over time energy for reform will fade away during the process of establishing the new organizational paradigm and that subsequently previously powerful actors will regain power by adapting their traditional means and strategies for exercising influence.

In contrast, federal systems are characterized by a pluralist power and resource structure with multiple hierarchies. They are therefore to a certain extent open to variations in the organizational paradigm. The intricate structure allows room for adaptation in processes of problem-solving without changing the whole system. The duplication or multiplication of decision units and communication channels that is inherent in federal systems makes dynamic self-regulating processes possible.[27] In West Germany this dynamic adaptation has taken place as a change from 'imperialistic' to co-operative intergovernmental relations in response to increasing demands for decentralization.[28] While the imperialistic approach meant growing intrusion of the federal government into the policy domains of states and municipalities, the co-operative version implies the opening of central decision-making processes to the participation of the states and local governments. Certainly, this adaptation is possible only within the framework of the existing power and resource structure, that is, without far-reaching changes of the distribution of functions and financial resources between levels of government.

The differences between decentralization and regionalization in unitary and federal systems can be viewed from still other regards. In France, decentralization represents a process of innovation defined as a conscious and active transformation of structures by changing the established organizational paradigm. Decentralization and regionalization in West Germany are adaptations, meaning that the system 'will respond to demands for change by the least change capable of neutralizing or meeting the intrusive process.'[29]

Innovation works against the inherent dynamics of the power and resource structure, whereas adaptation uses these dynamics of the system structure.

With respect to the different approaches of decentralization and regionalization discussed in the first section, the preceding analysis of the processes of structural change is disillusioning. Reforms intended to change the distribution of power and resources and to enhance the political autonomy of regional or local units are very difficult to realize in both centralized and federal states. The experience with decentralization in France and West Germany give rise to the expectation that regionalization and decentralization will ultimately be confined to extending the possibilities of the participation of decentalized units in central policy-making. In both France and West Germany, trends toward further intergovernmental entanglement are encouraged by intensified competition for scarce resources, by the growing aspirations of local governments and regions to participate in central decision-making, and by efforts of the central government to evade accountability for decisions made. Therefore, decentralization and regionalization, meaning greater local or regional autonomy – as proposed by liberals, regionalists, and socialists alike – are unrealistic goals. There is little hope for abolishing the interdependence and intermingling of functions and responsibilities between different levels of government in modern welfare states. Greater decentralization leads, at the best, to more participation of lower units in central policy-making but not to separation of functions between central, regional, and local governments.

But these trends also give rise to opportunities for decentralized policy-making. They open possibilities for adaptation, distortion, or stalemate in intergovernmental policy-making, leading to intensified tensions in the system, thus enhancing the likelihood of structural changes. Together with the formulation of a new organizational paradigm of decentralization, active politics from below will improve the prospects for decentralization and regionalization.

Conclusion: Implications for Further Research

This chapter has dealt with decentralization and regionalization in different structural contexts. The results suggest that federal systems are in a better position to react to demands for decentralization and to regionalist challenges than are unitary states. The network-like structure, that is, the multiplicity of decision points, communications channels, and power relations, advances centralization and decentralization simply by adapting the existing interaction structure of the system.

Because the investigation concentrated on the differences between unitary and federal states, thus focusing on structural characteristics as determinants of intergovernmental dynamics, it gave only passing attention to the influence of socioeconomic and cultural variables. The impact of socioeconomic developments on the power and resource structure has been mentioned above; nevertheless, the processes of forming the organizational paradigm and of changing the interaction structure are dependent also on societal factors.[30]

To a certain degree, the divergences of decentralization and centralization in Canada compared to the structural dynamics in the federal system of West Germany (or the United States) may be the result of different socioeconomic or cultural frameworks. Since the Second World War, federal systems in Canada and in West Germany have moved in opposite directions. In Canada, the provinces gained power at the expense of the federal government, while West Germany became increasingly centralized until the mid-1970s. In general, the difference between the Canadian and West German federal systems can be explained above all by the economic structure, the degree of geographic concentration of ethnic minorities, and the position of the country in the international system.[31]

Further investigation into this subject will be necessary to improve our knowledge of the process of centralization and decentralization. Generally, researchers on federalism should devote more attention to the dynamics of federal systems. Studying federal states in comparative and historical perspectives will contribute to a better understanding of the functioning of federalism in modern welfare states, of its adaptability and its structural flexibility, as well as of the difficulties of changing the system according to abstract goals.

The theory of federalism should take into account the fact that the problem-solving capacity of states is to a considerable extent dependent on their ability to adapt and to change their structures and to react to changed conditions. Therefore regionalization and decentralization should not only be discussed in normative perspective but also taken as indicators of processes of necessary adaptation and self-transformation of the intergovernmental system in the welfare state.

NOTES

1 See Maureen Covell in this volume.
2 Laurence J. Sharpe ed *Decentralist Trends in Western Democracies* (London, Beverly Hills: Sage 1979)
3 Garth Stevenson *The Unfulfilled Union* (Toronto: Gage 1979); Donald V. Smiley *Canada in Question* (Toronto: McGraw-Hill Ryerson 1980)

4 See e.g. Samuel H. Beer 'Federalism, Nationalism and Democracy in America' *American Political Science Review* 72 (1978) 9; Gerhard Lehmbruch *Parteienwettbewerb im Bundesstaat* (Stuttgart: Kohlhammer 1976); Fritz W. Scharpf, Bernd Reissert, and Bernd Schnabel *Politikverflechtung: Theorie und Empirie des kooperativen Föderalismus in der Bundersrepublik Deutschland* (Kronberg: Scriptor 1976); Harold Seidman *Politics, Position and Power* (Oxford: University Press 1970); David B. Walker *Towards a Functioning Federalism* (Cambridge, Mass.: Winthrop Publishers 1981). For a remarkable critique of the central-rule approach see Herman R. van Gunsteren *The Quest for Control* (London: John Wiley 1976).

5 See as an interesting approach in this context Albert Breton and Anthony Scott *The Economic Constitution of Federal States* (Toronto: University of Toronto Press 1978).

6 See e.g. J. Kenneth Benson 'Organizations: A Dialectical View' *Administrative Science Quarterly* (1977); Wolf Heydebrand 'Organizational Contradictions in Public Bureaucracies: Towards a Marxian Theory of Organizations' *Sociology Quarterly* (1977); Gerald Zeitz 'Interorganizational Dialectics' *Administrative Science Quarterly* (1980).

7 Arthur Benz 'Zur Dynamik der föderativen Staatsorganisation' *Politische Vierteljahresschrift* 25 (1984) 53-73; Arthur Benz *Föderalismus als dynamisches System. Zentralisierung und Dezentralisierung im föderativen Staat* (Opladen: Westdeutscher Verlag 1985) 92-9

8 See Richard Simeon *Federal-Provincial Diplomacy* (Toronto: University of Toronto Press 1972).

9 Michel Crozier and Erhard Friedberg *Macht und Organisation* (Königstein: Athenäum 1979)

10 Brinton H. Milward 'Interorganizational Policy Systems and Research on Public Organizations' *Adminstration and Society* (1982) 472

11 Richard Harvey Brown 'Bureaucracy as Praxis: Towards a Political Phenomenology of Formal Organizations' *Administrative Science Quarterly* 23 (1978) 373

12 Benson 'Organizations' 6

13 Garth Stevenson 'Federalism and the Political Economy of the Canadian State' in Leo Panitch ed *The Canadian State* (Toronto: University of Toronto Press 1977) chap 3; Charles H. Levine and Paul L. Posner 'The Centralizing Effects of Austerity on the Intergovernmental System' *Political Science Quarterly* 96 (1981) 67-85

14 Dietrich Fürst, Joachim Jens Hesse and Hartmut Richter *Stadt und Staat* (Baden-Baden: Nomos 1984) 36

15 See e.g. Anthony Downs 'Up and Down with Ecology – the "Issue-Attention Cycle" *Public Interest* 23 (1978) 38-50; Stephan Rub-Mohl *Reformkonjunk-*

turen und politisches Krisenmanagement (Opladen: Westdeutscher Verlag 1981); Heribert Schatz 'Staatsbürokratie im Wandel' in Wolf-Dieter Narr ed *Politik und Ökonomie* (Opladen: Westdeutscher Verlag 1975).

16 The following sections are based on a comparative study dealing with the changing intergovernmental relations in four welfare states (the United States, West Germany, France, and Great Britain). This research project is attached to the Research Institute of Public Administration at the Graduate School of Administrative Science, Speyer (Joachim Jens Hesse, Arthur Benz).

17 Pierre Grémion *Le pouvoir périphérique* (Paris: Edition du Seuil 1976)

18 Yves Mény 'Les rélations Etat-Régions en France: L'échange inégal' in Yves Mény ed *Dix ans de régionalisation en Europe* (Paris: Cujas 1981) 161

19 Grémion *Le pouvoir périphérique* 211–42

20 Jean-Claude Thoenig 'La rélation entre le centre et la périphérie en France' *Bulletin de l'Institut international d'administration publique* (1975) 77–124; Jean-Claude Thoenig 'State Bureaucracies and Local Government in France' in Kenneth Hanf and Fritz W. Scharpf eds *Interorganizational Policy Making* (Beverly Hills, London: Sage 1978) 167–97

21 Douglas E. Ashford *British Dogmatism and French Pragmatism* (London: Allen & Unwin 1982)

22 Thoenig 'Bureaucracies' 186

23 Scharpf, Reissert, and Schnabel *Politikverflechtung*

24 Hellmut Wollmann 'Implementation durch Gegenimplementation von unten?' in Renate Mayntz ed *Implementation politischer Programme II* (Opladen: Westdeutscher Verlag 1983)

25 Benz *Föderalismus als dynamisches System* 203–10

26 Benz *Föderalismus als dynamisches System*; Fürst, Hesse, and Richter *Stadt und Staat*

27 Martin Landau 'Federalism, Redundancy and System Reliability' *Publius* 3 (1973) 173–96

28 Dietrich Fürst and Joachim Jens Hesse 'Zentralisierung und Dezentralisierung politischer Problemverarbeitung? Zur Krise der Politikverflechtung in der Bundersrepublik' in Joachim Jens Hesse ed *Politikverflechtung im föderativen Staat* (Baden-Baden: Nomos 1978)

29 Brinton H. Milward and Cheryl Swanson 'Organizational Response to Environmental Pressure' *Administration and Society* 11 (1979) 140

30 Benz *Föderalismus als dynamisches System* 99–103

31 Milton J. Esman 'Federalism and Modernization: Canada and the United States' *Publius* 14 (1984) 21–38

Part Three

POLICY AND POLITICS IN
FEDERAL SYSTEMS

9 / Federalism and Political Parties

WILLIAM M. CHANDLER

Federalism provides for a formal division of authority in which at least two levels of government coexist side by side in a self-rule, shared-rule relationship.[1] Although both federal and unitary states vary a great deal in degrees of effective decentralization, only federal systems share a constitutionally legitimated and protected basis for the dispersion of power on a territorial basis. Divisions of authority are realized in two ways: through constituent sub-units and through jurisdictional/functional allocations between levels of government.

The essential role of political parties in democratic systems rests not on a territorial distribution of legitimate authority but on the mechanisms for guaranteeing responsibility and accountability. Parties, through elections and representative institutions, serve as intermediaries between citizens and the state and provide the most important channels for the recruitment and circulation of political élites. Despite this centrality for governing, parties usually enjoy only a quasi-official status. Unlike federal arrangements, they are neither constitutionally prescribed nor legally created.[2]

These political differences should not disguise the extensive overlap between party politics and federalism resulting from their sharing of a crucial political function. Both structure the way in which individual preferences are brought to bear on collective choice.[3] Each shapes the range of options open to individuals to alter or maintain the terms by which collective public goods are provided.[4] Both federalism and parties determine participants, power relations, and arenas for political struggle. Whether in territorial/jurisdictional terms or in social/factional terms, they structure the allocation of legitimate authority. Thus federalism and party systems necessarily interact to the extent that they both organize conflict.[5] The federal distribution of authority permits party competition in both national and regional units but also imposes constraints, especially where competition at one level shapes partisan issues and organization at the other. Reciprocally, parties help to determine the effective working relations of federal politics as they maximize votes, build coalitions, and set policy agendas.[6]

To gain perspective on this two-way relation between federalism and party politics, it is best to go a step beyond formal-legal structures to examine the social and economic bases of politics. In the context of any discussion of federalism it is critical to take into account whether and to what extent tastes and resources vary along regional lines. Some economic justifications for the federal dispersion of powers are predicated on the existence of significant differences in regional tastes and/or resource endowments.[7] Federal societies suggest political systems in which territorial units coincide with the lines of dominant political conflict and policy preferences.[8] Where this applies, tensions and strains can be managed through decentralization of power and direct representation of regional interests at the centre.[9] One function of federal arrangements is to control potentially destructive conflict by granting limited autonomy to regions so that permanent national minorities may become regional majorities.

Beyond the debate about the incentives involved in 'federal bargains,'[10] it is evident that the degree of regional conflict and the territorial basis of political cleavage vary greatly and can significantly determine not only the character of partisan conflict but also the structure of the public sector. Whether federal societies adequately explain the origins of federal institutions is not at issue here. Even if this theory is accurate, over time the socioeconomic bases for regionally distinctive political interests may erode through long-term processes of economic growth, urbanization, and population mobility – all of which tend to nationalize and homogenize political cleavages. Constitutional arrangements, in contrast, often prove remarkably durable and through adaptation, amendment, or judicial interpretation can long outlive their social bases. Among modern régimes it is immediately observable that some (like Canada, India, Belgium, and Switzerland) remain profoundly influenced by territorial divisions. Others (like the United States and West Germany) have experienced the waning of regionalism as a political force. Our question here is how variations in regionalism or territorial politics impinge on the role of political parties within federal systems and how political parties in turn shape the forces of regionalism.

Although analysis will not explore all the implications of regionalism for the study of federalism, it recognizes that territorial variations in the social and economic bases of both party politics and federal institutions profoundly influence party-federal interaction. Any comparative analysis of this phenomenon must remain sensitive to this socioeconomic context.[11]

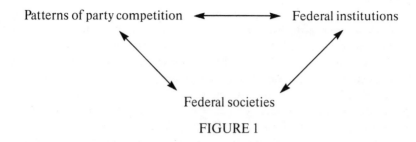

FIGURE 1

Figure 1 depicts the general implications of territorial politics and is intended to suggest its relevance for understanding the link between federalism and party politics.

Federal Impact on Party Politics

The link between federalism and partisan conflict is found in the structural incentives that an institutional arrangement creates for élites in their quest for political control. These are elucidated by the dynamics and constraints of the 'political games'[12] in the struggle for power. The multiple arenas of semi-autonomous decision-making found in federal systems provide parties and élites with special opportunities, not available in unitary states, to respond to regionally distinct electorates. These opportunities for representation are dualistic. They include constitutionally guaranteed regional political units, where regional majorities can directly shape those policy sectors primarily within their jurisdiction. They include also means of direct representation for regional interests at the national level.

The distinction between interstate and intrastate forms of federalism[13] is useful for understanding the varying roles of parties given alternative modes of representation. 'Interstate' refers to representation of territorial interests through provincial or state governments and often takes the form of quasi-diplomatic state-to-state relations. "Intrastate' connotes a pattern of representation within the institutions of the central policy-making apparatus. Here territorial interests but not governments are directly represented at the centre.[14] Both modes of representation, by allowing for some partial veto power for regional minorities, imply consensus-building rather than majority rule for resolving conflicts.

In establishing the basis for the general hypothesis of federal effects on party competition we must acknowledge several obstacles to making these effects immediately identifiable. First, such effects are multiple, overlapping, and occasionally even contradictory. Second, federal impact occurs at two interrelated levels – in an electoral context, where it influences party organizations and patterns of competition, and in an élite decision-making context, where effects involve styles of governance. Of course, the policy-making and electoral levels of politics themselves interact, blurring even further distinctions among effects. Third and finally, and perhaps most important, federal impact is only one subset of a larger complex of party-system determinants. Studies of party-system change[15] have convincingly demonstrated both the immediate effect of electoral laws and the enduring effects of changes in social structure. By comparison, federal arrangements are properly viewed as a residual category of determinants, but one having its own distinctive and stable influence on the conduct of party competition.

With all these provisos in mind, it is further useful to distinguish between the status and the quality of federal systems. Status refers to the general régime categories of federal versus unitary, where comparison is designed to describe broad conducive features associated with the existence of a federal order. Qualitative distinctions suggest comparisons among federal cases that demonstrate how institutional effects may vary depending on the structuring of federal arrangements. Because federal effects are interrelated, they may be parsimoniously grouped under two general headings. The first involves competitive patterns; the second stresses tendencies within the policy process.

Patterns of Competition

In terms of party competition, a federal régime can be conducive either to multi-partism, to flexible catch-all parties, or to the rise of minor parties. Not all of these tendencies occur together. Moreover, regionally one may observe counter-effects such as one-party dominance within certain provinces or states. With these important qualifications, the general argument is that federalism, where based on territorial pluralism, will encourage distinctive regional majorities or coalitions within regional units. If so, federalism may also stimulate divergent pressures on national parties, undermining internal cohesion and inhibiting the establishment of coherent national organizations.

Whatever the balance between regionalized multi-partisan and national catch-all groupings, federalism creates incentives for regional élites to establish parties that may be both regionally dominant and federally minor (the CCF-NDP and Social Credit are prime Canadian examples). Still others remain purely provincial formations, but often with tacit alliances with federal parties (Social Credit in British Columbia, the Union nationale in Quebec). In West Germany the Bavarian CSU is an intriguing mix of these two patterns. It operates at both levels – as a dominant party within Bavaria and directly in Bonn but as an ally of the CDU, which in return does not contest elections in Bavaria.

At first glance American partisan traditions appear to run counter to the multi-party thesis. In a nominal sense this is correct, for one finds Democratic-Republican competition everywhere. However, national bipartism surfaces only periodically for purposes of presidential elections. As ongoing organizations, American parties persist only at state and local levels. Congressional parties do exist as legislative instruments, but political success in exercising congressional power depends primarily on strong local-state roots and only rarely on caucus discipline. Presidential contests plus first-past-the-post plurality elections have created the façade of national parties and have successfully created barriers to numerous (often regionally inspired) third party experiments. Generally, American federalism has provided continuing incentives for political élites to build power bases and effective organizations locally and regionally.

To the extent that federal multi-partism depends on regional grievances and identifications, it is undoubtedly true in the American case that the potential for this type of party has diminished with the erosion of traditional north-south divisions, the decline of prior regional disparities due to the new prosperity of the Sunbelt, and the gradual homogenization of national political debate. None of this, however, has destroyed the local basis of party organization.

Federalism may also encourage very loose, non-programmatic catch-all formations that can accommodate divergent regional interests.[16] At the national level, the incentives for such pragmatic alliances will of course limit the spread of regionally autonomous parties. However, within states/provinces the weight of political incentives is more likely to be in favour of regional parties. Incentives for broad, loose party coalitions at the national level may coexist with federalist encouragement of a non-national multi-party system, that is, a complex mix of smaller parties, each with a regional stronghold but with limited appeal in other parts of the country. Canada illustrates the simultaneous realization of large catch-all formations and regional parties. It has often been observed that no federal party is truly national in character. Each relies on a strong regional base while failing adequately to represent some other region.[17] Added to this is the persistence of regionally unique provincial parties (e.g. in Quebec the Union nationale until the 1970s and later the Parti québécois; Social Credit in British Columbia and previously in Alberta).

Reference to American and Canadian experience underscores the difficulty of disentangling federal effects and leaves unanswered the question of when to expect federalism to be conducive to catch-all alliances and when to regionalist parties. Given decentralization of authority, regional élites working through local or regional parties are able to offer voters distinctive sets of policy packages.[18] Nationally, élites may also have positive incentives to respond to regional interests within the federal order. Where there are politically salient regional cleavages, federalism provides regional arenas for their expression and national mechanisms for direct representation at the centre. However, where there are strong regional forces but weak means for representation, either through national party organizations or policy-making structures, tensions and strains will be exacerbated.[19] As noted below, federal encouragement for minor parties need not always be confined to regionalist movements, but the impetus is likely to be strongest where regional demands underpin partisan divisions. More generally, it can be assumed that the probability of regionalist party formation depends on the territorial diversity of federal societies.

Regional opinion and regional élites may also be found within unitary states. But in contrast to the case in federal régimes, such interests are likely to achieve representation only as factions within a larger party or at most as stable regional allies of larger parties. Because the unitary structure of government affords little alternative to direct representation, influence must be sought within a national political force. It is sometimes argued that states with a strong unitary tradition inimical to the principle of regional representation tend to repress regionalist sentiments only to see them periodically explode in separatist demands and violent protest. Belgium, Spain, France, and Italy, all sharing a centralist tradition, have from time to time experienced the consequences of this. All these states over the past decade or more have shown themselves increasingly sensitive to decentralist trends and have made significant efforts to regionalize, if not federalize, their structures of government.[20]

Alongside the debate about the proclivity of federalism for some complex mix of regionalist multi-partism and broad, pragmatic alliances within parties, there exists an additional argument concerning the rise of minor parties. The general thesis is that federalism provides special opportunities for political oppositions.[21] The argument is not that federalism is a fundamental cause of new parties. It is rather that federal arrangements afford opportunities for minor parties, especially for those that do not represent immediate threats to the ruling party or coalition at the federal level. Sub-national legislatures provide arenas in which new forces may find lower barriers to entry than normally apply nationally.[22] This obviously applies to regionalist movements but can be an advantage for any new party proposing a distinct set of public goods and services. The recent success of the Greens in West Germany provides an excellent example.

Their early victories occurred in local, then Land, elections at a time when they were unable to win the necessary 5 per cent nationally to enter the Bundestag.[23] Federalism facilitated repeated Land successes. These gains permitted the Green party to attract new voters and to solidify its electoral base. By 1983 the movement had sufficient support to elect 27 Bundestag members.

Styles of Governing

Shifting from party competition to the role of parties in the policy process permits the identification of at least two additional federal effects. The first involves the transformation of partisan conflict into federal-provincial arenas. The second purposes that federalism encourages a style of policy-making based on consensus-building.

A virtue of federalism is that by decentralizing decision-making it compartmentalizes political tensions and therefore allows for the coexistence of varying majorities.[24] Territorially divergent majorities suggest the probability of politically incompatible governments among states and between national and state levels. This means that the competition for political power may be carried on simultaneously by élites building diverse popular coalitions within sub-sets of the political system. The decentralization of function makes regionally tailored policy packages politically attractive. What is less obvious but of greater significance is that this incongruence may then in turn constitute an incipient source of tension. It creates the possibility of federal-provincial relations being defined in partisan terms and provides opposition forces with an incentive for using regional arenas as a means of challenging the legitimacy of an existing federal majority party or coalition. Where majorities are congruent, there is no partisan basis for federal-provincial conflict. There still may be a strong regional basis for this type of conflict, which frequently in Canada has been the case. Generally, regional conflict presumes some degree of territorial pluralism, which unavoidably will create strains within parties.[25]

Incongruent majorities can be viewed in a far more positive way both at the individual voter and system level. For the individual it can maximize the opportunities for representation and for locating parties in power that reflect one's own preferences.[26] At the system level it provides for countervailing powers.[27] As will be seen below, the direction and character of these effects may depend on the quality of federal arrangements. One can note initially that federal systems have had very different experiences concerning this aspect of federal-partisan links. In Canada, parties have tended to develop separate organizations and bases of support at each level of government.[28] In West Germany by contrast there has emerged a strong integrating pressure for parties as a result of which Land elections are routinely taken to be mini-tests of national party popularity. In the United States, undisciplined cadre parties, combined with an absence of parliamentary party government, have rendered insignificant the issue of partisan incompatibility across levels.

With respect to policy-making, Gerhard Lehmbruch has argued that federal relations are inherently ones of a complex bargaining process in which conflicts are resolved not by imposing the principle of majority rule but by consensus-building and accommodation.[29] This implies concessions to opposition forces and to regional governments.[30] Where federal and parliamentary traditions are combined within one régime, two distinct sets of 'rules of the game' will intersect. This is especially so in the Westminster model, where the principles of parliamentary supremacy and party government stress conflict resolution according to majority rule. Hence one-party government is the norm, and government versus opposition structures political debate, yet federalism implies conflict resolution through bargaining and consensus-building.[31] The problem then is not so much one of incongruence in ruling majorities at different levels but one of styles of governance.[32]

Related to the issue of a consensus versus majoritarian style of governance is the normative view that federalism may weaken the link between citizens and the state that parties and elections are intended to provide. Federalism involves multiple decision points, division of authority, and interdependence. Thus lines of accountability are confounded and the principle of responsible government is undermined. In modern federal orders, where the scope of the public sector has necessitated large, complex governing machinery, debates over basic political priorities may take a back seat to considerations of procedures, rules, and the effective distribution of power.[33]

Variations in the Quality of Federalism

To this point discussion has been confined to those party system effects associated with the existence of a federal as opposed to a unitary system of government. However, federal systems are not alike, and analysis remains incomplete without consideration of variation among them. Federal régimes are often compared in terms of degrees of decentralization and, less frequently, by the extent of interdependence.[34] Implicit in what has already been discussed is the fact that the fragmenting or centrifugal effects at work within federal régimes will be accentuated by the extent of real decentralization of authority. Conversely, centripetal trends are likely to be fostered by the constraints of interdependence. What often remains unnoticed is a third fundamental dimension for comparison identified by distinctions in the purpose and effect of federal authority, in terms of divisions of jurisdictions versus divisions of labour. In those federal régimes organized primarily on the basis of jurisdictional principles, the object is to create two levels of authority, each with its own well-defined policy sectors, operating semi-autonomously. The entire machinery of governments tends to be duplicated at each level, and there is a presumption that each level can and should manage its own affairs. In its simplest form, this model suggests 'water-tight' compartments, or in Wheare's classic formulation, an arrangement in which each level is co-ordinate and independent.[35]

Of course, given the expansion of the public sector, this pattern of jurisdictional separation constitutes an ideal type rather than an accurate empirical description. Today in all federal systems, including those originating from something like 'water-tight' compartments, complex interdependence within major policy sectors is common. Yet many systems remain organized primarily along jurisdictional lines,[36] which implies that the political authority of sub-units is formally autonomous.

The second model stresses a very different concept of federalism based not on a division of tasks but on a division of labour (or horizontal federalism). It, too, involves some allocation of policy primacy to one level or the other; but what it proposes as the essence of federation is that for most major, ongoing policy concerns one level of government will be primarily concerned with the formulation and development stages in the policy process and the other level with implementation and control. This type of division of authority does not produce replicas of the machinery of government at both levels. Instead, given some policy sector, it allocates sub-sets of the decision-making process to one level or the other. Significantly, this functional division of authority presumes extensive interdependence and therefore a need for a stable pattern of direct sub-unit participation in policy-making as is typically found in interstate federal modes of representation. Thus, as in West Germany, the central government may be predominantly concerned with policy initiation, formulation, and legislation, while regional units may be heavily weighted in favour of policy implementation and administration.[37]

Functional federalism tends to spawn elaborate patterns of consultation and bargaining both politically and administratively, for neither level of government will succeed in providing policy or resolving conflicts without the help of the other. There is therefore a strong institutional bias in favour of a complex meshing of political and bureaucratic interests. To the extent that functional federalism does not allocate policy fields to a single level of government, the regional distinctiveness of policy packages will be less than under jurisdictional federalism. However, it must also be remembered that a functionally oriented division will allocate some policy sectors to one level primarily, for example, education, police, and municipal affairs in West Germany. As a result, one should not assume that regional elections are all alike in terms of issues, policy options, and the like, even though they will tend to involve national issues and national parties on a regular basis.

In contrast, jurisdictional federalism tends to encourage each level to go it alone wherever possible. Interdependence may be the reality, but disentanglement remains the ideal.[38] Further, the fact that decision-makers at each level possess a fully developed policy apparatus means that when conflicts prove intractable, unilateral action remains an alternative – often a politically attractive one. Unlike in functional federalism, provincial/state electoral politics rarely mirror national divisions. Given this important structural distinction, it remains to identify how jurisdictional federalism may shape the character of parties and party systems. Generally, we may expect it to expand the incentives for political élites to exploit regional conflicts and to politicize federal-provincial relations. There can be little doubt from Canadian history that there are political advantages for provincial leaders in fighting Ottawa. Popular support can usually be maximized by casting Ottawa as the enemy and portraying the provincial governing party as the sole defender of regional interests. This has the additional benefit of making provincial oppositions appear irrelevant.

It can further be argued that jurisdictional federalism facilitates patterns of one-party dominance, whereas functional federalism has no direct relationship. As Lévesque and Norrie have shown, overwhelming provincial majorities occur whenever major federal-provincial conflicts are present or anticipated. If intergovernmental relations are more harmonious, domestic issues will play a greater part in the outcome of the election. In this case the greater dispersion of most preferred positions on intraprovincial matters would suggest a much smaller plurality for the winning party and a higher vote for the opposition forces.[39]

With functional federalism, parties distinguish themselves not in terms of provincial rights or in terms of credibility in resisting the centre but by alternative sets of policy options for national government. Thus intergovernmental issues are likely to be of lower salience to voters. If so, the dispersion of preferences external to the region is less likely to differ significantly from the dispersion over intraregional issues than in jurisdictional federalism. One-party dominance reflects the tendency for the politicization of provincial governments in the intergovernmental policy process. That is, provinces act as if they were in a partisan opposition role vis-á-vis the federal government. From this follows the proposition that jurisdictional federalism tends to displace parties in intergovernmental relations; functional federalism integrates parties into the process.

Interdependence of policy sectors makes intergovernmental relations essential, but these may constitute decision arenas in which the traditional functions of parties have little place. In the case of jurisdictional federalism this generates intergovernmental relations based primarily on executive-bureaucratic bargaining.[40] These operate largely extra-constitutionally, and often on an ad hoc basis, outside the normal arenas of party activity – elections and parliament. In this way parties may be displaced and made peripheral to much of the policy process despite strong political traditions of parliamentary supremacy and party government.

In functional federalism the displacement of parties is less likely because regional-provincial élites have little incentive to structure federal-provincial conflict in terms of government versus opposition. Without this adversarial motive there is little impulse for these élites to take on partisan-like roles (just as there is no strong impetus for patterns of provincial one-party dominance). The centrality of parties in the federal bargaining process may also be guaranteed by the integrative effects of functional federalism on party organization,[41] as will be discussed below.

The West German experience provides an example of the integration of party influence within federal structures. Prior to the Third Reich, a bureaucratic-executive style of government enjoyed power and prestige while parties suffered from questionable legitimacy and severe fragmentation.[42] This situation was radically transformed by the post-war creation of the Federal Republic, in which parties assumed the role of defender of democracy while virtually monopolizing the recruitment of governing élites. More significant for understanding the workings of federalism, the concentration of the party system, along with the transformation of ideological movements into convergent Volksparteien, biased West German parties increasingly toward building broad majority-oriented coalitions and toward a governing role. These changes were part of what Germans refer to as the party-state (Parteienstaat) in which party and bureaucratic élites mutually interpenetrate in a two-way flow of influence.[43] The significance of this pattern of partisan development is that despite the fact that the policy process is characterized by highly developed networks of bureaucratic consultation and bargaining, parties are never excluded from this process. Quite the contrary, they are deeply embedded in it. Party organizations have internally taken on some of the characteristics of large-scale bureaucracy and have recruited a substantial portion of elected officials from the public service.[44]

Jurisdictional federalism encourages the bifurcation of party organization, while functional federalism facilitates organizational integration.[45] A functional division of labour necessitates co-operative bargaining over policy differences and a stable process of co-ordination/consultation. It also provides a strong incentive for co-ordinated party positions and alliances between levels of government. For example, from the early years of the Federal Republic, as the modern post-war party system was evolving, there was an early effort associated with Konrad Adenauer's majority-building to pressure Land politicians into coalitions parallel to that at the federal level.[46] A crucial factor in this process was the need of the federal government to assure the political compatability of the Bundesrat. Thus there has developed a strong incentive on the part of federal politicians to intervene in Land elections. This often has involved the parachuting of national leaders into Land politics. it has also meant that Land elections are fought, to some degree, over national rather than provincial issues, making these elections tests of national party support. In terms of élite recruitment, the Länder have been an important source of future national leaders.[47]

Generally, it can be said that regional party élites are tightly integrated and have an active voice within the federal party organization, a fact that complements and reinforces the formal role of Land governments in the Bundesrat. In sharp contrast to Canada or the United States, West Germany can be said to have nationally integrated party organizations.

In Canada, territorial politics combined with jurisdictional federalism has generated centrifugal effects that have accentuated strains within national parties.[48] Politicians at either level have found it costly to be too closely associated with the policies or stances of their counterparts at the other level. Typically, federal and provincial parties coexist and overlap, but they remain largely autonomous as organizations. Further, there are no strong structural incentives to create parallel majorities as there are in West Germany. Provincial elections are never interpreted as votes of confidence in the federal governing party. Federal politicians do not normally intervene in provincial contests, while provincial premiers do so to only a limited degree federally.[49]

Federalism commonly produces shifts in partisan support across two levels of elections. However, the significance of this phenomenon varies, depending on whether it occurs within a jurisdictional or a functional framework. There are two competing explanations for inconsistency in federal versus provincial voting behaviour. One derives from models of public choice and suggests that voters support different parties at the two levels of government as they seek to maximize their preferences. A decentralized system allows voters to select different policy packages as they are offered by parties at the two levels.[50] The second explanation is based on a countervailing powers model in which it is held that voters will seek to limit the powers of a national governing party by electing its political opponents at the provincial/ state level. Thus it is held that there is a balancing effect (and in some formulations a cyclical pattern in which opposition support builds over time to depose the existing federal majority party).[51]

Such inconsistent voting patterns exist, for example, in both Canada and West Germany. A comparison of the two demonstrates the utility of the two models and the importance of the federal context in interpreting this electoral phenomenon. Within functional federalism the phenomenon of voters supporting regionally a party they did not support federally can be interpreted as a shift in partisan support. As the West German example suggests, such electoral swings are partial indicators of changes in national public opinion and serve to caution or reinforce ruling coalitions in Bonn. Repeated losses at the Land level can provoke a government crisis in Bonn. The routine Canadian occurrence of a federal governing party losing votes in all provinces would be politically untenable in Germany because, due to party system integration, these are votes for the national opposition party. In the West German context, electoral splitting as a signal to the federal majority must also be seen from a second perspective. Given the strong interstate federal representation in the Bundesrat, Land elections can directly alter the partisan composition of the second chamber and produce dramatic constraints on the chancellor and his coaltion. This means that Land electoral shifts can literally enhance the weight of federal opposition parties. Unlike Canada, this occurs within the constitutionally defined federal policy process rather than in extra-constitutional intergovernmental arenas.

Thus regional elections within functional, integrated federalism do not provide incentives for regional élites to portray themselves as defenders of regional interests. Nor do they encourage the distinctiveness of regional policy packages. More typical is the pattern of federal issues structuring to some degree political debate within regional elections. Hence policy options offered by national parties provide a basis for regional voting choice. By contrast, it is far more plausible that in a jurisdictionally based federal order voters split their vote in order to seek distinctive policy packages. Further, given the tendency for jurisdictional federalism to encourage the bifurcation of party organization and to tolerate partisan incongruence in governments across levels there is no reason to think that such vote splitting predicts an eventual turnover in governing party at either level.[52]

Party Systems' Effect on Federalism

The structuring of conflict through parties provides them with an influence on the policy process and on the effective character of federal arrangements. It is therefore important to consider directly the ways in which party system traits are likely to shape federalism. In recognizing that parties and party systems in Western democracies vary greatly in organizational features, ideological distinctiveness, social and economic bases, and competitiveness, our task becomes one of isolating those partisan traits that are directly relevant to understanding the workings of federal institutions and processes.

Many of the hypotheses put forward in the previous sections contain hints of the reciprocal nature of the federalism-party system relationship. For example, patterns of highly fragmented, multi-party competition or party organizations built around regional power barons and local strongholds can certainly reinforce the decentralizing potential of federal structures. Beyond this, there appear to be two general competitive trends, concentration and convergence, that suggest particularly important consequences for the federal political process.

The concentration of a party system refers to the transformation from complex multi-partism to a simpler, bipolar configuration, where competition is dominated by two large partisan blocs. Generally, concentration facilitates conflict resolution by majority rule and therefore may generate ongoing tension within federal régimes built on bargaining and consensus. To the extent that party competition becomes concentrated, it will increase élite incentives for organizational integration and for parallel patterns of competition at national and regional levels. This may limit the likelihood of incongruent majorities but need not imply the elimination of all minor parties. As the West German experience shows, third parties like the FDP may survive and play a vital balancing role alongside two political 'giants.'

The shift toward bipolar structuring of conflict in the party system encourages majority rule as the legitimate basis for conflict resolution[53] and fosters single-party government and occasionally one-party dominance. However, the rationale for decision-making in all federal systems is one of the protection of minority or regional interests through intergovernmental bargaining or intragovernmental sharing of power. Thus it may be argued that some degree of multi-partism is conducive to the workability of federal régimes.

The concept of convergence is based on the ideological space of partisan conflict (rather than the number of competing units) and refers to the centripetal tendencies in party competition.[54] Party system convergence expands the consensual base of political conflict and is broadly compatible with federal modes of conflict resolution.

The classic formulations of convergence models are those associated with 'brokerage politics,' the 'end of ideology,' and the 'waning of opposition.'[55] In Downsian terminology, convergence in party competition means the maximization of electoral support from the centre.[56] Divergence or polarization suggests that party élites have incentives to differentiate themselves not just from their ideological opposites but from their political neighbours as well. Where such centrifugal effects are based on regional demands, federalism provides a means of depolarizing political conflict by guaranteeing territorial autonomy. In contrast to polarized pluralism, fragmented (multi-party) but convergent party competition implies moderated competition with a proclivity for coalition building after elections based on elaborate bargaining and power-sharing arrangements. It is sometimes argued that the incentives for gaining power in this type of party system approximate the incentives for co-operative bargaining that are essential for a smoothly working federal system. Conflict resolution that does not violate the spirit of federal bargains must allow for considerable consensus-building and for guarantees for minority interests through partial veto powers. This style of governance prescribes complex procedures for assuring that decisions will be arrived at without violating vital regional interests. Lijphart has drawn important parallels between this style of federal bargaining and the operative principles of consociational democracy.[57] Lehmbruch has most directly posed the dilemma for federal systems that may arise when party competition becomes increasingly concentrated and when the rules of decision-making become increasingly based on the majority principle rather than consensual bargaining.[58]

An important post-war trend in Western European politics has been the rise of so-called catch-all parties. It should be noted that both the fit of federal policy-making styles with multi-party bargaining and the trend toward bipolar concentration can be modified by the growth of catch-all parties because they allow for much internal fragmentation of opinion and rest on loose organizational bonds. This development has been clearest where the tendencies toward ideological convergence and concentration have been combined. Whether in a bipolar or a multi-polar context, the flexible style of catch-all parties appears relatively conducive to bargaining modes of conflict resolution and therefore is compatible with the consensus-building style found within federal structures.

Federalism, Parties, and Democratic Politics

Political systems may be judged by the degree to which citizen preferences are satisfied by the public sector. In one stream of democratic thought, for this to occur there must be responsible government, clear lines of accountability, and means of translating public preferences into public policy. Popular control through elections and parliamentary representation makes party government a tenet of a democratic order. Responsible parties are therefore an essential component of this model.[59]

In a second stream of democratic theory, satisfaction of citizen preferences is held to be maximized via dispersion of authority and the presentation of alternative sets of public goods and services.[60] From this perspective federalism facilitates the ability of citizens to signal their preferences through multiple levels of government. However, the more centralized the party system, the less likely it is that voters will be able to select among distinct options at different levels or across regions.[61] In this model of democracy, countervailing powers and pluralism, not party government, are the goals of institutional arrangements. What is important to recognize is that the comparative study of parties and party systems has tended to stress the first conception of democracy. The literature on federalism has stressed the second. The dilemma emerging from these two models is found in the apparent contradiction between the principles of accountability based on party government and citizen choice based on countervailing powers. It is a dilemma that confronts virtually all proposals for the reform of federal systems. Decentralization may allow policy-makers to tailor packages to a closer fit with voter preferences, but it creates the need for bargaining and log-rolling. And this in turn undermines organizational cohesion and discipline of parties and impairs their capacity to act in a 'responsible' way.

A second problem for federal systems arises when one views political parties as institutions designed to limit the diseconomies of decentralization. The logic of decentralization in a federal system fosters the undersupply of public goods with interjurisdictional (regional) spillovers,[62] often prompting calls for greater consultation and collaboration among governments.[63] Political scientists have naturally looked to parties as critical institutions for alleviating these shortcomings.[64] Political parties may serve as integrative mechanisms, which through formal and informal ties can prevent regional parties from neglecting the interests of those outside their own jurisdiction. National parties may thus constrain their regional affiliates in the pursuit of local objectives. They also provide a mechanism for regional representation within the national policy process. However, the capacity of parties to perform both these functions depends on their own internal characteristics and the structure of partisan competition through which they operate.

In some federal systems, like Canada's, parties have not effectively performed this integrative function, while in others, like West Germany, they have. It should be clear from the distinction between jurisdictional and functional federalism that in the jurisdictional case incentives favour the bifurcation of party systems. As previously indicated, there is by contrast in the functional case minimal division by jurisdiction, and therefore fewer policy choices can be differentiated at the regional level. The general point is that there exists within functional federalism an integrative tendency, for regional parties cannot systematically differentiate their positions from those of the national party leadership. By comparison, under jurisdictional federalism, and especially where there are deeply rooted territorial divisions, the absence of ties to a national constituency means that regional parties will be likely to impose costs on those outside the region. Although the limits to integrative politics have been particularly prominent in Canada, the acceptance of functional federalism remains improbable given a heritage of deeply rooted regional sentiments and an adversarial style of conflict resolution that pervades most Canadian legal, economic, and political institutions.

NOTES

1 Thomas J. Courchene 'Analytical Perspectives on Canadian Economic Union' in M.J. Trebilcock et al eds *Federalism and Canadian Economic Union* (Toronto: University of Toronto Press 1983) 72
2 Parties are of course constrained by electoral laws, conditions of public party finance, consitutional freedoms, and the like.
3 See for example J.R.S. Prichard with Jamie Benedickson 'Securing the Canadian Economic Union: Federalism and Internal Barriers to Trade' in Trebilcock et al *Federalism* 1–50.
4 Mark Sproule-Jones *Public Choice and Federalism in Australia and Canada* (Canberra: Australian National University 1975)
5 Theodore Lowi 'Party, Policy, and Constitution in America' in W.N. Chambers and W.D. Burnham eds *The American Party Systems: Stages of Political Development* (New York: Oxford 1967) 238–76; S.J.R. Noel 'Political Parties and Elite Accommodation: Interpretations of Canadian Federalism' in J. Peter Meekison ed *Canadian Federalism: Myth or Reality* 3rd ed (Toronto: Methuen 1977) 64
6 David B. Truman 'Federalism and the Party System' in Arthur W. MacMahon ed *Federalism: Mature and Emergent* (New York 1962); and Morton Grodzins 'American Political Parties and the American System' *Western Political Quarterly* 13 no 4 (December 1960) 974–98
7 J.R. Melvin 'Political Structure and the Pursuit of Economic Objectives' in Trebilcock et al *Federalism* 132–5; R.W. Boadway and K.H. Norrie 'Constitu-

tional Reform Canadian Style: An Economic Perspective' *Canadian Public Policy* 6 no 3 (summer 1980) 497. Even those who challenge the idea that regional diversity explains the origins of federalism acknowledge that diversities mean higher organizational costs, containing implications for the operation of the federal system. On this see Albert Breton and Anthony Scott *The Economic Constitution of Federal States* (Toronto: University of Toronto Press 1978) 9.

 8 Donald V. Smiley *Canada in Question: Federalism in the Eighties* 3rd ed (Toronto: McGraw-Hill Ryerson 1980) 1–5 and W.S. Livingston 'A Note on the Nature of Federalism' in Aaron Wildavsky ed *American Federalism in Perspective* (Boston: Little, Brown 1967)

 9 Richard Rose *The Territorial Dimension in Government* (Chatham, NJ: Chatham House Publishers 1982)

10 William H. Riker *Federalism: Origin, Operation, Significance* (Boston: Little, Brown 1964). Theories of federal bargains usually focus on identifying the origins of federal systems. In the context of the debate over federal societies, it is important to distinguish between models of the origins of federalism and models of the workings of federalism. Our concern here is entirely with the latter.

11 On the federal societies debate, see William S. Livingston *Federalism and Constitutional Change* (Oxford: Clarendon Press 1956); also Alan C. Cairns 'The Governments and Societies of Canadian Federalism' *Canadian Journal of Political Science* 10 (December 1977) 695–726.

12 Michael Trebilcock, Douglas Hartle, J.R.S. Prichard, and Donald Dewees *The Choice of Governing Instruments* (Ottawa 1982)

13 Donald V. Smiley and Ronald L. Watts *Intrastate Federalism in Canada* (Toronto: University of Toronto Press 1985) and Alan C. Cairns 'From Interstate to Intrastate Federalism' (Kingston: Queen's University, Institute of Intergovernmental Relations 1979)

14 Roger Gibbins *Regionalism: Territorial Politics in Canada and the United States* (Toronto 1982) 45–6; Donald Smiley 'Federal-Provincial Conflict in Canada' in Meekison ed *Canadian Federalism* 9–10

15 General sources on the determinants of the shape of party competition include Maurice Duverger *Les partis politiques* (Paris: Colin 1954); Giovanni Sartori *Parties and Party Systems* (London: Cambridge 1976); and Alan C. Cairns 'The Electoral System and the Party System in Canada, 1921–65' *Canadian Journal of Political Science* 1 (March 1968) 55–80.

16 Klaus von Beyme *The Political System of the Federal Republic of Germany* (New York: St. Martin's Press 1983) 165–7

17 On the regional character of national parties, see Gibbins *Regionalism* chap 6; Mildred A. Schwartz *Politics and Territory* (Montreal: McGill-Queen's University Press 1974) chap 3; and F.R. Flatters and R.S. Lipsey 'Common Ground

for the Canadian Common Market' (Queen's University 1981), quoted in Prichard and Benedickson 'Securing the Canadian Economic Union' 37. Canadian 'landslide' elections, like 1958 and 1984, create large party majorities that are national in scope. But the predominant pattern in Canadian federal politics is for all three parties to be strong in certain regions and weak in others. For Australia, see J. Holmes and C. Sharman *The Australian Federal System* (Sydney: Allen and Unwin 1977) chap 4.

18 Albert Breton *The Economic Theory of Representative Government* (Chicago: Aldine 1974) 114–15

19 Richard Simeon 'Regionalism and Canadian Political Institutions' *Queen's Quarterly* 82 no 4 (winter 1975) reprinted in Richard Schultz et al *The Canadian Political Process* 3rd ed (Toronto: Holt, Rinehart and Winston 1979). See also Prichard and Benedickson 'Securing the Canadian Economic Union' 37.

20 On regionalist political movements, see L.J. Sharpe ed *Decentralist Trends in Western Europe* (London: Sage 1979); Charles R. Foster ed *Nations without a State* (New York: Praeger 1980); Sidney Tarrow, P.J. Katzenstein, and L. Graziano eds *Territorial Politics in Industrial Nations* (New York: Praeger 1978).

21 Carl Friedrich *Trends of Federalism in Theory and Practice* (New York: Praeger 1968) 58–69; Maurice Pinard *The Rise of a Third Party* enlarged ed (Montreal: McGill-Queen's University Press 1975)

22 Albert Breton and Anthony Scott *The Economic Constitution of Federal States* (Toronto: University of Toronto Press 1978) 9 argues that local or regional entry points may entail lower signalling costs for new participants. See also Jonathan Lemco and Peter Regenstrief 'The Fusion of Powers and the Crisis of Canadian Federalism' *Publius* 14 no 1 (winter 1984) 114–15.

23 On the origins and early growth of the German Greens, see Klaus Troitzsch 'Die Herausforderung der etablierten Parteien durch die Grünen' in Heino Kaack and Reinhold Roth eds *Handbuch des deutschen Parteiensystems* 1 (Opladen: Leske 1980) 260–94 and William M. Chandler and Alan Siaroff 'Post Industrial Politics in Germany and the Origins of the Greens' *Comparative Politics* 18 (1986) 303–26.

24 Anthony Scott 'An Economic Approach to the Federal Structure' in *Options: Proceedings of the Conference on the Future of the Canadian Federation* (Toronto: University of Toronto Press 1977)

25 Edwin Black 'Federal Strains within a Canadian Party' in Hugh G. Thorburn ed *Party Politics in Canada* 4th ed (Scarborough: Prentice-Hall 1979) 89–99

26 Sproule-Jones *Public Choice* 42

27 R. West and Stanley Winer 'The Individual, Political Tension and Canada's Quest for a New Constitution' *Canadian Public Policy* 6 (winter 1980) 7

28 Smiley *Canada in Question* 129–39; Reginald Whitaker *The Government Party:*

168/William M. Chandler

Organizing and Financing the Liberal Party of Canada 1930–58 (Toronto: University of Toronto Press 1974)
29 Gerhard Lehmbruch *Parteienwettbewerb im Bundesstaat* (Stuttgart: Kohlhammer 1976)
30 Klaus von Beyme 'Do Parties Matter?' *Politische Vierteljahresschrift* (December 1981) 344
31 Gibbins *Regionalism* 78 argues that 'Canadians have tried to combine parliamentary and federal forms of government. The marriage has not been successful. Parliamentary forms have dominated and, as a consequence, national institutions have become too majoritarian in character, too insensitive to the diverse and pluralistic interests of a federal society.' See Smiley and Watts *Intrastate Federalism in Canada* 117–44 and Douglas Verney 'The Reconciliation of Parliamentary Supremacy and Federalism in Canada' *Journal of Commonwealth and Comparative Politics* 21 no 1 (March 1983) 22–44.
32 Lehmbruch *Parteienwettbewerb* 11–16
33 Simeon 'Regionalism' 299
34 Kenneth Hanf and Fritz W. Scharpf eds *Interorganizational Policy-Making* (London: Sage 1978)
35 K.C. Wheare *Federal Government* (London: Oxford 1946) 11–15
36 Nevil Johnson *State and Government in the Federal Republic of Germany* 2nd ed (Oxford: Pergamon 1983) 118–25
37 For general sources on German federalism see Heinz Laufer *Der Föderalismus der Bundesrepublik Deutschland* (Stuttgart: Kohlhammer 1974) and R.I. Mathews ed *Federalism in Australia and the Federal Republic of Germany* (Canberra: Australian National University Press 1980)
38 Task Force on Canadian Unity *A Future Together* (Ottawa: Supply and Services Canada 1979) 89
39 Terrence J. Lévesque and Kenneth H. Norrie 'Overwhelming Majorities in the Legislature of Alberta' *Canadian Journal of Political Science* 12 no 3 (September 1979) 466
40 Smiley *Canada in Question* 146ff
41 Although functional federalism, by its stress on interdependence, may reinforce the bureaucratization of intergovernmental relations and may minimize overt politicization of these relations, it does not necessarily reduce the role of parties in the process. The West German federal example suggests that partisan influence within executive-bureaucratic frameworks may be maintained in part through partisan penetration of the higher levels of the public service. There may also be a reverse flow of bureaucratic influence on parties through the recruitment of elected officials from bureaucratic ranks. For a detailed treatment of this phenomenon see Kenneth Dyson *Party, State and Bureaucracy in Western Germany* (London: Sage 1977).

42 Gordon Smith *Democracy in Western Germany* (London: Croom Helm 1979)

43 Dyson *Party, State and Bureaucracy* 9–11, 20ff

44 The Bundesrat is the pinnacle of a vast intergovernmental decision-making apparatus and must be understood as such. For this reason, outside observers who see in the Bundesrat model a possible replacement for the Canadian Senate are likely to be disappointed. Its role is not primarily that of a parliamentary upper house but rather that of a legitimizing public forum for an elaborate style of intergovernmental decision-making that allows for the simultaneous integration of partisan-administrative interactions with purely intergovernmental relations.

45 See David E. Smith *The Regional Decline of a National Party* (Toronto: University of Toronto Press 1981) 51–111.

46 Lehmbruch *Parteienwettbewerb* 125–32

47 Chancellors Kiesinger and Kohl both served as Land minister-presidents, Brandt was mayor of Berlin, and Schmidt had an early career in Hamburg politics.

48 Black 'Federal Strains'

49 Some important exceptions to this are noted by Smiley *Canada in Question* 143–4.

50 Breton *Economic Theory* 114–15; Sproule-Jones *Public Choice and Federalism in Australia and Canada* 76

51 The balance theory was first proposed by Frank Underhill in 'Canadian Liberal Democracy in 1955' in G.V. Ferguson and Frank Underhill *Press and Party in Canada* (Toronto: Ryerson Press 1955) 39–40. See Smiley's discussion of the debate over balancing in *Canada in Question* 123–9 and Steven Muller 'Federalism and the Party System in Canada' in Wildavsky ed *American Federalism in Perspective* 144–61.

52 Lawrence LeDuc and Harold D. Clarke 'Partisan Instability in Canada: Evidence from a New Panel Study' *American Political Science Review* 78 no 2 (June 1984) 470–84

53 Lehmbruch *Parteienwettbewerb* 126 provides the most systematic formulation of this thesis; see 7, 11–17, 126.

54 On theories of convergence and polarization, see Sartori *Parties and Party Systems* part II.

55 Daniel Bell *The End of Ideology* (Glencoe, Ill.: The Free Press 1960); Otto Kirchheimer 'The Waning of Opposition' in Dahl *Political Opposition* 237–59

56 Anthony Downs *An Economic Theory of Democracy* (New York 1957)

57 Arend Lijphart 'Consociation and Federation: Conceptual and Empirical Links' *Canadian Journal of Political Science* 12 no 3 (September 1979) 499–516

58 Lehmbruch *Parteienwettbewerb* 158–77

59 The Committee on Political Parties of American Political Science Association

Toward a More Responsible Two-Party System (New York: Holt, Rinehart and Winston 1950)

60 Vincent Ostrom, Robert Bish, and Elinor Ostrom *Local Government in the United States* Workshop in Political Theory and Policy Analysis, Indiana University 1980; see also Vincent Ostrom 'Can Federalism Make a Difference?' *Publius* 3 no 2 (fall 1973) 197–237.

61 Riker *Federalism* 129 provides a different but related formulation of this general proposition.

62 Prichard and Benedickson 'Securing the Canadian Economic Union' 20–6. See also B. Grewel et al eds *The Economics of Federalism* (Canberra: Australian National University Press 1980).

63 Gérard Vielleux 'Intergovernmental Canada: Government by Conference? A Fiscal and Economic Perspective' *Canadian Public Administration* 23 no 1 (spring 1980) 33–53; Donald J. Savoie *Federal-Provincial Collaboration* (Montreal: McGill-Queen's University Press 1981); Richard Simeon ed *Confrontation and Collaboration – Intergovernmental Relations in Canada Today* (Toronto: Institute of Public Administration of Canada 1979)

64 Smiley *Canada in Question* 143–8

10 / Federalism and Interest Group Organization

WILLIAM D. COLEMAN

Conclusions concerning the effect of federalism on interest associations are mixed. The dominant opinion is that federalism generally weakens the cohesion of interest associations and in doing so ultimately harms their effectiveness. The classic position is found in David Truman's proposition that interest associations operating in a federal system tend to take on a federal form themselves.[1] Given certain spheres of local autonomy, a federated association establishes and sanctifies sub-centres of power. In doing so, it weakens the internal cohesion of the organization and hence its ultimate effectiveness. Helen Dawson adds that a contradictory dynamic develops within 'federated' interest associations because the federal-level organization needs the strong support of the related provincial associations in its domain if it is to be effective.[2] However, if these provincial associations entertain too strongly a national point of view, they are likely to alienate their own membership which, of course, forms the constituency of the federal-level organization.[3] But if the provincial organizations become too self-centred, the federal organization will never be able to develop consensus positions and thus will remain weak and ineffectual in its dealings with the national government.

Certain patterns of interaction between national and regional governments further complicate the life of interest associations. In his study of highway transport regulation in Canada, Schultz shows how an association can be literally torn apart in situations where the two levels of government are at loggerheads.[4] A government at one level will tend to use associations in its attempts to broaden its powers at the expense of the other level. On the other side, associations will try to influence the division of powers in a federal system to enhance their own organizational strength.[5] In doing so, the association at one level will weaken its counterpart organization at the other level. Still another scenario is sketched out by Simeon, who sees the realm of intergovernmental realtions as one that can easily exclude associations completely, thereby giving them no chance to be effective.[6]

Although less prominent in the literature, a minority opinion has developed that sets federalism in a more positive light. The classic statement here is Grodzin's 'multiple crack hypothesis.'[7] In multiplying the number of governments, a federal system multiplies the number of access points where associations can bring pressure to bear on decision-makers. Schultz finds this hypothesis to be more credible when relations between levels of government are quiescent or co-operative.[8] Bucovetsky's study of the Canadian mining industry illustrates how both provincial and national mining associations and chambers of mines used all relevant access points in an ultimately effective attack on proposals for tax reform.[9] Even so, when the relations between governments are competitive and conflictual, federated organizations need not be torn apart as Dawson and Schultz suggest. In his study of vocational training in the West German construction industry, Streeck finds associations to be a co-ordinating, even reconciling force between federal and Land governments.[10]

The core argument needs to be examined by questioning its key assumption that associations in federal régimes take on their own federated structures.[11] Some account must be made of the fact that unitary, cohesive associations are found in federal systems, even in sectors like food processing or construction where jurisdiction is divided between governments. In addition, federated organizations are common in non-federal régimes. This chapter extends the critique of this key assumption by expanding the field of analysis to include a functional federalist régime, West Germany, two jurisdictional federalist systems, Switzerland and Canada, and a 'union' state, the United Kingdom. This comparison indicates that within the same sectors, differences among association structures in all four countries are relatively small. Further, where differences appear, they do so at the level of regional associational systems. Such systems occur both within and across economic sectors in jurisdictional federal régimes, within particular sectors in Britain's union state, and not at all in the functional federal West German system. In the conclusion to the chapter, I shall discuss the likely consequences of this order of differences for association effectiveness.

The Approach

The analysis of the relationship between constitutional and associational structures will be conducted by studying business interest associations in two economic sectors, industrial chemicals/pharmaceuticals and construction. These two are chosen because of their significant differences in industrial organization and the interaction of these differences with constitutional arrangements. The chemical industry is generally populated by large, capital-intensive firms strongly oriented to national and international markets. The construction industry is composed of many very small firms that are labour intensive and tend to operate in local markets. Accordingly, in federal systems, regional and local governments are more likely to be involved with the construction industry than with the chemical industry.

Elsewhere, we have suggested a typology of territorial differentiation by which associations may be distinguished.[12] At one extreme is the unitary association, which shows no differentiation along territorial lines. A single organization cares for member interests at all levels of government, federal, regional, and local. At the other extreme is a series of independent regional associations. Operating independent of one another, these associations deal with their corresponding regional governments and, in a totally unco-ordinated fashion, interact on their own with the national government.

Between these two extremes, five other categories of associations can be distinguished. In each case, the association has a distinct organizational presence at both national and regional levels. However, the autonomy of the regional instance from the national organization will vary in each case. Autonomy can be gauged by the following factors: whether the regional organization has its own constitution, hires and employs its own staff, administers its own budget, interacts with regional governments on its own without direction and consultation with the national organization, and the membership status of individual firms within the regional and the national organizations. Using these indicators, five categories can be defined.

Unitary association with regional sub-units. This type operates as a unitary organization but for purposes of administrative convenience has created a number of regional branch organizations. If these branches have permanent staff, it is allocated by the central body. The branches would have no independent source of funds, collect no dues of their own, and have no separate constitution. Generally speaking, they would not interact on their own with regional governments. Members would belong to and identify with the national organization.

Unitary association with regional sub-units, one or more of which enjoys an enhanced status. This is similar to the previous type except that one or more of the branches enjoys a greater degree of autonomy. Such branches are delegated responsibility for interacting with their corresponding regional governments on a substantial range of issues and are granted greater resources to carry out these tasks. At the same time, these enhanced branches remain constitutionally subject to the national organization.

Federal association. Here a classic division of labour exists between the national and regional levels of the association, with each granted autonomy to interact with its corresponding government. Normally, the division of powers within the association parallels that of the political system at large. The regional instances in this case have sufficient autonomy to be called associations in their own right; they employ their own staff and administer their own budgets. However, member firms belong to the association as a whole, being members of both the regional and national organizations, and usually pay one set of dues that is then divided between the two levels. The constitutions of the regional organizations are modelled on and perhaps even constrained by that of the national organization.

Confederal association. For this type, the regional organizations are virtually independent associations in their own right. They hire and fire their own staff, collect their own dues, and administer their own budgets. They have their own constitutions, which do not necessarily correspond to that of the national organization. The latter has a peak or umbrella organization composed of the regional associations. Individual firms then belong directly to the regional associations only and pay their fees to them. The regional associations pay a levy, usually based on membership, to the national group. Often, in this type of association, the regional organizations antedate the founding of the national body.

Affiliated associations. For all intents and purposes, these regional associations are independent organizations in their own right. However, in order to have a voice at the national level, they 'affiliate' to a national organization, usually by paying a nominal fee. Through affiliation, they obtain access to information from the national association and some say in its deliberations. However, they are not members of the national association as in the confederal case; the national association recruits its own firm members directly. Individual firms then might belong either to the national association, to the regional association(s), or to both. The national association exerts no authority over the regional associations, nor does it have a monopoly on access to the national government, as is the norm in federal and confederal arrangements.

Our task then will be to use this categorical scheme to examine the degree of regional differentiation in business associations in the four chosen countries. These countries vary in the degree of decentralization in their régimes. Probably the most centralized of the four is the United Kingdom, which has been characterized by Rokkan and Urwin as a 'union state.'[13] Such a state is basically centralized but because of the way in which it was formed also has areas of decentralized administration. 'The United Kingdom is the prototypic union state with an accumulation of disparate historical variations. The centre has responded with ad hoc proposals for specific problems as they arose, without any overall strategy, and in this way has sought to maintain a middle ground between a unitary structure and federalism.'[14] Overall responsibility then for economic development and international trade belongs to the central government. It therefore has the greatest impact on the British chemical industry. However, within this union state, Scotland, with its own legal system, has retained its own building regulations and a different system for house purchasing. This leads us to expect a greater degree of regional differentiation within construction associations.[15]

The federal system in West Germany would appear to fall between Canada and Switzerland on the one side and Britain on the other in terms of the degree of decentralization. Described sometimes as 'functional federalism,' the German system favours the federal government when it comes to making policy. Johnson writes: 'It is clear that the division of legislative competence under the Basic Law confers the bulk of the responsibility for law-making, and *a fortiori* for policy-making in the broadest sense, on the federal authorities. The Länder have effectively a residual competence and their more or less exclusive powers are by subtraction concentrated in three spheres: education (up to university level), police, and the general framework of local government.'[16]

From the point of view of interest associations, then, there is an incentive to have a strong presence at the federal level. This need is reinforced by the fact that in the orders of business for federal ministries the interests affected by any proposed measures must be heard.[17] At the same time, the powers of the Länder to determine how laws are to be implemented and administered gives them an important discretionary power over the content of policy. In order to influence these processes, associations need some regional presence as well. These pressures toward regional differentiation in West German associations should be more intense in the construction industry than in chemicals because the Land governments are responsible for the construction and maintenance of most locally used public infrastructure.[18]

In contrast to the British and West German cases, the Swiss and Canadian versions of jurisdictional federalism are more decentralized still. The policy-making powers of the Swiss cantons and the Canadian provinces are more extensive than those possessed by the German Länder or the Scottish Office. Being within jurisdictional federations, the regional governmental units have their own well-defined policy sectors and operate quite autonomously from the central government. Of particular importance to this study, in both countries, the cantons/provinces are primarily responsible for policy affecting the construction industry and for the erection and maintenance of most public infrastructure. This is not to say that the Swiss and Canadian systems are identical. In comparing the two countries in the light of the two sectors at issue in this chapter, the Swiss system is the more centralized and hence is likely to give a greater incentive to stronger federal-level organizations than the Canadian one. The Swiss federal government has wider powers over commerce and over the regulation of food and drugs than its Canadian counterpart.[19] In addition, article 32 of the federal constitution states that 'the appropriate economic organizations' are to be heard before federal laws are made.[20] As in West Germany, this notification procedure is a powerful stimulus to the development of strong associations at the federal level. Such a constitutional provision does not exist in Canada.

The data on internal structures of associations are drawn from an international comparative project on the associative action of business co-ordinated by Philippe Schmitter and Wolfgang Streeck.[21] The information for the four countries being studied in this chapter was collected in 1981 and 1982 by research teams in the respective countries and is based on intensive interviews with the associations as well as documentary materials supplied by them.

The Chemical Industry

The data on associations in the chemical industry do not cover all of its sub-sectors but are restricted to the important industrial chemicals and pharmaceuticals sub-sectors.[22] Both have industrial structures that favour unitary arrangements. They are characterized first of all by high product diversity.[23] Thousands of different chemicals are produced by large firms that are vertically integrated in the sense that they manufacture basic petrochemicals and inorganic chemicals, intermediate materials such as synthetic resins, and processed end materials. The high capital intensity of production and the importance of a large research and development capacity have favoured high concentration in the industry. In Britain, a single company, Imperial Chemical Industries, accounts for 35 per cent of the output alone.[24] The top four companies in Switzerland and Canada produce 69 per cent and 63 per cent of the output respectively.[25] The three West German giants, Bayer, BASF, and Hoechst, are responsible for 26 per cent of West Germany's output. They are also the three largest chemical firms in the world.[26] Firms producing industrial chemicals in the four countries export on the aggregate well over 50 per cent of their output. The same is true for the pharmaceuticals sector in all of the countries except Canada, where the industry exports only between 5 and 7 per cent of its

TABLE 1

Regional differentiation of business interest associations in the chemical industry

Association regional structure	Canada	Switzerland	West Germany	United Kingdom
Unitary	8	13	1	6
Unitary with regional sub-units	1	0	2	1
Unitary with regional (enhanced) sub-units	0	0	0	0
Federal	1	0	0	0
Confederal	0	0	0	0
Affiliate	0	0	0	0
Unaffiliated regional associations	0	0	0	0

output.[27] Large firm size and the orientation to international markets are characteristic of firms in these two sub-sectors and are conducive to nation-wide, unitary associations.

Generally speaking, government policies directed to the sub-sectors reinforce the tendency toward unitary structures. The industries are regu-lated, first of all, in order to protect both air and water environment against chemical wastes. In addition, governments regulate pharmaceuticals manu-facturers so as to ensure that drugs are safe, efficacious, and reasonably priced. With only slight exceptions, the powers to formulate these regulatory systems rest with the national, not the regional governments, in all four countries.[28] A third policy area, occupational health and safety, is a respons-ibility of national governments in all of the countries except Canada, where the provinces have jurisdiction. Finally, a state of overcapacity in the industrial chemicals industry world-wide has created an additional interest by national governments in the industry as rationalization plans have become increasingly necessary.

Table 1 categorizes the association structures in these sub-sectors in the four countries. As expected, the associations tend to the unitary pole of the contiuum. None of the Swiss associations is regionally differentiated. The two principal German associations, the peak Verband der Chemischen Industrie and the Bundesverband der Pharmazeutischen Industrie, do have regional sub-units. These sub-units' principal role is to maintain contact and liaison with politicians and officials at the Land level and nothing more.[29] The principal British association in the industry, the Chemical Industries Association, also has regional branches. These sub-units give a collective focus to regional concentrations of the British industry and provide a mechanism for aggregating demands and implementing the results when the CIA negotiates a national framework agreement with trade unions.[30]

The Canadian case departs furthest from the unitary pattern, with one association, the Canadian Fertilizer Institute, having a federal structure and the other, the Canadian Agricultural Chemcials Association, having regional sub-units. These departures appear to be linked to the fact that agriculture is a concurrent responsibility of the federal and provincial governments in Canada. Hence field personnel who advise farmers on the use of fertilizers and pesticides are normally employed by provincial governments. The associations have regional branches for dealing with provincial agriculture departments, which are important intermediaries with farmers. In addition, fertilizer production (unlike agricultural chemicals) takes place within regional markets, with regional-based farmers' co-operatives having a strong position in the industry in each region.[31] This fragmentation of the markets of the industry has given rise to the more autonomous provincial associations of fertilizer manufacturers.

The Construction Industry[32]

In contrast, the structural characteristics of the construction industry appear to favour regional differentiation within associations. Firms are overwhelmingly small, with close to 90 per cent employing fewer than twenty workers. These small firms operate within markets that are local in scope, seldom embracing more than a large metropolitan area or a small group of cities and towns near one another. Construction work draws on a variety of different trades and is highly labour intensive. As a consequence, unlike in chemicals, industrial concentration is much lower than in most manufacturing sectors. The only exception to this general pattern comes in civil engineering construction work – road building, bridge erection, pipeline laying, and the like – where firms tend to be larger, markets regional (in the case of Britain, national), and concentration levels higher. Generally speaking, however, one would expect associations to have viable local branches to serve members in their particular markets and to cultivate solidarity as a counter to the natural competitiveness and mutual suspicion in the sector.

Actions of governments affect association structures in this industry in two ways. First, governments may constitute the most important customer for the industry. In each of the four countries, governments account for about one-third of the work volume. Within the construction sector, governmental contracts can have a differential incidence, accounting for around 75 per cent of civil engineering work, about 40–50 per cent of non-residential building, and 10 per cent or less of residential building. This government 'business' is a further factor that works in favour of regional differentiation within associations. In Canada, the provinces have responsibility under the constitution for all works of a 'local nature,' and hence the provinces or their delegates, the municipalities, contract with the industry for the bulk of construction work. In West Germany and Switzerland, the constitutional responsibility of the Länder and the cantons respectively for administering and implementing policy makes those governments the prime focal points for the industry when it comes to government contracts. In the United Kingdom, local governments also are important contractors for construction work. The 'business' side then of relations with government, regardless of constitutional arrangements, creates important incentives for the establishment of autonomous, well-resourced regional units within construction associations.

Second, the content of public policies directed toward the industry will have a variable affect on regional differentiation among our four countries. The stimulus to the growth of autonomous regional associations is greatest in Canada. Industrial relations, including occupational safety policy, is primarily a provincial responsibility in Canada, and collective agreements, with only a tiny number of exceptions, are province-wide or even local in scope. In the other three countries, this policy area is dealt with by the national government, and collective bargaining takes place within a national framework. A second important policy area for the sector, vocational training, also has a differential impact on association structures. In the three federations, education is constitutionally a responsibility of the regional governments. In Canada and Switzerland, this responsibility has had the effect of making the provincial and cantonal governments the main policy actors in the field. However, in West Germany, using its overall responsibility for economic development, the federal government passed in 1969 a vocational training law (Berufsbildungsgesetz) which has had a muddying effect, as the two levels of government have sought means to share jurisdiction over the field.[33] In effect, associations are forced to be attentive to both levels of government in this policy area. In Britain, training has tended to be primarily a responsibility of the national government.

Table 2 summarizes the regional differentiation found within construction industry associations in the four countries. As is expected, associations are much more regionally differentiated in each of the countries than was found in the chemical industry. The several cases of unitary associations that occur in each country have some common origins. First, they represent (usually civil engineering) industries oriented to national or international markets: pipeline contractors (Canada and West Germany) and oil and chemical plant

TABLE 2

Regional differentiation of business interest associations in the construction industry

Association regional structure	Canada	Switzerland	West Germany	United Kingdom
Unitary	4	6	2	2
Unitary with regional sub-units	0	0	2	4
Unitary with regional (enhanced) sub-units	0	0	1	3
Federal	3	2	1	1
Confederal	1	0	4	0
Affiliate	0	0	0	0
Mixed (federal and affiliate)	0	0	0	1
Mixed (confederal and affiliate)	1	0	0	0
Unaffiliated regional associations	21	2	0	0

constructors and constructional steelwork (Switzerland and Britain).[34] Second, they are found in sub-sectors of the industry that are very specialized and sufficiently limited in the number of firms to preclude regional differentiation – oil-well drilling contractors in Canada, chemical damp-course manufacturers in Britain, scaffolding contractors in West Germany, and underground services contractors in Switzerland. Third, in West Germany and Switzerland, there are unitary associations organizing larger firms only.[35]

These cases aside, the tendency in each of the countries is for the most powerful construction associations to show considerable regional differentiation. In the United Kingdom, the largest association is the Building Employers Confederation. Representing the whole of the building industry, the BEC has both a federal structure, with ten autonomous units in England and Wales, and an affiliate relationship in Scotland.[36] The Scottish Building Employers Confederation is an independent, regional peak association, totally self-financing, that has affiliated to the BEC in order to establish a single wage-negotiating body for the whole of the British building industry. The particular characteristics of Scotland have also led to enhanced sub-units in associations for specialist sub-contractors and scaffolding contractors. These phenomena are related to the fact that Scotland has a separate 'sponsoring ministry' in the Scottish Office, a separate and distinct legal system, and a different system for house purchasing.[37]

In West Germany, the two largest and dominant associations in the industry, the Hauptverband der Deutschen Bauindustrie (HDB) and the Zentralverband des Deutschen Baugewerbes (ZDB), are confederations. The former represents larger firms, while the latter has as its members artisanal, usually smaller, firms. The central organization of the ZDB has authority over the regional association members on matters of policy. Some member associations of the ZDB do not have domains parallel to Land boundaries and exist primarily to provide solidarity goods and selective services to members in their local context. The HDB is a more complex case because the central organization is dominated in turn by the regional member association in Nordrhein-Westfalen. The other member associations of the HDB, however, are similar in function to those of the ZDB. Similar confederal structures are found in the associations representing roofing and garden, landscaping, and sports-field contractors. One West German association, representing demolition contractors, has a federal structure.

To a degree, the Swiss case is similar to the West German one in that the two pre-eminent associations, the Schweizerische Baumeisterverband (SBV) and the Schweizerische Zimmermeisterverband (SZV) (carpenters), are confederal. The cantonal associations in these two groups have less say over policy than the federal association. In distinction to the West German case, the linguistic division in Switzerland between French- and German-speaking cantons adds an extra degree of differentiation. In the woodworking and carpenters' sub-sector, the associations in the partly or completely French-speaking cantons belong not to the SZV but to their own higher-order association, the Fédération Romande des Maîtres-Charpentiers, Ebénistes, Menuisiers, Fabricants de Meubles et Parqueteurs (FRM).[38] The FRM itself has a confederal structure and is one of two regional construction associations that is unaffiliated to any national construction association.

The associations in Canada show the higheest degree of decentralization. The Canadian Construction Association (CCA), which is the largest in the industry, has a mixed structure. Provincial building associations and road-building associations in all provinces except Quebec have a confederal relationship with the CCA. The Quebec associations maintain only an affiliate relationship with the CCA. The Canadian case also contains three federal associations that represent housebuilders, roofers, and masonry contractors. The greater centralization in these three cases derives from federal-government involvement in the housing industry, particularly in the area of materials standards and building codes. Perhaps the most distinctive characteristic of the Canadian case in Table 2 is the existence of twenty-one unaffiliated regional associations, which come mainly from the province of Ontario. Whereas in each of the three other countries virtually all regional

construction associations are members of a national-level association, this is less true in Canada and suggests an additional consequence of a more decentralized federal structure.

The key phenomenon here is that of an integrated regional associational system: autonomous regional associations draw together to form their own regional peak association, which operates, in turn, independent of any national-level association. Such systems might develop within a given sector or across a variety of sectors. We would expect it to occur in those sectors where powers are sufficiently decentralized to favour the growth of several regional associations and of a significant regional bureaucracy dealing with the sector in the regional government. Within Canada, such a sectoral regional associational system has developed in the Ontario construction industry. The system is headed by a peak association, the Council of Ontario Contractors Associations, and includes within it seventeen of the unaffiliated regional associations listed in table 2. Somewhat less-developed sectoral associational systems are found in the other Canadian provinces. Such systems also exist in Switzerland, but not in the more centralized West German federation. However, the devolution of powers in the construction industry to the Scottish Office in Britain has been sufficient to favour the growth of a sectoral associational system in Scotland. There an organization called the Scottish Construction Industry Group, which brings together construction business associations, the design professions, and trade unions, is the peak grouping, and it is recognized as the spokesman for the industry in Scotland.

The devolution of power in Britain is much more restricted than is the case in Canada and Switzerland. In these jurisdictional federations, where decentralization affects a variety of sectors, an additional phenomenon not found in Britain or in West Germany occurs, regional intersectoral associational systems. In Switzerland, for example, in the canton of Zurich, the regional associations of the building contractors (SBV) and the carpenters (SZV), along with similar associations from other sectors, join cantonal intersectoral associations. These latter belong to the two national intersectoral peak associations – VORORT, representing industry (larger firms), and the Association of Small Businesses and Trades (Gewerbeverband). One finds then a miniaturized mirror image of the national-level associational system at the canton level. This type of broader regional associational system occurs most fully in Quebec among the Canadian provinces, through the peak association called the Conseil du Patronat du Québec, but also in British Columbia, under the auspices of the Business Council of British Columbia. However, unlike the Swiss case – and this probably reflects the greater decentralization in the Canadian system – these intersectoral associational systems are not mirror images of the national system. In fact, they are almost completely decoupled from the national system.

Conclusions

The relationship between constitutional structure and association structures is complex. There is no simple one-to-one relationship where one can say that unitary régimes have unitary associations and federal régimes have federal associations. Within any given régime type is found a variety of association types. Critical to understanding the relationship then is the interaction between the domain and hence the sector(s) that the association organizes and the policy stances and division of powers as they bear upon that domain. We have seen, for example, that in sectors where the division of powers is not a factor, (chemicals) associations assume similar structures, irrespective of the régime type. In fact, the variation in territorial differentiation among associations may be greater between sectors in the same country than it is between countries in the same sector. However, where policy responsibilities are divided in a sector, those countries that are more decentralized in this respect will have more decentralized associations. Further, there appears to be a critical point in régime decentralization. When decentralization passes this critical point in a sector, as it did in the construction industry in Canada, Switzerland, and the United Kingdom, integrated regional sectoral associational systems arise. When decentralization passes this point across a range of sectors, as it did in the jurisdictional federations of Canada and Switzerland, integrated regional intersectoral associational systems may develop.

This chapter has provided direct evidence not on the effectiveness of associations but only on a set of factors presumed to be related to effectiveness. The presumption here, drawing from the research surveyed at the beginning of this chapter, is that where interests vary by territory in an association's domain, the effective association will be the one that can differentiate itself sufficiently to take those variations into account and at the same time integrate its actions to produce a single meaningful stance on a policy issue. By this criterion, a unitary association may not be the most effective, if that unitary structure represses rather than gives voice to territorial interests. At the other end of the continuum, confederal or affiliate associations are likely to be less effective than federal ones or unitary ones with regional sub-units because of the obstacles they will experience to integrating varying points of view. Finally, the evidence does not allow us to say that federal associations are less effective than unitary ones with regional sub-units. In this respect we can only assume these structures to be equally conducive to effectiveness.

If these distinctions among categories of associations are granted, several further implications relevant to the effectiveness of associations may be drawn from the analysis in this chapter. The likelihood of effective associations in a country will vary by sector. The pressures toward decentralization were much greater in the construction industry than in the chemical industry, with the result being more associations with confederal or affiliate structures in the former than in the latter. Second, the more decentralized the régime structure in a sector, the more decentralized the associations, and hence the less effective they are likely to be. Within the construction industry, the Canadian associations were the most decentralized, thus likely to be the least effective, and this appeared to be the direct consequence of the greater decentralization of the Canadian federal system.

However, I have shown also that régime decentralization is a critical factor in the development of regional associational systems. The presence of such systems may, in fact, counter the weakened effectiveness of the individual associations belonging to that system. Hence the more decentralized constitutional arrangements found in jurisdictional as opposed to functional federations favour both the development of more autonomous, regional associations within national umbrella associations and integrated systems of these regional associations within the region. An integrated regional system may, in fact, be a very effective entity when it interacts with regional governments. Certainly what preliminary evidence exists suggests that the Coucil of Ontario Contractors Associations, the Scottish Building Employers Group, and their cantonal siblings in Switzerland have been very successful within their regional jurisdictions. At the same time, they may constitute very formidable obstacles to the development of a national consensus in a sector or across all sectors. Assessments of association effectiveness in federal systems have taken no account of such regional associational systems to date. This lacuna will need to be filled in future research on the problems of association effectiveness in federal systems.

NOTES

1 David B. Truman *The Governmental Process* (New York: Knopf 1951) 112ff
2 Helen J. Dawson 'National Pressure Groups and the Federal Government' in A.P. Pross ed *Pressure Group Politics in Canada* (Toronto: McGraw-Hill 1975) 29–58; M. Schwartz 'The Group Basis of Politics' in J.H. Redekop ed

Approaches to Canadian Politics (Scarborough: Prentice-Hall 1978) 323–46; Graham K. Wilson 'Why Is There No Corporatism in the United States?' in G. Lehmbruch and P.C. Schmitter eds *Patterns of Corporatist Policy-Making* (Beverly Hills: Sage, 1982) 224

3 Dawson 'National' 31

4 Richard Schultz *Federalism, Bureaucracy and Public Policy: The Politics of Highway Transport Regulation* (Montreal: McGill-Queen's University Press 1980) especially chap 8

5 David Kwavnick 'Interest Group Demands and the Federal Political System' in Pross ed *Pressure Group Politics* 70–86

6 Richard Simeon *Federal-Provincial Diplomacy* (Toronto: University of Toronto Press 1972) 144

7 Discussed in Schultz *Federalism* 148

8 Ibid passim

9 M.W. Bucovetsky 'The Mining Industry and the Great Tax Reform Debate' in Pross ed *Pressure Group Politics* 89–114

10 W. Streeck 'Die Reform der beruflichen Bildung in der westdeutschen Bauwirtschaft 1969–1982. Eine Fallstudie über Verbände als Träger öffentlicher Politik,' Discussion Paper IIM/LMP 83–23 (Berlin: Wissenschaftszentrum Berlin 1983)

11 W. Coleman and Wyn Grant 'Regional Differentiation of Business Interest Associations: A Comparison of Canada and the United Kingdom' *Canadian Journal of Political Science* 17 no 1 (1985) 3–29

12 Ibid 6–7

13 Stein Rokkan and Derek Urwin *Economy, Territory, Identity: Politics of West European Peripheries* (London: Sage 1983)

14 Ibid 181

15 Coleman and Grant 'Regional Differentiation' 33–4

16 Nevil Johnson *Government in the Federal Republic of Germany: The Executive at Work* (New York: Pergamon Press 1973) 105

17 Ibid 86

18 B. Reissert and G.F. Schäfer 'Intergovernmental Relations in the Federal Republic of Germany' in Y. Mény and V. Wright ed *Centre-Periphery Relations in Western Europe* (London: Sage 1984) 4

19 G.A. Codding *The Federal Government of Switzerland* (Boston: Houghton Mifflin 1965) 43

20 Jürg Steiner *Amicable Agreement versus Majority Rule: Conflict Resolution in Switzerland* (Chapel Hill, NC: University of North Carolina Press 1974) 110

21 The research design from which the nine country teams worked was published. See P.C. Schmitter and W. Streeck, 'The Organization of Business Interests,' Discussion Paper IIM/LMP 81–13 (Berlin: Wissenschaftszentrum Berlin 1981). The variables are described in the appendices to the design.

186/William D. Coleman

22 Because of the large number of associations in the British and West German chemical industries, only a sample of groups was studied in each case. The universe was studied in the Swiss and Canadian cases. The same procedure was adopted for the construction sector discussed below.

23 Thomas L. Ilgen '"Better Living through Chemistry": The Chemical Industry in the World Economy' *International Organization* 37 no 4 (1983) 649

24 Wyn Grant 'The Organization of Business Interests in the UK Chemical Industry,' Discussion Paper IIM/LMP 83-3 (Berlin: Wissenschaftszentrum Berlin 1983) 3

25 Statistics Canada *Industrial Organization and Concentration in the Manufacturing, Mining and Logging Establishments in Canada* (Ottawa: Statistics Canada 1979); the Swiss figures are based on the annual reports of Ciba Geigy, Hoffman La Roche, Sandez, Lonza, and Merck and were supplied to the author by Hanspeter Kriesi, the director of the Swiss team in the project.

26 M. Groser 'Die Organisation von Wirtschaftsinteressen in der chemischen Industrie der Bundesrepublik Deutschland,' Ms Berlin 1983, 14

27 Figure calculated by the author using data furnished privately by Statistics Canada

28 The Canadian provinces have some jurisdiction over environmental matters. The German Länder have become quite important in this area; they have moved to administer environmental legislation.

29 Groser 'Die Organisation' 77-8

30 Coleman and Grant 'Regional Differentiation' 15-16

31 Canada, Department of Industry, Trade and Commerce 'The Canadian Fertilizer Industry,' Sector Profile Discussion Paper (Ottawa: Department of Industry, Trade and Commerce 1978)

32 Not all the construction industry was covered in the research project. Only associations in the non-residential building, residential building, and civil engineering sectors were studied. This choice leaves aside the installation of fittings and fixtures and building completion work. In a general sense, this section of the chapter draws on three larger reports in the international project: W. Coleman 'The Political Organization of Business Interests in the Canadian Construction Industry,' Discussion Paper IIM/LMP 84-11 (Berlin: Wissenschaftszentrum Berlin 1984); Wyn Grant 'The Organization of Business Interests in the UK Construction Industry,' Discussion Paper IIM/LMP 83-25 (Berlin: Wissenschaftszentrum Berlin 1983); and Hanspeter Kriesi and Roland Schaller, *Wirtschafts verbaende im Schweizer Bauhauptgewerbe* (Zürich: Soziologisches Institut der Universität Zürich 1984). In addition, my treatment of the West German case has profited from discussion of it with Wolfgang Streeck.

33 For further discussion, see Streeck 'Die Reform der beruflichen Bildung.'

34 Other examples following the same logic are the Federation of Civil Engineering

Contractors in Britain, road builders in Switzerland, and manufacturers of prefabricated houses in West Germany.

35 Thus in West Germany, there is an association that organizes only middle-sized firms (Bundesvereinigung Mittelständischer Bauunternehmen) and one in Switzerland for large firms. Two Canadian associations with unitary structures exist specifically for federal-provincial co-ordination: Construction Specifications Canada and the Roads and Transportation Association of Canada. For details, see Coleman 'Canadian Construction Industry.'

36 Coleman and Grant 'Regional Differentiation'

37 Ibid

38 To add further complication, the carpenters association in the canton of Vaud belongs to both the FRM and the SZV.

11 / Federalism and Agricultural Policy

GRACE SKOGSTAD

The agricultural industries in Canada and the United States have evolved in an analogous fashion. Both are capital-intensive and technologically advanced and, particularly since the early 1970s, have faced similar problems. Canadian and American farmers, and consequently their governments, have attempted to come to grips with the altered international and domestic economic situation in the 1970s and 1980s: a growing export demand for grains from 1973 to the end of the decade, considerable instability in prices and costs owing to uncertain markets and supplies, and in the 1980s slow growth in world demand and a decline in the price of traded agricultural goods. Given these similarities, it is perhaps not surprising to discover that Canadian and American agricultural policies are remarkably similar substantively. However, the agricultural policy-making process in the two countries is markedly different, reflecting the effect of institutional differences between Canada and the United States.

Differences in the way in which power is organized within the national and regional governments[1] have affected each country's policy process and the role of producer groups in shaping agricultural policy. These institutional differences include the weak Canadian parliamentary committees versus the autonomous US congressional committees, tight party discipline in Canada in contrast to weak party solidarity in the United States, and executive dominance of policy-making in Canada versus the dispersion of policy-making authority in the United States. These disparate institutional contexts, in conjunction with jurisdictional and constitutional factors, have resulted in major differences in the relative strength and legitimacy of the central and local governments in the two federal systems. The cumulative impact of the American institutional framework has been to produce a system of effective intrastate federalism, wherein the interests of specialist regional groups are heeded. In Canada interstate federalism is stronger, and the joint effect of the federal, parliamentary, and party systems on regional producer groups has been less uniform – creating opportunities for some, raising obstacles for others.

In both Canada and the United States, the national government predominates in agricultural policy. Despite the fact that provinces enjoy concurrent jurisdiction, they have almost unanimously urged the Canadian government to use its larger purse to assume the greater financial responsibility for agriculture. Provinces have left to Agriculture Canada the major responsibility for providing producers with low-cost credit, capital assistance, and commodity price support, for funding research to enhance agriculture's productivity, and for establishing and regulating quality control in production and marketing. The result has been that since 1951 federal expenditures for agriculture have been about double those of the provinces.[2] While Agriculture Canada delivers many of its programs directly to Canadian farmers and other recipients, some nationally funded programs are developed in co-operation with provincial officials and administered by them. Two major examples are the shared-cost crop insurance plan and the regional development projects individually tailored to each province's needs. Here and in several other areas, provincial and federal officials work closely to administer programs, funded in the largest measure by the national government.[3] The continuous bureaucratic interaction is supplemented by consultation at the level of first ministers, institutionalized in their annual meeting.

The US government's dominance in agriculture is even greater, not being jurisdictionally limited. Beginning in the nineteenth century, but especially following initiation of price support programs in the depression-ridden 1930s, the US Department of Agriculture has been virtually exclusively responsible for formulating and financing agricultural programs. While state governments play a co-operative role in assisting to implement and administer federal programs, they enjoy nothing like the active and equal partnership in agricultural policy-making that provincial governments exercise in some aspects of Canadian agricultural policy. Even in the administration of their programs, the federal agencies have tended to bypass state authorities, and decentralized federal bureaus work directly with producers to implement programs.[4]

To what extent are the differing roles of provincial and state governments in agricultural policy-making manifestations of the alternative evolution of federalism in the two countries? The Canadian federal system, it is persuasively argued, has evolved in the direction of interstate federalism,[5] while the American system approximates intrastate federalism. In interstate federalism, the collective interests of citizens in the regions ('regional interests') are represented primarily by the governments of the constituent units, intergovernmental conflict is pervasive, and regional conflicts are resolved by intergovernmental negotiations and bargaining. By contrast, in intrastate federalism, regional interests are represented and regional conflicts are resolved within the national decision-making structures. In the United States, Congress is seen to be the linchpin by Gibbins: 'It is the congressional party system that gives members the independence to stand up for territorial interests, but it is the very complex congressional committee system ... that gives members the *strength* to effectively do so, by conferring significant power and influence on virtually all members of the House and Senate.'[6] The result, says Esman, is that 'most regional interest groups can be assured of a hearing in Washington in one or several congressional or executive branch forums.'[7]

As Canadian provincial governments have become more active and economically and politically stronger in the last two decades, they and the federal government have become locked in seemingly countless political struggles. 'Federal-provincial competition,' says Alan Cairns, 'is not abnormal, or sporadic. It is frequent and widespread.'[8] Few would disagree with Cairns's description of the pervasiveness of intergovernmental conflict in Canada, but there is a difference in the relative emphasis that different scholars place upon the roots of this conflict and on the motives behind the provincial activism and aggressiveness that have heightened conflict of late. For Cairns, intergovernmental conflict is largely the result of institution-building at both levels of government.[9] Behind the desire of bureaucrats and politicians 'to enlarge the scope of their functions'[10] and to extend 'their tentacles of control, regulation, manipulation into society,'[11] are motives of electoral self-interest and personal aggrandizement. With politicians at both levels endeavouring to augment their own personal and their government's economic and political power, they have sought to bring more policy areas under their authority and launched 'pre-emptive strikes' into policy fields when the other level is inactive.[12]

Cairns acknowledges but does not stress Donald Smiley's view that provincial policy activism has come about because provinces are engaged in long-run economic development projects and come into conflict with other governments whose policies and actions have spillover effects that impede the successful execution of their own projects.[13] Garth Stevenson places greatest stress on the clash of economic goals, arguing that federal-provincial conflict is rooted in the political economy of Canada.[14] The existence of regional economies, says Stevenson, 'increases the probability that a particular sector of the economy will be largely concentrated in one province and will exercise significant economic and political power within the province.'[15] As the provincial government responds to that dominant economic group, by formulating policies to advance its interests, it is likely to come into conflict with other provinces and, indeed, with the national government, which oppose provincial economic nationalism as contrary to the national economic interest in unrestricted interprovincial trade and economic interdependence across provincial borders.[16]

Richard Simeon's view of the sources of intergovernmental tensions is closer to Cairns than to Stevenson. Simeon plays down the reality of regional interests, including economic ones, and suggests that politicians define non-regional issues as regional issues because it serves their political goals and because the federal system facilitates such a definition.[17] On the latter, virtually all scholars are in agreement and point to the territorial division of jurisdictional authority in the Canadian political system as a factor that in itself has contributed to provincial policy activism and in turn to interstate federalism and federal-provincial conflict. The emergence of provincial governments as 'the almost exclusive vehicles for the representation of their area's interests'[18] owes much to the failure of the national government to demonstrate that it can articulate and accommodate the diverse goals of people in all regions of the country. The reasons for this weak intrastate federalism are many and include the workings of the electoral system, executive dominance of policy-making, and rigid party discipline. Regional interests that do not receive a hearing in central government institutions have turned to provincial governments, which have by default assumed the representational task.

The inquiry here attempts to determine which of these many themes are substantiated in the instance of agricultural policy in the two countries. Canadian agricultural policy is examined first. A brief historical review, followed by an examination of the most significant themes in Canadian agricultural policy in the past decade, demonstrates that while intergovernmental controversy is certainly no stranger to agricultural policy-making, its nature and intensity are not entirely what federalism scholars suggest. First, federal-provincial conflict less often arises over a struggle to exercise jurisdication than it does over an attempt to avoid it. Second, interprovincial and interregional conflicts are as frequent as federal-provincial struggles and probably an even greater barrier to policy co-ordination. And third, harmony, not tensions, best characterizes government, especially bureaucratic relations. In terms of the debate as to the origins of interprovincial and federal-provincial conflicts, the evidence tends to support Stevenson's veiw that intergovernmental conflicts are often rooted in disparate economic and ideological goals. The subsequent examination of agricultural policies and policy-making in the United States does confirm the appropriateness of the label of effective intrastate federalism to describe that system.

Canada to 1970:
National Predominance, Differentiated Governmental Roles

The federal government's traditional predominance in agricultural policy dates from the National Policy of 1879. Populating western Canada and promoting the western wheat economy confirmed Canada's hegemony over the region and provided a market for central Canadian industrial goods. Governments responded to prairie farmers' petitions for regulation of the inequitably high railway freight rates and monopoly control in the transportation and grain-marketing system 'in order to encourage the further development of the great grain growing provinces of the west, on which development of the future of Canada in a large measure depends.'[19] In regulating the handling, rate structure, and sale of grain in interprovincial and export markets, the federal government used the full scope of its jurisdictional authority. Section 92.10(c) of the constitution allowed it to bring 'works' – such as local railway lines or grain elevators – under federal authority, simply by declaring them to be 'for the general advantage' of Canada. In addition, section 92.10(a) and (b), in conjunction with the 'Trade and Commerce' power in section 91.2, gave the federal government the authority to regulate interprovincial transportation. Sir John A. Macdonald's Conservative government (1867–73, 1878–91) repeatedly used the federal power of disallowance to prevent provincial governments from usurping its monopoly of transportation.

The two most significant policies to emerge from the concerted lobbying by producers and prairie governments were preferential freight rates for grains and flour (the Crow's Nest rates, 1897) and a compulsory export grain marketing board (the Canadian Wheat Board, 1935). Subsequent attempts by federal governments, private grain traders, and railways to dismantle these structures were resisted by a combination of fortuitous circumstances, which included the political vulnerability of the national government, the severe economic dislocation of the 1930s, and the presence of prairie spokesmen in the federal cabinet.[20] Orderly grain marketing persisted, and the Crow's Nest rates remained intact until 1984 in spite of, rather than because of, a philosophical commitment to both by Ottawa.[21]

Like prairie grain farmers, producers of other commodities also turned to government to protect them from the perceived injustices of the marketing system. At the height of their distress, in the Depression, two major instruments were used to assist producers to cope with the chronic problems of low and unstable incomes: price and/or income stabilization programs and regulated marketing structures. The federal price support and income maintenance programs were continued and made permanent and mandatory by John Diefenbaker's government (1957–63) with the passage of the Agricultural Stabilization Act in 1958. Orderly marketing was the other major device used to enhance farmers' bargaining power in the market-place. Before 1972 it was the one important policy area where the federal jurisdictional arm did not reach and where provincial legislation was significant. Judicial rulings in 1937 denied the central government the unilateral authority to empower producers directly to create compulsory marketing boards that could effectively regulate marketing on a national basis.[22] Thereafter, most provincial governments delegated their legal authority over the regulation of local marketing and production so as to enable producer boards to operate on a province-wide basis. The federal government co-operated with provincial marketing boards, passing the Agricultural Products Marketing Act in 1949, thereby enabling them to extend their existing powers into extraprovincial and export marketing. In 1957 it amended this act to allow the delegation to provincial boards of federal authority to raise levies and so allowed these boards to circumvent a judicial ruling that threatened their economic viability and existence.[23]

The 1960s was a decade of transition in which the differentiation of federal and provincial roles began to disappear. The intergovernmental co-operation displayed in regulated marketing became evident in other programs. The two levels co-operated in crop insurance and regional economic development projects (the Agricultural Rehabilitation and Development Act and the Fund for Regional Economic Development). The administration of each was decentralized and largely in the hands of provincial officials. And finally, provincial agricultural colleges and schools continued to disseminate to producers the results of the extensive research activities of the federal Department of Agriculture.

In summarizing the impact of the federal system on agricultural policy in the pre-1970 period, a number of points may be made. First, the federal government tended to assume the major responsibility for agriculture and to incur the bulk of expenses associated with that responsibility. Not only did provincial governments accept federal paramountcy, they often lobbied for it. They did so on the grounds that the national government enjoyed the exclusive or effective legal authority to act, possessed the financial resources to cope with the problem, and/or was morally obligated to act on behalf of an industry of national importance. Second, provincial programs relating to production, marketing, and education and extension tended not to overlap with federal schemes. And third, the intergovernmental discord that surfaced tended to centre on provincial complaints about the federal government's failure to assume even more responsibility for such things as shielding producers from unstable and low incomes and seeking out export markets.

Canada since 1970: Concurrent Jurisdiction

The federal system had a changing effect on agricultural policy and policy-making in the 1970s as some provinces exercised more fully their concurrent jurisdiction for agriculture and their control over intraprovincial production and marketing. The record of joint provincial and federal legislative and regulatory activity with respect to agriculture has been mixed. In some areas policy co-ordination has been achieved; elsewhere, independent and unco-ordinated programs coexist.

Unco-ordinated Policy-Making: Commodity Stabilization

Federal predominance in agricultural commodity stabilization gave way to joint occupancy of this policy area as first British Columbia (1973), then Quebec (1975) and Ontario (1976), implemented comprehensive commodity stabilization programs and other provinces stabilized selected commodities. They did so primary for economic reasons – to repair the damage to their local economies wrought by the inability of federal programs to shield producers from the market instability and cost-price squeeze of the early 1970s. Already familiar with the problem in the 1960s, in the early 1970s farmers faced mounting costs for their supplies while simultaneously experiencing rapidly fluctuating and uncertain market prices. When combined provincial and producer lobbying failed to persuade the national government to broaden its commodity support, a few provincial governments took action. The entry of some but not all provinces into commodity stabilization raised fears about the economic repercussions of these unco-ordinated programs. Unlike the federal Agricultural Stabilization Act, the provincial programs of British Columbia, Ontario, and Quebec tried to stabilize producer incomes rather than commodity prices. The federal price stabilization program attempts to reduce producer losses during years of low prices by assuring the producer a minimum price for a given commodity. A typical program would guarantee the farmer a proportion of the average market price of the commodity over the previous five or ten years (for example, 90 per cent of the previous ten-year average). By contrast, income stabilization programs, such as those of British Columbia, Ontario, and Quebec, recognize that producer incomes fluctuate as a result of variations not only in commodity prices (the focus of price stabilization programs) but, as well, in the cost of purchased inputs such as labour, fuel, machinery, land, and feed. Hence, such a program tries to guarantee the farmer that his net income in a given year will not fall (because of higher costs, lower market prices, or both) below a certain proportion of what it has averaged in previous years.

The example of the provincial schemes, combined with pressure from producers in provinces where governments were reluctant to, or financially incapable of, instituting income maintenance plans, led the federal government to modify its own stabilization program to make it more analogous to provincial schemes. But the changes did not allay concern in Ottawa and some of the provinces that the significant differences in provincial programs were upsetting natural market forces and creating distortions in the national agricultural economy. The fear that the overall efficiency of Canadian agriculture would be eroded, combined with the fact that some commodities remained outside the umbrella of mandatory federal support, led to talks aimed at harmonizing federal and provincial plans. Initiated in 1977, the discussions bogged down in 1978 and then again in 1980. Renewed efforts by the producers and governments of Saskatchewan, Ontario, and Alberta in 1981 to procure a provincial-federal-producer agreement to deal with the crisis in the red meat sector likewise resulted in deadlock in 1983. British Columbia and Quebec remained unwilling to comply with the federal government's condition that provinces abandon the right to 'top-load' – to subsidize local producers when they enjoy mandatory support under a federal program. In this sense the impasse was a federal-provincial one, since Agriculture Minister Eugene Whelan refused to negotiate unless Ottawa was assured a paramount role. But the provinces were in discord and unable to mount a united front. Nor has the greater flexibility in the stabilization bill passed in June 1985 by the national Conservative government, which gives provinces five years to phase out their stabilization programs and makes their producers eligible for a joint provincial-federal-producer program in the interim if they agree to do so, sufficed to resolve the issue. While the prairie provinces and Ontario tend to agree with the principle of federal paramountcy in income stabilization as a way to ensure their comparative advantage in red meat production, producers in Quebec, British Columbia, and the Maritimes oppose it, since their competitiveness is contingent upon subsidization. They refuse to terminate their own programs to make their producers eligible for the tripartite program. Thus the competing economic interests of their producers have constrained provinces' capacity to abdicate their authority and thereby to harmonize their stabilization schemes.

Co-ordinated Policy-Making: National Supply Management

Since the early 1970s, beginning first with Quebec and Ontario, and by 1 April 1974 encompassing all the provinces, federal and provincial governments have co-operated to establish a national dairy program that includes supply management and federal price support measures. In the poultry sector the same provincial and federal co-ordination has occurred; three national agencies (the Canadian egg, chicken, and turkey marketing agencies) regulate the national production and marketing of eggs, chickens, and turkeys. Institutional mechanisms ensure the smooth operation of national supply management plans. In the dairy industry, the Canadian Milk Supply Management Committee brings together representatives of provincial milk boards to advise the federal Canadian Dairy Commission on dairy policy, including such crucial matters as provincial market shares and federal subsidy levels. In the poultry sector, annual marketing seminars draw together the chairmen and/or representatives of provincial and national marketing councils (which supervise the boards). Co-ordination is largely the work of bureaucratic officials, but should major differences and difficulties occur, conferences of agricultural ministers will be called to allow for the airing of grievances.[24]

The national dairy and poultry marketing agencies are good examples of how federal and provincial co-operation can overcome jurisdictional hurdles posed by the Canadian federal system. In the poultry sector, a federal-provincial agreement provides for the mutual delegation of governmental marketing authority to the producer-controlled agency and for provincial sharing of the national market for the regulated commodity. As noted previously, co-operation is necessary because of the division of jurisdiction for marketing in the Canadian federal system. Provinces cannot legally prevent other provinces' commodities from moving into their province and so are unable to avoid out-of-province dumping that could cause local farm prices to drop. It is only the federal government that can regulate the movement of commodities from province to province. The federal-provincial agreement is a contractual arrangement among the provinces to establish terms for the interprovincial movement of the agricultural commodity.

The bargaining over provincial market shares demonstrates one of the chief limits of co-operative federalism in agricultural policy: interprovincial competition. A national marketing plan requires that provinces share the national market (demand) for the regulated commodity. Sharing does not come easy to all or indeed any province, since producers and their provincial governments not unnaturally prefer to preserve the local market for local producers and are also seeking to expand their share of the national market. Provincial protectionism of this sort delayed the creation of the national broiler marketing agency and has to date prevented formation of an Eastern Canada Regional Potato Agency. In the three poultry agencies already in place, provincial representatives on the national agencies have found it virtually impossible to agree to shares of growth in the national market. This conflict is severe enough to threaten the very existence of the national agencies. It is reminiscent of the interprovincial competition in commodity stabilization, where one province's measures to offset a disadvantage for local producers damage the comparative advantage of another province's farmers.[25]

Their exercise of concurrent jurisdiction has given provinces considerable input into federal agricultural policy and tended to minimize federal-provincial governmental conflict. One major reason why shared jurisdiction has not led to combative intergovernmental relations has undoubtedly been the fact that governments at both levels are largely pursuing similar agricultural goals. While they quibble about the best means to realize these goals, they share with varying degrees of enthusiasm two beliefs: that the government has a role to play in protecting farmers from the vagaries of the market-place and assisting them to realize more stable and more adequate incomes, and that, while doing so, governments should not interfere unduly with farmers' freedom of decision-making on the farm. This unanimity of perspective unites governments behind producer marketing boards; such boards shield producers from a market-place that is unpredictable and often unfair and do so without government interference in farmers' daily business.

With the creation of producer-operated marketing boards, governments have removed themselves directly from the affairs of marketing and so lessened the opportunities for intergovernmental conflict. Instead of divided jurisdiction in marketing exacerbating intergovernmental tensions, as Richard Schultz predicts is likely when federal and provincial regulatory agencies have responsibility for different aspects of an economic activity,[26] co-operation and co-ordination have been forced on governments if they are to accede to producers' goals of supply management. For provincial governments relinquishing authority to national agencies (the Canadian Dairy Commission, the national poultry agencies) is eased by provincial representation and influence on these agencies.

Nonetheless, disagreements do arise between authorities in the different capitals. Such disputes are usually rooted in the different contexts, constraints, and influences on the policy-makers and approximate Stevenson's description of clashes of economic provincialism and economic nationalism. While federal agricultural policy is shaped within a national and international context, provincial agricultural positions bear the impact of narrower, local economic and political interests. The current disagreement over provincial top-loading in stabilization can be viewed as a conflict between Ottawa's definition of how best to serve the national interest and provincial governments' view that the national interest is best promoted by furthering the interests of all the individual regions. For Agriculture Canada, serving the national interest means meeting the concerns of producers in every region for a fair share of Canadian agricultural production, as well as serving consumers' wish for low-cost food. Moreover, the federal obligation to the nation as a whole to sell products abroad prohibits it from sanctioning income support plans that give Canadian producers unfair subsidization and invite other nations, especially the United States, to retaliate with their own protectionist measures.

For their part, provincial governments, being geographically closer to their producers, see and hear producers' problems at first hand. Whereas the federal government may feel that the 'fairest' response to producers' economic distress is to let the market decide, social, economic, and political imperatives may deny provincial governments the luxury of a 'hands-off' approach. Particularly in the major agricultural provinces, a provincial government's economic well-being, and consequently its political livelihood, may suffer if producers' problems are not addressed. Such economic and political calculations led provincial governments to enter the policy void created by an inadequate federal response, first, to the cost-price squeeze in the early 1970s and then, in the early 1980s, to bankruptcy problems for producers resulting from high interest rates and reduced producer incomes. Once having committed themselves to assisting producers, governments like those of British Columbia and Quebec find that the undesirable political and economic consequences of withdrawing support make them reluctant to abandon their producers to a less supportive federal proposal.

In conclusion, the examples of commodity stabilization and regulated marketing show that some agricultural policy-making approximates inter-state federalism. But contrary to Cairns's depiction of the situation in other policy areas, most provincial governments have not actively sought to compete with the federal government by encroaching on federal policy territory and rivalling federal agricultural programs with their own equally or more attractive policies. Rather than showing a desire to supplant the paramount federal role in agriculture, provinces have almost unanimously urged greater federal responsibility for agricultural matters and tried to avoid undertaking costly expenditure commitments themselves.[27] Only when they have believed that they had no alternative but to respond to pressure from producers to shore up incomes and stabilize the province's agricultural economy have they moved to fill the policy vacuum created by the federal failure to address compelling problems. The possible exception to this pattern is the Parti québécois government: its policies to enhance the productivity and diversification of Quebec agriculture can be properly regarded as 'province-building' projects, designed to promote Quebec's self-sufficiency in foodstuffs as a step on the road to sovereignty-association.[28] However, the Liberal government which replaced the Parti québécois in December 1985 seems determined to practise fiscal restraint, and the province-building approach to agriculture, which imposed a severe drain on the provincial treasury, is likely to wind down.

Canada: Weak Instrastate Federalism

The characterization of contemporary Canadian federalism as weak intrastate federalism has previously been noted. It remains to test the appropriateness of this description with respect to agricultural matters. Has the national government lost the capacity to represent and seek a balance among regional agricultural interests? And, if so, have provincial governments stepped into the breach? The test case examined here is the national government's resolution of the problems confronting the western grain transportation system in the 1970s and 1980s.

As early as the 1960s, the railways had sought removal of the Crow's Nest freight rates, the rates at which prairie grain moved out of the prairie region to terminal ports. The impetus for change became particularly acute after 1973, when export demand for grain greatly increased and it became clear that the existing facilities for handling and transporting grain were inadequate to cope with the increased traffic. The federal government, convinced by the railways that the latter would have the incentive to move larger volumes of grain more quickly only if they were compensated for the full cost of moving grain, began the task of persuading prairie farmers that the Crow rates, which had remained unaltered since 1925 and hence were not covering the railways' full costs, were the root cause of the problem and must be abandoned. It met with a wall of resistance in western Canada. Not all prairie farmers accepted the argument of the railways and the federal government that the Crow rates were responsible for the deterioration of the transport infrastructure. Even those who did were divided as to who

- the railways, the federal government, or the shippers - should bear the financial burden of the cost of upgrading grain-handling and transportation facilities and higher freight rates.

A major cleavage arose between the livestock sector (predominant in Alberta) and export grain producers (the largest sector of Saskatchewan's economy) as evidence mounted that the low Crow rates discriminated against the former in favour of the latter and were impeding the expansion and diversification of Alberta's economy.[29] In an effort to appease the vociferous opponents of change, the federal government drew agricultural groups into the policy process, commissioning first Emmett Hall (1975-7) and later Clay Gilson (1982) to solicit the views of western producers as to the appropriate railway system and freight rate structure to replace the Crow rate. Still later, in the summer of 1983, it gave agricultural groups and provincial governments a final opportunity to appear before House of Commons Transport Committee hearings in western and central Canada. Intensive lobbying by grain producers led the federal government to soften the blow of higher producer freight costs with government subsidies. But the livestock and grain producers remained at odds over who should receive the federal payment, with livestock producers preferring producer payments, on the grounds that they would immediately lower grain prices on the prairies and so benefit themselves as consumers of feed grains, and the grain growers wanting payments to go to railways. With their livestock and grain producers divided, the Conservative provincial governments attempted to stay out of the limelight and especially tried to avoid taking a public stand on the method of payment of the federal subsidy. Even the New Democratic Party governments in Saskatchewan and Manitoba, although loudly opposed to the elimination of Crow rates, found themselves unable to make claims of representing their entire provincial constituencies, as prairie farm groups became internally divided over what policy and tactics they should take in the debate. The absence of a regional consensus ruled out a co-ordinated and united stand by prairie premiers and prairie agricultural and transport ministers and left each province to pursue independent and often antagonistic strategies.

The disunity of the western agricultural community was in stark contrast to the unity of Quebec's agricultural interests. Quebec farmers opposed payments to producers, fearing that they would lower grain prices on the prairies and thereby give prairie livestock, egg, and dairy competitors the advantage of lower feed costs and hence a less costly final product. Their cause was championed by the 74 Quebeckers in the federal Liberal caucus. The 1 February 1983 proposal of federal Transport Minister Jean-Luc Pepin to replace the Crow rate with federal subsidies to be split equally between the railways and the farmers was reversed three months later as a result of combined pressure by the Quebec caucus and the prairie wheat pools. Intensive lobbying before the Transport Committee by cattlemen and the Alberta government, and filibustering by Conservative MPs on the floor of the House of Commons, succeeded in procuring an amendment to establish a committee to begin an immediate review of the method of payment. This amendment notwithstanding, the passage of the Western Grain Transportation Act and its replacement of the Crow rates with higher producer freight bills and government subsidies to railways left prairie cattlemen, prairie provincial governments, and large numbers of grain producers angry and bitter at the change wrought by a national government lacking representation west of Winnipeg.

The discord surrounding changes in grain transportation policy tends to confirm the ineffectiveness of national political institutions in accommodating all territorial interests. The pessimistic conclusion of analysts of the Canadian system – that groups and regions without representation at the national level will be shortchanged on policy – seems warranted. To its credit, the federal Liberal government tried to overcome the liability of no elected prairie members in its caucus by providing opportunities for unrepresented interests to appear before royal commissions and Transport Committee hearings in the region. But the final policy outcome demonstrated that provinces and groups with representation inside the government caucus, especially Quebec interests, inevitably fared better than those without advocates. The federal Liberal government left many westerners with the impression that serving the national interest was nothing more than serving the Liberal party's partisan interest of keeping onside the region most electorally significant to it. As with the experience of Lower Inventories for Tomorrow (1971) and C.D. Howe's grain policies, 'Westerners concluded that the public interest (for which they read central Canada's) and their own conflicted and that the federal government, at least when the Liberal party was in power, invariably was the servant of one and not the other.'[30]

For its part, the House of Commons proved somewhat more effective as a forum of intrastate federalism, as filibustering by opposition MPs resulted in a number of amendments to the Western Grain Transportation bill of symbolic and money-saving importance to grain farmers. But opposition parties, too, were handicapped by the diversity of interests in western Canada and faced the same real difficulty as the government in finding a compromise that all groups could live with.

The grain marketing experience suggests that when the federal government is untrammelled by the need to appease premiers and free to pursue its own partisan interests, it will do so. This indictment may not be wholly fair. The issue of freight rate reform may be too severe a test of the capacity of national institutions to accommodate regional interests and resolve territorial conflict. The high economic and symbolic stakes of change, plus the lack of regional consensus, made the issue particularly divisive. The fact that the positions of provincial governments and their producers are rooted in considerations of economic self-interest has stymied efforts of the national Conservative government since 1984 to persuade parties to compromise on the method of payment of the Crow benefit subsidy. Nevertheless, it is useful to ask whether the degree of controversy would have been less and the resolution of the issue more palatable to western Canada had Ottawa and the provinces shared jurisdiction. The question takes us to the effectiveness of provincial governments not only in representing producers within their provinces but also in finding compromises that lessen intersectoral and interprovincial conflict.

On the issue of western grain transportation, and in other matters, provincial governments have attempted to perform the role of territorial representation. When they share the philosophical view of a commodity group of considerable significance to the provincial economy, they have been most likely to depict themselves as the lone defenders of local producers before a federal government preoccupied with serving antagonistic groups. For example, Allan Blakeney and the Saskatchewan New Democratic Party not only made opposition to federal freight rate change the dominant theme of their 1982 election campaign but also depicted the issue as an instance of federal discrimination that had to be resisted by the local government. When a provincial government has found itself less in tune philosophically with the goals of a neglected local group, or been confronted with a divided community, it has been much less willing and able to provide territorial representation. Accordingly, Saskatchewan's Devine and Alberta's Lougheed governments, beset with one or both of these conditions, devoted fewer resources and publicity to denouncing the federal freight rate policy.

The effectiveness of provincial efforts to articulate the interests of locally significant 'class fractions'[31] is hindered by the small number of issues upon which there is unity of interest of agricultural producers. In most provinces, there is a range of commodity groups whose economic interests and ideological preferences are not necessarily mutually congruent; hence some are likely to be at odds with the philosophical perspective of the provincial government. Faced with such diversity and a consequent difficulty of finding compromises among disparate producer goals, provincial governments may opt for inaction and readily 'pass the buck' to the federal government by describing a problem as a federal responsibility. Differences among provinces handicap their joint claim to represent those regional interests that the national government is unable to represent because of a dearth of MPs from a particular region.

A further reason why provincial governments have not emerged as the sole defenders of locally based producer groups is the fact that producer organizations themselves have been active participants in agricultural policy-making. In western grain transportation, producer groups played a paramount role, lobbying the federal government in order to achieve their goals. Indeed, during the Crow reform debate, their extensive involvement in policy formulation was at the request of the governments themselves.

The United States:
Strong Intrastate Federalism

American agricultural policy is more complex than Canadian, being made up of an incredibly confusing plethora of commodity bills. The basis of farm policy is laid out every four years in the farm bill – the 1973, 1977, and 1981 Food and Agricultural Acts, for example – and beginning in 1986, the five-year Farm Security Act. Historically as well as currently, a major component of these farm bills consists of the programs to support commodity prices and producer incomes. Some instruments to maintain prices are similar to those found in Canada; others differ. The American dairy policies entail, as do the Canadian, floor price supports, production controls, import controls on dairy products, and a blended pricing formula for industrial and fluid milk. For the grains sector, the major instruments of government support have been the following: export subsidies to encourage foreign markets to absorb local grain surpluses (until 1972 and recommencing in 1986); a government non-recourse loan program[32] linked to an acreage-reduction or set-aside scheme; 'target prices' that 'guarantee producers that most of their production costs will be covered, at the same time they allow markets to clear at a lower price';[33] and a loan storage program designed to hold grain off the market in times of poor prices. Until the 1970s, the concept of parity formed the basis of government support for the six basic crops of wheat, corn, rice, cotton, peanuts, and tobacco that were guaranteed price protection after 1938. While the concept of parity was intended to guarantee that the price of an agricultural commodity would yield an equivalent buying power, in terms of goods and services bought by the farmer, to what the commodity had earned in the 1910–14 period, only rarely did farmers receive full parity, and, as was the case in Canada, government support was not intended to guarantee the farmer his costs of production.[34]

A major substantive difference between Canadian and American agricultural policy has been the greater willingness in Canada to intervene in the marketing system. Aside from the six basic commodities, many of the most important American commodities are exempt from programs to regulate prices or production. This includes soybeans, oilseed crops, most fruits and vegetables, forage crops for livestock, hogs, broilers, and livestock. Supply management exists for flue-cured tobacco and for peanuts 'where production above specified levels must be sold at a reduced price'[35] and on a local and regional basis for milk, fruit, and vegetables. While producers have been able since the Agricultural Marketing Agreement Act of 1937 to approve of marketing orders by vote and to have those orders binding thereafter, the orders they have chosen to establish have largely lacked supply control features and price-influencing powers and deal only with grades and standards on a local basis. The reluctance of most American farmers to give the necessary two-thirds plebiscite approval to implement compulsory marketing can be explained by a strong ideological preference for a laissez-faire market system. In 1962, American wheat producers voted to defeat President John Kennedy's plan to institute compulsory marketing for wheat.[36] Unlike Canadian grain producers, who very early sought orderly marketing for export grains, Americans sell and ship grain in a system dominated by a handful of multinational grain companies subject to few regulations.

While Americans have eschewed compulsory supply management, their commodity support programs tend to be linked to production controls. These have been voluntary in the sense that a farmer could refuse to set aside cropland from production, but in so doing he would forgo price supports. Even so, he would benefit from the commodity support programs without participating in acreage reduction, since the support programs guaranteed a floor market price.

Changes in Canadian and American commodity support programs since the early 1970s shed light upon the differing impact of the policy-making systems in the two countries. Beginning in 1973, the US Agricultural and Consumer Act began a general thrust, which the 1977 and 1981 bills continued, of freeing the farmer from production controls so as to allow him to take advantage of the growing export demand and of reducing the role of government in agriculture generally. Over the last decade, support prices for wheat and all the major field crops dropped, and American farmers 'have been left more vulnerable to fluctuations in the market place while program costs have been cut to a fraction of what they averaged from 1945 to 1970.'[37] In Canada, by contrast, governments showed more responsiveness to farmers' cost-price squeeze problems and market instability. As noted, the federal government revised its stabilization program to embrace a cost-of-production component and to make it more sensitive to fluctuations in prices. In Canada, interstate federalism and shared jurisdiction put pressure on federal authorities, whereas in the United States it could be argued that the national government has not been forced to approximate state programs in a bid for producer loyalty, since state governments have not shown the same activism, willingness, and fiscal capacity to supplement producer incomes and challenge federal hegemony as have their Canadian counterparts.

However, American producers do not appear to have suffered historically by not having state governments as courts of second appeal. The US Department of Agriculture (USDA) and Congress have been responsive to farmers' concerns. As early as the nineteenth century, when local committees of the Farm Bureau Federation gained control over the Extension Service of the Department of Agriculture, decentralized administration of USDA programs gave farmers significant involvement in agricultural policy implementation.[38] In addition, farm groups have received a hearing in Washington in the House and Senate agriculture committees and sub-committees. House sub-committees represent individual commodities; for example, in 1975, there were six House sub-committees for each of cotton, dairy and poultry, livestock and grains, oilseeds and rice, tobacco, and forests.[39] They consider legislation prior to its examination by the full committee. 'Uninhibited by the Presidency or by party discipline, sub-committee personnel carve out independent centres of power ... They are open to inputs from representatives of organized interest groups, including members of Congress attempting to serve the particularistic needs of their constituents and regions.'[40]

Log-rolling within the House Agriculture Committee offsets the numerical minority of rural representatives and ensures the passage of the commodity bills that are collectively bound together in the farm bill. Three different strategies of log-rolling have developed.[41] First, members have engaged in intra-agricultural commodity trading. With the price support programs for the three biggest commodities (feed grains, wheat, cotton) having been part of one omnibus farm bill since 1965, southern Democrats have supported the feed grains and wheat programs promoted by Midwest Republicans in exchange for the latter's endorsation of programs to bolster prices of cotton, tobacco, and peanuts and rice. This practice prevailed throughout the 1950s and 1960s and was virtually 'automatic' by 1977.[42] The geographic distribution of agriculture facilitated the aggregation of votes. With production of the three largest commodities geographically sectionalized (feed grains being produced in the middle corn belt states, wheat in the Great Plains and Pacific northwest, and cotton in the south and southwest), a package bill was able to elicit votes from rural House representatives in several parts of the country.[43] In short, the omnibus nature of the farm bill, which brings all commodities under one act, has allowed for alliances across geographical regions and parties.

The second log-rolling strategy has been facilitated by another feature of the farm bill. Since 1964, the food stamp program has been part of the farm bill, making possible the trading of congressional rural votes in favour of food stamps in exchange for urban votes in favour of commodity support programs. A third alliance has been forged between rural representatives and urban labour representatives, who in 1973 found common ground with the former's backing of minimum wage and food stamps for strikers in return for labour's backing of farm price supports and subsidies.[44] The three log-rolling strategies have enabled farmers, a mere 4 per cent of the population, to escape domination by the urban-consumer society. The intra-agricultural alliance has had the effect of equal treatment for all commodities, a consequence reinforced by the traditional dominance of southerners as chairmen of the House Committee on Agriculture until the 1970s. The latter especially meant that some of the less nationally economically significant commodities like cotton, tobacco, and peanuts received 'solicitous attention'[45] and support at price levels similar to those of other commodities.

The equitable treatment of commodities and regions that results from congressmen's perceptions of their representational role and from their log-rolling skills contrasts with allegations of preferential treatment of certain sectors and producers by Canadian national decision-makers. A further feature of the US system, namely, the separation of powers, also works to promote agrarian interests. While a Canadian cabinet minister whose government enjoys a majority in the House of Commons is relatively immune from opposition to his policies in all but the rare instance when the opposition comes from within his own government, by contrast, the executive can be blocked in the United States, as President Carter discovered when his efforts to reduce subsidies in the 1977 farm bill were impeded by Congress.[46]

The manner in which weak party discipline and the separation of executive and legislative powers in the United States have served to promote instrastate federalism raises the question of whether a stronger committee system and weaker party discipline would have similar effects in Canada.[47] In terms of the example discussed earlier, the debate to reform the Crow's Nest freight rates, the effect of weaker party discipline is difficult to assess. Party cohesion was not a barrier to territorial representation by Quebec MPs during the Crow rate debate (since their threat to break party ranks prevailed). Moreover, insofar as the government party had no rural representatives from western Canada, party discipline was not an issue. The impact of a committee system with members free from party ties may perhaps be assessed by looking at the behaviour of the opposition Conservative MPs from western Canada during the debate and their efforts to work with their Alberta provincial counterparts to find a compromise with which both livestock and grain growers could live. While their attempt suggests that greater accommodation of regionally based groups might be forthcoming with a reformed and more partisan-free committee system, it is also quite likely that the net policy outcome of a more independent committee system would have been no change in policy at all. For some producers that would have been a desirable policy outcome; for others, it would have been completely unwelcome. What the behaviour of federal MPs during the Crow debate does demonstrate is that parties and members that are ideologically pragmatic have more incentives to seek compromise solutions when they individually or collectively represent areas within which there are conflicting interests and goals. This being the case, the best safeguard for territorial representation at the centre is national political parties.

Summary

The example of Canadian agricultural policy has a number of implications for current popular analyses of contemporary Canadian federalism and its effect on policy-making. It suggests that scholars have tended to overemphasize the degree of intergovernmental, especially federal-provincial, strife and have underemphasized the extent and degree of co-operation and policy co-ordination. In highlighting governmental tensions, attention may have been somewhat misfocused on federal-provincial conflicts, to the neglect of interprovincial differences. In agricultural matters, genuine differences of economic interest and ideological perspective separate the provinces from one another (and from the national government), create potential conflicts, impede policy harmonization by provinces collectively, and incapacitate the national government in its attempt to formulate national policies. In recognizing these roots of governmental discord, Stevenson's portrait of contemporary Canadian federalism is more compelling than one that emphasizes political and institution-building causes of strife.

In agricultural policy, institutional factors have not always contributed to federal-provincial conflict. The existence of eleven governments, even when some provincial governments enjoy considerable bureaucratic and financial resources, does not necessarily give rise to competitive federalism. This is because such factors as tradition and philosophy create differences among governments in their willingness to deploy their resources, especially their financial resources, in a given policy field. The record in agricultural policy-making suggests that provinces will not be anxious to replace national predominance when policy leadership entails considerable financial responsibility. Insofar as national policy hegemony rests upon the exercise of the federal spending power, perceived federal niggardliness is likely to occasion provincial legislative thrusts that challenge the philosophy and role of the central government in policy-making.

It is important to dwell a moment on the significance of federal spending for agricultural programs. The federal assumption of financial responsibility for agriculture is an indication to producers and provincial agriculture ministers that the central government shares their belief in the national importance of the agricultural industry. In spending for agriculture, Ottawa affirms the contribution to the national well-being of the client group and the region in which it resides. When this shared perspective of agriculture's significance entails mutual goals, it can contribute to client and governmental harmony. And, as the example of national marketing suggests, it can be a potent catalyst to overcoming a constitutional barrier like shared jurisdiction.

In terms of policy outcomes, Canadian federalism has been a mixed blessing for producers. The division of jurisdiction over marketing has made it necessary for interest groups to lobby both levels of government, but, at the same time, it has afforded them two points of access. The experience of stabilization legislation demonstrates that groups ineffective at the national level have a second 'kick at the can' with provincial officials. The double blockage afforded by divided jurisdiction over marketing has also been exploited by many interest groups. Western cattle and hog commodity groups and Prince Edward Island potato processors have effectively vetoed supply management plans for their industry. These examples demonstrate, as Dawson suggests, that specialized groups may benefit more from divided jurisdiction in being able to undercut general farm groups, especially if the former wield significant economic clout at a local level.[48] But concurrent jurisdiction may be costly to some producers, as prairie cattlemen have discovered. The producers most hurt by provincial activism in commodity and general agricultural support have been those that enjoy a natural advantage in a market without government subsidies. It is not their own provincial governments but rather those of their less competitive counterparts that have shown the greatest willingness to implement income assurance plans. The consequence is that the natural advantage of some producers is slowly being eroded away.

Concurrent jurisdiction has other limitations. If governmental co-operation and unanimity are prerequisites to program development, then the formulation of needy programs can be frustrated, as the cases of red meat stabilization and a regional potato marketing agency demonstrate. To the extent that this results in joint unco-ordinated federal and provincial programs, economic inefficiencies may develop. Government programs may interfere with the allocation of production among regions according to the principle of comparative advantage, undermine Canadian economic integration, and lessen the efficiency of Canadian agriculture.

But if the Canadian system of shared jurisdiction has imperilled the Canadian common market in agricultural goods, one should not necessarily expect national predominance to yield a more integrated economy or efficient agricultural industry. Interestingly and importantly, American agricultural economists fault intrastate federalism for producing similar economic consequences. Cochrane and Ryan say that the omnibus strategy of legislation has contributed to an overall increase in the total costs of commodity programs,[49] and Paarlberg argues that the commodity approach to legislation has resulted in 'a fragmentation of the national interest.'[50] Gardner notes the protectionist tendencies of local regions; while restrictions on interstate trading are legally forbidden in the United States (as in Canada), 'ways to limit interregional competition have been found.'[51]

While shared jurisdiction in Canada has failed producers at times and possibly not always integrated the nation's economy, unilateral national authority for agriculture does not seem a welcome alternative. National political institutions, in provoking regional antagonism, have not served the country. Only time will tell whether recent changes to enhance the independence of parliamentary committees will undercut executive dominance of policy-making and ensure attention to the interests of Canadian farmers, who comprise less than 5 per cent of the Canadian population.

In spite of the very different processes of policy-making in the two countries, the substance of Canadian and US agricultural policy is likely to continue to be very similar, at least in the near future. In the United States, the growing influence of urban and consumer interests at both executive and congressional levels, the executive's concern about the costliness of farm commodity programs (hence its move to let the market set prices in the 1970s), and the changes in the leadership and make-up of agricultural congressional committees have lessened the influence of the agricultural sector as a whole and special sub-sectors (located in the south) in particular. Dale Hathaway makes the argument: 'During the 1950s and 1960s, agricultural policy was made by a tightly knit group that evolved from within the USDA. It agreed with, and was highly susceptible to, domestic commodity groups and like-minded congressional committees. Now the participants in agricultural policy decisions appear to come from a sprawling, ill-defined group that seems to be beyond the access of farmers and commodity groups.'[52]

However, while its willingness and capacity to articulate agricultural interests may have declined, Congress continues to be an important bulwark on behalf of American agriculture. Thus consumer advocates, supported by President Reagan, were successful in preventing a rise in the level of milk price supports in the 1981 farm bill but failed to realize their objectives with respect to the peanut, tobacco, and sugar programs.[53]

Congress, led by the Democratic majority in the House of Representatives, was also able to prevail against Reagan's determination to phase out target prices in the 1985 farm bill. The latter maintained target prices for wheat, corn, cotton, and rice at current levels for 1986 and 1987, after which they will decline slowly. The Reagan administration did realize its objective of reducing loan rates for wheat, corn, cotton, and rice, but this change was supported by some farm groups that saw the move as necessary to make American commodities more competitive in world markets. The lowered loan rates, combined with the reintroduction of export subsidies, reflected the effect of the international economy on American domestic agricultural policy; both are meant to send a message to the European Community that the US treasury will be used to protect American farmers against the Common Market's protectionism.

In Canada, the thrust of the Mulroney government is also toward a more efficient, competitive, export-oriented industry within which farmers will replace reliance on government subsidies with higher returns in the market-place. The Mulroney government is determined to reduce its expenditures for agriculture and to persuade provinces to assume an increasing share of the financial burden. To achieve this, it has committed itself to stronger intrastate federalism. Greater provincial input into the formulation of national agricultural trade and domestic policy is an important recognition of the province's expectations for such a voice but will be used by the provinces to pressure the national government not to abandon its responsibility for agriculture. If provinces succeed, harmonious intergovernmental relations will ensue. However, if Ottawa remains firm in its desire to divest itself of a large degree of financial responsibility for agriculture, and if the agricultural industry continues to experience the economic downturn that has plagued it in recent years, provinces will have to face producers' charges of being accomplices to federal inaction, or they will have to step into the breach. If the latter, the result is likely to be further splintering of the Canadian economic union. Should this happen, in the 1980s, as in the 1970s, federalism and the regional structure of Canada's agricultural industry will continue to contribute to a splintered agricultural policy that rewards some producers in some provinces and penalizes others in other provinces.

NOTES

1 Donald V. Smiley 'Public Sector Politics, Modernization, and Federalism: The Canadian and American Experience' *Publius* 14 (winter 1984) 39–59
2 Task Force on the Orientation of Canadian Agriculture *Report* Volume 1A (1977) 243
3 Ibid. See Table 9.3, 249–51, for a list of federal programs. In its last year in office, the federal Liberal government sought changes in the delivery of the regional development programs that would 'bypass provincial governments' (page 5) and result in provincial and federal governments separately delivering services directly to recipients. While the two governments would co-operate in planning economic development programs, the federal government wanted to deliver services, previously largely dispersed by provincial governments, in order to 'clarify in the public mind which level of government is responsible for a program or policy'; as quoted from *Annual Report of the Ministry of State for Economic Development 1982-3* 8–9 by Bruce G. Pollard, in *The Year in Review 1983: Intergovernmental Relations in Canada* (Kingston: Institute of Intergovernmental Relations 1984) 64. Preliminary evidence suggests that the minister of agriculture in the national Conservative government elected in September 1984 (John Wise) is intent on eliminating any friction in federal-provincial agricultural relations that the Liberal direct delivery policy may have created.
4 Ross B. Talbot and Don F. Hadwiger 'Federal-State Relations in Agriculture' in *The Policy Process in American Agriculture* (San Francisco: Chandler Publishing Co. 1968) chap 13
5 Donald V. Smiley 'The Structural Problem of Canadian Federalism' *Canadian Public Administration* 14 (fall 1971) 325–43; Donald V. Smiley 'Federal-Provincial Conflict in Canada' in J. Peter Meekison ed *Canadian Federalism: Myth or Reality* (Agincourt: Methuen 1977) 2–18; and Alan C. Cairns *From Interstate to Intrastate Federalism in Canada* (Kingston: Institute of Intergovernmental Relations 1979)
6 Roger Gibbins *Regionalism: Territorial Politics in Canada and the United States* (Toronto: Butterworths 1982) 52
7 Milton J. Esman 'Federalism and Modernization: Canada and the United States' *Publius* 14 (winter 1984) 29
8 Alan C. Cairns 'The Other Crisis of Canadian Federalism' *Canadian Public Administration* 22 (summer 1979) 191
9 Ibid. and Alan C. Cairns 'The Governments and Societies of Canadian Federalism' *Canadian Journal of Political Science* 10 (1977) 695–725
10 Cairns 'Governments and Societies' 703
11 Ibid 706
12 Cairns 'The Other Crisis' 189

13 Smiley 'Federal-Provincial Conflict' 12–13
14 Garth Stevenson *Unfulfilled Union* rev ed (Toronto: Gage 1982) 67–8
15 Garth Stevenson *Unfulfilled Union* (Toronto: Gage 1979) 183
16 Stevenson *Unfulfilled Union* rev ed 105
17 Richard Simeon 'Regionalism and Canadian Political Institutions' in J. Peter Meekison ed *Canadian Federalism: Myth or Reality* (Agincourt: Methuen 1977) 292–304
18 Donald V. Smiley 'Territorialism and Canadian Political Institutions' *Canadian Public Policy* 3 (autumn 1977) 452
19 Order-in-Council No. 886 (5 June 1925), as quoted in Howard Darling *The Politics of Freight Rates* (Toronto: McClelland and Stewart 1980) 69
20 In 1925, when the Crow's Nest rates were given statutory enactment, the minority Liberal government faced an imminent election in which it hoped to capture the 38 out of 43 western seats held by the Progressive party. In 1935 the spectre of the CCF and Social Credit capitalizing on farmers' economic frustration with the collapse of the wheat pools was important in the permanent establishment of the Canadian Wheat Board prior to the election of that year. In 1949, when the monopoly authority of the board was extended, the St Laurent government faced an election and had reason to be worried about its political support. The agriculture minister, Jimmy Gardiner, had won his seat in the 1945 general election only on a recount. Prairie cabinet spokesmen included Liberal Gardiner (1935–57) and Conservative Alvin Hamilton (1957–63).
21 The best documentation is provided by C.F. Wilson *A Century of Canadian Grain* (Saskatoon: Western Producer Prairie Books 1978) 472–4 and 783–5 especially. See also V.C. Fowke *The National Policy and the Wheat Economy* (Toronto: University of Toronto Press 1957) 268–9. Murray Beck *Pendulum of Power* (Scarborough: Prentice-Hall 1968) argues on p. 210 that it was pressure from the Liberal opposition on R.B. Bennett's Conservative government that resulted in the compulsory features of the bill to establish the Canadian Wheat Board being made optional. David Smith *The Decline of a National Party* (p. 26) states: 'The Conservatives under R.B. Bennett grudgingly accepted responsibility only after the free market had proved itself incapable of meeting the emergency and when they were convinced there was no alternative.'
22 *Attorney-General for British Columbia* v. *Attorney-General for Canada* (1937). See A.E. Safarian 'Agricultural Marketing Legislation: A Case Study' in Meekison ed *Canadian Federalism* 430–9
23 *Re the (Ontario) Farm Products Marketing Act* (1957)
24 In response to the request of Ontario's minister of agriculture and food, Dennis R. Timbrell, for a meeting of the signatories to address what Timbrell felt were unfair procedures for allocating provincial quotas, the federal agriculture minis-

ter, Eugene Whelan, called a signatories' meeting in March 1983. The subsequent provincial agricultural ministers' conference in July 1983 in Prince Edward Island agreed to co-operate on ways to address Ontario's grievances.

25 R.E. Haack et al *The Splintered Market* (Toronto: Lorimer 1981) 33–8; E.W. Tyrchniewicz ed *Proceedings of the Annual Meeting of the Canadian Agricultural Economics Society 1982 (June 1983)*: essay by Elmer L. Menzie 'Free Interprovincial Trade or Provincial Self-Sufficiency in Agricultural Products' 108–23 and discussion by G.A. MacEachern 123–8

26 Richard Schultz 'The Regulatory Process and Federal-Provincial Relations' in G. Bruce Doern ed *The Regulatory Process in Canada* (Toronto: Macmillan 1977) 141.

27 Alberta, Saskatchewan, and Ontario turned repeatedly to the federal government between 1974 and 1976 to demand that it assume responsibility for the beef crisis. They argued that the impact of the beef industry on the Canadian economy necessitated federal action. Saskatchewan premier Allan Blakeney said that it was unfair for the Saskatchewan people to bear the financial burden of saving the cattle industry when it was significant to all Canada. See *Western Producer* 21 (October 1976) 8. A communiqué issued at the Western Premiers' Conference earlier in 1976 declared: 'The fact that provincial governments have had to develop individual and provincial support programs ... is in the view of the Western Premiers a reflection of an obvious abdication by the federal government of their national responsibility.'

28 Quebec's goal in passing its Farm Income Stabilization Act was to 'increase agricultural production, particularly in those commodities which we now have to import in huge quantities from other provinces and from other countries.' See Gaetan Lussier 'Welcome to Quebec' *Canadian Journal of Agricultural Economics* CAES Workshop Proceedings (March 1976) 28. This interpretation was confirmed by interviews with Agriculture Minister Jean Garon and the assistant deputy minister of planning in the Quebec Ministry of Agriculture, François Dagenais, in July 1979. However, the Quebec government historically supported producer incomes to a far greater degree than other provinces. See W.M. Drummond et al *A Review of Agricultural Policy in Canada* (Ottawa: Agricultural Economics Research Council of Canada 1966) 377–8, Table 90.

29 See Gordon MacEachern *Retention of the Crow Rate and the Alberta Livestock Economy* (Ottawa: Agricultural Economics Research Council of Canada 1978); David R. Harvey *Christmas Turkey or Prairie Vulture* (Montreal: Institute for Research on Public Policy 1980); M.S. Anderson and W.H.C. Hendriks *A Review of the Crow Rate Implications for Alberta Agriculture* (Edmonton 1978). The argument is that Alberta's livestock-, meat-, and oilseed-processing industries have not expanded as they would without low export freight rates.

The prairie livestock grower has had to pay relatively more for his feed than his American competitors, and processed products have higher freight rates than unprocessed materials.

30 David Smith *The Regional Decline of a National Party* (Toronto: University of Toronto Press 1981) 145
31 Stevenson *Unfulfilled Union* rev ed 68
32 Dale E. Hathaway 'Government and Agriculture Revisited: A Review of Two Decades of Change' *American Journal of Agricultural Economics* (December 1981) 779–87
33 Bruce L. Gardner *The Governing of Agriculture* (Lawrence, Kan.: University Press of Kansas 1981) 25
34 Ronald D. Knutson, J.B. Penn, and William T. Boehm *Agricultural and Food Policy* (Englewood Cliffs, NJ: Prentice-Hall 1983) chap 9
35 Gardner *Governing* 26
36 James Johnson and Kenneth Clayton 'Organization and Well-Being of the Farming Industry: Reflections on the Agriculture and Food Act of 1981' *American Journal of Agricultural Economics* (December 1982) 947–56
37 Michael S. Lyons and Marcia Whicker Taylor 'Farm Politics in Transition: The House Agriculture Committee' *Agriculture History* 55 (April 1981) 128–46
38 Grant McConnell *Private Power and American Democracy* (New York: Alfred A. Knopf 1967) 235–7
39 A. Desmond O'Rourke *The Changing Dimensions of US Agricultural Policy* (Englewood Cliffs, NJ: Prentice-Hall 1978) 30
40 Esman 'Federalism and Modernization' 29
41 John G. Peter 'The 1977 Farm Bill: Coalitions in Congress' in Don F. Hadwiger and William P. Browne *The New Politics of Food* (Lexington, Mass.: D.C. Heath and Co. 1978) 23–35
42 Ibid 24
43 Weldon Barton 'Coalition-Building in the US House of Representatives: Agricultural Legislation in 1973' in James E. Anderson ed *Cases in Public Policy* (New York: Praeger 1976) 101–2
44 Charles M. Hardin 'Agricultural Price Policy: The Political Role of Bureaucracy' in Hadwiger and Browne *Politics* 8
45 Willard W. Cochrane and Mary E. Ryan *American Farm Policy 1948–1973* (Minneapolis: University of Minnesota Press 1981) 114
46 Don Paarlberg *Farm and Food Policy Issues of the 1980s* (Lincoln and London: University of Nebraska Press 1980) 49
47 Donald V. Smiley 'Territorialism' 453
48 Helen Jones Dawson 'National Pressure Groups and the Federal Government' in A. Paul Pross ed *Pressure Group Behaviour in Canadian Politics* (Toronto: McGraw-Hill Ryerson 1975) 30–5

49 Cochrane and Ryan *Farm Policy* 115
50 Paarlberg *Farm and Food Policy* 46
51 Gardner *Governing* 53
52 Hathaway 'Government and Agriculture' 784
53 Knutson et al *Agricultural and Food Policy* 237

12 / Federalism and the Canadian Economic Union

MICHAEL J. TREBILCOCK

The purpose of this essay is to evaluate how well the Canadian constitution protects the integrity of the internal common market by constraining the adoption of policies by either level of government that distort or inhibit internal flows of goods, labour, services, and capital. When we examine the historical origins of Confederation, we can have little doubt that whatever weight was assigned to goals of political and cultural autonomy and national security, it was widely accepted by the Fathers of Confederation that a sine qua non for the realization of these goals was the development of a viable economy with an east-west axis north of the US border. To this end, strategies were required to open up the agricultural hinterland and to promote a manufacturing sector in the more populous centres of central Canada. The construction of the transcontinental railway lines with substantial government subsidies (and later partial government ownership), the fostering of large-scale immigration through assisted passages and homesteading grants, and the erection of protective tariffs to encourage the development of a domestic manufacturing sector in central Canada were important ingredients in what came to be identified as the National Policy (1879) and were important elements of the Confederation compact.[1]

While it may be true that the National Policy did not reflect the closely worked out and coherent development strategy that some historians have tended to ascribe to it,[2] it seems an accurate generalization that economic integration and regional specialization were conceived of as central presuppositions of Confederation. At least at the rhetorical level, they have remained such to the present day; at times, concern over the growth of interprovincial economic distortions has clearly been much more than rhetorical. The major focus of the Rowell-Sirois royal commission in the late 1930s[3] was the so-called tax jungle that provincial tax policies had created as provinces vied for economic activities (and jobs). This prompted a number of federal-provincial initiatives following the Second World War that quite successfully sought to ensure a high degree of tax harmonization between and among the different levels of government in Canada.

During the constitutional reform debates of the late 1970s and early 1980s the effectiveness of constitutional protection of the Canadian economic union was again explicitly questioned, principally by the federal government, which pointed to a number of examples of provincially induced barriers to interprovincial trade ('beggar-thy-neighbour' policies, more pejoratively) that were claimed to be multiplying in scale and frequency and to be reflective of increasing balkanization of the Canadian economy.[4] A similar sentiment had been earlier expressed by Safarian in an influential study, *Canadian Federalism and Economic Integration*.[5] Both the federal government and Safarian argued that the Canadian constitution provided fewer protections of Canada's internal common market than the Treaty of Rome did for the European Community or the US constitution did for the United States, with the expansive interpretation given by the US Supreme Court to the federal government's interstate commerce power.

While subsequent analysts have questioned whether greater centralization of powers is necessarily highly correlated with reduction in internal trade-distorting policies, citing the case of Britain,[6] the Canadian federal government's posture in the constitutional reform debates was to argue for a stronger prohibition on both tariff and non-tariff barriers to the interprovincial movement of goods, capital, and labour than that currently embodied in section 121 of the Constitution Act, 1867. Section 121 provides: 'All articles of the Growth, Produce or Manufacture of any one of the Provinces shall from and after the Union, be admitted free into each of the other Provinces.' This provision applies only to tariff barriers (not non-tariff barriers) to the interprovincial movement of goods (not capital, services, or labour) and probably applies only to provincial, not federal action. Alternatively, the federal government proposed greater centralization of economic powers in the federal government, given the rather restrictive judicial interpretation of the federal parliament's trade and commerce power.[7] The constitutional reforms that were subsequently enacted (and reviewed below) were not responsive in any major way to either proposal, although the appointment in 1982 of the Royal Commission on the Economic Union and Development Prospects for Canada (which reported in late 1985),[8] and the announcement of free trade negotiations with the United States, have served to maintain a strong public policy focus on issues pertaining to interprovincial and now continental free trade and to relationships between the two.

Defining Internal Trade Distortions

Despite the casualness with which the term is often used, defining a trade distortion in a conceptually rigorous way is a far from straightforward exercise. As an initial presumption, economists would tend to define a distortion as any government policy that changes the relative prices of goods, capital, or labour so that resources are no longer allocated to their most highly valued uses. In the context of the Canadian economic union, either federal or provincial policies that induce spatial allocations of activities that forfeit those gains from specialization and scale that unimpeded market forces would have reflected would tend to be viewed as interprovincial (or inter-regional) barriers to trade. The unexploited gains from specialization and scale will be reflected in a lower national income or gross national product.

There are a variety of difficulties with this kind of definition.[9] Some of these are of a relatively technical nature. For example, provincial policies that respond to externalities generated by other jurisdictions, while superficially impeding interprovincial trade flows, may increase national welfare. Examples would include a policy of penalizing directly or indirectly upstream pollution of a river originating in one jurisdiction but passing through another or charging residents from one jurisdiction for access to parks or other public goods financed by residents of another. Again, the theory of second-best cautions against assuming that removing one trade-distorting policy will increase economic output if other trade-distorting policies are left in place. Indeed, in particular cases where one province has introduced a trade-distorting policy (e.g. export subsidies to local producers of a particular class), countervailing subsidy policies by other provinces with rival producers may lead to more efficient allocation of resources, even though in a first-best world there would be no subsidies of any kind.

More fundamentally, maximizing national wealth (output or gross national product per capita) has been convincingly critiqued by philosophers as an ethically incoherent and indefensible normative imperative.[10] Social or economic abstractions such as 'wealth' provide no index of whether underlying individual welfare has in all cases been enhanced. If this becomes the touchstone, one is then remitted to a utilitarian normative framework. That itself, of course, is highly problematic in important ethical respects and leads one to ask a number of questions that the simple objective of maximizing national income obscures. In a utilitarian framework, one would be bound to define a distortion in a way that related to the capacity of the institutions of government in a state to maximize the satisfaction of the preferences of its citizens. Assuming heterogeneity of preferences, it becomes obvious why a federal system offers advantages in realizing this goal.

Prichard identifies the following potential advantages of decentralization of state functions.[11] (1) Interest groups that may be minorities nationally are more likely, mathematically, to become majorities locally. (2) The greater the homogeneity of interests on a geographical basis, the more often minorities become majorities as decentralization increases. (3) Decentralization of functions in a hierarchical way disaggregates policy packages and allows a citizen to cast different votes on different components of public policy (i.e. 'full-line forcing' is reduced). (4) Decentralization, by creating a diversity of jurisdictions, allows a better matching of preferences and policies through the ability of citizens to 'vote with their feet.'[12] (5) Decentralization may reduce 'signalling' costs entailed in citizens articulating their preferences by reducing 'distance' among electors and between electors and their representatives and thus reducing information and participation costs faced by citizens wishing to influence political outcomes.[13] (6) Decentralization may encourage innovation in the provision of public services or policy development; interjurisdictional competition increases the number of sources of policy ideas, while simultaneously reducing the risk of a system-wide error.[14]

However, centralization of state functions also has virtues in terms of the ability of government to maximize the satisfaction of the preferences of as many of its citizens as possible.

1. Centralization may be able to internalize the externalities associated with policies adopted by lower-level jurisdictions when such policies impose costs on (or less typically) generate benefits for other jurisdictions. Obviously, there are political attractions for politicians in one jurisdiction in the adoption of policies that impose costs on citizens in another jurisdiction to whom the policy-makers are not politically accountable, although, in fact, most such policies also impose costs on local taxpayers or consumers. These 'spill-over' or 'beggar-thy-neighbour' tendencies may arguably be reduced by vesting decision-making in a central authority that must account to all citizens benefitted or harmed by its policies, although geographically differentiated power bases may lead to disproportionate weighting of costs and benefits.

2. Centralization may permit economies of scale to be realized in the provision of public goods. Obviously, if every decentralized jurisdiction felt obliged, for example, to maintain its own standing army, defence costs in aggregate are likely to increase dramatically. Similar, albeit less dramatic, examples may include the provision of postal or police services or major transportation infrastructures and external relations with foreign powers.

3. Centralization may permit the fuller realization of the distributional preferences of the majority of a country's citizens. In the absence of a strong central authority, most of the wealthy citizens of the state may group themselves in a particular lower-level jurisdiction and thus be able to avoid redistributional burdens that a majority of citizens in the country as a whole regard as appropriate. However, decentralization also limits the counter-vailing risk of unfair expropriation of minorities by majorities, although some theory of rights lying outside the conventional utilitarian framework is required to identify such forms of unfairness.

These various considerations bearing on the advantages and disadvantages of centralization and decentralization of state functions suggest a very complex set of trade-offs not well captured in the simple criterion of maximizing national income. Obviously, a variety of institutional arrangements are conceivable for striking particular trade-offs. In the international trade literature, it is conventional to identify six degrees of economic integration.[15] (1) A *free trade area* involves removal of customs tariffs and quantitative restrictions such as quotas on trade between the member countries, but with each of them retaining its own distinct barriers against non-members. (2) A *customs union*, in addition to (1) standardizes such barriers by member countries against non-members (i.e. adopts a common external tariff). (3) A *common market*, in addition to (2), removes restrictions on the movement of labour and capital between member countries. (4) An *economic union*, in addition to (3), involves varying degrees of harmonization of national economic policies in order to remove discrimination due to disparities in these policies. (5) A *federal state* is a form of union in which the central government and the provinces or states each exercise exclusive jurisdiction in some major areas of policy and shared jurisdiction in others. (6) In a *unitary state*, the central government has sole jurisdiction over economic and other major policies.

Obviously, this classification reflects a spectrum of degrees of integration, and any set of existing institutional arrangements under study is unlikely to fit neatly into one category. Canadian federal arrangements reflect features of (2) through (5). Courchene has attempted to capture these arrangements graphically on an integration spectrum (Figure 1).[16] Courchene views the Canadian federation as being located toward the decentralized end within the federal range on the spectrum. However, he properly cautions against viewing the Canadian federation, even in conventional economic terms, as merely a degenerate form of economic union. He argues persuasively that even if one accepts the maximization of national incomes as the touchstone that defines whether given government policies are distorting or not, there is no reason to suppose that governments in unitary states will not face

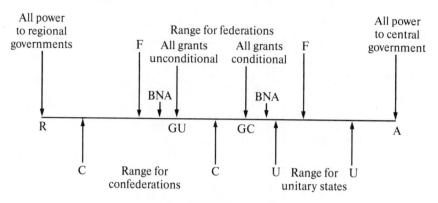

FIGURE 1
The centralization-decentralization spectrum

incentives to distort the internal allocation of resources.

For example, in the case of Britain (a unitary state, as conventionally defined), a combination of regional subsidy policies, bail-outs and often nationalization of lame-duck industries in economically disadvantaged and politically sensitive regions (coal mining, steel, autos, shipbuilding), and public housing policies administered by local governments and subsidized by the central government that make it costly for workers to relocate have almost certainly impeded adjustment processes and distorted the internal allocation of resources to a much greater extent than has ever been the case in Canada. Courchene argues that Canadian federalism contains a set of checks and balances between the different levels of jurisdiction that offsets distorting impulses that may arise at any given level of government. For example, if the federal government chooses to subsidize regional development, provinces other than the favoured regions can (and often do) offer countervailing industrial subsidies that largely undo the effects of the federal subsidies. While this may be a second-best outcome (the first-best from an efficiency perspective might be for no government to offer regional industrial subsidies), the economic distortions that result are likely to be significantly attenuated.

It also follows from Courchene's analysis that not only should we not assume more internal economic distortions in a federal state than in a unitary state, but we also should not assume a greater proclivity on the part of provinces in the Canadian federal system to distort the efficient internal allocation of resources than the federal government, despite the thrust of the federal government's claims during the constitutional reform debates.

TABLE 1

Destination of goods by province, 1979

	Total		Within province		Rest of Canada		Exports	
	Value ($000)	Percentage	Value ($000)	Percentage	Value ($000)	Percentage	Value ($000)	Percentage
Newfoundland	2,312,630	100	638,090	28	495,260	21	1,179,280	51
Prince Edward Island	367,170	100	147,800	40	143,120	39	76,250	21
Nova Scotia	4,114,910	100	1,650,180	40	1,400,920	34	1,063,810	26
New Brunswick	3,923,590	100	1,148,770	29	1,116,090	29	1,658,720	42
Quebec	45,969,900	100	21,922,850	48	13,115,810	28	10,931,230	24
Manitoba	6,149,200	100	2,142,550	35	2,503,720	41	1,502,930	24
Saskatchewan	6,644,170	100	1,681,270	25	1,900,400	29	3,062,500	46
Alberta	26,259,410	100	10,186,630	39	9,056,800	34	7,015,990	27
British Columbia	21,742,550	100	9,882,080	45	3,158,520	15	8,701,950	40
Yukon and NWT	656,990	100	201,310	31	54,480	8	401,200	61
Canada	202,841,450	100	89,602,780	44	53,865,860	27	59,372,790	29

SOURCE: Statistics Canada, Input-Output Division, Interprovincial Trade Flow Data, 1979

NOTE: Total may not add to a hundred because of rounding.

TABLE 2

Source of goods by province, 1979

	Total		Within province		Rest of Canada		Exports	
	Value ($000)	Percentage	Value ($000)	Percentage	Value ($000)	Percentage	Value ($000)	Percentage
Newfoundland	2,576,130	100	638,090	25	1,526,240	59	411,800	16
Prince Edward Island	601,020	100	147,810	25	391,900	65	61,340	10
Nova Scotia	5,786,830	100	1,650,170	29	2,156,050	37	1,890,620	33
New Brunswick	5,109,040	100	1,148,780	22	2,197,990	43	1,762,880	34
Quebec	50,593,240	100	21,922,860	43	12,564,480	25	16,105,890	32
Ontario	87,302,180	100	40,001,260	46	14,797,690	17	32,503,300	37
Manitoba	7,092,600	100	2,142,540	30	3,214,940	45	1,735,110	244
Saskatchewan	6,400,660	100	1,681,270	26	3,339,230	52	1,380,170	22
Alberta	21,555,330	100	10,186,620	47	7,047,430	33	4,321,280	20
British Columbia	22,085,430	100	9,882,070	45	6,238,300	28	5,965,050	27
Yukon and NWT	664,730	100	201,310	30	391,640	59	71,780	11
Canada	209,767,190	100	89,602,780	43	53,865,850	26	66,298,620	32

SOURCE: Statistics Canada, Input-Output Division, Interprovincial Trade Flow Data, 1979

Courchene outlines six alternative objective functions for the central government in a federal state:[17] (1) Maximize national output. (2) Maximize national output, subject to the constraint (a) that there be a minimum level of income for all Canadians. (3) Maximize national output, subject to the constraints (a) above, and (b) that regional income disparities be narrowed. (4) Maximize national output subject to the constraints (a) and (b) and, further, (c) that provincial income disparities be narrowed. (5) Maximize national output subject to the constraints (a) and (d) that regional production disparities be reduced. (6) Maximize national output subject to the constraints (a) and (d) and, further, (e) that provincial production disparities be narrowed.

In a Canadian context, where the power bases of the major federal parties (at least until recently) have been sharply regionally differentiated, it is obvious why the central government will often face strong political incentives to adopt policies that gravitate toward stage 6 on the scale, despite the fact that national income is likely to fall progressively as the central government adopts objective functions at lower stages on the scale.

The analysis to this point suggests reasons why one might, in a federal system, expect to observe both provincial governments and the federal government on occasion engaging in trade-distorting policies but why significant offsetting effects may be involved that are likely to reduce the net efficiency losses from these policies. I now turn to a review of the empirical evidence to date on these issues in a Canadian context.

Measuring Internal Trade Distortions

Interprovincial Trade Flows

The magnitude and patterns of interprovincial and international trade flows with respect to goods are depicted in tables contained in the Report of the Macdonald Commission.[18] The overall picture that emerges is that about one-quarter of all provincially produced goods and resources are shipped interprovincially, only slightly less than the percentage exported outside the country. See tables 1-3. For six of the provinces, the provincial market is more important than interprovincial sales or exports (Quebec, Ontario, British Columbia, Prince Edward Island, Nova Scotia, and Alberta). Three provinces (Newfoundland, New Brunswick, and Saskatchewan) and the Northwest Territories find their largest markets outside Canada. Only Manitoba's sales to other provinces are greater than sales within the province and sales abroad. Ontario, in 1979, accounted for nearly 40 per cent of all inter-regional shipments in Canada, and Quebec for another 25 per cent.

TABLE 3

Trade balances on goods by province, 1979

	Balance with other provinces	Balance on external trade	Overall balance
Newfoundland	-1,030,980	767,480	263,500
Prince Edward Island	-248,780	14,910	-233,870
Nova Scotia	-755,130	-826,810	-1,581,940
New Brunswick	-1,081,900	-103,560	-1,185,460
Quebec	551,330	-5,174,660	-4,623,330
Ontario	6,123,040	-8,724,370	-2,601,330
Manitoba	-711,220	-232,180	-943,400
Saskatchewan	-1,438,830	1,682,330	243,500
Alberta	2,009,370	2,694,710	4,704,080
British Columbia	-3,079,780	2,736,900	-342,280
Yukon and NWT	-337,160	329,420	-7,440

SOURCE: Calculated from Statistics Canada, Input-Output Division, Interprovincial Trade Flow Data, 1979

Alberta contributed 17 per cent of interprovincial Canadian trade in goods, largely in the form of energy. No other province recorded more than 6 per cent of the interprovincial total.[19]

With respect to personal mobility, between 1972 and 1984, an average of 380,000 persons a year changed residences by moving across provincial boundaries (i.e. about 15 for every 1,000 Canadians).[20] The proportion of population five years and over living in the same province as at birth in 1981 is shown in Table 4.[21] The interprovincial patterns of internal migration flows are shown in Table 5.[22] Data are unavailable on the amount of capital located in particular provinces whose owners reside in other provinces or on the amount of investment in a province financed by savers in other provinces. However, Table 6 indicates net capital inflows (from whatever sources) and outflows by province in recent years.[23]

In terms of any generalizations that the foregoing data might support, the important point can be made that interprovincial trade in goods is as important in value as goods sold into export markets. Obviously, also, internal migration and capital flows are very significant phenomena. Thus, a very substantial body of economic activity in Canada stands to be prejudiced by internal trade distortions. Moreover, a secondary cost from fragmented domestic markets is likely to be loss of returns from scale and specialization that reduce Canadian competitiveness in international trade. In this respect, internal barriers to trade are importantly linked to international trade performance.

226/ Michael J. Trebilcock

TABLE 4

Proportion of population five years and over living in the same province as a birth, 1980

	At birth (%)	Born abroad (%)
Canada	61.1	13.3
Newfoundland	83.0	2.4
Prince Edward Island	56.0	5.5
Nova Scotia	59.7	6.8
New Brunswick	63.0	5.0
Quebec	87.9	6.4
Ontario	62.8	19.5
Manitoba	60.2	8.4
Saskatchewan	66.4	6.2
Alberta	35.0	11.8
British Columbia	37.9	18.6
Yukon	10.6	11.4
Northwest Territories	23.1	8.6

SOURCE: Calculations made using data from Statistics Canada, *Mobility Status*, Cat. No. 92-907 (Ottawa), vol. 1, table 6, pp. 6–1 to 6–6

TABLE 5

Percentage distribution of interprovincial migration by province of origin and destination, average for 1971–2 to 1982–3

Province	Origin	Destination
Newfoundland	3.3	2.7
Prince Edward Island	1.0	1.0
Nova Scotia	5.6	5.7
New Brunswick	4.5	4.6
Quebec	13.9	7.6
Ontario	25.8	23.4
Manitoba	7.8	6.3
Saskatchewan	6.9	6.2
Alberta	15.8	22.5
British Columbia	13.6	18.2
Yukon and NWT	1.8	1.7
Total	100	100

SOURCE: Statistics Canada, based on data from *International and Interprovincial Migration in Canada*, Cat. no. 91–208 and Cat. no. 91–210 (Ottawa: various years)

TABLE 6

Net capital inflows (+) and outflows (–) by province
($ billions)

Province	Cumulative 1961–76	1974	1975	1976
Newfoundland	+6.9	+0.8	+0.9	+0.9
Prince Edward Island	+1.4	+0.2	+0.2	+0.1
Nova Scotia	+8.9	+1.0	+1.2	+1.1
New Brunswick	+7.0	+0.9	+1.2	+1.2
Quebec	+10.7	+2.2	+4.1	+4.0
Ontario	–16.3	–1.5	–0.4	–1.3
Manitoba	+3.1	+0.3	+0.2	+0.5
Saskatchewan	–0.4	–0.8	–0.6	+0.1
Alberta	–4.5	–2.5	–2.3	+1.6
British Columbia	+2.4	–	+0.1	+0.1
Total	+19.2	+0.6	+4.6	+8.3

SOURCE: *Quebec's Access to Financial Markets: A Report in the Series 'Understanding Canada'* (Ottawa: Ministry of Supply and Services 1979) 26

The Significance of Specific Distortions

Provincially Induced Distortions

A previous study[24] recently developed a comprehensive catalogue of provincial policies that appear to have a tendency to distort interprovincial trade flows and thus reduce national incomes (employing this as the only tractable definition of a distortion for purposes of measurement). The catalogue is lengthy and detailed. With respect to goods flows, it includes government procurement policies; non-uniform trucking regulations; agricultural marketing boards (often operating under federal legislative authority); divergent agricultural produce standards and grading practices; natural resource policies that confine access to local residents through licence or lease conditions or provide subsidies to local processing activities; and provincial liquor policies that entail preferential mark-up or stocking policies for local products.

With respect to personal mobility, distortions include preferential hiring policies applied by provincial governments in favour of local residents; non-recognition of extraprovincial occupational or professional credentials; limited portability of pension entitlements; and restrictions on access to welfare and social service programs. With respect to mobility of capital, distortions include restrictions on extraprovincial land ownership; restrictive

228/ Michael J. Trebilcock

investment policies requiring government investment funds such as the Alberta Heritage Savings Trust Fund or government pension plans or insurance companies doing business in a province to give priority to local investments; provincial crown corporations which, because of subsidized capital requirements and tax-exempt status, face a lower cost of capital than comparable private-sector enterprises; an enormous array of forms of financial assistance and agricultural and industrial incentives in various sectors; and various tax incentives designed to encourage provincial taxpayers to invest in locally based companies.

Federally Induced Distortions[25]

In the case of federally induced distortions of interprovincial trade, significant sources of distortion include, with respect to goods, the National Energy Program (now largely abandoned) and prior restrictions on the price of energy sold interprovincially and restrictions on exports; the national tariff that has forced western consumers to buy manufactured goods from central Canada behind the tariff wall; federal transportation policies such as the Crow's Nest Pass subsidies to prairie grain producers; and federal-provincial agricultural marketing board schemes. With respect to capital mobility, distortions include regional and industrial subsidy programs such as those formerly administered by the Department of Regional Economic Expansion, now the Department of Regional and Industrial Expansion, and business bail-outs in politically sensitive regions. With respect to labour mobility, equalization payments reduce the tax price of public goods in recipient provinces and in this sense discourage efficient relocation. However, to the extent that interprovincial migration may be induced by superior public goods packages financed from energy rents, this fiscally induced migration may be inefficient in that it does not necessarily reflect a higher marginal product of labour in the province of destination (indeed it may be lower).[26] Regionally differentiated unemployment insurance benefits have effects similar to equalization payments in discouraging efficient relocation.

Whalley's empirical analysis in the foregoing study of the magnitudes involved in these provincial and federal distortions of interprovincial trade yielded two significant conclusions. First, the economic costs associated with federally induced distortions, especially with respect to energy policy and the national tariff, overwhelmed the economic costs associated with provincially induced distortions (despite the length of the catalogue in the latter case). Second, even given the first point, taking federal and provincial distortions together, the total economic costs seem relatively modest. Estimates of welfare losses for 1974 fell between a low of $130 million, or 0.11 per cent of gross national product (GNP), and a high of $1.75 billion, or 1.54 per cent of GNP, depending on the assumptions made.[27]

These figures have prompted divergent interpretations. Even if the estimates are taken as given, there is room for difference of opinion as to whether these are 'small' or 'large' numbers. While Whalley views them as small, Anthony Scott pointed out to the Macdonald Commission that 1 per cent of GNP is 'equivalent to the G.D.P. of Newfoundland, not a trivial sum.'[28] Other analysts have questioned whether the estimates capture all relevant economic costs. For example, Courchene argues[29] that because they are static and not dynamic measures of efficiency losses, they do not reflect resources spent over time in rent-seeking and rent-maintenance activities (e.g. lobbying to secure or maintain distorting policies that are beneficial to special interests) or losses over time from reduced levels of innovation that less protected economic environments may encourage. Further, in measuring potential distorting effects they take existing interprovincial trade flows as given when, in the absence of existing interprovincial barriers to trade, it is possible that a significantly higher percentage of firms would find it worthwhile to engage in interprovincial trade. In addition, fragmenting production within the domestic market may entail forgone returns from scale and specialization that undermine Canadian competitiveness in international trade. Moreover, these estimates do not take account of the potential for increased levels of mutual retaliation over time and an unravelling effect quickly gathering momentum under suitable provocation if not effectively constrained. Observers point to the recent decision by Alberta to impose its own corporate tax and a threatened decision by British Columbia to do the same and increasing use of the tax system by various provinces to provide incentives for taxpayers to invest in local companies. These developments are said to carry analogies to the tax 'jungle' of the 1930s, which prompted appointment of the Rowell-Sirois Commission.

Thus current estimates of the welfare losses from interprovincial trade distortions must be accepted as somewhat conjectural, although the Macdonald Commission concluded, with Whalley, that the economic costs are currently relatively small and do not call for major constitutional reforms.[30]

Proposals for Better Securing the Canadian Economic Union

In the recent constitutional reform negotiations, the federal government proposed that the constitution include an expanded section 121, which would read as follows:[31]

121 (1) Neither Canada nor a province shall by law or practice discriminate in

a manner that unduly impedes the operation of the Canadian economic union, directly or indirectly, on the basis of the province or territory of residence or former residence of a person, on the basis of the province or territory into which or from which goods, services or capital are imported or exported.

(2) Nothing in subsection (1) renders invalid a law of a legislature enacted in the interests of public safety, order, health or morals.

(3) Nothing in subsection (1) renders invalid a law of Parliament enacted pursuant to the principles of equalization and regional development to which Parliament and the legislatures are committed or declared by Parliament to be in an overriding national obligation undertaken by Canada.

(4) Nothing in subsection (2) or (3) renders valid a law of Parliament or a legislature that impedes the admission free into any province of goods, services or capital originating in or imported into any other province or territory.

However, nine of the ten provinces at the 1980 Constitutional Conference rejected this provision as involving both unacceptable constraints on provincial powers and unacceptable extensions of federal power. In particular, the provinces viewed the proposed section 121(3) as authorizing the federal government to do precisely what the section forbade the provinces from doing – promoting regional development (a prime provincial concern) – and taking all the political credit for such policies.

In the result, the Constitution Act, 1982, largely abandoned any effort at strengthening constitutional protections of the Canadian economic union. Only section 6, which deals with personal mobility rights, directly addresses barriers to any form of mobility:

6 (1) Every citizen of Canada has the right to enter, remain in and leave Canada.

(2) Every citizen of Canada and every person who has the status of a permanent resident of Canada has the right

a) to move to and take up residence in any province; and

b) to pursue the gaining of a livelihood in any province.

3) The rights in subsection (2) are subject to

a) any laws or practices of general application in force in a province other than those that discriminate among persons primarily on the basis of province of present or previous residence; and

b) any laws providing for reasonable residency requirements as a qualification for the receipt of publicly provided social services.

4) Subsections (2) and (3) do not preclude any law, program or activity that has as its object the amelioration in a province of conditions of individuals in that province who are socially or economically disadvantaged if the rate of employment in that province is below the rate of employment in Canada.

The section is framed in very qualified terms – it appears only to apply to individuals and not corporations, and it explicitly authorizes provinces to create interprovincial barriers to labour mobility where the rate of employment in the province creating the barriers (e.g. preferential hiring policies) is below the national average.

Moreover, section 36 of the Constitution Act enshrines a constitutional commitment (of uncertain legal force) to equalization of economic opportunities and to the principle of equalization payments:

(1) Without altering the legislative authority of Parliament or of the provincial legislatures, or the rights of any of them with respect to the exercise of their legislative authority, Parliament and the legislatures, together with the government of Canada and the provincial governments, are committed to
(a) promoting equal opportunity for the well-being of Canadians;
(b) furthering economic development to reduce disparity in opportunities; and
(c)providing essential public services of reasonable quality to all Canadians.
(2) Parliament and the government of Canada are committed to the principle of making equalization payments to ensure that provincial governments have sufficient revenues to provide reasonably comparable levels of public services at reasonably comparable levels of taxation.

This outcome of the constitutional reform debates suggests little prospect for the foreseeable future of significant constitutional strengthening of protections of the Canadian economic union.

The Macdonald Commission proposed an alternative approach to advancing this goal. It suggested that both levels of government commit themselves to the development of a Code of Economic Conduct which would identify unacceptable barriers to interprovincial trade. The responsibility for developing the code would be vested in a Federal-Provincial Council of Ministers for Economic Development, assisted by a Federal-Provincial Commission on the Canadian Economic Union. The latter would consist of a group of experts appointed by the council to collect complaints from governments and others as to existing barriers to trade, propose constraining rules to the ministerial council, and thereafter undertake public inquiries into complaints of violations of these rules. The commission would make public recommendations for action to the ministerial council. At least initially, no direct legal force would attach either to the code or to adjudications made thereunder. Instead, the force of recommendations in particular cases would reside in the publicity that they would attract.[32]

These proposals seem a useful start to establishing a sharper political and public focus on interprovincial barriers to trade. They recognize the complex and inherently political trade-offs involved in constraining the jurisdictional powers of governments in the service of the rather elusive concept of non-distorted internal trade flows. By attempting to structure a political process that will yield some constraints on the most overt and costly forms of distortion, the proposals avoid the dangers inherent in an expansion of section 121 of vesting in a non-expert, non-political, and non-accountable court a largely uncharted discretion to invalidate a potentially wide sweep of federal and provincial economic policies. Without the benefit of a complementary institutional structure to provide an environment in which some systematic set of constraints can be bargained out with a degree of specificity and enforced in an equally systematic fashion, such a process seems likely to prove crude and unpredictable.

However, the weakness in the commission's proposals is clearly their lack of legal sanctions. Short of a constitutional amendment that would give legal force to the institutional arrangements that the proposals contemplate – analogous to the directive power vested in the Council of the European Community under the Treaty of Rome – another option deserves further exploration. As I have argued elsewhere,[33] there may be room within the context of existing federal-provincial fiscal arrangements for a 'trade' to be negotiated between the federal government and the provinces. The federal government, with respect to most shared-cost social programs (e.g. health and education), would agree to remove conditions on provincial expenditures, simply providing cash or tax room to the provinces (in the interests of vertical fiscal balance), leaving them to decide for themselves which social programs to underwrite and on what terms. Given limited economic spillovers from most of these programs, this approach would foster innovation and experimentation – one of the major virtues of a federal system. However, in exchange, the federal government would attach conditions to all equalization payments and vertical transfers, requiring adherence by the provinces to the Code of Economic Conduct negotiated and enforced much as the Macdonald Commission proposed. Failure to adhere to the code or adjudications thereunder would result in financial penalties analogous to those entailed in the recent extra-billing prohibition with respect to medical services enacted in the Canada Health Act, 1982.

This approach would have an additional virtue that reflects the relationship between internal and international trade distortions. As the Macdonald Commission pointed out, one of the difficulties that the federal government faces in negotiating international trade liberalization treaties (such as a bilateral Canadian-US free trade agreement) is that it is far from clear that it has the constitutional ability to bind the provinces with respect to constraints on non-tariff barriers to trade induced by provincial policies.[34] Under the approach here proposed, there is the potential that constraints negotiated in such international trade treaties could be embodied in the federal-provincial Code of Economic Conduct and enforced by way of conditions attaching to equalization payments and vertical transfers.

By viewing the issue of internal barriers to trade as closely linked to the issue of international barriers to trade, another problem might potentially be mitigated. Under the proposals I have advanced above for enforcing a Code of Economic Conduct against the provinces, there is no mechanism (except constitutional amendment) for legally enforcing the code against the federal government. Yet as we saw earlier in this essay, federal government policies have been responsible for more costly distortions of the internal common market than provincial policies. However, under a bilateral free trade agreement with the United States, many of the federal policies responsible for inducing interprovincial distortions are likely themselves to be constrained, e.g. national tariff policy, national energy policy, industrial subsidies. Thus the two tiers of legally enforceable constraints – against the federal government under any bilateral free trade agreement with the United States, and against the provinces under a domestic Code of Economic Conduct – would deal, in a complementary way, with both internal and international barriers to trade.

The inducements for the provinces to accept these constraints are, first, the right to participate in the Federal-Provincial Council and Commission that would develop and enforce the constraints; second, the freedom from federal conditions on expenditures with respect to shared-cost social programs; and, third, under further proposals of the Macdonald Commission, generous adjustment assistance to displaced workers with respect to retraining, relocation, early retirement, and, for example, loss of resale value on houses in dependent communities.[35] The Transitional Adjustment Assistance Program (TAAP) proposed by the Macdonald Commission should obviously encompass adjustments required by the removal of both international and internal trade barriers if the economic and hence political costs associated with their removal are to be mitigated.

All of this is to suggest that there seems to be the potential for a federal-provincial 'deal' – admittedly complex and difficult to consummate – for realizing simultaneously freer international and internal trade. The inherently political nature of this deal seems well beyond the reach of a bald but vague, judicially enforced constitutional prohibition on internal barriers to trade and implies that in the future many of the most important 'constitutional' arrangements governing federal-provincial economic relations will increasingly be resolved outside the bounds of Canada's formal constitution.[36]

NOTES

1 Garth Stevenson *Unfulfilled Union* (Toronto: Gage 1982) chaps 1 and 2
2 See Michael Bliss 'The Evolution of Industrial Policies in Canada' Economic Council of Canada 1982.
3 Royal Commission on Dominion-Provincial Relations *Report* (Rowell-Sirois Report) (Ottawa: King's Printer 1940)
4 See Jean Chrétien, Minister of Justice *Securing the Canadian Economic Union in the Constitution* (Ottawa: Department of Supply and Services 1980)
5 A.E. Safarian *Canadian Federalism and Economic Integration* (Ottawa: Information Canada 1974)
6 See T.J. Courchene 'Analytical Perspectives on the Canadian Economic Union' in M.J. Trebilcock, J.R.S. Prichard, T.J. Courchene, and J. Whalley eds *Federalism and the Canadian Economic Union* (Toronto: Ontario Economic Council and University of Toronto Press 1983)
7 See Michael Penny 'Existing and Proposed Constraints on Provincially Induced Barriers to Economic Mobility' in Trebilcock et al eds *Federalism*
8 Royal Commission *Report* on the Economic Union and Development Prospects for Canada (Macdonald Report) (Ottawa: Supply and Services 1985)
9 See J. Robert S. Prichard with Jamie Benedickson 'Securing the Canadian Economic Union: Federalism and Internal Barriers to Trade' in Trebilcock et al eds *Federalism* 8ff
10 See Ronald Dworkin 'Is Wealth a Value?' *Journal of Legal Studies* 9 (1980) 191; Anthony Kronman 'Wealth Maximization as a Normative Principle' ibid 227; Ernest Weinrib 'Utilitarianism, Economics and Legal Theory' *University of Toronto Law Journal* 30 (1980) 307
11 Prichard and Benedickson 'Securing' 17ff; on theories of federalism see also Kenneth Norrie, Richard Simeon, and Mark Krasnick *Federalism and the Economic Union in Canada* (Macdonald Royal Commission Research Study 1986) 58.
12 See C.M. Tiebout 'A Pure Theory of Public Expenditures' *Journal of Political Economy* 64 (1956) 416.
13 See A. Breton and A. Scott *The Economic Constitution of Federal States* (Toronto: University of Toronto Press 1978).
14 See E. West and S. Winer 'The Individual, Political Tension, and Canada's Quest for a New Constitution' *Canadian Public Policy* 6 (1980) 3; P. Weiler 'The Virtues of Federalism in Canadian Labour Law' in *The Direction of Labour*

Policy in Canada, 25th Annual Conference, 1977 (Montreal: Industrial Relations Centre, McGill University 1977)
15 See Safarian *Canadian Federalism* 2.
16 Courchene 'Analytical Perspectives' 77
17 Ibid 99
18 Macdonald Report III 104, 106, 108
19 Ibid 103, 105
20 Ibid 124
21 Ibid
22 Ibid 126
23 Taken from John Whalley 'Induced Distortions of Interprovincial Activity' in Trebilcock et al eds *Federalism* 184
24 Trebilcock, Whalley, Rogerson, and Ness 'Provincially Induced Barriers to Trade in Canada: A Survey' in ibid chap 6
25 See John Whalley 'The Impact of Federal Policies on Interprovincial Activity' in ibid chap 5.
26 Robin Boadway and Frank Flatters *Equalization in a Federal State: An Economic Analysis* (Ottawa: Economic Council of Canada 1982)
27 Whalley 'Induced Distortions' 190ff; Macdonald Report III 120
28 Macdonald Report III 120
29 Courchene 'Analytical Perspectives' 95ff
30 Macdonald Report III 120, 133, 134; further estimates of the welfare losses from internal trade distortions appear in J. Whalley *Regional Aspects of Confederation* vol. 68, Macdonald Commission Research Study 1986
31 See Michael Penny 'Existing and Proposed Constitutional Constraints on Provincially Induced Barriers to Economic Mobility in Canada' in Trebilcock et al eds *Federalism* 526.
32 Macdonald Report III 135ff
33 Michael J. Trebilcock 'The Politics of Positive Sum' in Thomas J. Courchene, David W. Conklin, and Gail C.A. Cook eds *Ottawa and the Provinces: The Distribution of Money and Power* II (Toronto: Ontario Economic Council 1985) 235ff
34 Macdonald Report III 151ff
35 Ibid 616ff
36 See Thomas J. Courchene 'The Fiscal Arrangements: Focus on 1987' in Courchene et al *Ottawa and the Provinces* I (Toronto: Ontario Economic Council 1985) 4–5.

13 / The Workability of Executive Federalism in Canada

J. STEFAN DUPRÉ

This chapter probes the workability of executive federalism in Canada. By workability, I do not mean the capacity of executive federalism, on any given issue or at any given time, to produce federal-provincial accord as opposed to discord. Because executive federalism is rooted in what Richard Simeon has succinctly labelled the 'political independence' and the 'policy interdependence'[1] of Canada's federal and provincial governments, it is these governments that make the fundamental choices to agree or disagree. Whether executive federalism works involves not whether governments agree or disagree but whether it provides a forum (or more accurately a set of forums) that is conducive, and perceived to be conducive, to negotiation, consultation, or simply exchange of information.

A major theme of this chapter is that the workability of executive federalism is to an important degree a function of the manner in which the executives of the federal and provincial governments operate. This is explored in an introduction – 'Executive Federalism and Intragovernmental Relations' – and probed further in the next two sections, 'Federal-Provincial Functional Relations' and 'Federal-Provincial Summit Relations.' These sections probe selective circumstances under which executive federalism has been a more or less workable mechanism of federal-provincial adjustment. The final section, 'Prescriptions for Workable Executive Federalism,' probes procedural and substantive directions that executive federalism might seek to follow for the balance of this century.

Executive Federalism and Intragovernmental Relations

The fundamental facts of Canadian constitutionalism are federalism and the cabinet-parliamentary form of government. The first means that the

Canadian territorial division of power takes the form of two constitutionally ordained levels of government, each endowed with distinct yet often overlapping jurisdiction. The second means that executive and legislative institutions, through the constitutional conventions of responsible government, are fused in such a manner that what Thomas Hockin calls the 'collective central energizing executive' (cabinet) is the 'key engine of the state'[2] within the federal and provincial levels of government.

The Canadian version of the rise of the modern administrative state yields progressively larger and more potent federal and provincial bureaucracies, formally subordinated to their respective cabinets, and growing federal-provincial interdependence as each of these levels of government, driven by its energizing executive, actualizes the jurisdictional potential conferred upon it by the constitution. With almost Sophoclean inevitability, the resulting need for a non-judicial mechanism of adjustment is met by what Donald Smiley so aptly calls executive federalism, 'which may be defined as the relations between elected and appointed officials of the two orders of government in federal-provincial interactions.'[3] Smiley includes relations among the elected and appointed officials of provincial governments under the umbrella of executive federalism, but this chapter will refer to such purely interprovincial relations as 'executive interprovincialism.' This is in part to stress the fact that relations between governments that share identical jurisdiction are different from relations between governments that share divided jurisdiction, in part to acknowledge that executive interprovincialism has not infrequently been a provincial response to executive federalism.

'The relations between elected and appointed officials of the two levels of government' are taken as the constant that defines executive federalism. Executive federalism has been categorized in the literature from the standpoint of results as co-operative or conflictual. From the standpoint of actors it has been called summit federalism (relations among first ministers and/or their designated ministerial or bureaucratic entourage) and functional federalism (relations among ministers and/or officials). From the standpoint of participating governments it has been labelled multilateral (the federal and all ten provincial governments), multilateral-regional (the federal government and the governments of some, normally contiguous, provinces), and bilateral (the federal government and a single province). These labels – and others – will be used where appropriate in the text of this chapter; all, however, are deemed conceptually secondary to the notion of executive federalism as embodying the relations between the elected and appointed officials of the energizing executives of Canada's federal and provincial levels of government.

It is this simple notion that permits me to observe that executive federalism, as a mechanism of federal-provincial adjustment, cannot be divorced from intragovernmental considerations, that is from the structure and functioning of the 'collective central energizing structure' with which the conventions of the constitution endow Ottawa and each of the provinces. Without altering one iota of the constitutional conventions that give them their central energizing force, cabinets can operate in vastly different ways. Thus, for example, at any given time, there will be differences in the manner in which cabinets operate in Ottawa, as distinct from large provinces, as distinct from small provinces. More important to a general consideration of executive federalism are historically distinguishable modes of cabinet operation. I shall distinguish three such modes of cabinet operation. The first, labelled the 'traditional' mode, is one in which cabinets can be said to operate primarily as what Jean Hamelin calls 'chamber(s) of political compensation.'[4] This mode antedates the rise of the modern administrative state and, for that matter, of executive federalism. Here cabinet ministers, given the limited scope of their respective governments, pre-eminently articulate and aggregate matters of regional or local political concern and are primarily in the business of dispensing patronage. The extent to which the federal cabinet, in this mode of operation, can itself provide a mechanism of federal-provincial adjustment has been aptly sketched by Donald Smiley.[5] The second and third modes of cabinet operation, which accompany respectively the rise and then the maturation of the modern administrative state, are the ones that are material to executive federalism. The second may be called the 'departmentalized cabinet,' and the third the 'institutionalized cabinet.'

The departmentalized cabinet at once reflects and abets the rise of the modern administrative state. Government departments, allocated among ministers as their respective portfolio responsibilities, are the prime depositories of public-sector expansion and of the special expertise that fuels and responds to expansion. The functions assigned to a department make it the natural focus of discrete client interests, and the inputs of these departmentally oriented clientele groups interact synergistically with the 'withinputs' of the department's expert bureaucrats. For ministers, this interaction breeds 'portfolio loyalty' both because they perceive that their effectiveness is judged by their departmental clienteles and because they depend on departmental expertise for policy formulation and implementation. Subject to greater or lesser degrees of prime ministerial direction, ministers are endowed with a substantial measure of decision-making autonomy which redounds to the benefit of their departmental clienteles and bureaucracies. In the departmentalized cabinet, a minister is of course always a member of what by constitutional design is a collectively responsible executive, but, as James Gillies puts it so well, 'the principle of Cabinet collective responsibility [is] based on the commonsense notion of confidence in one's colleagues, rather than on the concept of sharing of knowledge or decision-making.'[6]

In the 'institutionalized' cabinet, by contrast, various combinations of formal committee structures, established central agencies, and budgeting and management techniques combine to emphasize shared knowledge, collegial decision-making, and the formulation of government-wide priorities and objectives. 'The major thrust,' Smiley writes, 'is to decrease the relative autonomy of ministers and the departments working under their direction.'[7] More than this, the institutionalized cabinet generates distinguishable categories of ministers – what Douglas Hartle calls the 'central agency' ministers and the 'special interest' ministers.[8] The portfolios of the former, in Hartle's words, 'cut across special interest lines for they reflect the several dimensions of the *collective* concerns of the Cabinet.'[9] Meantime, the ministers in the second category continue to pursue, 'as they are expected to pursue, the special interest of special portfolios.'[10] In this setting, intragovernmental decision-making not only becomes collegial but also acquires a competitive, adversarial flavour.

The original Canadian home of the institutionalized cabinet is the Saskatchewan of Premier T.C. Douglas (1944–60), and its best documented manifestations are those of the Pearson-Trudeau-Clark-Trudeau era (1963–84) in Ottawa. With substantial variations both spatially and temporally, the institutionalized cabinet has as its theme the quest to make contemporary government decision-making manageable. It arises initially as the response to the perceived defects of the departmentalized cabinet in the face of the range, complexity, and interdependence of the decisions that contemporary governments are called upon to make. Once in place, it can be adjusted into a variety of configurations as the quest to make contemporary decision-making manageable continues to be pursued with all the intensity of the quest for the Holy Grail. From one perspective, effectively articulated by Peter Aucoin, the institutionalized cabinet subjects special interests to the welcome challenge of greater scrutiny and increased competition.[11] From a contrary perspective, articulated with like effectiveness by James Gillies, the institutionalized cabinet can so dissipate the input of special interests into the policies that affect them that it threatens to undermine the doctrine of government by consent.[12]

Which perspective is more nearly correct (and both may have enormous elements of validity) is less important for our study of the workability of executive federalism than the stark fact that the intergovernmental relations between elected and appointed officials of our two levels of government cannot but be affected by the very different intragovernmental relations that characterize the departmentalized and institutionalized modes of cabinet operation. To expound, let us consider federal-provincial functional relations and federal-provincial summit relations. In each instance, the transition from the departmentalized to the institutionalized cabinet has fundamental implications.

Federal-Provincial Functional Relations

From the 1920s into the 1960s, the Canadian story of income security, social services, health care, vocational education, transportation infrastructure, and resource development is a tale in which federal-provincial functional relations play a starring role. True to the operation, at each level of government, of the departmentalized cabinet, executive federalism rests upon relations between program officials, deputy ministers, and ministers from federal and provincial departments with overlapping or complementary missions. The relations are financially lubricated by numerous conditional grants which apply the federal spending power to individual programs that frequently but not invariably aspire to national standards. When categorized in terms of outcomes, federal-provincial relations are justifiably labelled 'co-operative federalism.'[13] The ingredients of these relations can be readily enumerated to yield what I choose to call the 'functional relations model' of executive federalism. Each element in the model is remarkably conducive to the formation and maintenance of what Albert Breton and Ronald Wintrobe call 'networks,' that is, 'trust relationships or trust ties,'[14] along intergovernmental lines.

1. The appointed federal and provincial program officials involved in functional relations share common values and speak in a similar vocabulary as a result of common training in a particular profession or discipline, e.g. public health, social work, or education.

2. Departmentalized cabinets make it likely that the commonalities that characterize functional relations at the level of program officials will percolate to the deputy ministerial and ministerial levels. In the departmentalized setting, deputy ministers will have commonly risen through the ranks of their deparments and thus share the outlooks of their program subordinates. As for ministers, the relatively uninhibited portfolio loyalties bred by the departmentalized cabinet induce a coincidence of views notwithstanding their diverse political and professional backgrounds. Further, the measure of decision-making autonomy that ministers enjoy as members of their departmentalized cabinets means that there is minimal likelihood that federal-provincial accord at the ministerial level will be questioned or reversed by first ministers or cabinets.

3. The trust relationships generated by elements 1 and 2 draw ongoing sustenance from the longevity of the federal-provincial structures within which functional relations are conducted. Enhancing as they do the likelihood of repeated transactions over long periods of time, these stable structures, to borrow the words of Breton and Wintrobe, 'increase the future return to investments in trust.'[15] They ensure that federal and provincial ministers, deputy ministers, and program officials, at any given time, have a stake in their future relationships.

4. The financial lubricant supplied by conditional grants aids and abets trust relationships in that the resulting program activity at the donating and recipient levels of government enhances bureaucratic careers and ministerial reputations. Such grants also insulate program activity from budgetary competition to the extent that they generate the familiar lock-in effect ('we are locked in by promises made to the provinces') at the federal level and the equally familiar carrot effect ('fifty-cent dollars') at the provincial level.

5. Special interests, e.g. those focused upon public health, welfare, or education, achieve virtual representation in the processes of executive federalism through the associational ties of department officials and the loyalty of ministers to their clientele-oriented portfolios.

If the four decades of federal-provincial functional relations from which the above model is derived can indeed be labelled an era of co-operative federalism, the evident exception is Quebec. But this exception supports rather than undermines the importance of the model's components. To the extent that Quebec's officials shared professional backgrounds similar to those of their counterparts from Ottawa and English-Canadian provinces, their distinctive academic formation was anything but tantamount to the common school ties, corresponding to the restricted number of professional faculties then found in English-speaking universities, worn by anglophone program officials. However, in Quebec's version of the departmentalized cabinet, ministerial autonomy was severely circumscribed by the prime ministerial style of Maurice Duplessis and by the government-wide objective, found on widely shared respect for classical as opposed to co-operative federalism, of protecting provincial jurisdiction and indigenous institutions. Again, in that Quebec did not uniformly exclude itself from functional arrangements, the longevity of federal-provincial structures, coupled with the open-ended availability of conditional grants, permitted selective shopping by the Quebec government and made it easier for it to select programs of its choosing, normally in the domain of income maintenance. Finally, with respect to special interests, the extent to which Quebec's self-imposed exclusion from federal-provincial functional relations enjoyed societal support is testimony to the segmentalist orientation,[16] driven by linguistic barriers, of this province's élites.

As the 1960s unfolded and blended into the 1970s, federal-provincial functional relations underwent a significant metamorphosis, which paralleled and reflected the transition within governments from the departmentalized to the institutionalized cabinet. The budgetary distortions that conditional grants generated through their 'lock-in' and 'carrot' effects, once discovered by rationalized budgetary processes, spelled the demise of these grants on a grand scale. Equally consequential was the extent to which functional relations had to adapt to broader governmental considerations and were forced to accommodate sudden shifts in personnel and structures. In the result, the model sketched above no longer reflected the reality of functional relations. These relations now defied generalization. How far they came to depart from the model is clear from examples like the following.[17]

In the realm of social assistance, the established federal-provincial channels of welfare ministers and officials were swamped when a comprehensive social security review in the early 1970s called for consideration of a guaranteed annual income. This eventually aborted innovation was one in which central agencies and non-welfare ministries at both levels of government had a stake. Its consideration injected into the welfare officials' network economists and employment specialists who shared neither their professional vocabulary nor their values. The workability of intergovernmental consultation foundered in a Babel of tongues and of intragovernmental disputes between and among central and special interest agencies.

In the realm of vocational education, which for decades faithfully reflected the functional relations model, the desirability of manpower training as an adjunct of economic policy wrought a clash between federal economists newly enlisted in the use of training as a job placement tool and provincial educationists intent on the role of education in personal development. The upshot was a federal-provincial conflict fuelled even more by diverging professional norms than by clashing jurisdictional claims. A telling by-product was recourse, through the Manpower Programs Committee of the Council of Ministers of Education, to 'executive interprovincialism' as a vehicle for insulating professional educationists and their institutional clientele from labour market–oriented objectives.

Finally, the realm of regional development, from the mid-1960s into the 1980s, featured staggering shifts in objectives from agricultural rehabilitation to alleviating rural poverty to urban job creation to identifying and exploiting 'economic opportunities' (whatever they might be). Regional development was the preserve of bilateral federal-provincial relations. But each shift in objectives occasioned in turn shifts in the professional orientation and home agency of the federal and provincial officials concerned, tests of strength between federal and provincial central agencies bent upon co-ordinating their respective governments at the expense of the other, and successive dissolutions of federal-provincial consultative and negotiating bodies, each dissolution aborting any trust ties that might be developing between federal and provincial officials.

If nothing else, what seemed clear by the 1980s was that the 'federal-provincial functional relations model' had been relegated to history. What about summit relations?

Federal-Provincial Summit Relations

Federal-provincial summit relations are epitomized in the media-haunted conferences of the eleven first ministers, but they have come to encompass a variety of central agency ministers and officials. This being so, they are strongly conditioned by the extent to which, within governments, the quest to make decision-making manageable is eminently prime ministerial. In this regard, first ministers are the chief architects of their own institutionalized cabinets, and they alone can elect to change or bypass the decision-making structures and processes of these cabinets at any given time and on any particular matter.

By the 1980s, federal-provincial summitry was in a state of disarray. The starring role in how this came about must be assigned to the all-too-familiar conflicting forces that first ministers so visibly articulated: Quebec nationalism/indépendantism, post-OPEC western Canadian assertiveness, Ontario's defence of its economic pre-eminence, Atlantic province resentments, and federal counter-offensives to perceived excesses of provincialism. All these forces roosted at the federal-provincial summit table during the constitutional review exercise of 1980–1. Their continuing saliency, exacerbated by the fact that the outcome of the constitutional review was declared illegitimate by the government and legislature of Quebec, found expression in the extent to which ministers had become prone to talk past each other from their respective capitals rather than with each other on the basis of their policy interdependence. But this was a recent phenomenon. If we examine summitry in the light of its longest-standing agenda item, fiscal relations, we can at once discern how it can be workable and appreciate the magnitude of its recent disarray.

The taxing, spending, and borrowing activities of government have always given a special status to departments of finance (or treasury). Long before the rise of the institutionalized cabinet and the coining of the term *central agency*, finance departments stood out as horizontal portfolios whose government-wide scope made them readily available adjuncts of first ministers. The war-conditioned initiation of tax rental agreements in 1940 gave to fiscal matters what turned out to be a regular quinquennial place on the agenda of federal-provincial summitry. By 1955, once the financial exigencies of recent and anticipated public-sector growth were apparent, the first ministers naturally turned to their finance officials so as to equip their fiscal conferences with an expert infrastructure. Thus was born the Continuing Committee on Fiscal and Economic Matters, to which was added a Tax Structure Committee of finance ministers in 1964 and then, beginning in the late 1960s, the still-ongoing practice of pre-federal budget formulation meetings of ministers of finance.[18]

With these underpinnings, federal-provincial summit relations, through the devising of the 1977–82 Fiscal Arrangements, achieved results that are well known: divorce of tax collection agreements from intergovernmental transfers and tax sharing; orderly reallocations of income tax room between the federal government and the provinces; unconditional equalization payments geared to provincial fiscal capacity as measured by a representative tax system; curtailment of conditional grants and the development initially of a shared-cost and then a block-funding approach to health and post-secondary education; and accommodation of income tax reform through federal revenue guarantees to the provinces.[19] The path to these achievements was often acrimonious. Thus, for example, the 1967–72 Fiscal Arrangements, while they did not provoke united provincial opposition, were never endorsed by a summit meeting;[20] the 1977–82 Arrangements, which did receive summit endorsement in December 1976, had previously provoked a provincial common front.[21] What remains constant is that first ministers, whether or not they endorsed a particular set of arrangements and however heated their periodic disagreements, had come to perceive their relations, underpinned as they were by finance ministers and officials, as workable. The elements of this workability can be readily enumerated so as to comprise a 'fiscal relations model' of federal-provincial summitry.

1. Financial issues are inherently tangible and quantifiable. Accordingly, the parameters within which they are discussed can often be delimited within the bounds of common-sense bookkeeping (e.g. the question of tax room for the provinces is conditioned by the fiscal capacity required to make federal equalization payments; the extent to which provincial natural resource revenues can enter into an equalization formulation is confined by reference to what constitutes a tolerable growth rate in the size of the federal equalization bill). Also, the bounds of any particular issue can be narrowed and even resolved through easily measured saw-offs (e.g. the provincial common front, which formed in 1976 around a revenue guarantee

termination payment of four personal income tax points, was bargained down to one point in tax room and one point in cash).[22]

2. Finance officials share not only the common vocabulary of macro-economic analysis but also the common outlook (the 'treasury mentality') bred by their roles as governmental fiscal managers. These characteristics, once situated under the umbrella of the long-lived Continuing Committee on Fiscal and Economic Matters, are conducive to the formulation of trust ties.

3. Network formation among finance ministers is facilitated by the trust ties among their officials and abetted by their common preoccupations with revenue and with managing the spending ambitions of their cabinet colleagues.

4. From first ministers down to finance officials, the fixed maximum five-year term of fiscal arrangements means that any particular configuration of issues, however disputed, must once again be opened to review. This simultaneously eases the climate of consultation ('nothing is forever') and invites reinvestment in trust ties.

What happens to this 'fiscal relations model'? Its effective operation remains abundantly apparent in the design of the 1977–82 Fiscal Arrangements and most particularly the Established Program Financing (EPF) feature of these arrangements. The block funding of health and post-secondary education disentangled federal rates of spending from provincial rates of spending, and vice versa. As such, EPF contributed to the quest to make the spending of each order of government manageable and is precisely what might be expected to emerge from an intergovernmental network of finance ministers and officials. The summit consensus of December 1976 testifies to the continuing influence of this network on first ministers, not least when two circumstances are recalled: the Parti québécois had come to power in the autumn of that year, and, the preceding summer, outright provincial rejection of Prime Minister Trudeau's minimalist constitutional patriation package had signalled the full awakening of western provincial governments to constitutional issues and their consequent rejection of the Victoria amendment formula.

But December 1976 marked the last hurrah of the fiscal relations model. Its outline is barely discernible in the fashioning of the 1982–7 Fiscal Arrangements. From David Perry's account, it is apparent that negotiation among finance ministers and officials had little impact on any component of these arrangements other than equalization.[23] Here the main result was a five-province representative average standard in lieu of the initial federal proposal for an Ontario average. For the rest, the fiscal relations model was inoperative. This is due in part to the weakening of the position of the Department of Finance within the federal government and more especially to the fact (perhaps because of this weakness?) that the government of Canada chose to pursue its counter-offensive against provincialism beyond the constitutional review and into the fiscal domain.

By the mid-1970s in Ottawa, the institutionalization of the federal cabinet had attenuated the hegemony of Finance as the key horizontal portfolio in fiscal and economic management. Indeed, competition among central agencies, notably Finance, the Treasury Board Secretariat, and the Privy Council Office, was a documented reality.[24] The emergence, at the end of the decade, of yet two more central agencies, the Ministry of State for Economic (later Economic and Regional) Development and the Ministry of State for Social Development, engendered further competition for Finance in the decision-making processes of the government of Canada. As Douglas Hartle asked pointedly in noting these developments, 'Is it credible that Finance has as much impact on federal-provincial fiscal relations and on economic and social development policies as it had when it was the overall 'economic manager' of the federal government?'[25]

The relative waning of Finance, and with it the fiscal relations model, in the devising of the 1982–7 Fiscal Arrangements was signalled with the appointment of the Parliamentary Task Force on Federal-Provincial Fiscal Arrangements (the Breau Task Force) in 1981. This innovation could be viewed – and justified – as a positive step because it involved members of Parliament in the pre-legislative process and opened the fiscal arrangements to interest group involvement. But it also unleashed an Ottawa-centred view of the Fiscal Arrangements, in particular of their EPF component. The EPF block cash payment was perceived as lacking an acceptable basis in accountability to Parliament. Moreover, the Breau Task Force proved to be a federal magnet for interest groups dissatisfied with provincial spending and policies in health care and post-secondary education. It met, as Rod Dobell has noted, 'the desire of provincially-based interest groups operating in areas falling within provincial jurisdiction to appeal to the federal government for action (standards, criteria, rules, whatever) to offset the impacts of provincial government spending (and legislative) priorities.'[26]

At this juncture, it became apparent at the highest political levels of the federal government that the abandonment of block funding could be pursued in the name of parliamentary accountability and responsiveness to interest groups whose demands were reinforced by polls demonstrating public antipathy toward user charges and extra billing by physicians for insured services. The upshot, after a stop-gap extension of EPF for the first two years of the 1982–7 Fiscal Arrangements, was the Canada Health Act of 1984. And the potent appeal, especially in an election year, of the values of accountability and responsiveness, was dramatically underlined by the all-party support given to the passage of this act in the House of Commons.

A starkly unilateral federal initiative endorsed by Prime Minister Trudeau, the Canada Health Act emerged not from Finance but from the collegial processes of cabinet decision-making served now not only by the Privy Council Office and its offshoot, the Federal-Provincial Relations Office, but also by the Ministry of State for Social Development. In essence, the act lays down a code of provincial government conduct toward insured hospital and medical services. User charges and extra billing by physicians are deemed a violation of the code and are henceforth subject to measured ·reductions in the EPF cash transfer to the offending provinces. Further, compliance with the code requires a province to enter into a formal agreement with medical practitioners and dentists with respect to their compensation and to the resolution of compensation disputes through conciliation or arbitration. Failure to comply entails reductions in the cash transfer that are left for the federal cabinet to determine.[27]

These details starkly spell the demise of block funding and with it the disentanglement of provincial from federal spending. Beyond spending, the very manner in which provinces choose to deal with health care practitioners becomes subject to federal fiscal intervention. What emerges is a fundamental reorientation of federal-provincial fiscal arrangements that has completely circumvented summit consultation and its underlying networks of finance officials and ministers. Thus does the disarray in federal-provincial summitry, exacerbated by the conflicting forces so apparent in the constitutional review, now embrace the fiscal arrangements that stood for decades as the staple agenda item of first ministers' conferences. One more point needs to be made.

The Canada Health Act fits the mould of federal counter-offensives to perceived excesses of provincialism. But in this instance the perceived excess at which the counter-offensive takes aim lies outside the mainstream of those that the government of Canada sought to counter in the constitutional review. There the perceived excesses converged around matters of economic policy. The slogan 'Securing the Economic Union' was the subtitle of the federal position paper on economic powers.[28] The economic union is to be secured from what are deemed to have been, for about a decade, balkanizing and unilateral provincial incursions into the economic realm in the form of a wide variety of protectionist measures and province-centred industrial and resource development policies. The Canada Health Act, for its part, has nothing to do with countering such provincial economic incursions. It constitutes a federal counter-offensive to provincial policies in the social realm of health care, policies that are a mixture of fiscal, cost-control, and professional compensation considerations. As such, the act is defensible in the name of accountability and responsiveness to interest group demands for equity. Meantime, however, the provincial incursions that have been perceived to affect the economic union are themselves defensible on the same grounds. Are not protectionism and province-centred development policies a reflection of provincial responsiveness to interest group demands and of the ultimate accountability of provincial governments to their electorates? Viewed in this light, the condition that leaves the eleven first ministers with their summit interactions in disarray is, if nothing else, deliciously ironic.

The recent condition of summit disarray casts a shadow over all manifestations of executive federalism. Nonetheless, especially under favourable assumptions regarding personalities and governing parties, it can be argued that this condition is not intractable. However, even allowing for the sweeping changes in the dramatis personae of first ministers, heralded by Prime Minister Mulroney's federal election victory of 1984 and by the advent in 1985 of new first ministers in Ontario, Quebec, and Alberta, the path to renewed workability does not lie in one more attempt to 'get the constitution right.' Any summit process called upon to devise the 'right' constitution is too likely to fail in the attempt. When we include the 1968–71 route to the aborted Victoria Charter along with the 1980–1 exercise that yielded, only after the Supreme Court's assistance, the Constitution Act, 1982, multilateral summitry has twice failed to achieve central institution reform, to disentangle the division of jurisdiction, and to recognize the historical mission of Quebec in the cultural domain. Setting aside whether or not these reforms were desirable in principle, a powerful explanation for this double failure lies in what I call a 'constitutional review model' of federal-provincial summitry that is the diametrical opposite of my fiscal relations model in all respects.

(1) Constitutional issues, being symbolic and abstract rather than tangible and quantifiable, are not amenable to readily measurable trade-offs. (2) The officials who underpin constitutional review deliberations include law officers who, to the extent that they view their respective governments as legal clients, may tend to magnify jurisdictional jealousies rather than reduce them on the basis of shared professional values. (3) The horizontal portfolio ministers most closely involved are federal and provincial ministers of justice and attornies-general, whose portfolios include recourse to adversarial processes before the courts and who are therefore prone to examine constitutional proposals in this light. (4) The whole process of comprehensive constitutional review focuses the attention on all participants, from first ministers down, on the 'one last play' that will be the constitutional

engineering feat of comprehensive change; the anticipated proximity of this last play depreciates investment in long-term trust. (5) Because it is known that the 'one last play' yields a quasi-permanent end result given the rigidity of the amendment process, negotiations are inherently more tension-ridden than when 'nothing is forever.'

The 'one last play' of the 1980–1 constitutional review, as it turned out, yielded a fundamental challenge: the task of legitimating the Constitution Act, 1982, in the eyes of the government and national assembly of Quebec. Elaborate proposals[29] advanced on this subject by the government of Quebec in 1985 are surely best pursued, for the time being, as matters for bilateral summitry between Ottawa and Quebec. They are not fit for the agenda of a multilateral federal-provincial summitry in need of convalescence.

Prescriptions for Workable Executive Federalism

Prescribing for the workability of executive federalism is first of all a matter of extracting the moral of my two tales of functional and summit relations. The history of federal-provincial functional relations demonstrates that there was a time, lasting until the 1960s, when these relations had sufficient commonality to be explained by a simple conceptual model. Thereafter functional relations galloped off in several directions as witnessed by abbreviated examples, which suffice to convey that wide variability in such relations has become a matter of fact. Summit interaction, for its part, involved relations which, when fiscal arrangements were on the agenda, could be explained by another model, valid as late as the mid-1970s. These relations then bogged down in a state of disarray.

What then is the moral of these tales? When all is said and done, it is that the formation and maintenance of networks, i.e. trust ties, between the appointed officials of the two orders of government play a fundamental role in the workability of federal-provincial interaction. Trust ties can be a function of shared professional training and norms, as in the functional relations model; they can be a function of the shared vocabulary of macroeconomic analysis and a common interest in managing the spending ambitions of operating departments, as in the fiscal relations model.

Trust ties are communicable to ministers, but more so when ministers possess a measure of decision-making autonomy in their portfolios than when they must be oriented to collegial decision-making processes within their cabinets. Finance ministers are a special case. Presiding as they do over the original and historically most potent central agency, they are in a position to capitalize on the trust ties among their officials to the extent that they have primacy of access to first ministers. Once this primacy is hedged by competing central agencies, especially by central agencies under other central agency ministers who vie for their own access to their first ministers, finance ministers are in danger of becoming 'central agency ministers like the others,' and the utility of finance officer networks will be dissipated.

The moral of my two tales is simple enough. If it evokes a sense of nostalgia for the 'good old days' of departmentalized cabinets, when operating department ministers enjoyed decision-making latitude and finance ministers presided over a horizontal portfolio unchallenged by insurgent central agencies, so be it. I happen to believe that future cabinet reorganizations, especially in Ottawa, can well afford a touch of nostalgia. I also believe, however, that in one form or another institutionalized cabinets are here to stay. The multiplicity, complexity, and interdependence of the decisions that contemporary governments are called upon to make demand both cabinet committees and central agencies. They ensure that the quest to make decision-making manageable will remain ongoing and will lead to continuing experimentation with forms and processes. And this will extend beyond the executive and into legislative assemblies if only because institutionalized cabinets, in attenuating the autonomy of 'special interest' departments and ministers, generate a need for new channels of interest group consultation, new adjustments designed to accommodate the desideratum of government by consent. All of this has implications for the workability of executive federalism to which first ministers especially should be sensitive and which can be addressed through a handful of practical propositions.

1. Central agencies per se are not inimical to the conduct of federal-provincial functional relations among ministers and officials. The key distinction to be observed is between occasional appearances to communicate or clarify general policy and ongoing participation in the process of consultation or negotiation. The latter is to be reserved for departmental ministers and officials.

2. Once central agents, and for that matter officials from different departments with different professional backgrounds, enter a domain hitherto the preserve of functional interaction among particular operating ministers and departments, as in the social security review, first ministers have reason to be concerned that the agenda item involved is too broad to be handled short of summit processes. Such an item is better placed before the first ministers themselves or before central agency ministers who have been given a specific prime ministerial mandate to co-ordinate the departments involved with the item concerned (e.g. a guaranteed annual income).

3. First ministers can virtually guarantee unworkable federal-provincial relations if, by design or inadvertence, the officials charged with articulating the positions of the two orders of government do so on the basis of the clashing norms of different professions. Manpower training is an excellent case in point. If professional norms clash and the matter cannot be confined to one professional group, intergovernmental consultation or negotiation by administrative generalists is to be preferred. Outstanding interprofessional differences are best left to fester or be resolved around each government's cabinet table.

4. When the possibility of internal governmental reorganization appears on a first minister's agenda, he should actively consider its potential implications for workable federal-provincial relations. An internal reorganization that nips incipient intergovernmental networks in the bud (witness the succession of organizational shifts in the domain of regional development) involves costs in forgone trust ties that might have been avoided if the desiderata prompting the proposed change (visibility, closer adherence to Treasury Board guidelines, whatever) had first been clearly communicated to the federal-provincial networks as criteria to which their interactions should adapt.

5. The institutionalization of cabinets means that departmental ministers and officials are less effective conduits for the claims of client interest groups than was once the case. By the same token, the capacity of special interests to achieve a degree of virtual representation in many forums of federal-provincial interaction has gone the way of the functional relations model. An enhanced use of parliamentary committees to ventilate group interests beckons on both counts. If recourse to such committees poses a particular problem in matters of federal-provincial interaction, this is because interest groups are not necessarily prone to follow the jurisdictional flag when the opportunity of open hearings presents itself. The more impressive problem that lurks behind parliamentary committees is asymmetry in group presentations. The Breau Task Force, implicated as it is in the current federal-provincial fiscal disarray, was a magnet for public spending coalitions; its companion Task Force on Pension Reform, another inherently federal-provincial matter, attracted groups closely identified with the case for fiscal restraint.[30] First ministers should consider, and indeed might well consult on, the manner in which legislative committees examining matters of federal-provincial import could be equipped with terms of reference that attract the widest appropriate spectrum of contending views. So that parliamentarians might themselves have the opportunity to view federal-provincial relations writ large rather than through the terms of any particular committee

assignment, there might be merit as well in making an annual federal-provincial relations debate a set feature of each legislature's agenda, as with the Throne Speech and the Budget.

The above propositions can as easily be considered by first ministers in their respective capitals as they can at a summit conference. There is much to executive federalism below the structured interaction of first ministers themselves, and my propositions are meant to convey to them that workable federal-provincial interaction begins with foundations that must be built at home.

As for channels of interaction, first ministers are well advised to supplement their formal conferences on specific topics (fiscal matters, energy, the economy, native rights) with an annual meeting, held as a matter of routine, whose agenda is open to any combination of pertinent subjects. Several considerations highlight the potential of routine annual summits for enhancing the workability of executive federalism.

1. Because the matters that could appear on the agenda of routinized meetings potentially embrace anything of federal and provincial concern, preparation for each such meeting will necessitate close and ongoing interaction on the part of senior central agency officials situated in first ministers' offices or cabinet offices. The pressure on these officials to 'show results' by extracting, on a continuing basis, manageable annual agendas from their vague mandate should abet the formation of trust ties and promote workable proceedings.

2. The nexus between federal-provincial interaction and intragovernmental organization, illustrated by the propositions addressed to first ministers above, provides a practical if not invariably palatable menu for interchanges among the very individuals who, at the apex of their respective cabinets, share incentives to make their own decision-making manageable and the formal powers of organizing and reorganizing their governments.

3. Regularly recurring events have the capacity to gather their own momentum and to evoke constructive patterns of behaviour. The latter range from mutual sensitivity in areas where governmental actions unavoidably overlap to identifying opportunities for disentanglement that might, in time, become the subject of individual constitutional amendments.

Supremely, I dare to hope that routinized summitry would breed and nurture among first ministers what J.A. Corry calls 'constitutional morality,'[31] a behaviour pattern that focuses on the norms as distinct from the mere legalities of federalism, that seeks simultaneously to capitalize on the socioeconomic forces that bind a federation and on those that demand decentralization.

A prescription that calls for routinized summitry is one that focuses on process, that is incremental, and that takes a long-run view of federalism. As for the matters of substance that are critically important in the near term, two sets of observations may be ventured. The first involves the importance of containing one's expectations of what might be called 'multilateral economic summitry' and of searching out economic agenda items that hold some promise of early success. The second, whose relative urgency is easily measured by the fact that the next set of fiscal arrangements spans the years 1987–92, seeks to galvanize fiscal summitry into renewed and reoriented coherence.

There are several reasons to contain one's expectations of what multilateral summit relations can achieve with respect to economic issues writ large. For one thing, there is the track record of summitry with respect to the regionally most divisive of the economic issues of recent years: energy. Here, the intractable manner in which Premier William Davis of Ontario chose to present the position of energy consumers, not least during the Clark government interlude, guaranteed that summit negotiations must be confined to bilateral interaction between Ottawa and the producing provinces rather than pursued on the agenda of the eleven first ministers.[32] For another, there is the elaborate exercise in multilateral economic summitry of 1978, complete with ministerial and other working groups. In Michael Jenkin's words, 'The Results of the conferences tended to be either agreements on general principles that later turned out to hide very real differences, or agreements on isolated issues which did not, in themselves, add up to a coherent program of political action.'[33] More generally, provincial premiers have been prone to use economic conferences as vehicles for charging the federal government with economic mismanagement, while the government of Canada has perceived many provincial economic positions as an affront to its primacy in the economic realm. It should also be borne in mind that any summit conference called in the near term to deal with 'the economy' is bound to be a major media event replete with opportunities for political posturing. Such a conference, if it is to have any chance of meeting public expectations, will be in need of restricted agenda items selected with an eye on their potential to elicit agreement and demonstrate movement.

One possibility lies in regional development, where a multilateral economic summit might well address in principle the future orientation of bilateral agreements. Michael Trebilcock, in a recent address to the Ontario Economic Council, suggestively raised the possibility that the thrust of future agreements might preferably concentrate on economic adjustment rather than development.[34] What he calls 'General Adjustment Agreements' would focus on adjustment costs arising from freer international trade and reduced barriers to internal trade. Then there is the possibility of seeking summit approbation of Michael Jenkin's proposal for a continuing structure at the level of ministers and officials which he calls the Canadian Council of Industry and Technology Ministers (CCIT).[35] Bearing in mind that within governments, notably within the federal government, tensions among economic portfolios have been painfully apparent, I do not foresee that a CCIT has the same potential for trust ties as the long-standing Continuing Committee on Fiscal and Economic Matters. It beckons, nonetheless, especially to screen what might or might not provide workable agenda items for future economic summits and to assist in staffing the more informal, routinized summit meetings.

My own favourite, subject to a heavy discount for this very reason, is the possibility of economic summit deliberations over manpower training. What could be sought here is what is within the capacity of first ministers, each in his respective capacity as head of government, to grant: federal-provincial interaction by ministers and officials concerned not with education but with training as an employment placement and economic adjustment tool. At the time, some twenty years ago, when manpower training bred federal-provincial conflict, employment and training for employment had not acquired the overtones of the moral and ethical imperative that they possess today. And now that non-university post-secondary institutions are firmly established and mature, they no longer justify provincial insulation from outside influences, be these called 'federal,' 'economic,' or 'labour market.'

Having delineated possible agenda items conducive to workable economic summitry in the near term, I conclude by addressing what I consider to be the most pressing matter of substance for the processes of executive federalism: the fiscal arrangements for 1987–92. The Canada Health Act, as I have already pointed out, leaves executive federalism in a position that is nothing if not deliciously ironic. Here is a federally devised code of provincial conduct, to be implemented through the application of the federal spending power, in the realm of social policy. This initiative came on the heels of a quite different federal thrust, one which, in the context of the constitutional review, sought to establish greater federal primacy in the realm of economic policy. Having largely failed in the latter, the government of Canada successfully undermined provincial primacy in the realm of social policy. Here surely is Corry's principle of constitutional morality turned on its head. And it has its own economic downside. As Courchene observes,

With health costs already representing over 30 percent of some provincial budgets and escalating rapidly, with the likelihood of even more cost increases arising from the combination of increasingly expensive diagnostic treatment and an aging population, and with a concerted effort by numerous health-related associations to be covered under the universal health plan, it would appear that increased innovation and experimentation is essential in order that more efficient ways of delivering health care can be found. Already much in the way of provincial experimentation is ongoing ... To the extent that the Canada Health Act serves to promote uniformity rather than innovation, it is clearly a move in the wrong direction.[36]

If we put Corry and Courchene together, it seems that the Canada Health Act is a massive thrust in the wrong direction. To be sure, it can be justified on grounds of accountability and responsiveness to interest group pressures. But so can any of a number of provincial interventions in the economic realm, including protectionist interventions that generate costs that are not simply imposed on provincial electorates but are borne elsewhere in the country. As Prichard puts it so well, the externalities that flow from such interventions 'are affected by a fundamental illegitimacy that does not apply, at least in theory, to federal intervention.'[37] The parallel illegitimacy of the Canada Health Act is that health costs are largely internalized within provinces and yet will be driven by a federal code. Thus a code applies where it has no basis in constitutional morality or economic rationality, while there is no code with respect to matters where one would be warranted.

It is this precarious and anomalous situation that, in my view, cries out for rectification in the fiscal arrangements of 1987–92. The outcome that is earnestly to be desired is one in which a code of provincial conduct is withdrawn from the realm of social policy and applied instead in the realm of protectionist economic policies. The long-standing network of finance officials and ministers must be galvanized to probe once again the relative roles of tax-sharing and fiscal transfers in matters of social expenditure. And if the federal spending power is to be used to secure adherence to codes of provincial conduct, let this be examined in the realm of conduct that has perverse economic consequences, not where decentralized experiments in cost control are to be desired.

I fully appreciate that to transpose codes of conduct from social to economic policy will be a matter of the utmost political delicacy. The toothpaste, so to speak, is well out of the tube on two counts: any federal prime minister knows that the Canada Health Act enjoys significant support, and any provincial first minister knows equally well the forceful stake of special interests in provincial economic protectionism. What will be central is nothing more or less than the extent to which first ministers, jointly and severally, can discern that grand abstraction, the public interest, as distinct from particular interests. The test I pose to executive federalism, from the level of finance officials to the summit, involves 1987–92 fiscal arrangements that will at least move in the direction of constitutional morality and economic rationality. The movement, as distinct from the outright resolution, if what is of supreme importance. Because in fiscal arrangements, as distinct from constitutional reform, 'nothing is forever,' the 1992–97 arrangements will present a further opportunity. What should be accomplished between now and 1987 is the movement, not without difficulty or even acrimony, as testimony to the reactivated workability of executive federalism.

NOTES

This chapter is adapted from my essay 'Reflections on the Workability of Executive Federalism' in Richard Simeon, research co-ordinator *Intergovernmental Relations*, vol. 63 in the series of studies commissioned as part of the research program of the Royal Commission on the Economic Union and Development Prospects for Canada (Toronto: University of Toronto Press 1985) 1–32.

1 Richard Simeon 'Intergovernmental Relations and the Challenges to Canadian Federalism' *Canadian Public Administration* 23 (1980) 21
2 Thomas A. Hockin *Government in Canada* (Toronto: McGraw-Hill Ryerson 1976) 7
3 Donald V. Smiley *Canada in Question: Federalism in the Eighties* 3rd ed (Toronto: McGraw-Hill Ryerson 1980) 91
4 Jean Hamelin *The First Years of Confederation* (Ottawa: Centennial Commission 1967), cited in Donald V. Smiley 'Central Institutions' in Stanley M. Beck and Ivan Bernier eds *Canada and the New Constitution: The Unfinished Agenda* I (Montreal: Institute for Research on Public Policy 1983) 36
5 Smiley 'Central Institutions' 28–9 and 34–5
6 James Gillies *Where Business Fails* (Montreal: Institute for Research on Public Policy 1981) 84
7 Smiley *Canada in Question* 277
8 Douglas Hartle *Public Policy Decision Making and Regulation* (Montreal: Institute for Research on Public Policy 1979) 72
9 Ibid
10 Ibid
11 Peter Aucoin 'Pressure Groups and Recent Changes in the Policy-Making Process' in A. Paul Pross ed *Pressure Group Behaviour in Canadian Politics* (Toronto: McGraw-Hill Ryerson 1975) 174–92
12 Gillies *Where Business Fails* 137

13 Donald V. Smiley *Constitutional Adaptation and Canadian Federalism since 1945* Documents of the Royal Commission on Bilingualism and Biculturalism 4 (Ottawa: Queen's Printer 1974) chap 8

14 Albert Breton and Ronald Wintrobe *The Logic of Bureaucratic Conduct* (Cambridge: Cambridge University Press 1982) 78

15 Ibid 75

16 Albert Breton and Raymond Breton *Why Disunity? An Analysis of Linguistic and Regional Cleavages in Canada* (Montreal: Institute for Research on Public Policy 1980) 58–60 and passim

17 For a detailed development of the examples summarized below, see J. Stefan Dupré 'Reflections on the Workability of Executive Federalism' in *Intergovernmental Relations*, vol. 63, research studies prepared for the Royal Commission on the Economic Union and Development Prospects for Canada (Toronto: University of Toronto Press 1985)

18 Smiley *Canada in Question* 95–6

19 Perrin Lewis 'The Tangled Tale of Taxes and Transfers' in Michael Walker ed *Canadian Confederation at the Crossroads* (Vancouver: The Fraser Institute 1978) 39–102

20 Richard Simeon *Federal-Provincial Diplomacy: The Making of Recent Policy in Canada* (Toronto: University of Toronto Press 1972) 259–62

21 A.S. Rubinoff 'Federal-Provincial Relations: Is Our Conduct Changing?' Unpublished paper presented to the annual conference of the Institute of Public Administration of Canada, Victoria, BC, September 1977, 17–18

22 Ibid 22

23 David B. Perry 'The Federal-Provincial Fiscal Arrangements for 1982–87' *Canadian Tax Journal* 31 (1983) 30–4

24 Richard D. French *How Ottawa Decides: Planning and Industrial Policy-Making 1968–1980* (Ottawa: Canadian Institute for Economic Policy 1980)

25 Douglas G. Hartle *The Revenue Budget Process of the Government of Canada: Description, Appraisal and Proposals* (Toronto: Canadian Tax Foundation 1982) 66–7

26 Rod Dobell 'Alternative Consultation Processes: Prospect for 1987 and Beyond' Notes prepared for discussion at the Ontario Economic Council Conference, 'Ottawa and the Provinces: The Distribution of Money and Power' Toronto, 14, 15 May 1984, 13.

27 Ibid 7–11

28 *Powers over the Economy: Securing the Economic Union*

29 *Draft Agreement on the Constitution: Proposals by the Government of Quebec* (Quebec 1985)

30 Dobell 'Alternative Consultation Processes' 2

31 J.A. Corry 'The Uses of a Constitution' in Law Society of Upper Canada, Special Lectures *The Constitution and the Future of Canada* (Toronto: Richard De Boo 1978) 1–15

32 Jeffrey Simpson *Discipline of Power* (Toronto: Personal Library Publishers 1980) 179–203

33 Michael Jenkin *The Challenge of Diversity: Industrial Policy in the Canadian Federation* Background Study 50, Science Council of Canada (Ottawa: Minister of Supply and Services 1983) 128

34 Michael J. Trebilcock 'The Politics of Positive Sum' Notes prepared for discussion at the Ontario Economic Council Conference, 'Ottawa and the Provinces: The Distribution of Money and Power' Toronto, 14, 15 May 1984

35 Jenkin *The Challenge of Diversity* 175

36 Thomas J. Courchene 'The Fiscal Arrangements: Focus on 1987' Notes for an address to the Ontario Economic Council Conference, 'Ottawa and the Provinces: The Distribution of Money and Power' Toronto, 14, 15 May 1984

37 J. Robert S. Prichard with Jamie Benedickson 'Securing the Canadian Economic Union: Federalism and Internal Barriers to Trade' in Michael J. Trebilcock et al eds *Federalism and the Canadian Economic Union* Ontario Economic Council Research Studies (Toronto: University of Toronto Press 1983) 49

14 / Managing Intergovernmental Relations

JOHN WARHURST

Policy-making in federal systems,[1] such as Canada and Australia, in which constitutional authority to raise revenue and to make policy is divided between central and regional governments, can be undertaken in practice only on the basis of joint action between governments.[2] In these parliamentary systems, in which responsibility in fact lies with the executive, effective joint action takes place between individual ministers and their administrations rather than between parliaments or between cabinets, in any but a formal sense. Therefore, to describe such relations as 'intergovernmental' is misleading. They are intergovernmental only in the sense that a very large number of individual acts of co-operation, viewed collectively, constitutes the pattern of relations within a federal system.

This pattern of intergovernmental relations, which I shall call 'co-operative-executive federalism,' became the norm in post–Second World War Canada and Australia.[3] Its modus operandi has been described by Donald Smiley as 'the piecemeal consideration of very specific matters.'[4] The following section will outline its characteristics in somewhat greater detail. Suffice it to say that it was the means (even its critics admit) by which in each country the programs that make up the modern welfare state were put into place. Judging by this standard, most commentators would say that it has served Canada and Australia well. Yet both its supporters and critics alike admit that it is an untidy, unorganized system, in which the effect of the whole on policy-making may be more than the sum of the parts. Its management is left in the hands of senior policy-makers, ministers and bureaucrats, in a score of departments at each level of government. As Smiley points out, in such a system program creation is in the hands of professionals: engineers, foresters, social workers, public health officials, and others.[5] Central co-ordination and control in such a system depend largely on the effectiveness of cabinets. Otherwise there is only financial management vested in the central department, usually named treasury or finance, responsible for preparing, and subsequently monitoring, a government's annual budget.

Over the past twenty-five years in Canada and the past twelve to fourteen years in Australia, central and regional governments, with few exceptions, have attempted to add a new dimension to this way of conducting intergovernmental relations: management by central agency at either the administrative or ministerial level, or both.[6] Governments have sought to make relations within the federal system more genuinely intergovernmental by imposing a 'whole of government' view on the most important of the joint actions. In Smiley's words, under such a régime, 'particularized problems are subsumed under more comprehensive concerns.'[7] Governments have been concerned, in particular, to guard their jurisdiction over their constitutional responsibilities. But they have generally been concerned only to add to the existing way of conducting intergovernmental relations, not to replace it. The mechanism created to perform this new function has been the intergovernmental affairs specialist, located the centre either in a separate department or as a group within an existing central agency.

The drive for central co-ordination in the conduct of intergovernmental relations contains a number of elements, as it derives its impetus from different sources. To understand these separate elements enables one to make judgments about whether or not this change is likely to be more or less permanent or merely transitory. First, the new development has been, in part, an offshoot of the general moves by governments toward building more powerful central agencies with a brief to impose stronger central co-ordination upon all policy-making. Inevitably, in federal systems, such ideas flow on into the conduct of intergovernmental relations. Second, it was in part a consequence of the emergence of bigger and more ambitious governments. As part of this growth there was rapid expansion of co-operative-executive federalism, as in more and more fields central and regional governments were both attempting to intervene. Third, it was associated with the rise of a more competitive and partisan brand of politics in which serious policy differences emerged between governments. Sometimes these policy differences related to fundamental issues, including constitutional disputes about the future of the federation itself. In Canada, the place of Quebec within the federation and the repatriation of the constitution document, the British North America Act, during Pierre Trudeau's years as prime minister placed great strains on the federal system.[8] Lesser, though still serious strains emerged in Australia about the same time, coming to a head during the prime ministership of Gough Whitlam.[9]

Co-operative-Executive Federalism

The development of co-operative-executive federalism in Canada and Australia occurred at about the same time. In both countries it is essentially
a post-1945 phenomenon, and the resulting patterns of intergovernmental
relations have a similar look. Canada did lead the way. Certainly the explosive
growth in the number and complexity of relations between governments
took place a decade or so earlier in Canada, in the early 1960s rather than
the early 1970s. Nevertheless, some of the key intergovernmental institutions,
including the annual meetings of first ministers and treasurers to reach
agreement on the fiscal aspects of federalism, became established earlier
in Australia.[10]

Co-operative-executive federalism has been defined as 'the relations
between elected and appointed officials of the two levels of government.'[11]
Such administrative and ministerial co-operation contains at least three
elements and is illustrated, for Australia, in Figure 1. First, there are the
formal and informal councils and conferences, held annually or more
frequently, at which government representatives share information, discuss
common problems, and contemplate joint action. Second there are the formal
and informal agreements, policies, and programs, often financed jointly by
participating governments, that emerge from or are confirmed by these
meetings. And third, there are day-to-day contacts between officers and
ministers, most often by telephone or telex, which sustain the relationships
and implement the programs. These contacts will occur not only between
each regional government and the central government, but among the regional
governments themselves. As there are ten of these in Canada and six in
Australia (plus territorial governments in both cases), the potential for
'relations' is very great. Much of it is so informal as to be beyond enumeration.

In Australia, each of the several attempts that have been made since
1975 to catalogue the extent of co-operative-executive federalism has led
to unease about the scope of the task.[12] Wiltshire has identified 330 separate
ministerial and departmental meetings and 43 Commonwealth-state councils
and committees, for the years 1970–8.[13] The Department of Prime Minister
and Cabinet, which published its own list in 1975, concluded that 'the majority
of the present arrangements have been established since 1973' (the first year
of the Whitlam government) and that much of this activity had occurred
in fields in which the Commonwealth had, since that year, created new
ministerial portfolios.[14]

In Canada, the number of such relations is even greater. The first attempt
to count them, in 1957, found 67 federal-provincial committees.[15] Later,
Veilleux estimated that in 1967 there had been 159 meetings of 119 separate

FIGURE 1

Examples of traditional co-operative arrangements between Commonwealth and state governments in Australia

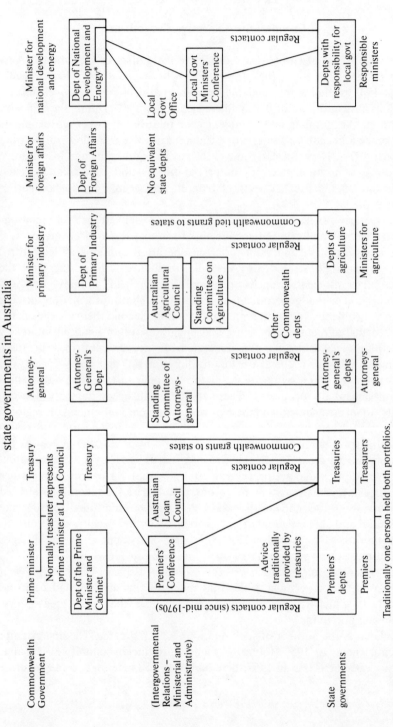

SOURCE: John Warhurst, *Central Agencies, Intergovernmental Managers, and Australian Federal-State Relations* (Canberra: Centre for Research on Federal Financial Relations, Australian National University 1983) 3

*In 1983 the Hawke government created a new department, Territories and Local Government.

federal-provincial committees.[16] The most detailed figures have been issued, since its establishment, by the Department of Federal and Intergovernmental Affairs in Alberta. By its count, for example, representatives of the government of Alberta attended 84 federal-provincial meetings and 89 interprovincial meetings in 1981.[17]

The beginning of co-operative-executive federalism was not only a consequence of central governments intervening in new fields of activity (although this was the case in Australia between 1973 and 1975). It was also a case of regional governments extending their involvement. In Canada, while the federal government took the initiative between the end of the Second World War and the early 1960s, from the mid-1960s provincial governments began to force the pace in fields in which they had not traditionally operated, including broadcasting, immigration, international banking, and economic relations generally.[18] Likewise, in Australia after 1975 state governments were extending their international activities.

This expansion began to cause disquiet among governments at both levels, especially as it seemed that no one possessed the range of vision to enable them to see the whole of the intergovernmental picture. Regional governments began to worry that their right to determine their own priorities and to make policy in their own jurisdiction was being subtly taken away from them with the agreement of their own officials in functional departments who, enticed by central government finance, were entering agreements with their counterparts in central governments. These professionals tended to have a very narrow focus. They shared, along with common interests and language,[19] 'a joint concern with maximising resources for that particular function.'[20] One consequence was that policy-making tended to be conducted in isolation, in 'water-tight compartments.'[21]

Intergovernmental Relations Specialists

The response of regional and central governments has been to appoint officials, and sometimes ministers, with specialist intergovernmental responsibilities. Depending on factors such as the size of the government and the seriousness of the need perceived, the ministers were either solely responsible for intergovernmental relations or held the portfolio along with a number of others, and the officials were either in a new department, formed a subdivision of an existing one, or in some cases were just one or two individuals. Almost always, when not in a new department, the officials were lodged in a first minister's department. In both countries such departments had expanded since the Second World War (late 1960s onwards in Australia) and so readily accommodated this new institutional development.[22]

Within federal systems several types of public servants might lay claim to be seen as intergovernmental specialists. In Canada, there are at least three types of officer with responsibilities in intergovernmental relations. First, functional departments make certain officers responsible for the department's relations with their counterparts in other governments. Ten federal government departments had specialist federal-provincial relations units in the mid-1970s.[23] Second, some federal-provincial committees have permanent specialist staffs. They may be located in federal operating departments (the staff of the Continuing Committees on Fiscal and Economic Matters is based in the Department of Finance), or they may be employed by independent councils, such as the Canadian Council of Resource and Environmental Ministers, which has its own secretariat.[24] Third, there are the officers in departments of Treasury and Finance who are responsible for the financial aspects of relations between the federal and provincial governments.

The new intergovernmental relations specialists are clearly different. The scope of their responsibilities is much wider than that of any of the three other types mentioned above. The new specialists are concerned neither with particular programs or policies nor with some aspects of all policies, but with the whole intergovernmental relations process. Their concern is with the way intergovernmental relations business is conducted, with what is being done across the whole range of government activity, and with how their government ought to do business with other governments.

There can be no argument about just when intergovernmental relations specialists began to appear in some governments, but in most cases the timing is quite clear. The record, as outlined for Canada and Australia in Tables 1 and 2, shows a wide variety of experience among governments. In Canada the introduction of specialists occurred in fits and starts over a period of almost twenty years between 1961 and 1979. Australian developments were more tightly bunched and took place, without exception, between 1974 and 1976.

The Quebec government took the first step in 1961, although the model that later stimulated most interest was that adopted by the third Canadian provincial government into the field, that of Alberta, which in 1972 created the Department of Federal and Intergovernmental Affairs. This department was given a legislative basis for its role as an interventionist intergovernmental co-ordinating department. The idea was later adopted by the Quebec government, when it chose to reinforce the powers of its Ministry of Intergovernmental Affairs, and by the Newfoundland govern-

TABLE 1

Intergovernmental relations specialists in Canadian governments (1984)

Government	Date created*	Responsible minister	Name/ location	Staff
Alberta	1972	Minister of Federal and Intergovernmental Affairs	Dept of Federal and Intergovernmental Affairs	25
British Columbia	1976†	Minister of Inter-governmental Relations	Ministry of Inter-governmental Relations	10
Manitoba	N/A	Premier and Minister of Federal Relations	Premier's Office	4
New Brunswick	1974	Premier	Cabinet Secretariat	3
Newfoundland	1973	Premier and Minister for Intergovernmental Affairs	Intergovernmental Affairs Secretariat	20
Nova Scotia	1979	Minister of Inter-governmental Affairs	Intergovernmental Affairs Office	4
Ontario	1965‡	Minister of Inter-governmental Affairs	Ministry of Inter-governmental Affairs	15
Prince Edward Island	1979	Premier	Executive Council Secretariat	3
Quebec	1961	Deputy Prime Minister and Minister of Inter-governmental Affairs	Ministry of Inter-governmental Affairs	20
Saskatchewan	1977§	Premier	Dept of Inter-governmental Affairs	15

SOURCE: The information has been extracted from T.B. Woolstencroft *Organizing Intergovern-mental Relations* Discussion Paper No. 12 (Kingston: Institute of Intergovernmental Relations, Queen's University 1982) and R.J. Zukowsky *Intergovernmental Relations in Canada: The Year in Review 1980. Volume One: Policy and Politics* (Kingston: Institute of Intergovernmental Relations, Queen's University 1981), supplemented by information obtained by the author from interviews in May and June 1982 and by the *Canadian Almanac and Directory* 1984 (Toronto 1984).

*These are the dates of the initial creation of specialist categories. In three instances signifi-cant further developments occurred later.

†In 1979 a full ministry replaced an existing Office of Intergovernmental Affairs in the Premier's Department.

‡In 1978 a full ministry replaced the secretariat in existence since 1965.

§In 1978 a full department replaced an Office of Intergovernmental Affairs in the Executive Council Office.

ment. These three governments contain the only specialists with a mandate in law as well as in practice. None of the Australian arrangements operates on this basis.

Arrangements within governments differ in a number of other ways. In Australia in each case where a separate intergovernmental affairs portfolio

TABLE 2

Intergovernmental relations specialists in Australian governments (1984)

Government	Date created	Responsible minister	Department	Name	Staff
Commonwealth	1975	Prime Minister and separate minister assisting the prime minister in federal affairs	Prime Minister and Cabinet	Community Development Branch	10
New South Wales	1974	Premier	Premier's	Senior Administrative Assistant, Government Branch	3
Victoria	1975	Premier	Premier and Cabinet	Inter-governmental Relations Branch	6
Queensland	1974	Premier	Premier's	Intergovernmental Projects Branch	7
South Australia	1976	Premier: between 1979 and 1982 the attorney-general also held the title of minister for federal affairs.	Premier's	Intergovernmental Relations Branch	3
Western Australia	1976	Premier	Premier and Cabinet	Director, Intergovernmental Relations	2
Tasmania	N/A	Premier	Premier's	Director of Policy Administration in Cabinet Division	1½ (2–3 part-time)

SOURCE: Information provided by responsible officers. Table constructed by G. O'Loghlin.

exists, it is now held by the premier, although in several states this has not always been the case. In Canada, this is so in five of the smaller provincial governments.

In Australia the specialists act both as a central agency responsible to the first minister and as a cabinet secretariat, thereby both reinforcing the traditional function of cabinet and serving the newer function of central co-ordination and control at the officer level. In Canada, there is a variety of practice. In six governments, including Alberta, Ontario, and Quebec, there are separate departments and ministers. The governments of New Brunswick and Prince Edward Island employ a dual-function cabinet secretariat, while British Columbia's government has the best of both worlds: specialists in both a dual-function cabinet secretariat and a separate intergovernmental affairs department.

The size of the groups of specialists varies markedly: in Australia between about two and ten; in Canada between about three and twenty-five. The difference stems not only from the slightly larger scale of government in some Canadian provinces but also from the fact that generally Canadian governments have taken the idea more seriously.

In both countries these units/departments also have international responsibilities (and sometimes municipal) and are therefore intergovernmental in another sense. These responsibilities include the overseas offices of regional governments. Most Australian and Canadian regional governments have London offices that derive from the Commonwealth connection. More recently, offices have been set up elsewhere, with the Australian governments tending to concentrate more on Asia and the Canadians on North America.

Three Canadian provinces, Alberta, British Columbia, and Saskatchewan also maintain offices in the national capital, Ottawa, with one or two of the other provincial governments employing a representative of some sort. The idea has been considered by some Australian state governments, but none has an office in Canberra, although the government of the Northern Territory did so for a time.[25]

The Role of the Specialists

The contribution of intergovernmental relations specialists to the conduct of intergovernmental relations has a number of aspects. The specialists provide a variety of services. They also set out to achieve far more than they actually do in practice.[26] It must be remembered that in most governments they are small in number in comparison with the functional departments, so their resources are often stretched.[27] Critics have sometimes overestimated their impact. Intergovernmental specialists have been a controversial innovation, although far more so in Canada than in Australia. In both countries they are the subject of a great deal of interdepartmental bickering, of a sort that is more or less standard in relations between central and functional departments. Line departments often object to the specialists' intervention (which they would see as interference) in their functional activities.

There has also been, in Canada, a great deal of public criticism from respected academic quarters.[28] Smiley has been probably the most outspoken critic: 'The role of the intergovernmental affairs specialist is to protect and extend the powers of the jurisdiction for which he works ... Despite the high-flown justifications that such persons make for their occupations, this is in fact their only important role ... In his stance towards other governments the federal-provincial relations specialist has a single-minded devotion to the power of his jurisdiction. And because his counterparts in other governments have the same motivations, conflict is inevitable.'[28] This line of criticism, which had enough support to become the conventional view, would seem with the benefit of hindsight to have been too much influenced by a peculiarly Canadian concern for national unity to be a balanced assessment. It is at most only part of the story. This view exaggerates the effect of the intergovernmental specialists and neglects their positive contribution to the efficient management of the system. And in its overriding concern with the avoidance of intergovernmental conflict, it forgets that the earlier 'golden age' of consensus among program officials owed as much to the broader consensus that existed in the federation at large as it did to purely institutional factors.[30]

The Alberta government's Department of Federal and Intergovernmental Affairs describes it 'basic objectives' as 'to represent Alberta's interests as an equal partner in Confederation and to ensure that the Province's relations with the Government of Canada, governments of other provinces and the governments of foreign countries or states are conducted in a coordinated and consistent manner.' That is a statement of objectives with which most intergovernmental specialists could agree, whatever their own approach to achieving such aims might be.

The activities of the various groups of specialists can be discussed under four headings. They include acting as the intergovernmental arm of the first minister, who is always the senior intergovernmental representative; collecting and distributing as widely as possible inside its own government information about developments in the intergovernmental field – in other governments and within parts of its own government; co-ordinating policy initiatives and responses within its own government; and exercising central control over initiatives and responses originating from functional departments. The balance between these different aspects and the style in which they are pursued vary greatly between governments in both countries.

The First Minister's Intergovernmental Arm

The most important responsibility of intergovernmental specialists is to serve their first minister in the role of leader of the government. Both formal protocol and political strategy demand that when intergovernmental relations are most serious, first ministers are involved.

This applies even in situations where the specialists are lodged outside the first minister's department, as in some Canadian governments. Not only is the support of the first minister necessary for success, but the specialists still work directly with the premier. The regular tasks of Alberta's Department of Federal and Intergovernmental Affairs include 'coordinating the preparation of briefing materials and strategy recommendations' for the annual premier's conference, the regional premiers' conference, and any other intergovernmental conference involving the first minister.[31] Similar roles are played by Australian specialists, often in collaboration with treasury departments.

The specialist's role in relation to premiers' conferences is matched by the informal support to the first minister given on a daily basis. There are some fields, such as foreign policy or trade policy, for which regional governments usually have no other responsible minister than the first minister. Generally, however, the participation of first ministers is an indication of the seriousness with which an intergovernmental issue is regarded by at least one government. And once one first minister is involved, then so must the opposite number be. A government may choose to escalate consideration of an issue by persuading its first minister to intervene. In practice, it is normally a regional rather than the central government that raises the level at which the business of intergovernmental relations is carried out by handing the issue to its premier.

Intervention by a first minister supported by intergovernmental specialists may occur with the concurrence of, or at the initiative of, the responsible functional minister, who sees an opportunity to add extra firepower to the argument. On other occasions, for which there are Australian examples in the fields of education and environmental policy, the first minister and department will clearly be 'pulling rank' over another minister and imposing a different point of view from the centre.[32]

Information Collection and Distribution

The first task of intergovernmental specialists after their emergence has often been to engage in a mapping exercise to establish for their government just what the terrain of co-operative-executive federalism looks like.[33] This then forms the basis of subsequent work. Understanding necessarily precedes intervention.

Once an administrative map has been provided, central agencies set out to use it by monitoring as closely as possible all the intergovernmental meetings that it was possible to attend, so that the centre would know what was being discussed for its own sake and for the sake of other departments with related interests. Central agencies also generally institute procedures by which other departments are asked to assist in this collation of information by passing all significant communications to the inter-governmental specialist.

Even when these efforts have been successful, which was unlikely, given interdepartmental rivalry and genuine ignorance, this did not resolve the situation. Much of the information desired by the specialists at the centre comes not from departmental sources but from non-governmental sources, including parliament and its committees, interest groups based in the national capital, and so on. Much of this information may be little more than gossip. Governments want, in effect, their own intergovernmental intelligence service.

This is the function served by the 'diplomatic' offices in national capitals, which operate as listening devices. Australian governments have thought such offices an inefficient use of resources, while recognizing that some benefits would accrue. The alternative chosen by state governments in Australia has been to pay the private sector to provide such information. Early in 1976 a news service with offices in the press gallery of Parliament House in Canberra was commissioned. It provided subscribers – mainly private business corporations – with daily air-freighted packages of information, including material from departments, political party headquarters, the Australian Government Publishing Service, parliament, and interest groups. After a year's trial, the South Australian intergovernmental specialists declared themselves well pleased, while recognizing that it was only a second-best solution. They concluded that 'this service does at least overcome an information lag in printed and released information.'[34]

Bilateral Intervention

Once central agencies become aware of the type of intergovernmental relations that exists they may choose to intervene and break off the relationship. Much of this intervention occurs by administrative fiat, with first minister and cabinet support for the termination of informal inter-governmental arrangements between departments. Australian examples of such action come from a variety of fields. On one occasion, intergovernmental specialists in several state governments found that professional judgment of local agricultural or industrial matters that was transmitted to the central government contradicted broader government policies on employment creation. On another occasion, professional educational judgment on cur-riculum materials was overruled by the intergovernmental specialists because of their allegedly 'strong centralist flavour.' On yet another occasion, one state government's functional departments were forbidden to deal with their central government counterparts because of the sheer weight of the demands being made upon them for information.

This power of veto comes in its strongest form in those three Cana-dian provinces – Alberta, Quebec, and Newfoundland – in which inter-governmental specialists were given legislative support. The relevant section of the Alberta act states:

Notwithstanding any other Act, an intergovernmental agreement to which this section applies is not binding on the Government of Alberta or any other agency or official thereof, unless

a) it is signed on behalf of the Government by the Minister of Federal and Intergovernmental Affairs, if the agreement is designated by the regulations as an agreement that is to be signed on behalf of the Government by the Minister of Federal and Intergovernmental Affairs only, or

b) it is agreed on behalf of the Government by the Minister of Federal and Intergovernmental Affairs in addition to any other Minister of the Crown authorized by law to sign it, if the agreement that is to be designated by the regulations as an agreement that is to be signed by the Minister of Federal and Intergovernmental Affairs in addition to another Minister of the Crown authorized by law to sign it, or

c) it is approved by the Minister of Federal and Intergovernmental Affairs, in any other case.[35]

While the department has generally been able to enforce its will, short of exercising a veto, which has been used very rarely, the legislation still remains a powerful lever.

Co-ordinating Diverse Views

In the growing number of fields of policy in which a number of departments each have a legitimate interest, intergovernmental managers must ensure production of a coherent policy that comes to terms with conflicts between departments before a government policy is presented to other governments. As the origins of the expanded first minister's departments were tied closely to the need to co-ordinate the domestic activities of their own functional departments, co-ordination of intergovernmental relations came as a natural extension.

Left to themselves, functional departments may proceed in intergovernmental relations without regard to the interests of other departments. They may do so out of ignorance. As the head of the New South Wales government's Federal Affairs Division said in 1975, 'People working in particular departments can be like a horse with blinkers. A request for information may seem straightforward in terms of that department. But when we look at it we may say 'Aha, but what about department A, B and C?' Or there may have been a change of policy they don't know about.'[36] However, the narrowness of vision may come from a faithful representation of clients' interests. For example, central government policies that encourage the domestic manufacture of motor vehicles may be supported by regional departments responsible for manufacturing industry but, quite naturally, opposed by regional departments of agriculture, whose concern is to minimize costs for their farmer clients.

Intergovernmental specialists may encourage co-ordination, or they may demand it. When the Commonwealth government in Australia set up a Task Force on Health and Welfare in 1976 to report on possible rationalization of health and welfare provision, state government intergovernmental specialists not only assisted the task force's access to state departments but also co-ordinated departmental responses. The intergovernmental unit in the South Australian government reported: 'This review required considerable cooperation from a wide range of South Australian Departments and authorities and the Branch organised a series of meetings which ensured that the responses of Departments and agencies were consistent with government policy.'[37]

Conclusion

The new style of central management of intergovernmental relations, epitomized in the work of intergovernmental relations specialists located in departments and units at the centre, is a substantial input to the working of federal systems. It has emerged in Canada and Australia in response to common features in the co-operative-executive style of intergovernmental relations in these countries. Nevertheless, even in Canada, where the number of such specialists is far greater, and where they have been the focus of considerable criticism, the new development has not transformed the management of intergovernmental relations in any government. (The only possible exceptions to this judgment would be Alberta and Quebec.) Rather, it has added a new ingredient, a small counterweight, to the traditional segmented approach to policy-making inherent in the co-operative-executive style.

The intergovernmental affairs specialists were, in their genesis, partly an urgent response to tensions within federal systems. They have been called into service by embattled governments. They may be perceived as less necessary in rosier times. As their role wins them few friends among functional departments, they may suffer reverses at the hands of governments that see less need to enhance their jurisdiction over intergovernmental policy-making. There is evidence of this in Australia between 1975 and 1983, when some of the specialist groups were disbanded.

The intergovernmental relations specialists should not, however, be seen as just a passing fad, born in a crisis situation and to be thrown away when the tension lessens. In Canada they appear to have become less important since 1982.[38] However, they will survive because their origins also lie partly in more deep-rooted concerns. The traditional unco-ordinated pattern of policy-making in co-operative-executive federalism has enduring features, which governments of whatever political colour will recognize and wish to ameliorate. The costs of allowing the traditional segmented system to continue unchecked have become larger as government as a whole has grown, leading to the expansion of intergovernmental relations. These costs not only are the result of one government interfering in the jurisdiction of another but also lead to policies that fail because they do not take into account the implications for other departments and whole governments of an otherwise admirable agreement between professionals in a single functional area.

Intergovernmental relations needs central management. What final form that management is likely to take is not certain. The precise mechanisms will vary from government to government. Should greater awareness and willingness to 'see the whole picture' develop within the constituent parts of governments, then intervention from the centre may be able to become less intrusive. But this is perhaps to be too optimistic and to neglect the institutional self-centredness to be found in most government departments and agencies.

NOTES

1 This chapter draws heavily on my previously published work on intergovernmental relations specialists in both Canada and Australia. A number of the
themes developed below are discussed more fully in the following publications:
'Canada's Intergovernmental Relations Specialists' *Australian Journal of Public
Administration* 42 no 4 (December 1983) 459–85; *Central Agencies, Intergovernmental Managers, and Australian Federal-State Relations* (Canberra:
Centre for Research on Federal Financial Relations, Australian National University 1983); and 'Intergovernmental Managers and Co-operative Federalism:
The Australian Case' *Public Administration* 61 no 3 (autumn 1983) 308–17.
2 For the sake of consistency and brevity, the term *central government* is used in
this chapter to mean the national or federal government; in Australia, the central government is more strictly referred to as the government of the Commonwealth of Australia. The term *regional government* is used for the governments
of the constituent units of the federation, which in Canada are known as provinces and in Australia as states.
3 This type or aspect of federalism is known in Australia as co-operative federalism, although it is recognized that as a term it has benign connotations that are
often quite misleading. The term has fallen into disuse in Canada for reasons
noted by D.V. Smiley *Canada in Question: Federalism in the Seventies* 2nd ed
(Toronto: McGraw-Hill 1976) 57. The term now commonly used in Canada is
executive federalism. See, for example, the Task Force on Canadian Unity *A
Future Together* (Ottawa: Ministry of Supply and Services 1979) 95. I have
chosen in this chapter to combine the two terms.
4 Smiley *Canada in Question* 79
5 Ibid 59
6 The major study of these developments in Canada is T.B. Woolstencroft *Organizing Intergovernmental Relations* (Kingston: Institute of Intergovernmental
Relations, Queen's University 1982).
7 Smiley *Canada in Question* 79
8 R. Gibbins, R. Knopff, and F.L. Morton 'Canadian Federalism, the Charter of
Rights and the 1984 Election' *Publius* 15 no 2 (summer 1985) 155–7
9 G. Sawer *Federalism under Strain: Australia 1972–1975* (Melbourne: Melbourne University Press 1977); G. Evans *Labor and the Constitution 1972–1975:
The Whitlam Years in Australian Government* (Melbourne: Melbourne University Press 1977)
10 See R.S. Gilbert *The Australian Loan Council in Federal Fiscal Adjustments
1890–1965* (Canberra: Australian National University Press 1973) and C. Sharman *The Premiers' Conference* (Canberra: Department of Political Science,
Research School of Social Sciences, Australian National University 1977)

11 Smiley *Canada in Question* 54
12 For the most recent and comprehensive attempt see Advisory Council for Inter-government Relations *Register of Commonwealth-State Cooperative Arrangements* (Hobart: Advisory Council for Intragovernment Relations 1982)
13 K.W. Wiltshire 'Australian State Participation in Federal Decisions' in R.L. Mathews ed *Federalism in Australia and the Federal Republic of Germany: A Comparative Study* (Canberra: Australian National University Press 1980) 105–30
14 Department of the Prime Minister and Cabinet *Australian-State Government Cooperative Arrangements* (Canberra: Department of Prime Minister and Cabinet 1975) 1 (in a separate accompanying foreword issued in July 1975)
15 K.W. Taylor quoted in Smiley *Canada in Question* 57
16 Quoted in ibid
17 Alberta Department of Federal and Intergovernmental Affairs *Ninth Annual Report to March 31, 1982* (Edmonton: Alberta Department of Federal and Intergovernmental Affairs 1922)
18 Smiley *Canada in Question* 55
19 G.J. Inns 'The Public Services and Cooperative Federalism' *Public Administration* (Sydney) 34 no 1 (March 1975) 35–7
20 R.N. Spann *Government Administration in Australia* (Sydney: Allen & Unwin 1979) 208
21 Foreword by Don R. Getty in Alberta Department of Federal and Intergovernmental Affairs *Inventory of Federal-Provincial Programs in Alberta, 1974* (Edmonton: Alberta Department of Federal and Intergovernmental Affairs 1974) i
22 For Australia see F.A. Mediansky and J.A. Nockles 'The Prime Minister's Bureaucracy' *Public Administration* (Sydney) 34 no 3 (September 1975) and J. Warhurst ed 'Perspectives on Premiers' Departments' *Politics* 17 no 1 (May 1982); for Canada, C. Campbell and G.J. Szablowski *The Superbureaucrats: Structure and Behaviour in Central Agencies* (Toronto: Macmillan 1979)
23 R. Schultz 'Prime Ministerial Government, Central Agencies and Operating Departments: Towards a More Realistic Analysis' in T.A. Hockin ed *Apex of Power: The Prime Minister and Political Leadership in Canada* 2nd ed (Scarborough: Prentice-Hall 1977) 234
24 R.J. Van Loon and M.S. Whittington *The Canadian Political System* 2nd ed (Toronto 1976) 372–4.
25 J. Warhurst 'The Northern Territory Government's Canberra Representative' *Australian Journal of Public Administration* 40 no 4 (December 1981) 363–5
26 Woolstencroft *Organizing Intergovernmental Relations* 79
27 Schultz 'Prime Ministerial Government' 231
28 Warhurst 'Canada's Intergovernmental Relations Specialists' 475–6

29 D.V. Smiley 'An Outsider's Observations of Federal Provincial Relations among Consenting Adults' in R. Simeon ed *Confrontation and Collaboration* (Toronto: The Institute of Public Administration of Canada 1979) 109–10

30 Warhurst 'Specialists' 476–80

31 Alberta Department of Federal and Intergovernmental Affairs *Ninth Annual Report* 2

32 Warhurst *Central Agencies* 16–17

33 See, for example, Department of Prime Minister and Cabinet *Australian-State Government Cooperative Arrangements* and Alberta Department of Federal and Intergovernmental Affairs *Inventory of Federal-Provincial Programs.*

34 South Australian Premier's Department *Inter-Government Relations Function* (Adelaide [1977]) 6

35 The Department of Federal and Intergovernmental Affairs Act, 1972, section 5(1)

36 D. Dale 'When the Feds Come NSW Is Ready' *National Times* 14–19 April 1975

37 South Australian Premier's Department *Inter-Government Relations Function* 4

38 K. McRoberts 'Unilateralism, Bilateralism and Multilateralism: Approaches to Canadian Federalism' in R. Simeon ed *Intergovernmental Relations* vol. 63 of the research studies prepared for the Royal Commission on the Economic Union and the Development Prospects for Canada (Toronto: University of Toronto Press 1985)

Part Four

CONCLUSIONS: THE FUTURE OF FEDERALISM?

15 / Alternative Models of Governance: Federalism, Consociationalism, and Corporatism

HERMAN BAKVIS

Problems confronting the modern state, federal or unitary, can be roughly classified into two categories: those stemming from cultural division or fragmentation, and those stemming from the increasing gap between shrinking resources on the one hand and continued demand for maintenance and even expansion of the welfare state on the other hand. Closely related to the second category is the quandary facing most modern industrial nations – stagnant or low rates of economic growth.[1]

On a broader plane, all systems must confront the problem of interest representation – that is, the manner in which societal interests can best be expressed and how governments respond to them. Some societies favour a plebiscitarian model that stresses direct links between governments or legislatures and individual citizens. Most, however, depend upon intermediary levels of government organization or political bodies to provide contact between citizens and the state; at the same time there is debate on how these levels or bodies should be organized and whether they should be part of the state apparatus or remain largely private.

Federalism is often seen as a means for resolving, or at least mitigating the effects of, some of these problems. By granting cultural minorities a high level of protection in crucial areas such as education through the federal distribution of powers, a system can alleviate problems stemming from cultural fragmentation. As well, difficult decisions can be handled at a lower level without involving the central government proper. With respect to the issue of shrinking resources, some economists and political conservatives have favoured decentralization, particularly as found in the classical model of federalism, as a way of restraining government activities so that economic and societal problems can be left to the private realm.

Federalism, however, is not the only form of governance dependent upon the norms of non-majoritarianism and decentralization. This chapter examines two additional models and their interrelationships: consociationalism, which involves accommodative behaviour on the part of élites, often in the face of discord at the mass level, and corporatism, which involves the devolution of political/legal authority to functionally or economically based quasi-governmental organizations and a high level of collaboration between them. Consociationalism, as practised in countries like Belgium and the Netherlands, is usually seen as a means for resolving cultural conflict, while corporatism, as exemplifed by Austria and Sweden, is perceived primarily as a means of resolving economic issues based on class differences. It is worth noting that in recent years corporatist solutions to economic problems have become even more attractive in light of the above-average economic performance and apparent ability of these countries to adapt quickly to changing economic conditions.[2] Federal solutions in turn tend to be found where differences, whether economic or linguistic, tend to have a territorial basis. Many federal systems also tend to be encumbered by policy problems stemming from regional disparaties and cultural or linguistic divisions rather than class divisions. At the same time, as we shall see, neither of the two so-called alternative models is necessarily incompatible with federalism or each other.

For some, these two alternative models are seen as techniques of social control, and in this sense they appear to imply a degree of centralization. But, in fact, both corporatism and consociationalism involves a significant degree of decentralization. According to Kenneth McRae, they share with federalism some basic similarities.[3] (1) The total burden of government is shared between at least two levels of government or arenas of decision-making or interest mediation. (2) Parliamentary parties and the interest groups associated with them are willing to relinquish certain areas of policy formation and implementation to organizations operating in other arenas such as a special economic decision-making body consisting of business and union representatives. (3) In these alternative arenas, issues are hived off from the central government's political agenda and resolved through negotiations between representatives of the relevant interest groups. McRae notes also that all three forms appear to require a minimum élite disposition toward co-operation for their proper functioning and that the position of élites within their own government or organization tends to be enhanced by virtue of the responsibilities and opportunities that arise as they interact and relate to the other groups or governments.

Although the term *alternative* is used here, it should be emphasized again that the three models are not mutually exclusive. Two or possibly all three forms can be in place simultaneously, and in certain circumstances the practices inherent in one can reinforce practices in another. Thus political scientists have detected consociational practices in federal Canada and have argued that these practices have contributed to the survival of the Canadian polity.[4] In the case of both Austria and the Netherlands, it has been suggested that acceptance of consociationalism has reinforced patterns of corporatist decision-making.[5] The links of consociationalism with both federalism and corporatism have been explored by a number of authors who note the compatability of consociational practices with the other two forms. However, in the case of federalism and corporatism, McRae notes that the links remain both difficult to discern and at the same time relatively unexplored. Some analysts have argued even that the two are essentially incompatible because the territorial division of powers in federalism inhibits the development of large-scale functional organizations necessary for the development of corporatist institutions and practices. Leo Panitch, for example, claims that this has certainly been true of the organized working class in Canada; a centralized and cohesive trade union federation, according to Panitch, is a necessary component in any corporatist or 'tripartite' arrangement involving government, business, and labour.[6]

Because the connections between federalism and consociationalism have been amply discussed elsewhere, this chapter stresses the relatively unexplored links between federalism and corporatism. Without necessarily disagreeing with Panitch's view of the limited applicability of the model to Canada, the argument will be made that federalism is not necessarily incompatible with corporatism in all respects. In the final section some of the possible ways of reconciling corporatism with federalism are assessed through an examination of recent efforts by the federal government in tripartite policy-making and a brief evaluation of the model put forward by Hugh Thorburn for implementing and institutionalizing economic planning in Canada.

Consociational Democracy

This model has been described most succinctly by Arend Lijphart: 'government by elite cartel designed to turn a democracy with a fragmented political culture into a stable democracy.'[7] Implicit in the model is the idea that certain societies have such pronounced cleavages that only deliberate joint efforts by élites can produce a stable political system. If élites do not act in concert, civil war can result or, in the case of federations, one or more of the component units may try to secede. The attractiveness of the model, particularly for prescriptive purposes, lies in the possibility that political integration can be achieved through the action of élites, in spite of dissension at the mass level. In order for a consociation to succeed, Lijphart stipulates, a number of conditions must be met: élites must have the ability to accommodate the divergent interests and demands of their sub-cultures; they must have the ability to transcend cleavages and to join in a common effort with the élites of rival sub-cultures; they must have a commitment to the maintenance of the system; and finally they must understand the perils of political fragmentation. As well, according to Lijphart, élite efforts at accommodation are greatly facilitated if certain rules of the game apply. These include the norms of secrecy, the rule of proportionality, the rule of sub-cultural autonomy, and the ability of a minority sub-culture to veto proposals it feels are inimical to its interests. The last two rules, it is worth noting, coincide with features formally built into most federal arrangements through the distribution of powers or non-majoritarian representation in a second chamber.[8]

The consociational model was first developed by Lijphart and others to decribe political systems such as the Netherlands, Belgium, Switzerland, and Austria, all relatively small countries with divided societies. In the Netherlands and Austria the main lines of cleavage are religion and class, while in Belgium and Switzerland language is also important. The extent of consociational practices has varied across these countries and over time, but in the case of the Netherlands between 1918 and 1967 virtually all of the practices and conditions noted above were in effect. Levels of sub-cultural segmentation were high, and sub-cultures enjoyed autonomy in important areas such as education and welfare activities, valued goods tended to be distributed proportionally across the different sub-cultures according to size, and élites succeeded in collaborating with each other and were able to do so in secret. Particularly with respect to the last, a generally deferential attitude on the part of most citizens gave élites ample opportunity for engaging in accommodative practices.[9]

Federalism and Consociationalism

It needs to be stressed that the sub-cultures in the Netherlands lack a territorial basis, which makes them rather different from those in a federation like Canada. Nevertheless, Lijphart has argued that in principle a federation can sometimes meet the conditions for consociation, for example, where a fragmented society combines with a decentralized federal arrangement to ensure the autonomy of the different segments. The consociational model, therefore, has been applied to Canada in a number of studies. Kenneth McRae, for example, has argued that examples of élite accommodation can be found in the period of the United Canadas between 1840 and 1867 as well as subsequent periods of Canadian history. The accommodation he cites is mainly that which prevailed between English and French élites, for example the bleu-Conservative coalition during the Union period and later the co-operation between the premiers of Ontario and Quebec.[10] More recently, accommodation among all provincial premiers over issues like the Canada Pension Plan has been cited as evidence of at least limited consociationalism in Canada.[11] There is, however, both confusion and debate over the definition of the sub-cultural blocs being represented by élites. McRae feels that the primary blocs are the French and English communities; these, it is claimed, come closest to being the equivalent of the sub-cultural blocs found in the small European democracies. Others such as S.J.R. Noel argue that the individual provinces can be treated as single cohesive blocs.[12] In the case of French-English differences, the primary arenas for élite accommodation would be the federal cabinet and to a lesser extent meetings between the first ministers on a bilateral as well as multilateral basis. In the case of provinces as the relevant units, the federal-provincial first ministers' conference is the obvious arena.

During the 1970s various advocates of consociationalism saw it as a means of preserving the Canadian federal union. Unfortunately, examples of élite accommodation have become more difficult to find. During the latter years of the Trudeau period the debate between Ottawa and the provinces became increasingly acrimonious, and the federal government became more inclined to threaten and actually resort to unilateral action. Under the Conservatives the federal-provincial climate has improved somewhat, and agreement between Ottawa and the provinces has been reached on a number of issues. Yet it is far from clear whether these agreements fall under the rubric of consociationalism, if only because the bargaining process has become much more open to public scrutiny and élites have become much more sensitive to what their electorates might think. In other words, political élites are finding it more difficult to move away from publicly stated positions or to bridge differences in public opinion. As well, a number of élites, and not just those from Quebec, have at times clearly lacked a commitment to resolving major issues. Further, one could argue that in some instances political élites have co-operated less from a sense of public duty than from a perception that the public was becoming impatient with intergovernmental bickering. In other words, the key dynamic in consociationalism – élite collaboration – has been lacking.

In short, many of the rules and conditions deemed conducive to consociationalism, such as secrecy and the ability of élites to control members of their blocs, are absent and unlikely to reappear in the near future. Moreover, some students of Canadian federalism have objected to the lack of popular participation implicit in the consociational model. It might also be argued that while élite accommodation is one way of bringing about needed co-operation within the Canadian federation, there are other, more democratic means available. To be sure, a process based on wider consultation with a variety of groups, greater accessibility at both federal and provincial levels, and closer scrutiny of the workings of executive federalism will mean more protracted bargaining and slower decision-making by federal and provincial leaders; but at the same time it can be considered a realistic alternative to models almost entirely dependent on élite accommodation. As a mode of governance, therefore, the prospect of consociational democracy in Canada appears dim. At the same time, close and comfortable relations among élites are also a hallmark of corporatist systems of governance, a subject to which we now turn.

Neo-Corporatism

It should be emphasized that what most modern proponents of corporatism have in mind is the so-called liberal, societal, or neo-corporatist version, which can be distinguished from older, authoritarian forms of state corporatism, of which Franco's Spain and Mussolini's Italy are seen as prototypes.[13] Sweden, Austria, and the Netherlands are often taken as the best examples of liberal corporatist systems, while West Germany and Switzerland, although considered weaker examples, nevertheless display pronounced corporatist tendencies.

Among the attractive features of these countries for many Canadian observers are their success in dealing with the economic crises of the late 1970s and the early 1980s and their very high level of industrial peace. Particularly in Austria and Sweden, collective bargaining is centralized, as are the employer and employee organizations involved in the collective bargaining process, and the result appears to be both harmony and stability in industrial relations.[14] Governments do have a role, direct or indirect, in producing wage settlements, but at the same time business and labour typically enjoy considerable influence with respect to government economic and social policy. This triangular relationship between the three has given rise to the term *tripartism*, though this concept, as will be noted later, may be misleading in its characterization of the links prevailing between the three bodies. Whether the alleged harmony between government, business, and labour in these three countries is actually due to corporatist institutions and practices and whether these institutions and practices can be transported to and adopted by other countries are subject to considerable debate.

Definitions of corporatism and what the concept entails abound. The one offered by Philippe Schmitter, though not necessarily definitive, provides a useful starting point: 'Corporatism can be defined as a system of interest representation in which the constituent units are organized into a limited number of singular, compulsory, non-competitive, hierarchically ordered and functionally differentiated categories, recognized or licensed (if not created) by the state and granted a deliberate representational monopoly within their respective categories in exchange for observing certain controls on their selection of leaders and articulation of demands.'[15]

The interest organizations referred to have the authority not only to act in their own spheres but also to act in concert with each other, that is, to negotiate agreements in areas like wage policy, or labour policy more generally, beyond the purview of popularly elected legislatures. These agreements would be valid in their own right or, alternatively, would constitute recommendations that governments would find very difficult to reject or alter, even in respect to minor features. This corporatist 'concertation' occurs in conjunction with, and in the interests of, the national economy as a whole, and, as Lehmbruch points out, it is this 'concertation' that distinguishes mere sectoral or partial corporatism from a national system of corporatist co-operation.[16] Also, as stressed by McRae, there would have to be at least tacit agreement by government and other interest groups to permit these organizations to make decisions in separate arenas. In Canada this would mean the concurrence of not just the federal parliament but also the ten provincial legislatures. Further, as in the case of consociationalism, for corporatism to work, there has to be close collaboration between élites, which in turn implies that élites have strong hierarchical control over the members of their organizations.

Most observers consider Austria the prototypical corporatist case, and therefore, if only for illustrative purposes, it merits discussion. Not only are corporatist practices of the Austrian 'social partnership' strongly entrenched and highly institutionalized, but the apparent benefits are the envy of many countries: low unemployment, price stability, sustained economic growth throughout the 1970s and 1980s, taxation levels second lowest among the small, advanced industrialized countries, and, of course, labour peace.[17] There are three main elements in this social partnership. First, associational interests are organized into three all-encompassing interest groups or 'chambers' – business, agriculture, and labour, respectively – 'which are statutory public corporations with compulsory membership' and constitute highly centralized bodies.[18] Second, co-operation between these three bodies has been institutionalized in a body called the Parity Commission for Questions of Price and Wage Regulation, which has representatives from the chambers and government, though the government representatives have only a 'deliberative voice' rather than decision-making power. Another body, the Advisory Council for Economic and Social Problems, has all its members appointed by the chambers and is responsible for economic forecasts on which many government decisions are based. The chambers are also well represented on the governing council of the national bank.[19]

Third, all chambers and related interest groups have the right to be consulted on all government bills, '*before* they are submitted to parliament.'[20] Not infrequently, bills concerning important subjects such as competition policy are negotiated by the chambers of business and labour and then ratified virtually unchanged by the Austrian parliament. Participation by the major chambers in these bodies is voluntary, but all have found it to their advantage to participate. A host of associational groups, academic and recreational for example, tend to be affiliated with one of the major chambers, an organizational pattern that tends to reinforce the strength and central role of the chambers, particularly those of business and labour. Business and labour are in fact the primary actors and operate on the basis of parity in all the aforementioned corporatist bodies. This parity also tends to be reflected in the role played by the two main political parties, the Socialists (spo) and the Conservatives (ovp), in the legislature and, especially, the bureaucracy.

Sweden and the Netherlands also tend to be placed in the corporatist category. In the latter country the major arena for deliberation between business, labour, and government is the Social-Economic Council, literally a tripartite body in that one-third each of the membership is appointed by the employers' organizations, labour, and the government respectively. These organizations lack the power of compulsory membership but by and large are centralized and comprehensive in their coverage of potential members.[21] Until the late 1960s, when corporatism in the Netherlands went into decline, which among other things involved a failure on the part of the council to reach decisions, the major groups represented in the Social-Economic Council were able to negotiate agreements on wage determination and other matters that were then acted upon by management and labour or tendered as recommendations to the government, which usually accepted and implemented them with little or no modification. In Sweden there is actually little in the way of formal institutional arrangements, but the highly centralized Trade Union Federation and Employers' Association have for many years succeeded in agreeing to and subsequently enforcing a highly egalitarian wage policy, with the government playing only a minor role.[22]

The corporatist arrangements in these three countries have, at various times, experienced difficulties, and indeed in the case of the Netherlands it has been argued that the country can no longer be considered a proper corporatist system.[23] The Dutch Social-Economic Council is no longer able to reach agreement on major issues, particularly those involving questions of economic restructuring. Within the combined Catholic-secular trade union federation, authority has devolved to lower levels, which has made it more difficult for the top leadership to speak effectively on behalf of all member organizations. In Sweden the primary trade union federation has remained highly centralized and cohesive, but relations between it and the Employers' Federation have become difficult as a result of the 'wage earner' issue, a policy favoured by labour, in which, over time, employees would become the major stockholders in their firms. Debate over this proposal has spilled over into the political arena, with the Employers' Federation becoming directly involved in election campaigns, something that hitherto it has rarely done. Nevertheless, on issues like wage determination the two organizations are still able to co-operate. Austria, in contrast, remains a shining example within the corporatist stable.

Additional features of neo-corporatist systems, as well as the conditions under which these systems operate, need to be stressed. First, in many of them there exist two levels of bargaining. In the first instance, negotiations occur between the major organized groups. Then, according to Lehmbruch, bargaining shifts to exchanges between the so-called cartel of these organized groups and the government. Interactions between government and the cartel, therefore, tend to be bilateral rather than multilateral. In contrast, in the case of multilateral negotiations such as in the United States and Canada, the government remains a key element, a 'turnplate,' in economic policy-making. In the case of bilateral negotiations, government has a much less active role.[24] To be sure, it still plays a role; in Austria, for example, government representatives on the 'parity' commission will let the other representatives know of government views and feelings on various matters. But these government representatives do not actively participate in the actual decision-making and do not enjoy voting rights. The key feature, thus, is the effective delegation of state power to the appropriate chamber. The term *tripartism*, sometimes used in connection with these arrangements, is actually misleading.

This bilateralism and two-stage bargaining also help to distinguish corporatism from pluralism. A concept of interest representation familiar to most political scientists, pluralism shares with corporatism a number of assumptions, including the recognition of the growth in the number and importance of formal associational units in the political process and their role in mediating between citizens and the state. The pluralist paradigm, however, offers more of a government-centred view of the interaction between interest groups and the state, if only because government deals not with a single cartel but with a variety of groups and does so on a multilateral basis. This does not necessarily make the government all-powerful; the opposite could well be the case. But certainly the load on government tends to be much greater. As well, under conditions of pluralism, the groups in question may be very influential, may be unrepresentative in the sense that they further only the interests of the rich and the powerful, and may even have captured part of the state apparatus, along the lines described by Theodore Lowi.[25] Further, within specific sectors there may be little or no competition between groups.[26]

Yet on the whole the American system, and to a lesser extent the Canadian and the British, are characterized by multiple groups, which recruit members on a voluntary basis and which, excepting professional associations such as medical societies, are not licensed by the state. In only very few sectors would a single organization enjoy a monopoly over all representational activity, and certainly not in any formal sense that is officially recognized by the state. In a corporatist system of representation, peak associations tend to be all-encompassing, hierarchically organized, and either differentiated into functional sectors (Austria) or, more commonly, composed of more sector-specific associations (Switzerland, West Germany, the Netherlands). These sectoral associations in turn, limited in number and usually encompassing workers or employers, work out their differences among themselves and present a common position to government; and the whole arrangement is accorded legitimacy by all the groups involved.

A second point to be stressed in connection with corporatist systems of governance is what Lehmbruch refers to as structural isomorphy: for corporatist patterns of decision-making in society to be effective they should be paralleled in the parliamentary arena. Since corporatist decision-making is by and large consensual and non-majoritarian, the same should hold true in parliament, which usually means coalition government. This has certainly been true in both Austria and the Netherlands, and this type of coalition behaviour is in conformity with the consociational pattern. In both countries more than economic issues have been at stake; conflicts stemming from the religious cleavage have traditionally been an important raison d'être for creating broad-based governing coalitions. The importance of this structural isomorphy concerns the reinforcement of practices in the one arena by those in the other. Thus in the Netherlands the decline in corporatism coincided with the decline in consociationalism in the later 1960s. In Austria the social partnership has survived the 1966 termination of the grand coalition between conservatives and socialists, which suggests that formal structural isomorphy is not a necessary condition. But reference is still made to the 'sectoral coalition' and the double parity rule in Austria, and it has been argued that the long period of the grand coalition allowed the transference of bargaining approaches in the political sphere to the economic sphere.[27]

Corporatism and Federalism

This relationship remains relatively uncharted territory. It is best, therefore, to begin with those federal systems that can be roughly classifed as semi-corporatist. West Germany and Switzerland are two such systems where corporatist practices exist, if only on an informal level, and the question arises whether corporatism in these systems would be even more pronounced in the absence of federal institutions or whether there may actually be some mutual reinforcement between the two. No definitive answers are provided here, but there is some evidence to suggest that in both West Germany and Switzerland federalism and corporatism are not necessarily at odds with each other.

Let us turn first to 'model Germany.' The hallmark of post–Second World War West German economic development was the 'social market economy,' brain-child of the first post-war economics minister, Ludwig Erhard, which stressed minimal government intervention and little in the way of formal participation by either business or labour in economic policy-making. Yet it would be misleading to say that there was an absence of either an industrial strategy or co-operation between significant economic groups. The West German mark was deliberately undervalued to facilitate exports, and the three largest banks orchestrated, in effect co-ordinated, industrial development strategies through the strategic use of their controlling interest in most available investment capital.[28] Restraint on the part of the trade unions, for which the government reciprocated by providing social welfare measures, was important in helping to bring about the economic miracle.

In 1966 the dominant Christian Democratic parties (CDU/CSU) joined with the Social Democratic Party (SPD) to form the Grand Coalition, an action reminiscent of consociational practices in Austria and the Netherlands. It was during this period that the government sought to institute corporatist practices on a more formal basis by the introduction of 'Concerted Action.' The Ministry of Economic Affairs began convening on a regular basis meetings of economic interest groups to deliberate on, and help formulate, incomes policy, which would essentially be respected and enforced by the 'autonomous' groups themselves. In contrast to the Austrian system, here the government was clearly taking a much more active role. It was also a far more complex process in that the number of participants was quite high, reflecting the more diffuse nature of interest group organization in West Germany. Although West German interest associations are highly centralized, according to Lehmbruch the degree of intersectoral concentration is lower than in Austria, for example. This is particularly true of the West German Trade Union Federation, which, unlike its Austrian and Swedish counterparts, lacks authority over its constituent industrial unions. The participants in Concerted Action were able to reach agreement during economic slumps, but not during periods of recovery or boom, and during periods of the latter there were instances of large-scale strikes. Nevertheless, the West German Trade Union Federation, as well as the most important industrial and white-collar unions, continued to attend meetings in spite of criticism from their rank and file. This state of affairs lasted until 1976, when the unions finally withdrew.

Whether either the limited success or the ultimate failure of Concerted Action can in any way be linked to West German federalism is not clear. Since the more tightly run corporatist systems are found in smaller economies, it is likely that size is an important determinant of the viability of any such arrangement. On several dimensions the West German economy is much larger and more complex, involving a greater variety of producers and hence interest group associations. Unlike Austria and Sweden, West Germany appears to be lacking the limited and highly centralized peak organizations apparently necessary for corporatism to work. Yet at the same time most collective bargaining does take place on an industry-wide basis, even if negotiations do not always go smoothly. In contrast, Canadian industry-wide bargaining (as opposed to bargaining within a single firm or plant) is a rarity. Beyond collective bargaining and wage settlements, most of the relevant West German economic interest groups, including labour, appear to be well integrated into the system as a whole. On this point, Klause von Beyme, among others, has argued that West German unions are integrated not at the centre but at the level of the plant, through mechanisms such as co-determination, which provides for worker participation in the management of enterprises.[29] Thus even though worker participation is not the product of élite bargaining, there is still a high level of consensus among workers and unions on the legitimacy of the basic economic framework and on many, if not all, the policies pursued within it. Finally, as William Coleman's chapter makes clear, since primary responsibility for policy-making rests with the federal government, and administration of policy rests with the Land governments, this provides a powerful incentive to interest organizations to have a strong and unified presence at the federal level.

Assuming substantial integration of workers at the plant level, and a high level of cohesion both through direct corporate control and through cartels at the level of industrial and commercial enterprises, then fairly extensive co-ordination of economic policy can be achieved. An article on Japan with the provocative title 'Corporatism without Labor'[30] suggests that it is possible to have a co-ordinated quasi-corporatist system without a centralized and concentrated trade union organization. In the Japanese case, the integration of workers also occurs at the level of the plant, although generally this is achieved by means of paternalistic techniques. The West German and Japanese cases stand in contrast with those of France and Italy. In the latter two countries, unions have a strong tradition of class conflict and ideological division. The extent of co-operation with employers at either plant or national level or with the state is typically low.

But where does federalism enter into this? In addition to the incentive provided by West German functional federalism for organizational cohesion at the federal level, a further feature of federalism has been the emphasis on secretive, behind-the-scenes bargaining between officials and politicians of both Land and federal governments.[31] This type of bargaining is characteristic not just of the federal process but in many respects of the West German political system as a whole. As Thomas Hueglin has noted, these practices may limit democracy by precluding broad-based popular participation. At the same time they are essentially non-majoritarian, which means that more than a simple majority of significant groups must concur with decisions that affect the interest of those groups. The emphasis is on achieving consensus.

West German federal practices in good part can be traced back to Wilhelmine Germany, when Bismarck used similar tactics to incorporate the smaller states and principalities into the German Reich. These traditions were effectively superseded during Weimar, when the 'Länder were left without the necessary financial powers to protect their interests, and, later, toward the end of Weimar, when power, effectively concentrated at the centre in Berlin, was captured by the National Socialists. The post–Second World War period saw a deliberate effort to incorporate some of the older non-majoritarian practices into the new constitution, the Basic Law. The resulting institutions and horizontal federal arrangement are of the intrastate variety, which, perforce, requires consensus building and co-operative behaviour if any degree of co-ordination is to be achieved. By and large, efforts in this direction have been successful, accomplished not only through the major political arena, the Bundesrat, in which the Länder are directly represented, but also through bodies such as the Council of Public Author-ities on Business-Cycle Policies (for federal and local authorities) and the

Council on Budgetary Planning (for federal and Länder governments). Co-operative practices in these bodies both parallel and help to reinforce similar practices among the so-called autonomous economic groups outside government.[32] Compared with Austria, the West German state does take a more active and visible role, and power is dispersed more widely among groups. But at the same time, most industrial sectors are highly concentrated and have been able to achieve a modus vivendi with both government and labour; and in doing so the West German federal system does not appear to have been a major impediment. In fact, given the emphasis on keeping matters at the bureaucratic level and on the avoidance of conflict, as fostered by federal practices, these industrial cartels have probably been helped by the federal arrangement.

Turning to Switzerland, even more than in West Germany we find an emphasis on the sanctity of the free-market economy and deliberate governmental preference for non-intervention in the economy. There has never been anything that can be termed a national wage determination policy by either autonomous groups working on their own or in conjunction with government. Only in the area of export promotion does the Swiss national government play an active role, what Peter Katzenstein has referred to as the Swiss version of Keynesianism.[33] At the same time, Switzerland is characterized by a high level of accommodation between the different sub-cultural segments through non-majoritarian practices, in large part fostered by the institutional arrangements of Swiss federalism and mechanisms such as the referendum procedure on federal legislation. The latter allows citizens in a minority of cantons to hold a national referendum on any federal legislation. Since the majority of referendum questions go down to defeat, it is seen as an effective instrument for protecting the interests of minority sub-cultures, whether religious or linguistic.[34] Swiss political élites engage in extensive consultation with the leaders of groups whose interests might conceivably be affected by proposed legislation, a practice sometimes referred to as the politics of avoiding the referendum. And these groups include economic interest groups, organized into cohesive, albeit informal, cartel-like arrangements.

Organized labour in Switzerland does not have a high profile, a situation that is paralleled in the parliamentary arena, though the left often has more influence than its numbers would suggest, largely as a result of the consociational elements built into the Swiss political system. In contrast, business, particularly internationally oriented business, is well organized and cohesive and enjoys easy access to government. As noted by Coleman, the Swiss constitution states that economic organizations are to be heard before federal laws are enacted. Further, even though Swiss federalism is somewhat similar to Canadian federalism in assigning separate policy-making powers to the two levels of government (jurisdictional federalism), the Swiss federal government does have much broader powers over commerce and the regulation of food and drugs. According to Coleman, these two features provide a powerful stimulus to the development of strong business associations at the federal level.

The interests of most industrial sectors, however, are held to be best served by minimal government intervention. In this respect the restructuring of the Swiss watch industry during the 1970s is instructive, an eight-year effort accomplished with virtually no help from government, other than some limited export subsidies. In conjunction with the banks, the industry was able to decide which firms should be phased out, what sort of technological and marketing innovations were necessary to meet Japanese competition, and where capital was best invested. Collectively and individually firms were also able to make arrangements with their workers as to layoffs, transfers, and retraining. As Katzenstein notes, all this was done after a certain amount of self-imposed centralization within the industry.[35]

The Swiss example highlights three points. First, there appears to be a spillover effect whereby consociational practices among political élites are replicated in other sectors of Swiss society, including the economic sector. Second, economic collaboration and decision-making above the level of the individual firm take place quite easily and without even implicit government direction, thereby perhaps giving new meaning to the term *societal corporatism*. Third, the Swiss federal system, which incorporates definite intrastate elements in the make-up of its federal council, the rotation of the presidency, and so on, along with the referendum system, promotes consociational bargaining.

The first and third points require further investigation as well as elaboration. Their potential importance in explicating the links between federalism and corporatism, however, can be illustrated by returning briefly to the Austrian example, even though Austria and Switzerland are seen as quite different examples of successful economic policy-making. Austria is generally regarded as a highly centralized state despite a federal constitution. Yet Lehmbruch, referring to the break-up of the government coalition betwween the Socialist and Conservative parties back in 1966, notes that nevertheless the 'majoritarian features of Austria today are not only mitigated by the importance of a powerful neo-corporatist inter-organizational network ... but also by the federal elements of the constitution.'[36] Important areas of economic and social policy are under the jurisdiction of the states, jurisdiction that can be overriden by a two-thirds majority of the national parliament. Although the national legislature can override initiatives at the state level, this does require a 'consociational' or concurrent majority, in that no single party is likely to have enough seats to meet the two-thirds criterion. Further, education is a 'joint' responsibility, which requires consent by both state and federal governments in order to validate any given piece of legislation. These institutional rules of the game ensure a high level of co-operation and extensive consultation, so that the necessary majorities can be put together, thereby helping to reinforce the basis of the Austrian social partnership.[37]

Corporatism and Federalism in Canada

Leo Panitch has argued that Canada lacks an ideological as well as a structural basis for corporatism. Notwithstanding the writings of Prime Minister William Lyon Mackenzie King, the ideas of the Progressives on group government, and the influence of Roman Catholic thought in Quebec during the inter-war period, very few actual efforts have been made to implement such ideas, and those that were made departed significantly from the corporatist model. In the post–Second World War period the Economic Council of Canada was modelled on the example of European tripartite councils and did provide for representation from organized labour. But the council has never been seriously involved in either economic planning or short-term economic policy-making, and it would be stretching matters to say that even at the most minimal level it helped develop a consensus between government, business, and labour on economic issues.[38]

Citing Clause Offe on the natural asymmetry between the established power position of business generally and the weakness of labour, Panitch argues that a cohesive and centralized labour movement is essential before one can speak meaningfully about the integration of the three elements into a tripartite arrangement. In contrast, 'the power of capital resides in the private ownership of means of production, and not its interest associations.'[39] In the Canadian case, therefore, one of the primary failings is the lack of an organized working class. Panitch notes that although business organizations in Canada also tend to be decentralized, 'the weakness and decentralization of labour in Canada must certainly be seen as a much more important factor in any explanation of the historical absence of corporatist arrangements in Canada and any consideration of future developments.'[40]

It can be argued, however, that Panitch perhaps dismisses the organizational dimension of business interests a little too readily. Corporatism is primarily an organizational phenomenon, and, the universal dominance of business in capitalist systems notwithstanding, there does appear considerable variation from country to country in the extent of centralization and concentration of business interests. Further, although on a normative basis one can argue that the role of labour in any corporatist arrangement should be considered only on the basis of equality, and that this can come about only when labour is strong and cohesive, there are other ways through which the integration of labour can be achieved. We have already noted the case of Japan, 'corporatism without labor'; we also noted the manner in which unions in West Germany enjoyed some participation in economic decision-making, in part through the mechanism of co-determination. Thus a plausible case can be made that if one wishes to establish a necessary condition for the success of corporatism, that condition must then be the organized concentration and centralization of business rather than labour interests. This is not to claim that Canada might qualify for corporatist status. Quite the contrary, for not only is organized labour in Canada fragmented, but so too are business interests. In spite of high levels of concentration in several important sectors, such as steel, transportation, and banking, the organization of business interests remains decentralized.

This state of affairs can be attributed in part both to the regional nature of the Canadian economy and to the policies pursued by federal and provincial governments.[41] Robert Salisbury, in commenting on the lack of cohesive peak organizations in the United States and hence the lack of corporatism in that country, attributes this to the unevenness of economic growth and the high level of competition within many industrial sectors.[42] Within Canada, growth has been uneven, particularly across regions. Further, there is considerable evidence of competition between regions within the same sector. Thus one major tire company, Michelin, in Nova Scotia, is pitted against tire companies based in Ontario. Michelin does not belong to the Canadian Rubber Manufacturers Association and does not share information with the association or any of its members. Provincial governments have actively supported the companies in their respective provinces.

Regional development policy as pursued by federal and provincial governments may also play a role. The three Michelin plants are encouraged to locate in Nova Scotia in part by means of generous grants offered by the then Department of Regional Economic Expansion (DREE). Coleman and Grant have pointed to the confederal character of many Canadian business associations, in which provincial member organizations remain highly autonomous. Their decentralized character does not necessarily preclude effective action at the national level, as illustrated by the successes of the Canadian Trucking Association and the Mining Association of Canada. However, this effectiveness comes about only under certain conditions, that is, when one level of government is indifferent or when both levels are generally of the same mind.[43] The situation is quite different when governments are in conflict. 'The greater autonomy of action enjoyed by the partners in confederal or affiliate associations makes it much easier for governments to split their ranks in these instances.'[44]

There is little doubt that the nature of Canadian federalism has played a role in fragmenting the associational life of business interests. But whether federalism, or at least the Canadian variant of it, is the only or even the main factor is very much open to debate. As the Swiss and West German cases demonstrate, business associations can overcome the institutional barriers of federalism, and, further, these barriers do not preclude development of cohesive peak organizations in the major sectors of the economy. What is clearly evident is the extent to which Canada lacks equivalent peak organizations. As Coleman notes, there is virtually no sector in Canada in which a single peak organization can be said to have a monopoly. Two competing bodies, the Business Council on National Issues and the Canadian Chamber of Commerce, both claim to speak for the general interests of business. Within the small-business sector, the Canadian Federation of Independent Business and the Canadian Organization of Small Business are in competition with each other. Although the Canadian Manufacturers' Association is sometimes thought to be an all-encompassing organization, it represents the interests of manufacturers only, excluding from membership firms in the resource, construction, transportation, and finance areas.[45] When examples of sectoral or intersectoral cohesion do occur, they are much more likely to be found at the provincial level. In summary, the fragmentation of economic associations and the resulting lack of policy capacity within business as a whole have profound implications for any efforts to introduce corporatist institutions and practices in Canada. Corporatist procedures and arenas, as in the case of consociationalism, need not be highly institutionalized; but corporatism is effective only when the organizations are both limited in number and at the same time all-encompassing.

Neither condition is met in Canada, as illustrated by efforts over the past decade to introduce corporatist practices. In the aftermath of the introduction of wage and price controls in 1976, the Canadian Labour Congress (CLC) put forward a proposal for a tripartite Social and Economic Planning Council, modelled on various European corporatist planning structures. The federal government countered with a proposal for a much larger multipartite structure with reduced powers, which would include representation from the provinces.[46] Although discussions were held with the private sector and, through the federal government, with provincial governments, the extent to which these business and provincial interests supported either of these initiatives remains unclear. Discussion effectively ceased in 1978, and both proposals died a quiet death.

The more significant effort in tripartite relations occurred during the period 1977–8 with respect to the problem of industrial restructuring. While discussing the problem of co-ordinated economic policy in a federal system with the provinces at first ministers' conferences in February and November 1978, the federal government, through the old Department of Industry, Trade and Commerce (IT&C), initiated twenty-three separate task forces, each dealing with a specific industrial sector. The discussions held by these sectoral task forces were referred to as tier I, and they were expected to report their recommendations by August 1978, at which point the tier II committee would attempt to distil all the recommendations into something more manageable. The whole exercise was preceded by extensive interviews with the private sector by IT&C, a project ambitiously entitled Enterprise '77, involving 5,000 interviews designed to elicit private-sector concerns.[47] The significance of the process resides in the fact that these task forces were each headed by a representative from the business sector in question and included representatives from labour; both federal and provincial officials participated, but only as observers. The 860 recommendations made in the tier I reports were distilled down to 46 recommendations in nine major areas by the tier II committee. This committee also drew on representation from business and labour as well as a number of academics, and its major task was to draw out the cross-sectoral concerns common to all the tier I reports.

Many of the recommendations were contradictory and, if taken seriously, would have involved several billion dollars either in tax cuts or in direct expenditures. Several differences between labour and management were also left unresolved. Equally critical was the government's reaction. As Richard French has noted, by the time the tier II committee delivered its report in the fall of 1978, both the government's industrial policy-making machinery and its agenda had altered radically. The Trudeau government was now engaged in drastic cost-cutting; any prospect of funds for industrial adjustment was now in abeyance.[48] If one of the more important elements in corporatist accommodation is stability and consistency in the government's position, it was clearly lacking in this instance.[49]

Very little of the spirit of tier I and tier II survived. The short-lived 1979–80 Conservative government of Joe Clark did not pursue the exercise, and neither did the subsequent Liberal government. Nor were any efforts made by the Mulroney government to link the earlier tier I and tier II discussions to the 1985 Economic Summit exercise, in which 150 participants from business, labour, welfare groups, the unemployed, and other groups, organized and unorganized, were brought together to discuss and consult, in a highly public forum, with the prime minister.

The tier I and tier II exercise was perhaps the closest Canada has come to tripartism; but the exercise also illustrated the enormous difficulties involved in attempting to develop a consensus involving a multiplicity of actors, including the ten provincial governments. In a recent book, Hugh Thorburn offers one novel solution to the problem of co-ordinating economic planning in Canada, in part animated by the failure of both executive federalism and the tier I and tier II experience: the creation of a federal-provincial planning institution.[50] This body would have equal representation from federal and provincial governments and would be responsible for producing a 'rational' master plan for the economy. It would be aided by experts and still remain accountable to the federal and provincial legislatures. However, without a direct role for business and labour, it cannot be considered a proper corporatist solution. These two bodies, presumably, could be represented only through the efforts of the different governments.

On the one hand, the Thorburn model demonstrates the gap between the possibility of corporatist institutions and specific designs for economic planning institutions produced by either academics or politicians. On the other hand, it underscores the fact that no proposed co-ordinating mechanism, corporatist or otherwise, can ignore the important role played by provincial governments in regulating and representing economic interests.[51]

The older form of executive federalism, sometimes described by the rubric of co-operative federalism, shares with corporatism certain elements, namely the quality of élite accommodation in the face of deferential or indifferent mass publics. Aside from the heightened competition between the two levels of government, as well as among some provincial governments, and the inclination of many provincial governments to intervene directly in economic matters, most governments can no longer depend upon their citizens remaining quiescent. In short, with or without the formal representation of economic interests, an economic planning or co-ordinating agency dependent on the participation of all provincial governments is likely to lack the essential ingredient of consociationalism. Even assuming that all governments are willing to participate, such a scheme is unlikely to have much practical effect.

Conclusion

The organizational fragmentation of economic interests, when combined with the Canadian variant of executive federalism, does not appear conducive to the adoption of corporatism in Canada. It might be argued, on the basis of our discussion of federalism in Switzerland, West Germany, and Austria, that the introduction of intrastate federalism in Canada, or at least some elements of non-majoritarianism in central institutions, could help matters. But this is not necessarily so. American intrastate federalism does not appear to have contributed to the development of corporatism in that country. Indeed in some respects it has probably contributed to the multiplicity and fragmentation of economic interests. The successful role of non-majoritarian techniques in Switzerland and Austria in bringing about co-operation presupposes the existence of large-scale, unified economic interests.

Leaving aside the question of federalism, in Canada there exists an additional institutional barrier, namely parliament and the executive-administrative branch and their roles in government decision-making. In corporatist arrangements government need not be actively involved in economic decision-making, but it still needs to have a single, coherent, and consistent point of view. In Canada this has been lacking, largely because of what Paul Pross has referred to as bureaucratic pluralism, a development that has multiplied over the past two decades.[52] The locus of power has shifted away from the mandarins at the top to the lower levels of the bureaucracy; but at the same time the influence of each policy actor is now so restricted that at most one can only veto the activities of other actors. Thus diffusion has resulted in confusion. One of the most striking developments has been the failure of central agencies or co-ordinating bodies, like the Privy Council Office, which were designed to provide the necessary control over the multifarious activities and decisions of the federal government. Ironically, various provincial governments, because of their smaller size and scale of operations, have been more successful in co-ordinating the internal activities of their executive-administrative branches.

According to Pross, competing federal government agencies have actively courted interest groups in order to enhance their influence within the bureaucracy, but with the effect of further diffusing power and thereby creating additional, often contradictory points of entry for pressure groups. Equally important, these developments have also led to what Pross claims has been the enhancement of parliament's role in the policy process. In part through default, parliament has become more prominent, and both agencies and interest groups have found the publicizing and legitimating capacities of parliament to be useful in furthering their goals.[53]

The implications of the failure of intragovernmental co-ordination for the possible broader co-ordination of the economic activities of business, government, and labour are obvious. In addition, however, Pross's perceptive analysis also points to some fundamental attitudes and changing preferences about the nature of public authority among both citizens and politicians. Panitch noted that the government's rejection in 1976 of the CLC's proposal for a tripartite Social and Economic Planning Council was based in part on its unwillingness to see the usurpation of parliamentary power.[54] Corporatism requires that popularly elected legislative bodies delegate part of their decision-making and legitimating authority to a separate arena. In this respect Pross, citing the work of Allan Kornberg et al, notes that among the general public, parliament as an institution is still held in high esteem, while the same cannot be said of civil servants.[55] In short, the unwillingness of the public to accord legitimacy to the administrative state, and by implication to the secretive practices that are a necessary component of corporatism, will probably help to forestall efforts to devolve parliamentary authority to a separate body.

Finally, the entrenchment of adversarial and majoritarian procedures, not just in parliament but also in collective bargaining, the courts, and other legal, economic, and social institutions, further militates against the adoption and subsequent reinforcement of corporatist practices in Canada. These are not the only norms and institutions that serve to hinder collaboration. For example, the organization of capital markets on the basis of traditional Anglo-Saxon practices prevents Canadian banks from pursuing an active co-ordinative role in questions of sectoral restructuring as is the case in countries like West Germany and Switzerland.[56]

Notwithstanding the above, there are still grounds for arguing that efforts can and should be made to improve co-ordination between governments and economic interests and to alter the climate within which labour relations are conducted. The point to be made, however, is that alternative means will have to be used. Some of these may be of the populist or plebiscitarian sort, as practised in part by Prime Minister Mulroney. At lower levels, it may be possible to promote quasi-corporatist practices, for example at the provincial level, if certain conditions are met, including the concentration of significant economic interests. Unfortunately, while efforts to reinforce corporatism at lower levels may succeed, this can occur at the expense of macro-level corporatism. According to Lehmbruch, the two are incompatible, in that strong associations at a lower or regional level will simply act to undermine the authority of national-level associations.[57] However, limited business and labour co-operation at the national level may be effective, if only be demonstrating to affiliated member organizations what can be achieved. The CLC and the Business Council on National Issues recently created the Canadian Labour Market Productivity Centre, the mandate of which includes study of issues such as worker participation in management.[58]

The merits and deficiencies of such efforts cannot be examined here. What can be said is that while 'the century of corporatism,' to use Schmitter's phrase, appears to have passed Canada by, alternative means designed to mesh with the realities of executive federalism and our parliamentary institutions may nevertheless help us reach the same objectives, albeit at a slower pace. Without dismissing out of hand all possible lessons for Canada stemming from Austrian, Dutch, West German, and Swedish experience, it does appear that as models both corporatism and consociationalism are of limited utility in helping Canadians chart future institutional developments.

NOTES

1 Gerhard Lehmbruch 'Federalism and Consociationalism: Some Comments' Paper presented to the American Political Science Association, Chicago, 1983.
2 See David R. Cameron 'Social Democracy, Corporatism, and Labour Quiescence: The Representation of Economic Interest in Advanced Capitalist Society' in J. Goldthorpe ed *Order and Conflict in Contemporary Capitalism* (New York: Oxford University Press 1984) 143–78; also Andrew Martin 'The Politics of Employment and Welfare: National Policies and International Interdependence' in K. Banting ed *The State and Economic Interests*, vol. 32 of the research studies prepared for the Royal Commission on the Economic Union and Development Prospects for Canada (Toronto: University of Toronto Press 1986) 157–241.
3 K.D. McRae 'Comment: Federation, Consociation, Corporatism – An Addendum to Arend Lijphart' *Canadian Journal of Political Science* 12 (1979) 520.
4 McRae 'Consociational Democracy and the Canadian Political System' in K.D. McRae ed *Consociational Democracy: Political Accommodation in Segmented Societies* (Toronto: McClelland and Stewart 1974) 238–61; S.J.R. Noel 'Consociational Democracy and Canadian Federalism' in McRae ed *Consociational Democracy* 262–8; Arend Lijphart *Democracy in Plural Societies* (New Haven: Yale University Press 1977) 129
5 Lehmbruch, 'Consociational Democracy, Class Conflict and the New Corporatism' in P.C. Schmitter and G. Lehmbruch eds *Trends Toward Corporatist Intermediation* (London: Sage 1979) 53–62; Alfred Diamant 'Bureaucracy and Public Policy in Neocorporatist Settings: Some European Lessons' *Comparative Politics* 14 (October 1981) 120–1
6 Leo Panitch 'Corporatism in Canada?' in Richard Schultz et al eds *The Canadian Political Process* 3rd ed (Toronto: Holt, Rinehart and Winston 1979) 53–72
7 Lijphart 'Consociational Democracy' *World Politics* 21 (1969) 216

8 Lijphart 'Consociation and Federation: Conceptual and Empirical Links' *Canadian Journal of Political Science* 12 (September 1979) especially 506–7

9 Lijphart *The Politics of Accommodation: Pluralism and Democracy in the Netherlands* 2nd ed (Berkeley: University of California Press 1975) especially chap 8

10 McRae 'Consociational Democracy and the Canadian Political System' 248–56

11 Richard Simeon *Federal-Provincial Diplomacy: The Making of Recent Policy in Canada* (Toronto: University of Toronto Press 1972) 291–2

12 Noel 'Consociational Democracy and Canadian Federalism' 265

13 Philippe C. Schmitter 'Still the Century of Corporatism' in Schmitter and Lehmbruch eds *Trends Toward Corporatism Intermediation* 22–4

14 John Crispo *Industrial Democracy in Western Europe: A North American Perspective* (Toronto: Lorimer 1978)

15 Schmitter 'Still the Century of Corporatism' 13

16 G. Lehmbruch 'Concertation and the Structure of Corporatist Networks' in J. Goldthorpe ed *Order and Conflict in Contemporary Capitalism* 60–80

17 Bernd Marin 'Organizing Interests by Interest Organizations: Associational Prerequisites of Cooperation in Austria' *International Political Science Review* 4 (1983) 201–3

18 Lehmbruch 'Consociational Democracy, Class Conflict and the New Corporatisms' 55

19 Ibid

20 Ibid

21 R. Singh *Policy Development: A Study of the Social and Economic Council of the Netherlands* (Rotterdam: University of Rotterdam Press 1972)

22 Lehmbruch 'Liberal Corporatism and Party Government' in Schmitter and Lehmbruch eds *Trends Toward Corporatist Intermediation* 165

23 S.B. Wolinetz 'Neo-corporatism and Industrial Policy in the Netherlands' Paper presented at the annual meeting of the Canadian Political Science Association, Vancouver, June 1983

24 Lehmbruch 'Consociational Democracy, Class Conflict, and the New Corporatisms' 54. The irony is that in countries like Austria and the Netherlands the 'state' looms much larger and appears to enjoy greater legitimacy than in North America. The point that needs to be stressed is that the concept of the state extends beyond government itself and that institutions such as the economic chambers and the 'parity' commission in Austria can be seen as part of the apparatus of the state even though distinct from and largely independent of the government. Where the boundary between state and society rests is far from clear, since, as Lehmbruch and others have pointed out, social, economic, political, and government organizations have become highly interdependent, particularly in Austria. For discussion of differences between European and North

American conceptions of the state see Kenneth Dyson *The State Tradition in Western Europe* (Oxford: Martin Robertson 1980). For the manner in which organized groups in many European states came to attain public legitimacy see Claus Offe 'The Attribution of Public Status to Interest Groups: Observations on the West German Case' in S. Berger ed *Organizing Interests in Western Europe: Pluralism, Corporatism, and the Transformation of Politics* (Cambridge: Cambridge University Press 1981) 123–59.

25 Theodore Lowi *The End of Liberalism: Ideology, Policy, and the Crisis of Public Authority* (New York: Norton 1969)

26 To take account of this middle ground between pluralism, defined as open competition between groups, and corporatism, as defined by Schmitter et al, Grant Jordan has introduced the term *corporate pluralism*, denoting cases of closed group-departmental relations and sectorized policy-making but where organizations are still segmented and not all-encompassing. Grant Jordan 'Pluralistic Corporatisms and Corporate Pluralism' *Scandinavian Political Studies* 7 (New Series) (September 1984) 137–53

27 Lehmbruch 'Consociational Democracy, Class Conflict and the New Corporatism 59

28 Andrew Shonfeld *Modern Capitalism: The Changing Balance of Public and Private Power* (London: Oxford University Press 1965); John Zysman *Governments, Markets, and Growth: Financial Systems and the Politics of Industrial Change* (Ithaca: Cornell University Press 1983) 251–65

29 Klaus von Beyme 'Neo-Corporatism: A New Nut in an Old Shell?' *International Political Science Review* 4 (1983) 178–9; Wolfgang Streeck 'Neo-Corporatist Industrial Relations and the Economic Crisis in West Germany' in Goldthorpe ed *Order and Conflict in Contemporary Capitalism* 291–314

30 T.J. Pempel and Keiichi Tsunekawa 'Corporatism without Labor? The Japanese Anomaly' in Schmitter and Lehmbruch eds *Trends Toward Corporatist Intermediation* 231–70

31 Ronald Burns 'Second Chambers: German Experience and Canadian Needs' *Canadian Public Administration* 18 (winter 1975) 541–68

32 Lehmbruch 'Liberal Corporatism and Party Government' in Schmitter and Lehmbruch eds *Trends Toward Corporatist Intermediation* 161

33 Peter J. Katzenstein *Corporatism and Change: Switzerland and Austria and the Politics of Industrial Change* (Ithaca: Cornell University Press 1984) 159

34 Ronald Rogowski *Rational Legitimacy: A Theory of Political Support* (Princeton: Princeton University Press 1974) 127–32

35 Katzenstein *Corporatism and Change* 224–36. Unfortunately, as Katzenstein points out (p. 250), many of the costs of the restructuring were born by foreign workers, perhaps the only group in Switzerland that lacks adequate representation and protection in the Swiss political and economic system.

36 Lehmbruch 'Federalism and Consociationalism: Some Comments'
37 Ibid; see also Peter Katzenstein 'Center-Periphery Relations in a Consociational Democracy: Austria and Kleinwalsertal' in S. Tarrow, P.J. Katzenstein, and L. Graziano eds *Territorial Politics in Industrial Nations* (New York: Praeger 1978) 123–69.
38 Panitch 'Corporatism in Canada?' 56–65
39 Ibid 67
40 Ibid
41 O.F.G. Sitwell and N.R.M. Seifried *The Regional Structure of the Canadian Economy* (Toronto: Methuen 1984); Garth Stevenson *Unfilled Union: Canadian Federalism and National Unity* (Toronto: Gage 1982) chap 4, especially 64–83
42 Robert H. Salisbury 'Why No Corporatism in America?' Schmitter and Lehmbruch eds *Trends Toward Corporatist Intermediation* 215
43 William D. Coleman and Wyn P. Grant 'Regional Differentiation of Business Interest Associations: A Comparison of Canada and the United Kingdom' *Canadian Journal of Political science* 18 (March 1985) 28
44 Ibid
45 Coleman 'Canadian Business and the State' in K. Banting ed *The State and Economic Interests*, vol. 32 of the research studies prepared for the Royal Commission on the Economic Union and Development Prospects for Canada (Toronto: University of Toronto Press 1986) 264–74
46 Panitch 'Corporatism in Canada?' 65–6
47 See Douglas Brown and Julia Eastman *The Limits of Consultation: A Debate among Ottawa, the Provinces and the Private Sector on an Industrial Strategy* (Ottawa: Science Council of Canada 1981); Richard French *How Ottawa Decides: Planning and Industrial Policy-Making 1968-1980* (Toronto: Lorimer 1980).
48 French *How Ottawa Decides* 123
49 Ibid 128–9. In late 1978 the tier II recommendations were turned over to the newly created Board of Economic Development Ministers (BEDM), which by April 1979 claimed to be making progress in meeting the objectives outlined in the tier I and tier II reports in a number of areas. French notes that the single major accomplishment of BEDM was probably the pulp and paper modernization program, consisting of federal-provincial agreements negotiated by DREE and the expenditure of $250 million. The policy represented the first national strategy for a specific sector, and it came about in part as a result of the deliberations of the tier I task force responsible for the forestry industry. This, however, would be the only success arising out of the whole consultative process.
50 H.G. Thorburn *Planning and the Economy: Building Federal-Provincial Consensus* (Toronto: Lorimer 1984)
51 On this point see Michael Jenkin *The Challenge of Diversity: Industrial Policy*

in the Canadian Federation (Ottawa: Science Council of Canada 1983) especially 101–41.

52 A. Paul Pross 'Parliamentary Influence and the Diffusion of Power' *Canadian Journal of Political Science* 18 (June 1985) 235–266

53 Ibid

54 Panitch 'Corporatism in Canada?' 66

55 Pross 'Parliamentary Influence and the Diffusion of Power'

56 Banks are required to maintain an arms-length relationship with firms to which they extend credit and, further, are not permitted to own more than 10 per cent of voting shares in any firm. See R. Schultz and A. Alexandroff *Economic Regulation and the Federal System*, vol. 42 of the research studies prepared for the Royal Commission on the Economic Union and Development Prospects for Canada (Toronto: University of Toronto Press 1985).

57 G. Lehmbruch 'Neocorporatism in Western Europe: A Reassessment of the Concept of Cross-National Perspective' International Political Science Association, 13th World Congress, Paris, 1985; A. Wassenberg 'Neo-corporatism and the Quest for Control: The Cuckoo Game' in G. Lehmbruch and P. Schmitter eds *Patterns of Corporatist Policy-Making* (London: Sage 1982) 83–108. On partial corporatism in Canada see M. Atkinson and W. Coleman 'Corporatism and Industrial Policy' in Alan Cawson ed *Organized Interests and the State: Studies in Meso-Corporatism* (London: Sage 1985) 22–44.

58 See Judy Steed 'Labor's Quiet Revolution' *Globe and Mail* 24 March 1984, 10. For a review of various efforts in business-labour consultation see Pierre Fournier 'Consensus Building in Canada: Case Studies and Prospects' in Banting ed *The State and Economic Interests* 291–335.

16 / The Future of Federalism

HERMAN BAKVIS

WILLIAM M. CHANDLER

Territorially based conflicts are certainly more visible within the context of a constitutionally enshrined division of powers. There follows, therefore, a natural tendency on the part of students of federalism to concentrate on these cases. However, it has become clear that in addressing issues surrounding the importance of federalism for the modern state, we are dealing with a range of questions that extends far beyond the borders of formal federalism. A first lesson that we can draw from the contributions to this volume, therefore, is that there should be recognition that the debate over federal questions cannot be so restricted as to exclude territorially based conflicts and federalizing trends within unitary states. As the chapters on decentralization, pressure groups, and corporatism demonstrate, on grounds of method alone data from non-federal systems provide a valuable comparative reference for testing propositions about federal systems.

But what have we learned of the workability of federalism itself? First, despite the centralist prophecies of three decades ago, the federal state has not whithered away, and decentralizing solutions in unitary systems have assumed new prominence. The reasons for this, as noted by our contributors, are both varied and complex. As stressed by Roger Gibbins, they relate in part to the resilience and durability of federal institutions, some of which were designed over two centuries ago. Further, as a well-tried means of resolving conflict, federalism has remained particularly relevant in light of the persistence of linguistic or ethnically based conflicts in modern societies like Belgium and Canada. Finally, the fact that decentralization, modernization, and economic development need not be incompatible also helps to affirm the adaptability and therefore the modernity of traditional federal institutions. More generally, it is also evident that the complexities of governance in advanced industrial systems may make the federal form more attractive, not less.

In a sense these findings reinforce arguments developed in other research. There are two areas, however, where the essays in this volume point to trends that either have received relatively little attention or have been underrated. The first concerns the link between decentralist solutions and the constraints of interdependence, which are essential for understanding the problem of governance in modern industrial societies. The second concerns the ways in which federalism makes a difference and the inherent limitations on the autonomy of the federal state. It would appear, on the basis of some of the findings in this volume, that a degree of revision in the state-centred paradigm may be required. Let us briefly recapitulate and summarize these themes.

Decentralization and Interdependence: Toward a Confederal Model?

Federal systems have been compared most frequently in terms of degree of centralization or decentralization; this dimension remains for many the starting point for comparative generalizations. In the era of 'classical federalism,' when the scope of the public sector remained restricted and when models of water-tight compartments of policy-making bore some resemblance to reality, the primacy of centralization as the dimension for comparison remained beyond dispute. The maturation of the large-scale interventionist state, which constitutes the most pervasive and consistent transformation common to all advanced industrial societies, has posed an inevitable challenge to this unidimensional view of federalism.

Advocates of decentralization must take account of the existing interdependence of governmental and administrative units, even where those units have autonomous sources of power and authority. In unitary states this is readily observable within the complexities of the administrative state. In federal states it is mirrored in complex intergovernmental relations vertically across two or more levels and, to a degree, horizontally among the regional units. Here, too, the autonomy of constitutionally distinct decision-makers has been irreversibly compromised by the imperatives of complex policy demands and solutions. While decision-makers may have considerable legal and even fiscal authority – indeed in some federations this authority may well have increased – in reality it is often based on the power to say no, to be able to veto proposed courses of action that depend upon co-ordination with, and the acquiesence of, other units.[1]

In other words, the debate over decentralizing trends cannot be evaluated accurately without recognizing the nature of the authority accompanying decentralization and the crucial constraints working against disentanglement. In this connection, efforts to redefine the sharing of power within federal arrangements take on a special meaning. Increasingly there appears to be an emphasis on the representation of regional interests in national policy-making as opposed to the simple question of the division of powers. For this reason, modes of representation and the nature of intergovernmental bargaining arenas have become especially significant.

The distinctive federal question about representation concerns the expression of regional interests and quite naturally is focused on the role of parties and parliamentary institutions. Here the distinction between intra- and interstate federalism is instructive, because in representational terms it identifies those systems in which regional interests are primarily represented within institutions (hence intra-) and those in which the federal units themselves formally articulate conflicting preferences through relations between levels of government (hence inter-). This distinction is especially compelling for Canadian politics because of its combination of strong regional pressures with an institutional structure affording only limited, ad hoc opportunities for intrastate modes of representation. Alan Cairns has recommended elsewhere that the present structure of Canadian interstate federalism be maintained, if only to avoid the further confounding of the authority and accountability of the different levels of government. But he has also favoured some form of proportional representation for the House of Commons as a means of securing greater regional balance and a reduction of sectionalism within parliament.[2] Arend Lijphart, while not advocating one particular solution over another, nevertheless notes that Canada is one of the few federations lacking a bicameral mode of regional representation. At the same time the existence of a second chamber would not necessarily guarantee regionally based non-majoritarian practices. Campbell Sharman's study of the Australian Senate demonstrates how, given certain political contexts, non-regional partisan or functional interests may override regional interests. Thus, while the answers are far from clear, the debate over second chambers has taken on considerable importance, particularly in those federal states, like Canada, where the mechanisms for effective regional representation have been historically faulty and where regional disaffection has prospered in the popular belief that certain regions and interests have been regularly denied an effective voice within central decision-making.[3]

In certain federal systems, the proliferation of intergovernmental relations, symptomatic of the spread of policy interdependence, has challenged the representational role of both parties and parliamentary institutions by creating parallel mechanisms of, in Smiley's term, 'executive federalism,' which bypass the normal mechanisms of democratic accountability. However, as the chapter on federalism and political parties has indicated, the extent of this exclusion will be a function of the degree to which intergovernmental relations are integrated within the constitutionally defined policy process at the national level. It will also be a function of the extent of partisan-bureaucratic élite interpenetration and whether or not the underlying rationale for the federal division of authority is rooted in a division of jurisdictions or in a division of labour.

On the whole, the question of regional representation looms large because as interdependence increases so, too, does the realization that the mere shifting of authority or responsibility from one level of government is unlikely to provide an adequate solution. Arthur Benz's findings in the case of West Germany are particularly instructive. He notes that recent efforts to devolve more authority to the lower-level units, rather than increasing the autonomy of these units, have instead resulted in these units becoming simultaneously more dependent upon the central government and more involved in central government decision-making. Lower-level units discovered that increased responsibilities required more in the way of monetary resources and therefore a new dependence on the central government; but they discovered also that increased authority resulted in greater overlap between their activities and those of the central government and the other Länder, which in their view could be dealt with satisfactorily only by enhancing direct influence on central government efforts to co-ordinate and control these activities. Although the aim in part was to reduce the load on the central government by devolving more authority to the Länder, an additional result proved to be increased participation of Land governments in central decision-making.

The functional, horizontal structure of West German federalism may help push developments there in a confederal direction, but there may also be a logic inherent in the operation of all modern federations. In Canada, a recent parallel is evident in the provincial pressure for direct involvement in the Canadian-us free trade negotiations. Provincial demands have set forth a level of participation that the federal government has been reluctant to grant. Increasingly, it seems, whether under the rubric of inter- or intrastate federalism, central government decision-making in many policy areas is subject to constraint from regional units or participants. Benz's analysis thus points to an important trend in modern federations: given the already entrenched position of lower-level units, the increasing interdependence over time between these units and the central government leads to confederal forms of decision-making.

This does not necessarily mean that central governments will become the creatures of the constituent units. As long as central governments retain their own basis of political authority, and given the persistence of conflicting claims among the constituents themselves, it seems likely that central governments will be able to insert their own autonomous will and vision into national as well as many local and regional policies. However, central governments can proceed only *inter*dependently, for there are few if any policy areas where they can operate effectively without, at a minimum, consulting lower levels of government.

Public Policy and the Federal State

One of the issues raised in this volume is the manner in which federalism makes a difference. This is obviously a policy-oriented question and is a theme running through a number of the comparative studies found here. When the question is posed in terms of whole systems, as in the tradition of William Riker, the answer remains indeterminant. Grace Skogstad, in her analysis of agricultural policy, notes that on the whole the substance of Canadian and American agricultural policies is surprisingly similar, even though the role of various producer groups in the policy process differs considerably both within and between the two countries. She attributes the stronger position of producer groups and the more or less equal treatment for all commodities in the United States to the existence of more effective intrastate federalism in that country. The sharp differences in both the treatment and the effectiveness of various specialized groups in Canada are attributed to the often ideological conflict between the federal government and the provinces and among the provinces themselves.

In short, at the level of particular outcomes or processes and with respect to specific features, we can discover evidence of how federalism does make a difference. Similarly, William Coleman has noted that differences between federations in the distribution of powers with respect to the regulation of commerce affect the extent of regional differentiation of business associations. At the same time, this may not hold for all industrial sectors, as indicated in part by decentralist trends in non-federal Great Britain. Thus some federalizing trends may be independent of whether the state is federal or unitary in structure. Michael Trebilcock, in turn, notes how in Canada the availability to provincial governments of several regulatory instruments in areas such as securities, professions, and land use, as well as the leverage inherent in government purchasing policies, permits the creation of impediments to the free flow of capital, goods, and labour within the Canadian economic union. But he notes also that the actual effects of these barriers have probably been exaggerated and, more important, that it is the federal government itself that is most prone to create impediments to factor mobility. Most suggestively he argues that some of the same internal barriers can be found in a unitary state like Britain.

Thus students of federalism should be sensitive to a distinction that for the most part remains implicit in most policy studies, that is, some policy problems are based in society, while others are not. Societal problems may antedate any particular government or régime, and they may outlast generations; or they may develop independently of government. Regional economic disparities and sub-cultural, linguistic or religious cleavages all tend to share this characteristic. Other policy problems are in a sense state-induced. That is to say they exist largely because of intervention by the state, often in an effort to respond to problems of the first type. These are modern problems that originally helped give rise to the growth of the state and currently inspire many of the policy dilemmas and conflicts of the federal state. Thus the array of issues that we normally associate with the welfare state, with the extractive capacity of the tax state, and with economic intervention or management are all of this order. Whereas the first policy type is deeply rooted in society, economic environment, or historic divisions, the second type is rooted in the state itself. These may therefore be said to be second-order, man-made policy problems.

Federalism and the 'Embedded' State

The notion that the activities and problems of the modern federal state are both generated and often resolved within the confines of the state itself is consistent with what we have called the state-centred view of federalism. It is a view most closely identified with Alan Cairns, who has stressed the capacity of governments 'to mould their environment in accordance with their own governmental purposes.' Subsequent works in political science, such as Eric Nordlinger's seminal book, *The Autonomy of the Democratic State*, have helped to reaffirm this view of Canadian federalism.[4]

Although few of the contributors directly challenge the state-centred paradigm, their findings are not wholly consistent with this view. Dupré remarks that politicians have local or provincial constituencies, which invariably affects or constrains their behaviour in federal-provincial conferences. Skogstad notes that the role of individual producer groups has been central to the formulation of agricultural policy. She further suggests that in some respects her findings fit better with the neo-Marxist paradigm as put forward by Garth Stevenson, which places primary emphasis on those economic groups or constituencies dominant in each province.[5] The question therefore arises whether the state-centred view, at least as formulated in the mid-1970s, is still an appropriate vehicle for capturing essential elements of the modern federation.

Intellectual climates do sometimes change in response to underlying social and political changes. Two important trends since the late 1970s are particularly worth noting. First, there has been increasing public awareness of government activities, combined with willingness on the part of a number of groups to pressure government in different arenas, using newer tactics. In turn governments have increasingly paid heed to public opinion, both in seeking to cultivate it and in many instances in following it. At least in selected policy problems – like the environment, energy, and consumer safety – governments have discovered the political necessity of taking heed of public opinion. Second, there is realization by virtually all governments, both in Canada and abroad, that there are distinct limits to what governments can achieve.

These changes are readily evident in comparing analyses of Canadian federalism and constitutional change over the past decade. In 1977 Alan Cairns wrote: 'Members of the public are little more than spectators, mobilized by competing elites at three-to-five year intervals for electoral purposes,' and he cited approvingly Richard Simeon's observation: 'Canada combines the British tradition of a strong executive and centralized leadership with a *relative* freedom from mass pressure and popular restraint.'[6] Nearly six years later, Keith Banting and Richard Simeon noted that this general climate of democratic élitism had been tempered by 'populist anger,' as revealed at the time of the constitutional negotiations.[7] It should be noted that such populist dissatisfaction occurred in conjunction with the activities of well-organized pressure groups such as the women's rights and native people's lobbies, both of which have been quite successful in mobilizing important segments of public opinion and in exploiting public arenas such as the joint parliamentary committee on the constitution.[8] They also have been able to make their influence felt even after the accord between Ottawa and the nine provinces had been reached. In all major policy sectors, both federal and provincial governments have engaged in extensive polling of citizens, making the perceived approbation of citizens an important factor in the calculation of a government's next move.[9]

In the economic sphere, the recession of 1982, culminating almost a decade of economic crisis and stagnation, brought home to governments around the world how limited they were in what they couuld accomplish by way of reducing unemployment and deficits or in preventing the decline or disappearance of industrial sectors. The highly 'dirigiste' Parti québécois government in Quebec admitted that its ability to shape its economic destiny was thwarted not just by Ottawa but also by the onslaught of international economic forces beyond the control of virtually any government. In Ottawa the ill-fated National Energy Program and the associated megaproject strategy illustrated that governments were capable of serious economic as well as political miscalculation, which in this instance was reflected in the defeat of the government. New economic realities have also reinforced energy policy, fiscal federalism, and, most recently, the debate over free trade with the United States as core issues on the Canadian intergovernmental relations agenda.

Developments in the economic realm have thus brought home the fact that national political economies are highly dependent upon the vagaries of international forces, which for Canada means particularly the influence of the American economy.[10] Realization of the relative incapacity of governments in federations, whether central or local, to steer clear of troubled waters has combined with a revival in neo-conservative thinking to justify the acceptance of a more limited role for government generally. Yet the popularity of such notions does not necessarily make life easier for those in power. Ironically the very actions of governments during earlier eras, when conceivably they thought themselves to be relatively unrestrained by public opinion, have created dependent links with client groups from which both politicians and civil servants are likely to find it very difficult to extricate themselves.

These dependencies, or more accurately interdependencies, between state and society have been described in a variety of ways. Daniel Bell and Jeffrey Simpson refer to the relentless pressure of perceived rights or 'entitlements.' Thus Simpson writes: 'Everywhere the government turns, it finds groups upset at having lost services, or fearful that they will lose services. The anger is compounded over time because the existence of these services allows beneficiaries to claim them as rights.'[11] Most recently Alan Cairns has coined the term *the embedded state* to describe the changed relationship between state and society.[12] Mancur Olson has referred to 'distributional coalitions,' that is, coalitions between management and labour or between government and interest groups that work to the benefit of the participants but to the detriment of the larger community. As political systems age they are more likely to be afflicted by socio-political sclerosis – a proliferation of distributional coalitions. The irony, according to Olson, is that while there may be a tacit admission by coalition members that the arrangement promotes inefficiencies, they are nevertheless reluctant to abandon the comfort and security that the coalition affords them. Indeed, in terms of economic self-interest it would be irrational for them to do so.[13]

Thus the penetration of any given governmental unit into its environment, whether on its own volition or as a result of competition with other governmental units, is not without consequences. In doing so the state as a whole generates expectations, greater awareness, and ultimately more critical scrutiny on the part of the media, citizens, and groups. Governments that undertake bold new initiatives without extensive consultation do so at their peril. Conversely, governments that do undertake to consult extensively may find themselves hamstrung by well-organized interests.

The import of the above is certainly not that the state-centred view of federalism need be abandoned. It is rather that the paradigm itself may require modification in order to reflect discoveries about the limits, and changes in those limits, of government activities. The relation between state and society is not constant; it varies from sub-unit to sub-unit, from nation to nation, and over time. The agents of change can be of two sorts. First, outside forces such as those stemming from changes in the international economy may reduce the resources available to one or more governmental units or interest groups. Second, any given relation between state and society may contain or generate within itself those features that sooner or later will result in alteration of that relation. Constituencies, although initially dependent upon the state, will gradually develop their own resources and capabilities; and the state in turn may become highly dependent upon the support of those constituencies. While purposeful and autonomous activity by the state may be easy to achieve in the first instance, subsequent alteration or cessation of that activity, like the removal of the proverbial fish hook, may be much more difficult.

In short, there appears to be a second logic affecting the operation of the federal state: interdependencies between state and society that have developed over time, often as the result of initiatives originally undertaken by government, serve to constrain further the activities of both levels of government.

The Future of Federalism

In an idea reminiscent of Lipset and Rokkan's notion of the 'freezing' of party alignments in the early decades of the twentieth century, and echoing the views of Alan Cairns,[14] Roger Gibbins has sought to explain the persistence and continuing viability of federalism. He generalizes: 'The federal systems, once put in place, are able to ensure their own survival' and, further, 'the fact that the underlying federal society might be profoundly transformed [are] largely irrelevant to their continuation. Federalism persists in the United States and Australia not because of the federal nature of the underlying societies, but because the constitutional status quo is resistant to change.'

This does not mean that the constitutional status quo prevailing in Canada, the United States, Australia, and elsewhere is unchanging or inflexible. As Gibbins notes, formal and informal constitutional amendments have sub-stantially altered the balance of power between federal and regional govern-ments; and in the case of Canada, where informal means have taken on particular prominence, some lament that the constitution has become too flexible. Nor does it mean that societal forces are irrelevant. Constitutional provisions and associated government activities must strike a responsive chord, positively or negatively, among at least certain groups or individuals in the environment, notwithstanding the possibility that these activities were taken on the initiative of government itself.

Thus the constitutional framework can be seen as a template originally designed to deal with particular problems and to mesh with the values held by founding fathers about the nature of representative institutions and the role of citizens. Over time this basic framework proved useful in resolving analogous problems at subsequent stages of development and, importantly, provided guidance where there was ambiguity. Governments in interacting with one another and with social groups have argued about the interpretation and manner of application of those features of the constitution that, over time, may have altered the balance of powers between governments without necessarily affecting the integrity of the basic framework itself.

In Canada of the 1980s the 'great debate' over the constitution has given renewed prominence both to provincial autonomy and to citizens' rights. Moreover, well before the constitutional accords, the predominant post-war trend in Canadian federalism was already decentralist in character. Some attribute it to 'province-building'; others prefer to discuss it in terms of the changing balance of federal-provincial relations. In either case there is no doubt that a significant institutional and political evolution has transpired which in its broad outlines is irreversible and is likely to continue in the future. Not only has the federal government lost some of its authority vis-à-vis the provinces, but, more important, in keeping with trends in other federations, Canadian politics has taken on increasingly a confederal form. This does not mean that we will not see reassertions of central authority; indeed in Canada the centralizing impulse was very much in evidence during the Trudeau years, in part as a direct reaction to regionalist and, from Quebec, separatist strains within the federal order. Irreversibility does suggest, however, that some new plateau of federal power sharing has been achieved that is likely to prohibit any swing of the pendulum back the other way. To pursue a risky metaphor a bit further, the pivot and the arc of the pendulum itself have been altered. We now find a far more complex set of intergovernmental processes in which numerous threads of policy interdependence constrain federal and provincial actors in ways unknown a generation ago.

For Canada, in contrast to federal systems such as the United States, Australia, and West Germany, constituent issues focusing on centre-periphery bargaining and executive federalism have been central to political debate and have prompted a noticeable degree of citizen awareness and, to a lesser extent, participation. With the important exception of the American civil rights movement in the 1950s and 1960s, such changes in other federations have had a lower profile, have tended to be less controversial, and have often been confined to discussion among bureaucratic élites or academic experts. The style of debate confined to bureaucratic circles and technical issues is perhaps best exemplifed in the workings of West German administrative federalism.

The relative lack of public controversy in federations other than Canada over the nature of intergovernmental bargaining points to a final condition for the workability of federalism, namely the extent to which citizens, politicians, and bureaucrats are willing to accord legitimacy to the federal state. It was noted in the chapter on corporatism and consociationalism that in Canada, while parliament as an institution enjoys considerable esteem, there is general mistrust of the administrative state and of the various arenas in which federal-provincial bargaining takes place. There appears to be a lack of congruence between citizens' attitudes and the reality of federal-provincial bargaining.[15] This cannot but help affect the nature and future course of executive federalism in Canada, particularly as citizens and groups have begun taking more active interest in inquiries conducted by task forces and parliamentary committees and in federal-provincial encounters as relayed by the media. The new Canadian Charter of Rights and the prospects of a more activist Supreme Court, as noted by Jennifer Smith, may also contribute to a more critical stance toward government by citizens. In West Germany and Switzerland as well as in quasi-federal and unitary European systems, there appears to be greater willingness to accept, if not necessarily embrace, a variety of governmental, intergovernmental, and paragovern-mental activities as a legitimate part of the state. In the United States, intrastate federalism allows much centre-periphery bargaining to take place within the confines of Congress, while at the same time the scale of government intervention in social welfare and related areas is proportionately much less than in Canada.[16] Australia, like Canada, may also suffer from the lack of legitimacy accorded to intergovernmental bargaining processes, but this problem is perhaps overcome more easily by virtue of the greater centralization common to Australian federalism.

In summary, the findings in this volume confirm not only the moulding effects of federal institutions but also the limitations on government actions. We will watch with interest the manner in which the interdependencies between the components of the federal state and societal interests, including the differing conceptions of the state held by citizens and élites, will affect the particular shape and role the federal arrangement will take in the future.

NOTES

1 For an analysis of this problem see A.P. Pross 'Parliamentary Influence and the Diffusion of Power' *Canadian Journal of Political Science* 18 (June 1985) 235–66.

2 Alan C. Cairns 'From Interstate to Intrastate Federalism in Canada' Discussion Paper, Institute of Intergovernmental Relations (Kingston 1979); 'The Electoral System and the Party System in Canada' *Canadian Journal of Political Science* 1 (March 1968) 55–80. There still remains confusion in how the terms *interstate* and *intrastate federalism* should be used, depending in part on whether the emphasis is directed toward the representational issue or the question of the jurisdictional division of power. For further discussion and examples of these concepts see D.V. Smiley and R.L. Watts *Intrastate Federalism in Canada*, vol. 39 of the research studies prepared for the Royal Commission on the Economic Union and Development Prospects for Canada (Toronto: University of Toronto Press 1985).

3 Smiley and Watts *Intrastate Federalism in Canada* 50–9

4 Alan C. Cairns 'The Governments and Societies of Canadian Federalism' *Canadian Journal of Political Science* 10 (1977) 699; Nordlinger *The Autonomy of the Democratic State* (Cambridge, Mass.: Harvard University Press 1981)

5 Garth Stevenson 'Federalism and the Political Economy of the Canadian State' in L. Panitch ed *The Canadian State: Political Economy and Political Power* (Toronto: University of Toronto Press 1977) and Stevenson *Unfilled Union: Canadian Federalism and National Unity* (Toronto: Gage 1982)

6 Cairns 'The Governments and Societies of Canadian Federalism' 707

7 Richard Simeon and Keith Banting 'Federalism, Democracy and the Constitution' in Banting and Simeon eds *And No One Cheered: Federalism, Democracy and the Constitution Act* (Toronto: Methuen 1983) 18; see also Keith Banting and Richard Simeon eds *Redesigning the State: The Politics of Constitutional Change in Industrial Nations* (Toronto: University of Toronto Press 1985).

8 Ronald J. Zukowksy *Struggle over the Constitution: From the Quebec Referendum to the Supreme Court* (Kingson: Institute of Intergovernmental Relations 1982) chap 8

9 Ibid chap 10
10 Denis Stairs and G.R. Winham eds *Canada and the International Political/Economic Environment* and *The Politics of Canada's Economic Relationship with the United States*, vols. 28 and 29 of the research studies prepared for the Royal Commission on the Economic Union and Development Prospects for Canada (Toronto: University of Toronto Press 1985); Peter J. Katzenstein ed *Between Power and Plenty: Foreign Economic Policies of Advanced Industrial Societies* (Madison: University of Wisconsin Press 1978); David R. Cameron 'The Expansion of the Public Economy: A Comparative Analysis' *American Political Science Review* 72 (1978) 1243–61
11 Jeffrey Simpson 'The Strength to Say No' *Globe and Mail* 28 February 1985, 6
12 Alan C. Cairns 'The Embedded State: State-Society Relations in Canada' in Banting ed *State and Society* 53–86
13 Mancur Olson *The Rise and Decline of Nations: Economic Growth, Stagflation and Social Rigidities* (New Haven: Yale University Press 1982)
14 S.M. Lipset and Stein Rokkan 'Cleavage Structures, Party Systems, and Voter Alignments' in Lipset and Rokkan eds *Party Systems and Voter Alignments: Cross-National Perspectives* (New York: Basic 1967); Cairns 'The Governments and Societies of Canadian Federalism'
15 Anthony H. Birch 'Political Authority and Crisis in Comparative Perspective' in Banting ed *State and Society* 87–130
16 Keith Banting *The Welfare State and Canadian Federalism* (Kingston: McGill-Queen's University Press 1982)

Note on Contributors

Herman Bakvis, Department of Political Science and School of Public Administration at Dalhousie University, is the author of *Catholic Power in the Netherlands* and *Federalism and the Organization of Political Life*.

Arthur Benz is associated with the Hochschule fur Verwaltungswissenschaften in Speyer, West Germany. He has published various works on German and comparative federalism, most recently *Föderalismus als dynamisches System*.

William M. Chandler, Department of Political Science at McMaster University, is co-author of *Public Policy and Provincial Politics* and has written extensively on Canadian and West German politics.

William D. Coleman is the author of *The Independence Movement in Quebec 1945–1980* and numerous articles. He is currently a participant in a cross-national research project on the political role of business associations and teaches in the Department of Political Science at McMaster University.

Maureen Covell, Department of Political Science at Simon Fraser University, has published widely on linguistic conflict and constitutional change in Belgium and is the author of *Madagascar: Politics, Economics, Society*.

J. Stefan Dupré is a member of the Department of Political Science at the University of Toronto. He is the author and co-author of numerous works on regulatory administration, research policy, and intergovernmental relations. He has served as member or chairman of numerous federal and provincial commissions and task forces, the most recent being the Ontario Task Force on Financial Institutions. He is the recipient of the Vanier Medal awarded by the Institute of Public Administration for outstanding public service.

Roger Gibbins, Department of Political Science at the University of Calgary, has among his numerous publications *Prairie Politics and Society* and *Regionalism: Federal Societies, Institutions and Political Systems*.

Thomas O. Hueglin is a member of the Department of Political Science at Wilfrid

Laurier University. Previously he taught at Konstanz University, West Germany, and in 1984–5 was the Skelton-Clark Fellow at Queen's University. He has written a book and several articles on the political thought of Johannes Althusius.

Arend Lijphart, Department of Political Science at the University of California in San Diego, is the author of several books and articles on modern democratic theory, electoral behaviour, and international relations. His most recent book is *Power-Sharing in South Africa*.

Campbell Sharman is a member of the Department of Politics at the University of Western Australia. He has held teaching and research posts at the Australian National University, the University of British Columbia, and the University of Victoria and has published widely on Australian politics and comparative federalism.

Grace Skogstad, Department of Political Science at the University of Toronto, has written *The Politics of Agricultural Policy-Making in Canada* as well as articles on marketing boards and the role of parliamentary committees.

Jennifer Smith is a member of the Department of Political Science at Dalhousie University. She has published a number of articles and book chapters on constitutional change and the role of the courts and is currently engaged in a biographical study of the Honourable Robert Stanfield.

Michael J. Trebilcock is director of the Law and Economics Program in the Faculty of Law at the University of Toronto. He has written extensively on the topics of economic union and the role of government in economic life. Among his recent works is *The Political Economy of Economic Adjustment*.

John Warhurst is head of the Department of Politics, University of New England, Australia. He has written *Central Agencies, Intergovernmental Managers and Australian Federal-State Relations*; *Machine Politics in the Australian Labour Party*; and *State Governments and Australian Tariff Policy*.